MEDIA, FEMINISM, CULTURAL STUDIES

Stepping Forward: Essays, Lectures and Interviews
by Wolfgang Iser

Wild Zones: Pornography, Art and Feminism
by Kelly Ives

Global Media Warning: Explorations of Radio, Television and the Press
by Oliver Whitehorne

'Cosmo Woman': The World of Women's Magazines
by Oliver Whitehorne

Andrea Dworkin
by Jeremy Mark Robinson

Cixous, Irigaray, Kristeva: The Jouissance of French Feminism
by Kelly Ives

Sex in Art: Pornography and Pleasure in Painting and Sculpture
by Cassidy Hughes

The Erotic Object: Sexuality in Sculpture
From Prehistory to the Present Day
by Susan Quinnell

Detonation Britain: Nuclear War in the UK
by Jeremy Mark Robinson

Julia Kristeva: Art, Love, Melancholy, Philosophy, Semiotics
by Kelly Ives

Luce Irigaray: Lips, Kissing, and the Politics of Sexual Difference
by Kelly Ives

Helene Cixous I Love You: The Jouissance of Writing
by Kelly Ives

The Poetry of Cinema
by John Madden

The Sacred Cinema of Andrei Tarkovsky
by Jeremy Mark Robinson

Disney Business, Disney Films, Disney Lands
Daniel Cerruti

Feminism and Shakespeare
by B.D. Barnacle

Wild Zones

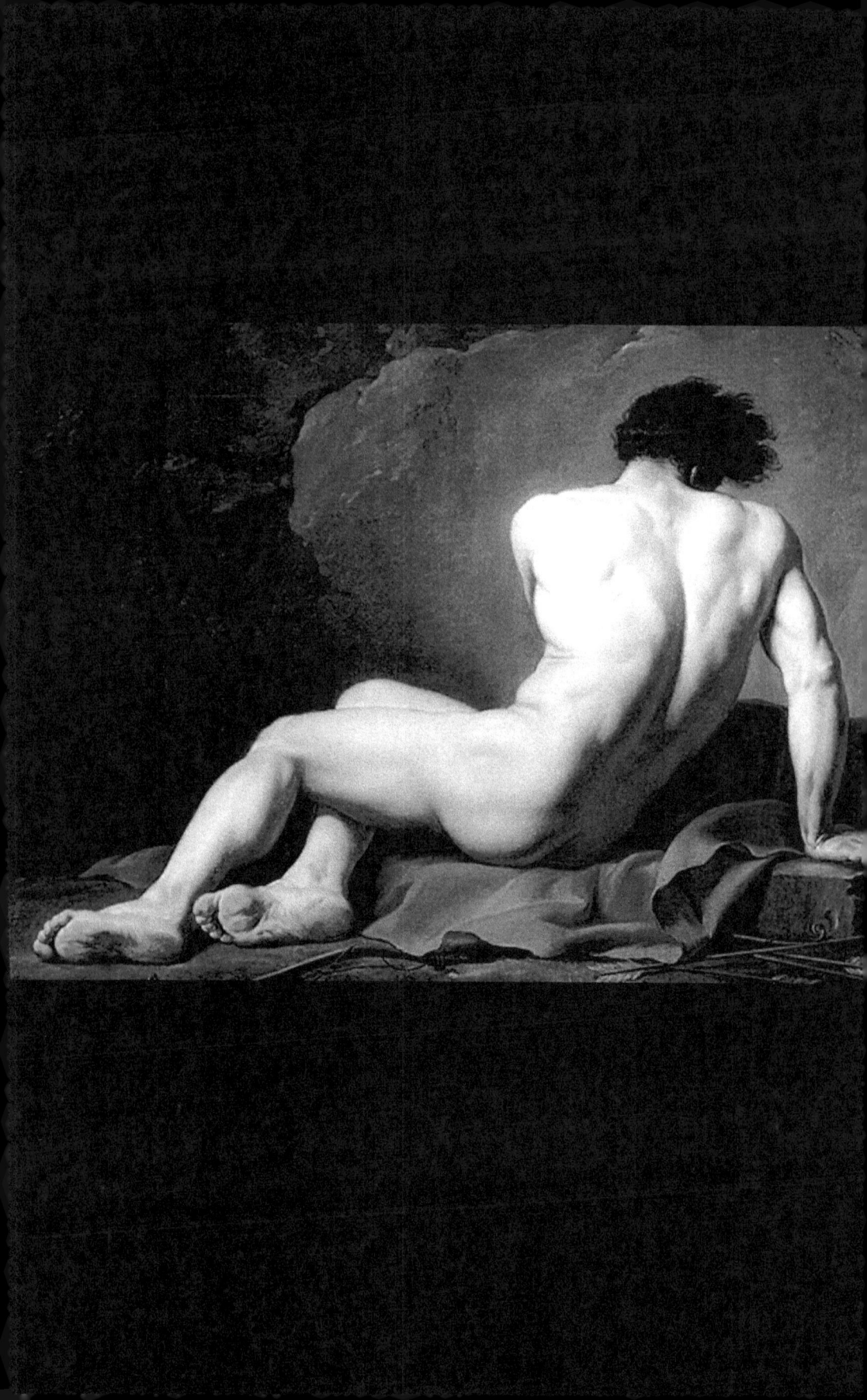

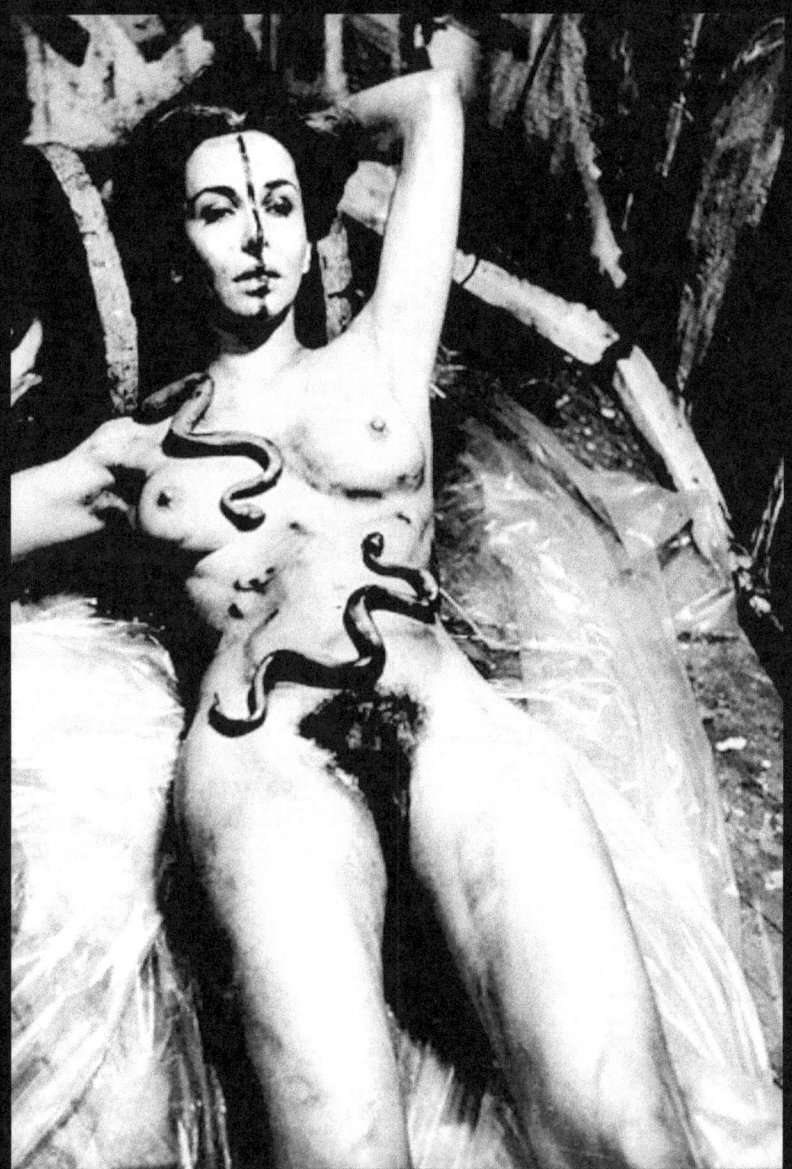

WILD ZONES
Pornography, Art and Feminism

Kelly Ives

Crescent Moon

CRESCENT MOON PUBLISHING
P.O. Box 393
Maidstone
Kent, ME14 5XU
United Kingdom

First published 1994. Second edition 2008. Fourth edition 2010.
© Kelly Ives 1994, 2008, 2010.

Printed and bound in the U.S.A.
Set in Book Antiqua 10 on 12pt .
Designed by Radiance Graphics.

British Library Cataloguing in Publication data

Ives, Kelly
Wild Zones: Pornography, Art and Feminism. – New ed.
I. Erotic Art. 2. Feminist Criticism
704.9'428

ISBN-13 9781861712929

CONTENTS

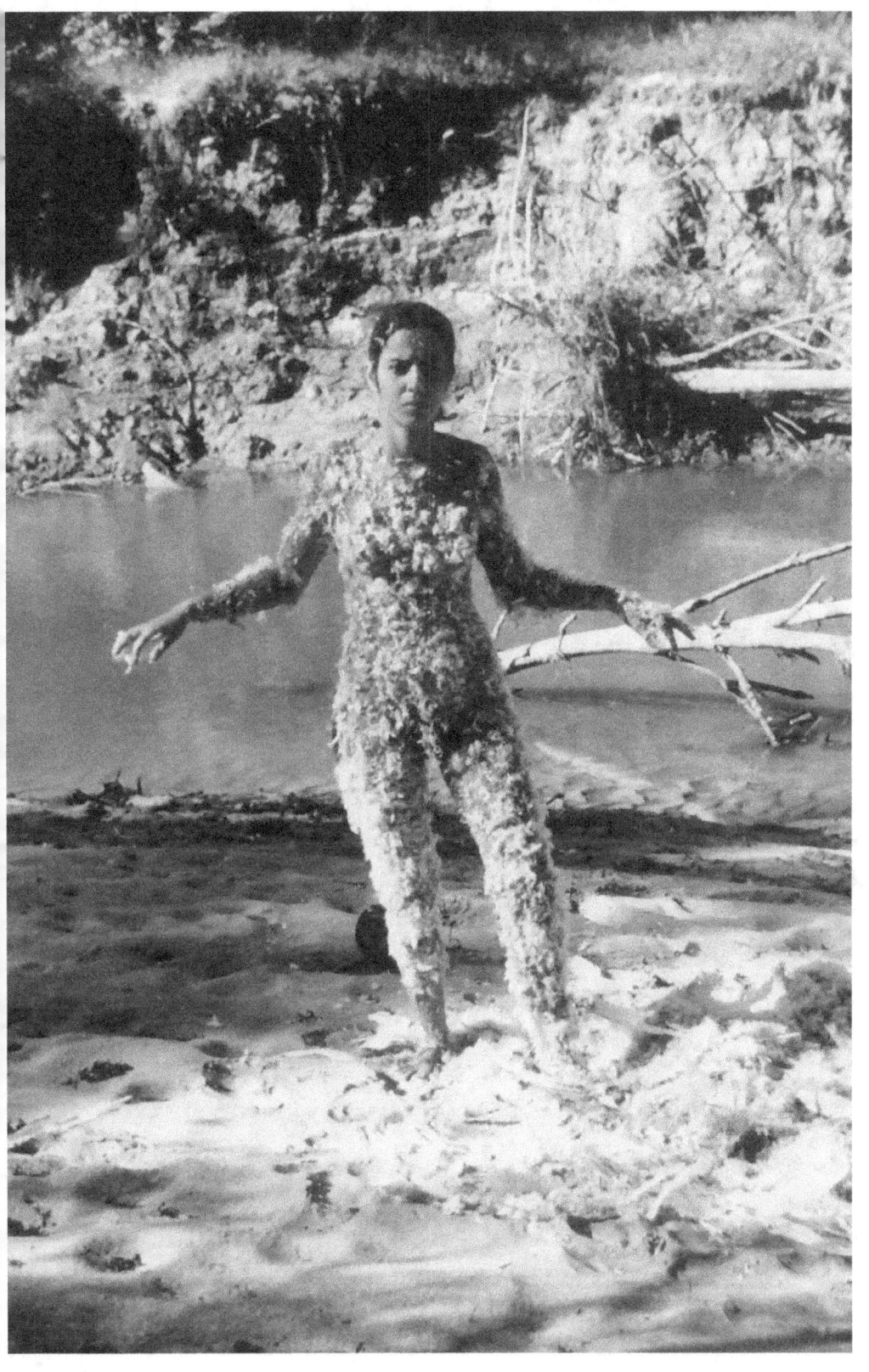

Ana Mendieta, Blood and Feathers, 1974

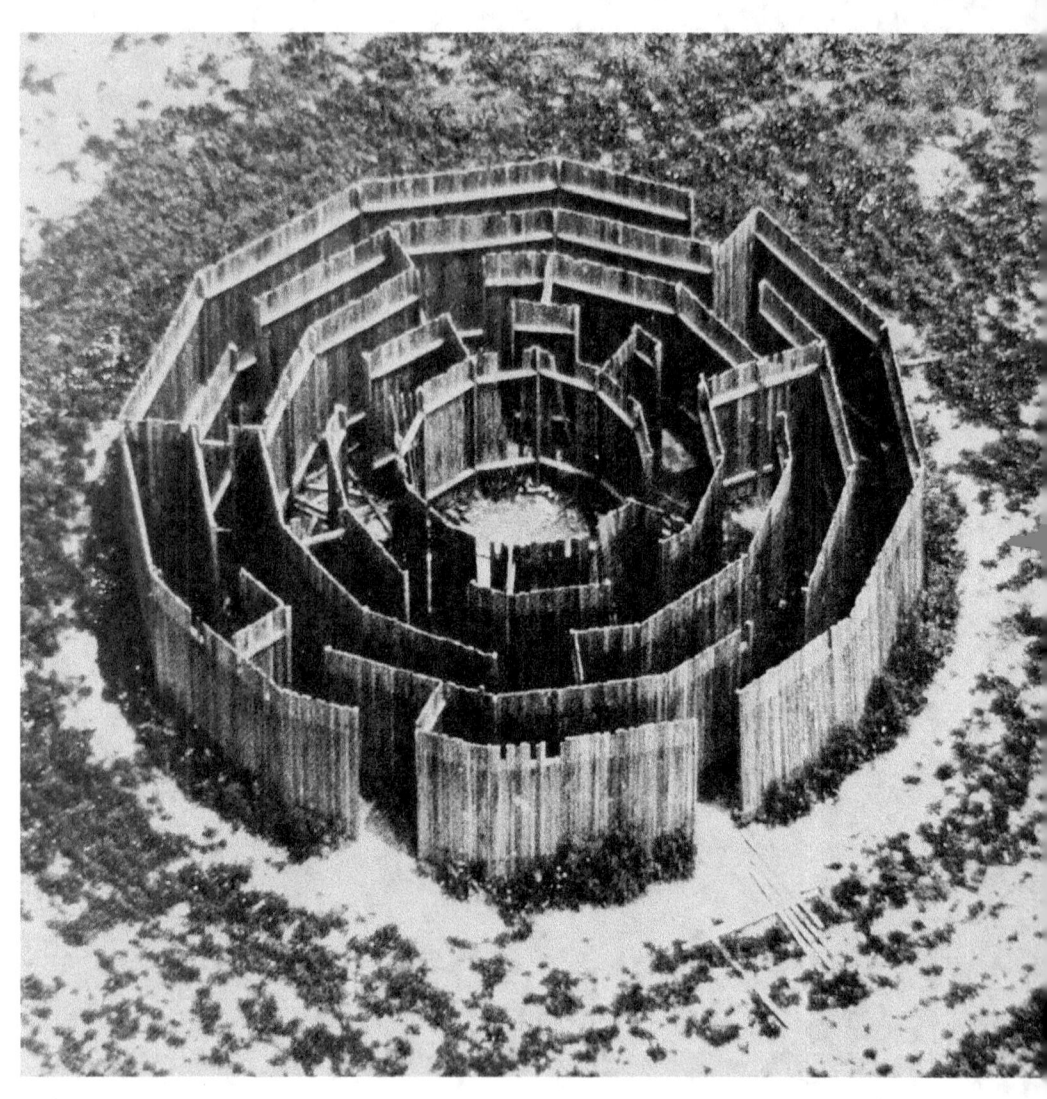

Alice Aycock, Maze, 1972

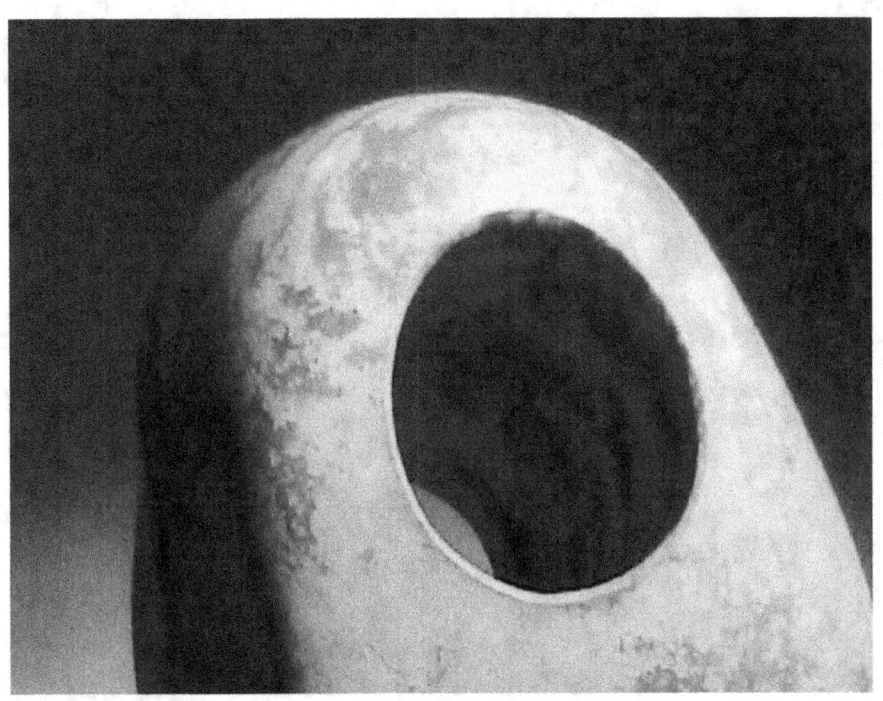

Barbara Hepworth, Pierced Form (April), 1968

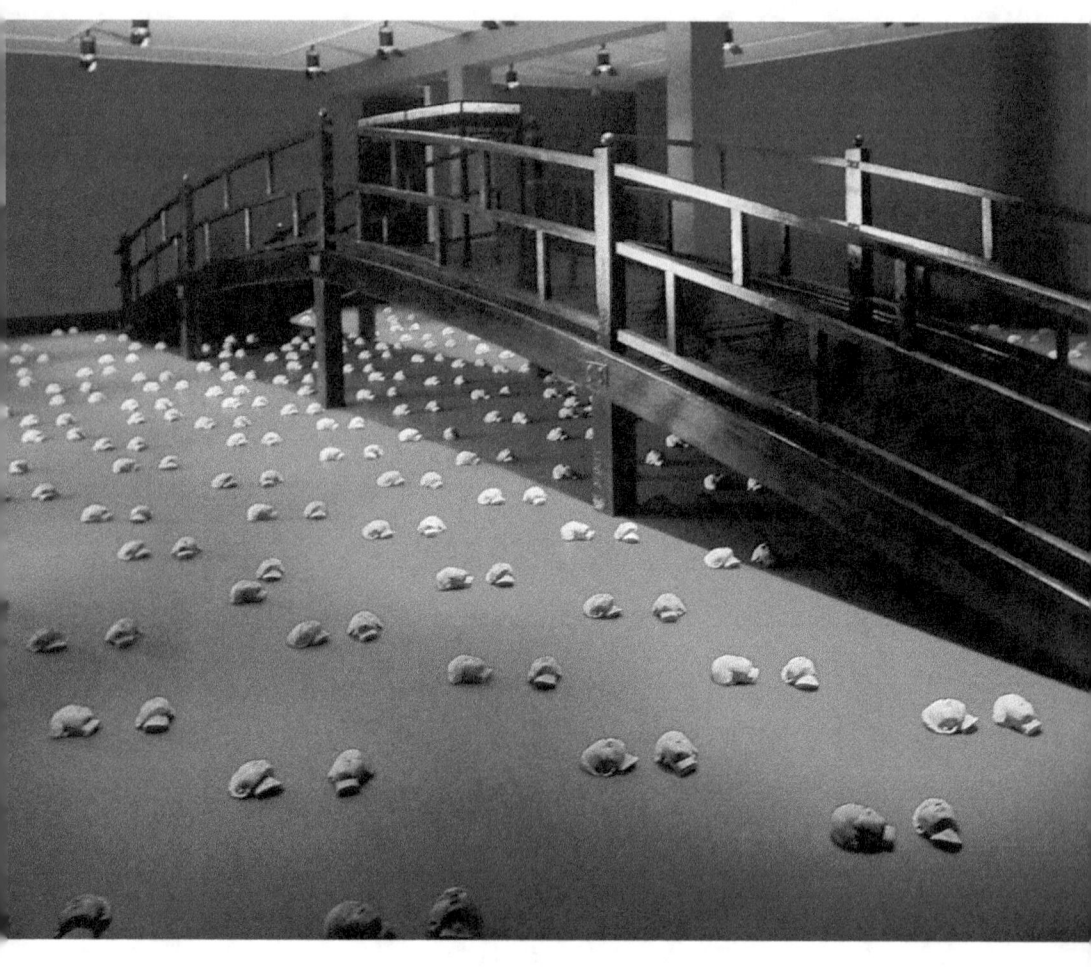

Barbara Bloom, Pictures From the Floating World, 1995

I

PORNOGRAPHY / ART / FEMINISM / CENSORSHIP

No study of a subject as vast as pornography and art can cover everything, so there are many aspects of the pornography and art debate and how it relates to feminism that will be left out here, for there are many many views on the matter. Also, this book focusses on Western culture, society and history. Firstly, there are as many definitions of art and pornography as there are people. Everyone has their own opinions, their own interests and realms to defend. There are the liberals who say that nothing should be censored, including pornography. Pornography is seen as part of artistic expression, and if people want to express themselves, they should, and if they want pornography, they should have it. This is the view of liberals such as Peter Webb, who campaigns for freedom of expression, and an art that should 'celebrate' eroticism.[1] This is a familiar viewpoint, which we have heard made many times. In the (male) liberal view, sex is OK, so sexual art must be OK, so that much of pornography must be OK. The 'experts' on sex, the so-called 'sexologists' (Eduard Fuchs, Richard von Krafft-Ebbing, Sigmund Freud, Wilhelm Reich) argue that sex is a normal part of life, so it is natural that it should abound in art. Fuchs wrote; '[a]rt has treated erotic themes at almost all periods... [it] lies at the root

---

1 See Peter Webb: *The Erotic Arts*, 1-9

of all human life.'[2]

Everyone seems to have their cut-off points, however, their 'standards' of 'taste' and 'decency'. It's a very subjective business, the debates between art and pornography, and between pornography and censorship. As Wendy Moore writes: '[c]ensorship like freedom is an entirely subjective term'.[3] What you like defines yourself. As Pierre Bourdieu put it: '[t]aste classifies, and it classifies the classifier.'[4]

Taste, choice, categorization and classification, then, defines the viewer, the reader, the consumer. Censorship, you might say, defines the culture. And 'sensitive' novelists are wary of writing 'sex scenes', because they know that what they write defines themselves. Yet sex is crucial to art, many artists say. As Gertrude Stein wrote: '[l]iterature – creative literature – unconnected with sex is inconceivable.'[5]

What emerges from the liberal, patriarchal view of art and pornography is that censorship is largely political: it is not concerned so much with 'taste' and 'offending' people as with political control. The history of censorship bears this out. As Catherine Itzin writes: '[t]he purpose of censorship from beginning to end has been *political*: suppression.'[6]

Some things still 'shock' people, upset them, disturb them. A survey for the Royal College of Midwives of November 1993 found that half of the men interviewed were opposed to breast-feeding.[7] Men don't want to see mothers breast-feeding in a restaurant, because it puts them off their food. They think it's 'embarrassing, unnecessary, exhibitionism, disgusting'. It's hard to believe, but men think breast-feeding is 'unnecessary'. 'Unnecessary'! It's 'unnecessary' to feed children, but it's OK for men to feed themselves in restaurants, but not for mothers to feed their

2 E. Fuchs: *Geschichte der Erotischen Kunst*, Albert Langen, Munich, 1912-26, I, 1

3 Moore: "There Should Be a Law Against It... Shouldn't There?", in Gail Chester & Julienne Dickey, eds., 141

4 P. Bourdieu: *Distinction: A Social Critique of the Judgment of Taste*, tr. Richard Nice, Routledge & Kegan Paul 1984, 6

5 Stein, in "A Conversation", John Hyde Preston, *Atlantic Monthly*, CLVI, August 1935, 191

6 Catherine Itzin: "Sex and Censorship: The Political Implications", in Gail Chester, 41

7 Chris Mihill: "Breast-feeding falls foul of men", *The Guardian*, 6 November 1993

children! Men are 'disgusted' by breasts even though they adore them and make jokes about them, and put them in their newspapers and magazines. As Andrea Dworkin writes in *Mercy*, 'what's so dirty to men about breasts so they put tassels on them and have them swirl around in circles and call them the ugliest names; as if they ain't attached to human beings' (298).

Religious images used 'blasphemously' still 'shock' some people. Salman Rushdie's *The Satanic Verses* and the death threat is probably the most notorious case of religious intolerance of recent years. Seven people died in anti-Rushdie riots in Pakistan and India in February 1989; ten people died in riots in Bombay; there have been other deaths, all sparked off by a book being published in the late 20th century.[8] Some people wouldn't have thought that there are those who could be so upset by such things, but they are.

Andres Serrano's photograph *Piss Christ* created a lot of controversy, for it depicted (here we go again) a fusion of sex and the sacred, eroticism and Christianity (Serrano's art is often very beautiful).[9] The activist group Guerrilla Girls said: 'the majority of exposed penises in major museums belong to the Baby Jesus."[10]

Serrano said that he wanted to be 'descriptive or literal' in his use of bodily fluids (yet, but in his later depictions of sex acts, using the iconography of pornography, Serrano seems to be enjoying sticking a finger up at the bourgeoisie. I remember seeing an exhibition by Serrano in New York City in 2009 of giant photographs of turds).[11]

Jean-Luc Godard's 1985 film *Hail Mary* created controversy

---

8 See W.J. Weatherby: *Salman Rushdie: Sentenced to Death*, Carroll & Graf, New York 1992; Paul Theroux: "What About Rushdie?", *New York Times*, 13 February 1992; "Islam zealots threaten Dante's tomb over Mohammed slur", *The New York Post*, 6 March 1989; S.J.D. Green: "Beyond the Satanic Verses: Conservative Religion and the Liberal Society", *Encounter*, June 1990, 12-20; John F. Baker: "A Rushdie Paperback?", *Publishers Weekly*, 13 October 1989; Salman Rushdie: "A Pen Against the Sword: In Good Faith", *Newsweek*, 12 February 1990

9 Andres Serrano: *Piss Christ*, 1987, Cibachrome photograph, Stux Gallery, New York

10 Quoted in Dubin, 136

11 Serrano, quoted in Dubin, 98; see Michael Brenson: "Andres Serrano: Provocation and Spirituality", *New York Times*, 8 December 1989, C1, 28

when it depicted the Blessed Virgin as garage attendant.[12] There were bomb threats, 5,000 protesters reciting the rosary to cinema queues, and the 'film bears the distinction of being the first ever condemned by a pope (Pope John Paul II), and being the first instance in 400 years that a pope directly intervened in the suppression of a work of art' (Steven Dubin, 93). Artistic transgressions of the Christian religion upset people immensely, it seems. Other religious fundamentalists give Christian bigots a run for their money when it comes to intolerance. Witness, for instance, the pathetic moaning of the clergy and the church about women priests. In 1984 an artwork of a crucified woman, *Christa*, was taken out of a church in New York because it was 'theologically and historically indefensible'.[13] A crucified *woman*, now there's a blasphemous image to conjure with. An artist superimposed the breasts and face of Marilyn Monroe over the Virgin Guadalupe and there were threats to burn down the Museum of Modern Art in Mexico City.[14] The pop star Madonna fused the sensuality of pop icon Miss M with the untouchableness and sanctity of the Virgin Mary. She dances in a wedding dress in the video for *Like a Prayer*, and wrote the song *Papa Don't Preach*, mocking male authority figures, and of course her products *Erotica* and the book *Sex* flirt playfully with pornographic images, and in Champaign, Illinois, over 300 people protested over the public library's decision to buy the book *Sex*.[15] Martin Scorsese's *The Last Temptation of Christ* kicked up a fuss, with cinemas being set on fire, thousands of people protesting in the streets, and TV executives banning it, etc, yet the film is clearly the work of a faithful Catholic, and

---

12 Godard: *Hail Mary*, 1985, France. See James Strong: "*Hail Mary* leaves council offended, box office booming", *Chicago Tribune*, 17 April 1986; Wes Smith: "Ecumenical crowd of protesters pans *Hail Mary*", *Chicago Tribune*, 5 April 1986; Michael Wilmington: "*Hail Mary*: A Godard Pirouette", *Los Angeles Times*, 20 November 1985
13 Kenneth A. Briggs: "Cathedral Removing Statue of Crucified Woman", *New York Times*, 28 April 1984
14 Larry Rohter: "Marilyn and Virgin: Art or Sacrilege?" *New York Times*, 2 April 1988
15 See Chuck Philips: "Anger Over Madonna Single", *Los Angeles Times*, 4 January 1991; "Clash Over Madonna", *New York Times*, 14 July 1990

Scorsese calls himself a believer in Christ as the Son of God.[16]

So much art has to be censored, edited, screened, so that nothing offends anybody. The list of television shows that have not been broadcast because of their political or sexual content is enormous. Huge numbers of TV programmes and documentaries have simply been ditched, usually banned by governments.[17] Prime-time shows in the US are pre-screened for executives and 'screeners', so that nothing offends.[18] The feminist Judy Chicago's *The Dinner Party* was reviled by critics because it focused on the vulva, what the art critic Robert Hughes called 'Chicago's relentless concentration on the pudenda'.[19] It's OK for male artists to paint the female genitals over and over (Pablo Picasso, for instance, or Hans Bellmer, or Egon Schiele), but not for female artists. For Hilton Kramer, *The Dinner Party* was 'vulgar',[20] while Robert K. Dornan called it 'ceramic 3-D pornography'.[21] When the American flag is burnt or used in a transgressive manner, some folk get upset. Politically subversive acts disturb people, but when political art is combined with erotic art, the effect can be too much for the moral majority. Erika Rothenberg produced an art installation called *Have You Burned America Today*, which contained

16 See Janet Maslin: "*Last Temptation*: Scorsese's View of Jesus's Sacrifice", *New York Times*, 12 August 1988; Aljean Harmetz: "7,500 Picket Universal Over Movie About Jesus", *New York Times*, 12 August 1988; Jorge Casuso & Charles Mount: "Protesters, fans flock to *Last Temptation*", *Chicago Tribune*, 13 August 1988; Barry Cronin & Tom Gibbons: "600 Picket as Christ film opens", *Chicago Sun-Times*, 13 August 1988; James Caryn: "Paul Shrader Talks of *Last Temptation* and His New Film", *New York Times*, 1 September 1988
17 See John Pilger: "Silence of the Lambs", *The New Statesman and Society*, 20 August 1993, 14
18 See Bill Carter: "Screeners Help Advertisers Avoid Prime-Time Trouble", *New York Times*, 29 January 1990
19 Robert Hughes: "An Obsessive Feminist Pantheon", *Time*, 15 December 1980, 85-6
20 Hilton Kramer: "Art: Judy Chicago's *Dinner Party*, Comes to Brooklyn Museum", *New York Times*, 17 October 1980. And see Carrie Rickey: "Judy Chicago, *The Dinner Party*, The Brooklyn Museum", *Artforum*, January 1981; Robert Pedersen: "The Bitter Taste of the *The Dinner Party*", *Los Angeles Times*, 5 November 1990; Jonetta Rose Barras: "UDC's $1.6 million 'Dinner': Feminist artwork causes some indigestion", *The Washington Times*, 18 July 1990; Cliff O'Neil: "House cuts D.C. Funding over Judy Chicago display", *Outweek*, 15 August 1990
21 *Congressional Record*, 101st Session, volume 136, no.98, 26 July 1990

a 'blonde couple' demonstrating how to use a DIY 'flag-burning kit' (see Dubin, 252). The Ridgeway Bennett group produced 'Cum Paintings', canvases shaped like triangles or crosses smeared with vinyl, wax and the sperm of the artists, spelling out the word 'cum'.[22]

D.H. Lawrence is, overall, typical of many in his view of pornography. For him, pornography demeans sex, makes it 'dirty', squalid, limited: '[p]ornography is the attempt to insult sex, to do dirt on it,' he writes in *Pornography and Obscenity*.[23] For Lorenzo, as for so many writers, poets, intellectuals and philosophers, sex is something holy, sublime and central to existence. One must have 'a proper reverence for sex', Lawrence wrote in "A Propos of *Lady Chatterley's Lover*".[24]

The problem with Bertie Lawrence, some commentators maintain, and you can say the same of Georges Bataille, Wilhelm Reich, Sigmund Freud, the Marquis de Sade, Henry Miller and others, is that he emphasizes sex too much; that, in *Lady Chatterley's Lover* especially, he reckoned a social revolution could only occur founded on a sexual revolution. Get right in your sex, Lawrence said, and everything else will fall into place. But many feminists also place sexuality at the centre of the feminist debate. As Catherine MacKinnon said, in her manifesto of feminist theory: '[s]exuality is to feminism what work is to marxism'.[25]

The problem of representation in pornography and the relation between representation and 'reality' is something we return to again and again in the pornography debate. The question of representation goes to the heart of the controversy surrounding art, feminism and pornography. Andrea Dworkin, for instance, believes wholeheartedly in the power of words. She believes that language can influence, persuade and corrupt, that words can be weapons. She says in her speech "The Power of Words":

> Words can be used to educate, to clarify, to inform, to illuminate. Words can also be be used to intimidate, to threaten, to insult, to coerce, to incite hatred, to encourage ignorance. Words can make us

22 Elizabeth Hess: "Gutter Politics", *Village Voice*, 3 July 1990, 89

23 D.H. Lawrence: *Pornography and Obscenity*, *This Quarter*, 1929, in *A Selection From Phoenix*, 313

24 Lawrence, in *A Selection From Phoenix*, 331

25 Catherine MacKinnon: "Feminism, Marxism, Method, and the State: An Agenda for Theory", in N.O. Keohane, *et al*, eds. *Feminist Theory: A Critique of ideology*, Harvester 1982

better or worse people, more compassionate or more prejudiced, more generous or more cruel. Words matter because words significantly determine what we know and what we do. Words change us or keep us the same. Women, deprived of words, are deprived of life.[26]

In Andrea Dworkin's system, men can use the whole of language as violence against women, not just so-called 'dirty' words such as *fuck* and *cunt*. It's not only these words that are verbal violence, for even the 'soft' words, like 'soft' or 'gentle' can be violence against women if employed in certain ways, in certain contexts, for all words can be strung together to form violence against women, a kind of linguistic or verbal rape. The choice for women, according to Andrea Dworkin, is 'lie or die'.

> Women have two choices: lie or die. Feminists are trying to open the options up a bit.[27]

The linguistic analysis of Andrea Dworkin and other feminists who propose that language is 'man-made', is too reductive and simplistic. They are over-simplifying a more complex problem. The analysis is always to be reduced to simple notions of 'masculine' and 'feminine'. So it's men who use words to exert power over and above women, it's women who are the 'victims' of men's ability to wield language as a weapon; but isn't this too simplified? Is language really that simple, and static, and powerful? After all, language mutates continually, and even one sentence or one word changes in different contexts, as Jacques Derrida has noted.[28] Texts are open, not closed or fixed, and thus pornography, like any literature, like any series of words, can be read in multiple ways. So that there is no single, fixed and sexist reading of pornographic films or magazines, but many readings. Notions of 'masculinity' and 'femininity' are too often regarded as fixed categories, whereas other feminists acknowledge the fragility and flux of sexual identities.[29] Indeed, the notion of sex difference in language is fraught with problems: it 'is not only a theoretical impossibility, but a political error' suggests Toril Moi (in ib., 153). Cheris Kramer, Barrie Thorne and Nancy Henley state: '[w]hat is notable is how

26 Dworkin: "The Power of Words", 1978, *Letters*, 30

27 Dworkin, "Nervous Interview", *Letters*, 60

28 Derrida: *Eperons: Les styles de Nietzsche*, Flammarion, Paris 1978

29 See Toril Moi: *Sexual/Textual Politics*, 154f; Shirley Ardener, ed. *Perceiving Women*, Malaby Press 1975

few expected sex differences have been firmly substantiated by empirical studies of actual speech';[30]

Everyone who says anything about pornography and art and censorship usually states, either overtly or by implication, what *they* think is 'acceptable' and what is 'obscene' or 'unacceptable'. Steven Marcus offers a typical viewpoint: art is about 'the relations of human beings among themselves' while 'sex in pornography is sex without the emotions'.[31] The view is that 'true' art (or 'high' art) is emotional, and therefore justifies its existence. Deep feelings or emotions in art connote æsthetic and philosophical authenticity. As one of the 'founders' of modern abstraction, Kasimir Malevich has it: 'the significant thing is feeling... Feeling is the determining factor',[32] while the prince of dreamy, escapist art, Odilon Redon, said: 'I speak to those who surrender themselves gently to the secret and mysterious laws of the emotions and the heart'.[33]

Pornography 'shocks' some people, but it shocks people for different reasons. Benoîte Groult writes that '[p]ornography has always existed and has never undermined anything. It has always given pleasure to the same men and the same women and shocked the same others.'[34] It may be the content of pornography that shocks people, i.e., the very fact that tits and asses and cocks and cunts exist. Or, more likely, what shocks people is the act or fact of depiction of these below the belt events. Genitals exist, and denying that fact is psychotic, mistaken and anti-human. What 'shocks' people about pornography, then, is *that* genitals are depicted; or it may be *how* sexual activities are depicted that 'offends' people. For some people think that sexual 'acts' are 'private' events, not – nay, *never* – to be seen in 'public'. Cultural theory and post-1960s feminism has demonstrated every which way that sexual acts are *not* 'private' acts but 'public', and political acts. Even though intercourse may occur under seventeen blankets in the missionary position in total darkness once a decade, it is socially and politically conditioned act. To ignore the cultural aspects of sexuality and to focus on the 'natural' aspects, in the

30 Cheris Kramer, Barrie Thorne and Nancy Henley: "Perspectives on language and communication", *Signs*, 3, 3, 640

31 Marcus: *The Other Victorians*, Corgi 1969, 283-4

32 Kasimir Malevich: *The Non-Objective World*, tr. Howard Dearstyne, Theobald, Chicago 1959, 67f

33 Odilon Redon: *A soi même: Journal (1867-1915)*, Corti, Paris 1961, 115f

34 Groult: "Le portiers de nuit", in E. Marks, 73

culture versus nature dialectic, misses out crucial dimensions of sexuality. Pornography, then, 'shocks' people possibly because it is 'shocking' or 'offensive' culturally, not 'naturally'. Mr and Mrs Public are perhaps 'offended' by pornography in public even though they may indulge in 'pornographic' acts in private. Denouncing pornography publicly looks good. It fits in with going to church and saying grace before a meal. In private, though, Mr and Mrs Public may consume pornography. Or Mr Public might, and his wife will politely ignore this consumption. One of the great hypocrisies in the pornography debate is this private consumption/ public hatred.

For some people, the walls of one's house are more than just physical. They do not simply shut out the noise and turmoil of the 'outside world', they are psycho-social barriers. Shut one's door and the horrors of the world won't get in. This is clearly wrong. There are no barriers of this sort, except in the mind. There are no distinct divisions between the public and private worlds. There are obvious ways in which the public impinges upon the private: the steady stream of radio, television and newspapers and advertizing and junk mail and letters and leaflets and packaging on food and miscellaneous items. But people are thoroughly socialized and enculturated anyway, without these outward manifestations of culture, these signs and logos and adverts and trailers and programmes and news bulletins. Even without the paraphernalia of culture, everyone is firmly and inextricably embedded in culture. There is no escaping culture, not in the Amazonian forest, not in Antartica, not six miles under the Pacific, not on the Moon or on Mars, not in deep space. This realization that culture is the environment of humans, just as much as, if not more than, nature, is crucial. People live in a psycho-social space as much as in a 'natural' space. People live in their bodies, but they also, increasingly, live in cities and towns, where they don't have to walk on grass or 'nature' ever, if they so wish. Humans can live in a city, and never see grass for real, if they wish. The debate about computerized 'virtual reality' technology or the internet is only another admission that we live in a media landscape, a psycho-social space that has an increasingly ambiguous relation to 'real' 'nature'. If people voice fears of computers and electronic technology and 'virtual reality' they are a bit late. This kind of construction of imaginary, fantastical worlds occurred thousand years ago. Sophocles and the Greek dramatists created imaginary worlds, and people must have told stories, creating alternative realities, way before the Classic Greek era. The creation of 'virtual reality', then, is nothing new. Pornography, then, is but one cog in this gigantic 'communications landscape'.

Perhaps pornography is 'offensive' because it reminds people about nature, about their bodies, about what their bodies can do. For they might have forgotten about or suppressed their bodies, which is not as difficult as you might imagine in a postmodern, Westernized, post-industrial world. Pornography may be a sudden inrush of the body into daily, technological life, unwanted because suppressed, unwanted because unknown.

Yet, at the same time, the world of desire that pornography evokes is yearned for. In pornography, fantasies run wild. Perhaps pornography is so popular, is such a big business ($8 million according to Andrea Dworkin, though less than $4 billion according to Forbes), because it deals with primordial, suppressed desires, that have no place in the day-to-day running of the world. Perhaps pornography is simply the 'return of the repressed', like all art. Perhaps pornography is simply an eruption of desire into the workaday, everyday, day-to-day world, an enshrinement of desire in glossy, garish and grotesque photographs and films and magazines. Perhaps pornography is an inrush of 'nature' into 'culture', and perhaps that's why it is so hated. For pornography depicts people going after one thing, orgasmic pleasure. It is supreme hedonism, it is supreme hedonism enshrined in expressive media. It uses expressive media (painting, photography, video, etc) to depict pure pleasure and fantasy. Perhaps pornography is hated so virulently by some people because it depicts unbridled pleasure. And it depicts it using the female body as the site and vehicle and means of pleasure; and, the anti-pornography lobby contend, the female body is subordinated, exploited, degraded, detested in and through pornography.

Speaking about pornography, it seems, forces people to declare their political allegiances, their views on the quality of life, their philosophies, their fears. Pornography is an emotive subject – this partly explains the widespread debates about it in the modern era (the modern era which we might define aptly as from de Sade onwards).

It should be remembered, too, that when people speak about pornography they are not simply offering dispassionate, deperson-alized, distanced accounts of something that is 'out there'. For pornography to work, like any art or communication, it needs a reader, a viewer, a consumer. You can't, then, ignore the critic's own part in the discussion of pornography and feminism, for the critic, whether feminist or not, is also a consumer. Jennifer Wicke writes that

> it needs to be accepted that pornography is not 'just' consumed, but is used, worked on, elaborated, remembered, fantasised about by its subjects. To stop the analysis at the artifact, as virtually all the current books and articles do, imagining that the representation is the pornography in quite simple terms, is to truncate the consumption radically, and thereby to leave unconsidered the human making involved in completing the act of pornographic consumption.[35]

It is not simply a case of critics, feminists and consumers on one side and pornography, art and culture on the other. Critics pretend they coolly analyze texts from a distance, whereas they are involved with them at many levels. Subjectivity and objectivity merge, and there is not an area of neutral ground between the consumer and what is consumed. As Wicke puts it:

> The academic market is hot for pornography because pornography is both the object and the subject of desire, the representation and the reader, the consumer and the consumed, one inextricable package. (ib, 79)

Feminists have many views on pornography. Some feminists advocate the abolition of pornography, while others see the banning of pornography as more political suppression. On the one hand, there must be no censorship in a truly 'liberating' socio-political stance. On the other hand, some feminists see much of pornography as violence against women. Probably the most powerful of commentators on pornography, and certainly the most incisive and relentless in her analysis, is Andrea Dworkin. Her book *Pornography: Men Possessing Women* is a landmark in sexual politics debates. It is a work of rage, in which pornography is seen as a manifestation of the exertion by men of power over women:

> In the male system, women are sex; sex is the whore. The whore is *porne*, the lowest whore, the whore who belongs to *all* male citizens:

---

35 Jennifer Wicke: "Through a Gaze Darkly: Pornography's Academic Market", in Gibson, ed, 70

the slut, the cunt. Buying her is buying pornography. Having her is
having pornography. Seeing her is seeing pornography. (202)

In a piece in *Letters From a War Zone*, Dworkin goes further:

Women mistakenly think that pornography is largely built on the
good girl/ bad girl or the Madonna/ whore theme. With rare
exceptions, it is not. It is built on the whore/ whore theme.[36]

Andrea Dworkin pinpoints the unceasing reductionism of
patriarchy, where people are sexualized or reduced to their
genitals. We see this all the time in pornography and culture. More
controversially, Jenny Diski suggests that a rape 'victim's' life need
not be utterly shattered after the rape, because it means we put too
much emphasis on sexuality: '[e]very act of physical violence will
have traumatic effects but what do we mean when we tell a young
woman that her sense of self-esteem can be destroyed by an act of
enforced penetration? Are we really meaning to say that a
woman's central identity resides in her genitals?'[37] For some
feminists, rape is not the utter obliteration of self and life.
Feminists, such as Camille Paglia, Naomi Wolf and Katie Roiphe
claim that 'bad sex' does not mean rape, does not mean *all* sex is
bad, and should not be practiced: for some feminists, not all violent
sex is rape: 'I don't feel that whenever a woman feels violated it is
rape' says Katie Roiphe, continuing: 'everybody has been date-
raped according to these definitions – namely verbal coercion,
manipulation and pressure. Most people I know have had sex with
somebody they didn't want to'. For Roiphe, bad sex ain't rape: 'we
need to separate bad sexual experience from rape' she says.[38]
   The genitals have replaced the soul as the site of a person's
core or essence. Pornography, and art, adds to this emphasis. On
the other hand, pornography does more than reduce people to
genitals: for some feminists, a definition of pornography must
include, for instance, history, sociology, economics. Anne Snitnow
writes:

A definition of pornography that takes the problem of analysis
seriously has to include not only violence, hatred and fear of women,

36 Dworkin, *War Zone*, 239
37 Jenny Diski: "Double jeopardy of the victim victim", *The Guardian*, 27
August 1993
38 Katie Roiphe, in ib.

but also a long list of other elements, which may help explain why we women ourselves have such a mixture of reactions to the genre... Without history, without an analysis of complexity and difference, without a critical eye toward gender and its constant redefinitions, some recognition of the gap – in ideas and feelings – between the porn magazine and the man who reads it, we will only be purveying a false hope to those women whom we want to join us'.[39]

Pornography has its own 'genres' of sub-categories: there is s/m, hard core, lesbian, gay, child pornography, soft core, and there is pornography geared to any number of fetishes; rubber, leather, boots, large breasts, mud wrestling, nurses, babies, foodie, bondage, etc. These sub-genres are institutions in themselves, with their own codes and structures, but their institutionalized sexual images do not express the real eroticism that people experience.

In the art criticism of the history of the painted nude, for example, attention is always drawn to the erotic nature of the naked body. David Hockney expresses a typical (patriarchal) view on this matter: 'Kenneth Clark points out in his book *The Nude* that there are bound to be elements of eroticism in any nude picture and I think he's absolutely right there.'[40] Kenneth Clark puts it thus: '[a]ll good nude painting and sculpture is sexually stimulating'.[41] Dworkin's' point, and the opinion of many feminists, is that men reduce people to their sexuality, to penises and clitorises. As Dworkin writes: '[t]he fact is that men can and do fetishize everything' (124-5). But this might apply to women too. So many writers are guilty of this incessant sexualizing of people, of seeing just the sexual aspect of someone, ignoring other aspects: D.H. Lawrence, Henry Miller, Dante Alighieri, Charles Baudelaire, the Marquis de Sade, Paul Éluard, Maurice Scève. Many many painters eroticize people, emphasizing the sexual element above all others: Pablo Picasso, Egon Schiele, Edgar Degas, Gustav Moreau, Hans Bellmer, Auguste Renoir, Eric Gill, Titian, etc. It seems male artists cannot make art without drawing attention at some time to a person's sexuality.

Many modern 'thinkers' have stressed sex above everything else: Georges Bataille, Sigmund Freud, Wilhelm Reich, Herbert Marcuse, etc. What happens is that people become genitals:

39 Snitow: "Retrenchment Versus Transformation: The Politics of the Anti-Pornography Movement", in *Women Against Censorship*, 117
40 Hockney, in Peter Webb, 376; Kenneth Clark: *The Nude*, Penguin 1960
41 Kenneth Clark: *The Nude*, John Murray, 1956, 6

women are reduced to 'cunt... our essence, our offense' as Kate Millet put it.[42] It's easier, feminists claim, for men to relate to a depersonalized fetishized object, such as a vagina, a boot, a stocking, a woman's torso bereft of head and personality, than to relate to a real person, which is infinitely more complicated. Pornography reduces women to sex objects, much as men manufacture sex toys such as blow-up dolls, which are the ultimate, in one sense, of erotic reductionism. The sex doll doesn't moan she has a headache, she is 'always ready' for sex, so the adverts run. As Elizabeth Carola writes: 'sexually 'relating' to a fetishized image is far easier than sexually relating to another human being.'[43] In some ways, then, pornography is the ultimate pleasure machine: it is a mirror, which reflects back the man's desire. The 'sex object', the woman, is a mirror, reduced, tailored and shaped to the consumers' needs, reflecting only what he desires: depersonalized sex, sex with no personality, no feedback, no empathy, no soul or emotion, no familial, social or political worries or responsibilities. Human-free sex, in other words, machine-like sex, with no effort required, like zombie-ing out in front of the TV, couch potato sex, computer sex, cel phone sex, i-Pod sex, now called 'virtual reality' sex, hyper-real sex, fucking without touching, without making contact with anything more demanding than a flickering computer/ video-generated retinal image.

Benoîte Groult describes the 'intellectual' books of high-class pornography – by Miller, Bataille, de Sade:

> No matter what book it is, we always find the same male hero who, with the same arrogance, takes his pleasure in some creature who for him is reduced to two holes in the bottom of her body, plus a third on the bottom of her face...[44]

According to Dworkin, the way women are treated in pornography reflects the way they are treated in society, although this view is questioned by some feminists. Pornography is the theory and social power is the reality, or as Robin Morgan put it:

---

42 Millet: *The Prostitution Papers*, Avon Books, New York 1973, 95

43 Carola: "Women, Erotica, Pornography – Learning to Play the Game?", in Chester, 172

44 Groult: "Les portiers de nuit", in *Ainsi soit-elle*, Grasset, Paris, 1975, and in E. Marks, 71

'pornography is the theory and rape is the practice',[45] adding:

> And what a practice. The violation of an individual woman is the metaphor for man's forcing himself on whole nations (rape as the crux of war), on nonhuman creatures (rape as the lust behind hunting and related carnage), and on the planet itself (reflected even in our language – carving up "virgin territory", with strip mining often referred to as a "rape of the land"). (Morgan, 88)

For radical feminists, such as Susan Griffin, Dworkin, Kate Millett and Susan Brownmiller, rape is sanctioned and sanctified in patriarchy.[46] Pornography helps to legitimize rape, to make it appear the norm, so that feminists see marriage as sanctified rape.[47] Rape is the law in society, from the top down, says Andrea Dworkin. In *Intercourse* she writes:

> In Christianity, attitude is everything; in Judaism, simple compliance is. In each faith, the man's authority means that he has a right supported by law – divine law – to fuck his wife; her legal duty to submit; and intercourse itself is a legally defined hierarchy in which the one who fucks has sovereignty over the one who submits. (193).

Avis Lewallen glosses Dworkin's persuasive rhetoric thus: 'Dworkin's pornography-equals-rape argument ignores all the other discourses through which power is mediated – of which pornography is just one, if important, constituent',[48]

Dominique Poggi writes: 'one of the principal functions of pornography: the purveying of an ideology of pleasure and enjoyment which urges rapelike relations, exalts rapists'.[49]

---

45 See L. Lederer, ed. *Take Back the Night: Woman on Pornography*, William Morrow, New York 1980

46 Susan Griffin: *Rape: the Power of Consciousness*, Harper & Row, New York 1979; Susan Brownmiller: *Against Our Will: Men, Women and Rape*, Simon & Shuster, New York 1975; D. Rhodes & S.McNeil, eds. *Women Against Violence Against Women*, Onlywomen Press 1985; J. Hammer & M. Maynard, eds. *Women, Violence and Social Control*, Macmillan 1987;

47 See C. Kramarae & P. A. Treichler, eds. *A Feminist Dictionary*, Pandora Press 1985

48 Avis Lewallen: "*Lace*: pornography for women", in L. Gamman & M. Marshment, eds. *The Female Gaze: women as viewers of popular culture*, Women's Press 1988

49 Dominique Poggi: "Une apologie des rapports de domination", *La quinzaine littéraire*, August 1976, in E. Marks, 77

Catherine MacKinnon's definition is aligned with Dworkin's: she says: '[p]olitically, I call it rape whenever the woman feels violated'.[50] Feminists such as Robin Morgan and Michael Moorcock concur with this view, but other feminists, such as Camille Paglia, Naomi Wolf and Katie Roiphe disagree vehemently, claiming that not all violent sex is rape: 'I don't feel that whenever a woman feels violated it is rape' says Katie Roiphe, continuing: 'everybody has been date-raped according to these definitions – namely verbal coercion, manipulation and pressure. Most people I know have had sex with somebody they didn't want to'. For Roiphe, bad sex ain't rape: 'we need to separate bad sexual experience from rape' she says (in ib.).

For Dworkin, pornography is about male power: '[m]ale power is the raison d'etre of pornography; the degradation of the female is the means of achieving this power.' (25) This power is exerted, claims Dworkin, physically, economically, psycho-logically, philosophically, ideologically, politically, socially, in every sphere of life. Dworkin uses pornography as a way of showing just how men control so many aspects of life, and how men express their hatred of women.

For the establishment, Dworkin's cultural analysis goes too far. For some feminists, it doesn't go far enough. Some feminists have been critical of Dworkin, and of Dworkin's and Catherine MacKinnon's anti-pornography bill in the US.[51] The problems begin when anti-pornography drives become as dogmatic and entrenched as pro-pornography agendas. The area is a minefield, continually paradoxical, with no clear dividing lines. There is massive confusion and ambiguity.

For some, Dworkin goes too far, or is too sweeping and generalized in her polemical statements. For Michael Moorcock, Andrea Dworkin is an inspiration. She does not dictate, Moorcock says, but simply reflects what is already there in contemporary culture:

> Dworkin says her books are not prescriptive but descriptive. While continuing to expand the boundaries of feminist, she argues from a

50 MacKinnon, quoted in John Cassidy: "[The] author who took on the feminists [interview with Katie Roiphe", *The Sunday Times*, 9 January 1994
51 See Lisa Duggan: "Censorship in the Name of Feminism", in Chester, 76-86; Varda Burstyn, ed. *Feminists Against Censorship*, Douglas & McIntyre, Toronto 1985; Liz Kelly: "Feminists v Feminists – legislating against porn in the USA", *Trouble and Strife*, 7, 4-10

humanistic and idealistic perspective both intellectually stunning and stylistically eloquent.[52]

For some feminists, focusing on the pornography issue means vital energy is directed at only one issue, when there are many others that need attention. 'Porn is just one product in the big social supermarket,' writes B. Ruby Rich. 'Why is pornography so important, finally? Is it important enough to be consuming all our political energy as feminists?... whether symptom or cause, pornography presents an incomplete target for feminists. The campaign against pornography is a massive displacement of outrage that ought to be directed at a far wider sphere of oppression.'[53]

The issue of pornography creates confusion and divides feminists as much as liberal intellectuals or politicians. As Julienne Dickey writes: 'why does the subject evoke on the one hand such passion, even hostility, and on the other hand an incapacitating confusion?'[54] Pornography is such a contentious issue, it seems no commentator can manoeuvre through it without sinking into some bog or other of moral ambiguity or hermeneutic conflict. Julienne Dickey says that there

> are also other dangers in making a centrality of the pornography position. Focussing so strongly on sexual imagery can lead to feminist struggle being co-opted by the right, thus defusing the very real threat that feminist ideas and practice pose to the patriarchal structures of society. It can divert feminist attention, resources and energy away from other sites of struggle, such as socio-economic problems, women's inequality in every sphere – and the appalling but non-pornographic content of the rest of the media.[55]

Another feminist, Claudia, says that the concentration on pornography as production displaces awareness of other important modes of labour by women:

> It is remarkable how sudden feelings of empathy and identification with 'exploited' women surge up in the breasts of feminists when they think of works in the sex-industry... It is even more remarkable

---

52 Michael Moorcock: *Casablanca*, Gollancz 1989, 134-5
53 B. Ruby Rich: "Anti-Porn: Soft Issue, Hard World", *Village Voice*,20 July 1982, in *Feminist Review*, eds., *Sexuality: A Reader*, 347-8, 350
54 Julienne Dickey: "Snakes and Ladders", in Chester, 161
55 Dickey, in Chester, 165

how feminists never identify in this way with cleaners, child-minders and factory works; that is, those 'hidden' women who create the conditions that keep the feminist in the 'alternative' lifestyle to which she has become accustomed'[56]

For feminists, the issue of pornography often involves the most extreme emotions, from virulent hatred to passion. As Sue George writes, '[f]or a feminist, therefore, to enjoy pornography is to feel doubly guilty.'[57]

Are you simply going to ban it outright, then? But what is 'it', who defines pornography, and how can you ban it? If people are affected they see and read, this would mean not simply banning pornography, but so much other forms of communication which encouraged, as Dworkin said, the 'subordination' of women. Julienne Dickey writes:

> There be no doubt that media sexism contributes to our feelings about ourselves and our expectations, inevitably placing limits on our achievements and our enjoyment of life. But if we were to ban things on the grounds that they contribute to women's lowered expectation and negative self-image, then surely we should ban anything which presents women in stereotyped roles. The portrayal of women as engaged solely in the service of men – at home, at work, at play – is all-pervasive, and arguably more damaging to women's self-estimation than the (statistically rarer) instances of explicit pornography. (ib., 164)

The Bobbitt case, where a woman cut off her husband's penis, reveals some of the powergaming and goals of the media and how it reports sexual violences. This extract is from the biggest selling Sunday broadsheet newspaper in the UK, *The Sunday Times*:

> In the early hours of June 23, 1993, the 5ft, six-and-a-half stone Mrs John Wayne Bobbitt claims that "an irresistible impulse" – or temporary insanity drove her to sever her husband's penis. Years of physical abuse by her husband, a US marine, led the slightly built manicurist to commit the act. On the night in question, she says, he raped her. At the time, she called the police from a pay-phone to say she had been raped and had fled the apartment in a panic. It was only while driving that she realised she was still clutching the penis in her

56 Claudia: "Fear of Pornography", in Assister, 133
57 Sue George: "Censorship and Hypocrisy: Some Issues Surrounding Pornography that Feminism has Ignored", in Chester, 111

hand. She then flung it out of the driver's window and went to the
same hospital where her husband was having surgery, to be treated as
a rape victim.

The dick-chopping case caught the imagination of America:
the newspaper report goes on to describe the merchandize that
people cooked up to cash in on the incident:

> Other T-shirts were for sale among the satellite trucks and live
> cameras set up from around the world. If you wanted a
> commemorative slogan you could choose from "You snooze, you
> lose", "He lost that loving feeling", "Hung jury", "What's up with
> you?" and "Clean-cut kind of guy". One enterprising vendor was
> hawking $10 gift packs of chocolate penises complete with knife. A
> prospective purchaser complained that the penises were broken.
> 'They're not broken, sir, they're sliced," was the reply. [...] Inside
> court, the debate boiled down to its essence. "A sleeping man's penis
> was amputated," stated the state persecutor (a man). "What we have,
> ladies and gentlemen," claimed the defence lawyer (a woman), "is
> Lorena Bobbitt's life juxtaposed against John Wayne Bobbitt's penis."
> The husband was the first witness to take the stand and his penis was
> an early exhibit. A photograph of what the police described as "the
> appendage" was quickly produced (prompting cheers, applause and
> roars of approval among reporters watching the trial in a nearby
> room). The photograph was not shown in close-up on national
> television. "It was just too gross," said Stephen Johnson, executive
> producer of Court TV.

What's interesting, and what many feminists would surely
comment on, is *how* the case was reported, how people discussed
the case. How, for instance, they concentrated on the comical
aspect of someone having their dick chopped off. How hilarious it
is. Yet how many men would utterly hate it happening them. For
the Bobbitt cock-topping case centres around docking the dick,
whereas the case is really about rape and domestic violence, about
a woman being brutalized over years, not just in one incident. Of
course it makes great copy for the media, but as in so many other
similar cases of women hitting back at men, it is blown out of
proportion. It is over-sensationalized, with male critics and
reporters drawing ridiculous conclusions about men being
'harassed' by women.

In the Bobbitt case, attention is neatly diverted from rape and
violence to the 'grotesque' act of mutilation. The media is provided

with a 'bizarre' angle or story which enables them to shirk the real point of the story, which is the sexual harassment and rape of a woman by a man. Further, the case enables wags and commentators, rightwing or leftwing or liberal or whatever, to lay into feminism, to blame feminism for such female acts of revenge. The woman is branded, as so often, as 'mad'. The man becomes a victim, and martyr. Poor devil, he just wants his penis back, his 'manhood', his pride and joy. Well, if patriarchal people keep exalting the penis and the erection, it's no wonder that the people they've hurt will go for their dicks when they're angry. While soldiers will go in for 'skull fucking', according to Vietnam War legend, where a woman's head after she's been killed is poked with a penis, so will battered women hit back by chopping off men's glories.

The bitter irony of the Bobbitt case is that men have perpetrated thousands of far worse acts than chopping off a penis. The number of men who have mutilated women throughout history must be something like 1000:1 or more compared to the number of women who have mutilated men. Statistics on these acts are difficult to find. In the Bobbitt case, the man emerged with his pride and joy sewn back on; in the case of thousands of women throughout history, many died, or suffered far worse fates. And, while one man had his dick cut off in America, there are thousands of clitorises being cut out around the globe even now.[58]

Extremist feminists, whether right, communist, liberal, or radical, never argue for the murder of men. That would be the most extreme act of feminist separatism. For, as Andrea Dworkin writes in *Mercy*: 'killing killed the one doing the killing and that killing killed something precious and good at the center of life itself' (168). However much the oppressed want to kill the oppressors, they are held back. All manner of things hold them back: laws, codes, parents, friends, the police, society itself. Punishment comes swiftly to those women who revolt and murder their oppressors, as in Thomas Hardy's *Tess of the d'Urbervilles*. Both men, Angel and Alec, treat Tess abominably: Angel exalts her as a 'pure', spiritual being, too innocent to know anything about

---

58 See Mary Daly: *Pure Lust*, 155f; Fran Hosken, ed. *Women's International Network News*, vol.1, no.3, June 1975, vol. 1, no.4, Oct 1975; J.A. Verzin: "Sequelae of Female Circumcision", *Tropical Doctor*, Oct 1975; Eugenio Lenzi: "Damage Caused by Infibulation and Infertility", *Acta European Fertilitatis*, vol. 2, no.47, 1970

'real', manly life, a pretty appendage to his plan of creating a farm business somewhere; Alec exalts Tess sexually, as, again, for him she's a pretty thing to fuck occasionally, when he feels like it. The outcome, as Hardy bitterly says, is that 'the woman pays' for the mistakes of men, society and patriarchal laws. Not just in the matter of death, but in the realms of sexuality, education, career, race, economy, class, status and family, there are rules and laws which say 'no'. The laws, for some feminists, favour men over women, and women receive more oppression than men. Sue Bridehead in Hardy's novel *Jude the Obscure* had also found out (the hard way) that there is some great voice from above which says 'Don't, Don't Don't':

> 'Then another silence, till she was seized with another uncontrollable fit of grief. 'There is something external to us which says, "You shan't!" First it said, "You shan't learn!" Then it said, "You shan't labour!" Now it says, "You shan't love!"'

There are many different kinds of pornography, as there are many different kinds of art or feminism. Seen through cultural or postmodern or deconstructionist or semiological theory, pornography can be viewed as a realm of codes, meanings, contexts, signifiers, values, attitudes, which are politically controlled, manufactured by social, economic and political needs and demands. Pornography is thus the *representation* of... something; maybe certain kinds of sexuality, maybe somebody's thoughts on certain kinds of sexuality. Pornography is not *sexuality in itself*, it is mediation, representation, communication. Representations of sexuality feed back into people's actual sexual identities, in their actual sex 'acts', and vice versa, as Suzanne Kappeler notes (2). As a series of representations, then, pornography can be seen as part of a *continuum* of other representations: TV, magazines, painting, writing, video, the web etc. Pornography is one area, one genre even, of representation, and is thus subject to the various mechanisms of political, social, economic, metaphysical and physical pressures that influence other forms of representation.

Most commentators, of whatever ideological or political persuasion, agree that pornography is full of conflict, hypocrisy and paradox, as well as heaps of desire. Catherine MacKinnon describes sexuality in a way that might apply also to pornography:

Sexuality is that social process which creates, organizes, expresses, and directs desire, creating the social beings we know as women and men, as their relations create society.[59]

For radical feminists, we live in a 'rapist' culture, a 'sado-spiritual' society, as Mary Daly called it, using her new terms which she invented to describe the phallocentric nature of Western society.[60] 'The fact is,' writes Daly, '

that we live in a profoundly anti-female society, a misogynistic 'civilization' in which men collectively victimize women, using us as personifications of their own paranoid fears, as The Enemy.[61]

Many feminists concur with Mary Daly's view of the West as phallocentric and violent. It seems to be 'us and them', as Ann Snitow notes: 'the brotherhood of the oppressors, the sisterhood of the victims'.[62] The problem with this view, of men against women, is that it reduces the conflicts too easily, too simply. Further, it ignores, as concentration on the pornography issue does, other issues, important issues of race, class, economy and politics. Pratibha Parmar glosses Ann Snitow's comment thus:

again this sisterhood of all women assumes that there are no significant differences between women, compared with the similarities of our experiences of pornography. I find such analysis both Eurocentric and nationalist. It is also insulting in its simplicity.[63]

For some feminists, the emphasis on the male-female antagonisms obscures issues of race, for instance, which some feminists regard as far more important than the usual issue of men against women. As Audre Lorde, 'an Afro-American lesbian poet

---

59 Catherine MacKinnon: "Feminism, Marxism, Method, and the State: An Agenda for Theory", op. cit.

60 Mary Daly: *Pure Lust: Elemental Feminist Philosophy*, Women's Press, 1984

61 Mary Daly: *Gyn/Ecology: The Metaphysics of Radical Feminism*, Women's Press 1978

62 Ann Snitow: "Retrenchment Verses Transformation: the Politics of the Anti-Pornography Movement", in Varda Burstyn, op. cit., 113

63 Pratibha Parmar: "Rage and Desire: Confronting Pornography", in Chester, 123

and philosopher'[64] wrote: '[f]or then beyond sisterhood is still racism.'[65]

When the establishment – politicians, the media, etc – speak of feminism they usually mean, without saying so, the white middle class feminism of France or Anglo-America. It is important to remember that however important issues such as pornography and men-women conflict are, the issue of racism is regarded by many feminists as much more important to address.[66]

For Susan Griffin, pornography stems from body hatred, an inability, found in many institutions, such as Christianity, to accept wholeheartedly one's own body. Griffin argues that 'pornography is an expression not of human erotic feeling and desire, and not of a love of the life of the body, but of fear of bodily knowledge, and a desire to silence eros.'[67] Certainly we find a lot of body-loathing in erotic art – in Picasso, Schiele, Bellmer, Toulouse-Lautrec, Magritte, etc. And Christianity is the king of all body-hating religions. Pornography may be seen as an inability of the people who make pornography (men) to accept fully the body in all its wildness and strangeness.

What happens, throughout history, is that wildness or madness is suppressed, repressed, sidelined, ignored, or, to use a term popular in early 21st century criticism, 'marginalized'. Wildness is marginalized, because it upsets the status quo; it usurps the societal and social norms. It is threatening. This is a continuing theme in the writings of Julia Kristeva. In "The True-Real" ("Le vréel"):

> We know… how logic and ontology have inscribed the question of *truth* within *judgement* (or sentence structure) and *being*, dismissing as *madness, mysticism or poetry* any attempt to articulate that impossible element which henceforth can only be designated by the Lacanian category of the *real*. After the flowering of mysticism, classical

64 Maggie Humm's description, in Maggie Humm, ed. *Feminisms: A Reader*, 137

65 Audre Lorde: "An Open Letter to Mary Daly", 1980, in *Sister Outsider*, Crossing Press, New York 1984

66 C. Moraga & G. Anzaldúa, eds. *This Bridge Called My Back: Writings by Radical Women of Color*, Kitchen Table, New York 1983; B. Christian: *Black Feminist Criticism*, Pergamon, Oxford 1985; P.H. Collins: *Black Feminist Thought*, Unwin 1990

67 Susan Griffin: *Pornography and Silence: Culture's Revenge Against Women*, Women's Press 1981

rationality, first by embracing Folly with Erasmus, and then by excluding it with Descartes, attempted to enunciate the real as truth by setting limits on Madness; modernity, on the other hand, opens up this enclosure in a search for other forms capable of transforming or rehabilitating the statues of *truth*. (in *The Kristeva Reader*, 217)

When feminists discuss the body and sexuality, the results are just as controversial as discussions of art vs. pornography. Many feminists speak of the sexual superiority of women. For instance, Xavière Gauthier says that

...witches [women] are bursting; their entire bodies are desire; their gestures are caresses; their smell, taste, hearing are all sensual. Their pleasure is so violent, so transgressive, so open, so fatal, that men have not yet recovered... Female eroticism is terrifying; it is an earthquake, a volcanic eruption, a tidal wave. It is disquieting and so is mystified. It is made a mystery.[68]

This transgressive, terrifying eroticism has not yet really been depicted in art or pornography. What we get is men's version of it – male ideas of wild eroticism, which is usually reduced to violence.

Women have an all-over, total body eroticism, say writers such as Anaïs Nin, Peter Redgrove and Luce Irigaray. 'But *woman has sex organs just about everywhere*. She experiences pleasure almost everywhere' writes Luce Irigaray.[69] Feminists have spoken of the wildness of women's eroticism and their fantasies. What this stance does is to uphold the eternal philosophical dualism of the West, setting women always against men, and using men to gauge women's sexuality. Feminists such as Hélène Cixous have argued, rightly, that masculine 'binary logic', which constantly opposes terms such as 'masculine' and 'feminine' is very limiting. It is two-term logocentrism, which reduces everything to 'yes' or 'no'.[70]

68 Xavière Gauthier: "Pourquoi Sorcières?", in *Sorcières*, 1, 1976, in E. Marks, 201-2

69 Irigaray: "Ce sexe qui n'en est pas un", in *Ce sexe qui n'en est pas un*, Minuit, Paris, 1977, and in E. Marks, eds., 103; see also: Jane Gallop: "*Quand nos lèvres s'écrivent*: Irigaray's body politic", *Romantic Review*, 74, 77-83; Elizabeth Grosz: "Philosophy, subjectivity and the body", in Carole Pateman & Elizabeth Grosz, eds. *Feminist Challenges*, Allen & Unwin, Sydney 1986, 125-43

70 Hélène Cixous & Catherine Clément: *The Newly Born Woman*, 63f

Julia Kristeva writes in *About Chinese Women* that:

> no other civilization seems to have made the principle of sexual
> difference so crystal clear: between the two sexes a cleavage or abyss
> opens up... Monotheistic unity is sustained by a radical separation of
> the sexes: indeed, it is this very separation which is its prerequisite.
> (*The Kristeva Reader*, 141)

The pornography issue emphasizes heterosexuality, whereas
there are many forms of eroticism. Reducing erotic identities to
male/ female or masculine/ feminine is limiting: eroticism is far
stranger, more diffuse, more focused and far wilder than
genderized categories suggest.[71] Hence feminists' emphasis on
difference: instead of always relating women's sexuality to men's:
some feminists stress that it is *different* – not just sexually, but
socially, economically, ideologically, racially.[72] Irigaray writes, so
simply yet so effectively: 'there are no grounds for paying less for
one body's work than for another's', but Irigaray does not believe
in full 'equality', the only sort of equality she deems possible is
economic, otherwise she argues for difference, but all feminists
agree that there is inequality and injustice in so many areas of life.
It can be pointless always blaming men, because that is not the
whole problem, and it's pointless always blaming sexuality, for
sexuality is only one part of human experience. It is not what is
desired in that pornography is unacceptable, says Gayle Rubin, but
the arrogant way that men *expect* certain things to be done. It is is
the fact that men think they can make these demands of people:

> it is the fact that men feel entitled to make these demands which is
> disgusting – not what they desire sexually. This is not caused by
> depiction of sex acts in pornography, but by a sexist society that does
> not afford women full human or sexual status.

For Andrea Dworkin, there is injustice where there doesn't
need to be injustice: she is not talking about the unfairness of
death, or the human condition as grounded in biology or nature;

---

71 See E. Newton & S. Walton: "The misunderstanding: toward a more
precise sexual vocabulary", in C.S. Vance, ed. *Pleasure and Danger*,
Routledge & Kegan Paul, Boston, Mass., *1984*
72 See Monique Wittig: "The category of sex", *Feminist Issues*, vol 2, no. 2,
1982, 63-8; Audre Lorde: *Sister Outsider*, op. cit.; Colette Guillaumin: "The
question of difference", *Feminist Issues*, vol 2, no.1, 1982, 33-52

she's talking about the injustices that people create. Unnecessary tortures, either physical or psychological, tortures which simply do not have to be there:

> The women's movement is like other political movements in one important way. Every political movement is committed to the belief that there are certain kinds of pain that people should not endure. They are unnecessary. They are gratuitous. They are not part of the God-given order. They are not biologically inevitable. They are acts of human will. They are acts done by some human beings to other human beings.[73]

Dworkin is surely right here, that there are things that people do to each other that are unnecessarily painful. So that feminism, in Dworkin's view, must be concerned, first and foremost, with the injustices that people gratuitously, unnecessarily create. For her, feminism pivots around the assumption that women are inferior: '[t]he movement is concerned first of all with this virtual metaphysical premise that women are biologically inferior.' (in ib., 135)

Feminists such as Elaine Showalter and Jeanne Roberts, taking their cue from Edwin Ardener,[74] propose that there is a female 'wild zone', as there is a male 'wild zone'. We know about men's version of wild zone eroticism, what Hélène Cixous calls 'glorious phallic monosexuality'.[75] The female 'wild zone' is beyond patriarchal space, beyond patriarchal representations.[76] Elaine Showalter writes:

> We can think of the "wild zone" of women's culture spatially, experientially, or metaphysically. Spatially, it stands for an area which is literally no-man's land, a place forbidden to men... Experientially it stands for the aspects of the female life-style which are outside of and unlike those of men; again, there is a corresponding zone of male experience alien to women. But if we think of the wild zone metaphysically or in terms of consciousness, it has no corresponding

73 Dworkin, "Feminism: An Agenda", *Letters From a War Zone*, , 134
74 Edwin Ardener: "Belief and the Problem of Women", in Shirley Ardener, ed. *Perceiving Women*, Halsted Press, New York 1978
75 Cixous, "The Laugh of the Medusa", in E. Marks, 254
76 Elaine Showalter: "Feminist Criticism in the Wilderness", in Showalter, 1986, 262-3; Jeanne Addison Roberts: *The Shakespearean Wild: Geography, Genus and Gende*r, University of Nebraska Press, Lincoln, Nebraska 1991, 1-5

male space since all of male consciousness is within the circle of the dominant structure and thus accessible to or structured by language. (in ib., 262)

Julia Kristeva and Luce Irigaray, among other French feminists, have spoken of something in 'women' or the 'feminine' that is 'unrepresentable', beyond art, beyond male culture. In *About Chinese Women*, Kristeva writes of the woman as a witch, someone outside of patriarchal discourse, or at least, thrown to the edge, the border between the known zone and the wild zone:

> ...woman is a specialist in the unconscious, a witch, a bacchanalian, taking her *jouissance* in an anti-Apollonian, Dionysian orgy. A *jouissance* which breaks the symbolic chain, the taboo, the mastery. A *marginal discourse*, with regard to the science, religion and philosophy of the *polis* (witch, child, underdeveloped, not even a poet, at best his accomplice). (*The Kristeva Reader*, 154)

Ann Rosalind Jones describes Kristeva's notion of the 'outsider' culture of women, of women as 'witches':

> Women, for Kristeva… speak and write as "hysterics," as outsiders to male-dominated discourse, for two reasons: 'the predominance in them of drives related to anality and childbirth, and their marginal position *vis-à-vis* masculine culture. Their semiotic style is likely to involve repetitive, spasmodic separations from the dominating discourse, which, more often, they are forced to imitate.[77]

Julia Kristeva's writings may be the most coherent and incisive account of the psycho-cultural 'wild zone'. Victor Burgin, describing Kristeva's philosophy, says that she positions

> the woman in society… in the patriarchal, as perpetually at the boundary, the borderline, the edge, the 'outer limit' – the place where order shades into chaos, light into darkness. The peripheral and ambivalent position allocated to woman, says Kristeva, had led to that familiar division of the field of representation in which women are viewed as either saintly or demonic – according to whether they are seen as bringing the darkness, or as keeping it out.[78]

---

77 Ann Rosalind Jones: "Writing the Body: L'Écriture féminine", in Showalter, ed, 363
78 Victor Burgin: "Geometry and Abjection", in John Fletcher and Andrew Benjamin, eds., 115-6

Saintly woman (the Virgin Mary is a typical example) keeps the amazing energy of the female wild zone out of men's lives; the demonic woman (Mary Magdalene, the *femme fatale*, vampire, 'devil woman') is the one who brings the wildness with her. Patriarchy of course prefers bland, mute, passive door-stops in women, people who will stop the darkness from coming in, who will sit there and say nothing and get on with society's housework.

André Breton said the 'existence is elsewhere'. French feminists say that 'woman' is elsewhere. 'She is indefinitely other in herself,' writes Luce Irigaray, maintaining that women

> are already elsewhere than in the discursive machinery where you claim to take them by surprise. They have turned back within themselves, which does not mean the same thing as 'within yourself'. They do not experience the same interiority that you do and which perhaps you mistakenly presume they share.[79]

Here, perhaps, in the female 'wild zone', some of the wildness and strangeness and ecstasy of 'female' eroticism may be experienced and depicted. Luce Irigaray also spoke in spatial terms of idealist feminism:

> We need both space and time. And perhaps we are living in an age when *time must re-deploy space*. Could this be the dawning of a new world? Immanence and transcendence are being recast, notably by that *threshold* which has never been examined in itself: the female sex. It is a threshold unto *mucosity*. Beyond the classic opposites of love and hate, liquid and ice lies this perpetually *half-open* threshold, consisting of *lips* that are strangers to dichotomy. Pressed against one another, but without any possibility of suture, at least of a real kind, they do not absorb the world either into themselves or through themselves, provided they are not abused or reduced to a mere consummating or consuming structure. Instead their shape welcomes without assimilating or reducing or devouring. A sort of door unto voluptuousness, then? Not that, either: their useful function is to designate a *place*: the very place of uses, at least on a habitual plane. Strictly speaking, they serve neither conception nor *jouissance*. Is this, then, the mystery of female identity, of its self-contemplation, of that strange word of silence; both the threshold and reception of exchange, the sealed-up secret of wisdom, belief and faith in every truth?[80]

---

79 Irigaray: *Ce sexe qui n'en est pas un*, Minuit, Paris 1977, 28-9
80 Luce Irigaray: "La différence sexuelle", *Ethiope de la différence sexuelle*, Minuit, Paris, 1984, and in Toril Moi, ed. *French Feminist Thought*,128

Many feminists suggest that women's eroticism cannot be represented, much as women themselves cannot be represented. Julia Kristeva writes: '[i]n "woman" I see something that cannot be represented, something that is not said, something above and beyond nomenclatures and ideologies.'[81] Other feminists echo this idea, that women cannot be fully represented in the traditional media of patriarchy. As Hélène Cixous writes:

> It is at the level of sexual pleasure in my opinion that the difference makes itself most clearly apparent in as far as woman's libidinal economy is neither identifiable by a man nor referable to the masculine economy.[82]

The unrepresentable in art and pornography, according to some feminists, is women's eroticism, their *jouissance*, that 'explosive, blossoming, sane and inexhaustible *jouissance* of the woman', as Julia Kristeva describes it.[83]

What we get in most Western art, from Greek and Roman sculpture through the glories of the Renaissance to the latest pornography, are male representations of female eroticism. Feminists say that there are no real depictions of female *jouissance* in art or literature. 'In my opinion,' writes Marguerite Duras, 'women have never expressed themselves.'[84] What she means, perhaps, is that women have expressed themselves thus far in terms and means defined by men. There is no 'feminine' or 'women's' writing, according to some feminists. Hélène Cixous reckons she's found only three 'inscriptions of femininity' the 20th century: Colette, Marguerite Duras and Jean Genet.[85]

Real sex, the French feminists argue, has not yet been represented. Women haven't done it because they work within the same patriarchal structures, codes and constraints as men. Men, generally, haven't got a hope of depicting authentic 'female' eroticism, although the authors of millions of pornographic products would claim they know everything about 'female' eroticism. On the other hand, in the mechanisms of cultural/

81 Kristeva: "La femme, ce n'est jamais ça", *Tel Quel*, Autumn 1974, in E. Marks, 135
82 Hélène Cixous: "Sorties", in E. Marks, 95
83 Kristeva: *About Chinese Women*, Marion Boyars 1977, 63
84 Duras, interview in *Signs*, Winter 1975, in E. Marks, 175
85 Cixous: "The Laugh of the Medusa", *Signs*, Summer 1976, in E. Marks, 249

postmodern theory, anyone, male or female, should be able to create a truly 'feminine' text. It shouldn't matter who the author is. If the French feminists are right, then nearly all of the art produced anywhere is orientated to the male and the masculine, even when it is created by women. Many women artists would dispute this. The notion of an 'authentic' 'women's'/ 'feminine' art continues to be hotly debated.

According to the French feminists, 'women's' or 'feminine' or 'female' art is created in the gaps and silences of a text, but not in the intentional space of the artwork. Mary Jacobus explains:

> The French insistence on *écriture féminine* – on woman as a writing-effect instead of an origin – asserts not the sexuality of the text but the textuality of sex. Gender difference, produced, not innate, becomes a matter of the structuring of a genderless libido in and through patriarchal discourse. Language itself would at once repress multiplicity and heterogeneity – true difference – by the tyranny of hierarchical oppositions (man/ woman) and simultaneously work to overthrow that tyranny by interrogating the limits of meaning. The 'feminine', in this scheme, is to be located in the gaps, the absences, the unsayable or unrepresentable of discourse and representation.[86]

For some feminists, philosophies based on the body are problematic, because to look for some essential nature of 'woman', some essence based in biology is dubious.[87] Indeed, Toril Moi writes that 'to define 'woman' is necessarily to essentialize her.' (*Sexual/ Textual Politics*, 139) What is 'woman', anyway? A 'writing-effect', for the feminist Alice Jardine, an element in culture or a text. It's important, as Monique Wittig notes, to make a distinction between the various interpretations 'woman' and 'women':

> Our first task... is thoroughly to dissociate "woman" (the class within which we fight) and "woman," the myth. For "woman" does not exist for us; it is only an imaginary formation, while "women" is the duct of

86 Mary Jacobus: "Is There a Woman in This Text?", in *New Literary Criticism*, Autumn, 1982, 14, 1
87 See Susan Rubin Suleiman: (Re)Writing the Body: The Politics of Female Eroticism", in Suleiman, 14f; Elizabeth Grosz: "Desire, the body and recent French feminism', *Intervention*, 21-2, 1988, 28-33; Alison M. Jagger & Susan R. Bordo, eds. *Gender/ Body/ Knowledge: feminist reconstructions of being and knowing*, Rutgers University Press, New Brunswick 1989; Naomi Schor: "This essentialism which is not one: coming to grips with Irigaray", *differences*, 1 (2), 38-58

a social relationship.[88]

Elaine Showalter writes of the biologic and genderized views of feminism:

> Organic or biological criticism is the most extreme statement of gender difference, of a text indelibly marked by the body: anatomy is textuality... Simply to invoke anatomy risks a return to the crude essentialism, the phallic and ovarian theories of art, that oppressed women in the past.[89]

Biology, though, is crucial, the body is crucial. Hélène Cixous writes: '[i]n censuring the body, one censures at the same time breathing and speech.'[90] But feminists such as Elaine Showalter are wary of biologist or essentialist philosophies. As Simone de Beauvoir put it, women are not born, they are made, meaning socially, culturally, politically, ideologically, psychologically, etc.

In pornography, the great signifier for anti-porn feminists is the phallus, while the site of pleasure is the woman's body. Reclining on a million couches in artists' studios, the female nude offers itself up as a country to be colonized. She is both a pleasure machine and a fantasy. The orchestrator of pleasure in this pornographic scenario is that little slip of flesh, the penis. The phallus is good, whole, true, unifying, as opposed to the bad, fragmented, impure, chaotic vagina.[91] The phallus is the emblem of male power, as many commentators, not only feminists, note: '[t]he supreme power is the power that prevails over mortality', and this power is 'reasonably equated with the phallus'.[92] For feminists, we live in a phallic/ phallocentric/ phallogocentric society, where the phallus, the sublime signifier, the most censored image in the West, is the beginning and the end of sexual pleasure. For Madeleine Gagnon, the phallus is an emblem of male narcissism: '[t]he phallus... represents repressive capitalist ownership, the exploiting

88 Monique Witting: "One Is Not Born a Woman", speech at the Feminist as Scholar Conference, May 1979, Barnard College, New York
89 Showalter: "Feminist Criticism in the Wilderness", in Showalter, ed, 250
90 Cixous: *Le Jeune Née*, Paris 1975, 179
91 See Toil Moi: *Sexual/Textual Politics*, 66f; Sandra M. Gilbert & Susan Gubar: *The Madwoman in the Attic: The Woman Writer and the Nineteenth Century Literary Imagination*, Yale University Press, New Haven 1979
92 Leo Steinberg: *The Sexuality of Christ in Renaissance Art and in Modern Oblivion*, Pantheon, New York, 1984, 90

bourgeois... The phallus means everything that sets itself up as a mirror. Everything that erects itself as perfection.'[93] Phallic power, as feminists know, must be rigorously defended, and the phallus is a power that must always remain secret, taboo, as Andrea Dworkin writes:

> The fathers know that taboo is the essence of power: keep the source of power hidden, mysterious, sacred, so that those without power can never find it, understand it, or take it away... the fathers maintained, as they always do, that the power of manhood is in the phrase: keep it covered, hidden; shroud it in religious taboos; use it in secret; on it build an empire, but never expose it to the powerless, those who do not have it, those who would, if they could but see its true, naked, unarmed dimensions, have contempt for it, grind it to nothing under their thumbs.[94]

Whole philosophic systems are based on the phallus, yet, as Juliet Mitchell notes:

> It's extraordinary what happens when you get rid of the centrality of the concept of the phallus. I mean, you get rid of the unconscious, get rid of sexuality, get rid of the original psychoanalytic point.[95]

If men reduce people to their sexual identities, as some feminists claim, then at the heart of this is the penis. Women are reduced to 'cunt', as Kate Millet notes, while men are all phallus. There are certainly no shortage of phallic symbols and artifacts about. You can't see the real thing in society, the real penis – it's not much to look at anyway – so men displace their phallic sexuality onto thrusting cars, trucks, missiles, bombs, towers, cameras, computers, guitars, cigarettes, telephones, swords, guns, eyes, etc. These things abound in (patriarchal) art, and throughout the history of art. The trouble is that the penis ain't much of a thing, after all, for many feminists. As Richard Dyer writes:

---

93 Gagnon: "Corps I", *La venue à l'écriture*, UGE, 10/ 18, Paris 1977; in E. Marks, 180
94 Dworkin, *Letters From a War Zone*, 216-7
95 Juliet Mitchell: "Feminine Sexuality: Interview with Juliet Mitchell and Jacqueline Rose", *m/f*, 8 (1983), 15

For the fact is that the penis isn't a patch on the phallus. The penis can never live up to the mystique implied by the phallus.[96]

For other women writers, the penis is loved, beloved, exalted. Tuppy Owens, who has worked in conventional soft-core pornography and the new 'women's 'pornography', writes loving of the penis:

Let's hope that my sex mag which *can't* show dicks (Smiths and Menzies won't allow them to be shown in their exciting, excited state), won't also be a waste of time. It's a travesty! Dicks are delectable, incredible biological structures. The whole apparatus, the size, the way it fits inside, and the precariousness of it all, makes me wonder why people bother to take an interest in anything else in life at all. That so many cocks go unloved and uncherished by women these days is an unbelievable waste of resources, and also senseless human cruelty.[97]

Tuppy Owens' exaltation of the penis is about as far away from many feminists' polemic anti-pornography stance as is possible. The idea that there are penises being 'unloved' in the world, which so disheartens Tuppy Owens, is obscene to some feminists. The phallus is precisely that 'transcendent signifier' that many feminists are trying to dislodge from its central throne in patriarchy.

The male nude can be seen as a phallus, as Gill Saunders writes: '[t]he male body, while not constructed as the site of sexual pleasure, is often symbolic of phallic power. The whole body, muscular, potent, active, may come to represent the phallus.'[98]

The penis isn't a phallus, so, to make up for the pathetic insufficiency of the penis, macho masculinity is demonstrated by bulging muscles, clenched fists, sturdy poses. The male nude poses with a body of 'rippling muscles', bizarrely exaggerated, or gripping a gun, or standing next to a motorcycle, a car, a machine, something that can connote phallic power.

The male nude is uncomfortable. He doesn't like his photograph or painting or sculpture to be looked at like female nudes. He doesn't like it. He is used to being the one doing the

---

96 Richard Dyer: 'Don't Look Now", *Screen*, vol. 23, 3/ 4, 1983, and in Angela McRobbie, 206
97 Owens: :Sex On My Mind", in Assister, 125
98 Gill Saunders: *The Nude*, 26

looking. When the roles are reversed, ambiguity and confusion seeps in. The male nude is set up as spectacle, and as a passive object. To counter the awkwardness of this passivity, the male nude is shown *doing* something. Running, throwing a spear, fighting, etc. It tries to engage a position of activity, because to be the 'looked-at' one, the passive sex object, is very disquieting. Further, the activity of the male nude, which you see everywhere, in photographs by Muybridge,[99] in sculptures by Michelangelo, in films, aims at portraying phallic power. 'Even in an apparently relaxed, supine pose,' writes Richard Dyer, 'the model tightens and tautens his body so that the muscles are emphasized, hence drawing attention to the body's potential for action. More often, the male pin-up is not supine anyhow, but standing taut ready for action' (Dyer, op.cit., 20).

For men, according to feminists such as Andrea Dworkin, sex boils down to the penis, the penis rubbing up and down, which, Dworkin claims, is the 'secret' and 'mystery' of sex:

> Commonly referred to as "it," sex is defined in action only by what the male does with his penis. Fucking – the penis thrusting – is the magical, hidden meaning of "it," the reason for sex… In practice, fucking is an act of possession – simultaneously an act of ownership, taking, force; it is conquering… In the male system, sex is the penis, the penis is sexual power, its use in fucking is manhood.[100]

Dworkin's analysis is partially accurate: the penis is that magical signifier which is always so curiously absent yet such an important component in any pornographic situation or image. In the feminist view, the pornographer creates with his penis – the paintbrush, camera or pen – these things are called 'tools', a common euphemism for penis, as is pencil, often used in William Shakespeare's plays. The quill, stylus or 'sharp projective' is a crucial element in the male's manufacture of art and pornography.[101] When painter Pierre Renoir was asked how he painted when his hands were crippled by arthritis he replied

---

99 See Linda Williams: "Film Body, an Implantation of perversions", *Cinétracts*, vol. 3, no.4, Winter 1981, 19-25

100 Dworkin: *Pornography: Men Possessing Women*, 23

101 See Jacques Derrida: *Spurs: Nietzsche's Styles*, tr. Barbara Harlow, University of Chicago Press, Chicago 1979, 37-9; on the penis as a paintbrush, see Carol Duncan: "The Esthetics of Power in Modern Erotic Art", *Heresies*, 1, 1977, 46-50

'[w]ith my prick'.[102] In pornography, the eye becomes the phallus, and looking is equated with caressing the obscure object of desire with the phallus. Throughout Western art the phallus is that visually absent but psychologically and ideologically present object. It is central in erotic art. Look at the Western nudes – by Titian, Picasso, Ingres, Boucher: the phallus is there even though you don't see it. It's the same in any number of books, poems, sculptures, plays.

It is the same in aspects of homosexual eroticism, which is defined in some ways, for feminists, by the phallus and the penis thrusting. For Andrea Dworkin, the structure of the laws policing homosexuality can be seen as also controlling women's sexuality. For Dworkin, the sodomy laws protect men from being treated like women: '[t]he sodomy laws are important, perhaps essential, in maintaining for men a superiority of civil and sexual status over women. They protect men as a class from the violation of penetration; men's bodies have unbreachable boundaries.' (*Intercourse*, 183) In Dworkin's view, men are never the fucked: rather, they *always* do the fucking. But she's wrong, because women do the fucking too, and many men are fucked.

Lesbian sex, it seems, is marked by the *lack* of the phallus. Hence, lesbian eroticism must always be 'deviant', because it departs from the patriarchal norms which exalt the phallus. Lesbianism must always be 'Other', sexually, and many feminists note that the otherness of lesbian sexuality is one of the reasons that men and their patriarchal institutions are very threatened by lesbianism.[103] Lesbianism undermines patriarchy at its powerbase. Men cannot control lesbians: '[l]esbians, by loving women and not men, pose a direct threat to the very basis of male supremacy', write Alice, Gordon, Debbie and Mary.[104] The lesbian is crucial, argues Monique Wittig, because she 'is the only concept that I

102 In J. Hobhouse, 135.

103 Ti-Grace Atkinson: *Amazon Odyssey*, Links Books, New York 1974; Alice, Gordon, Debbie and Mary: "Separatism", in Sarah Lucia Hoagland & Julia Penelope, eds. *For Lesbians Only: A separatist anthology*, Onlywomen Press 1988, 31-40; Adrienne Rich: "Towards a woman-centred university", in *On Lies, Secrets and Silence*, Novotny, New York 1979; Jill Johnston: *Lesbian Nation: The Feminist Solution*, Simon & Shuster, New York 1974; S. Rowbotham: *Beyond the Fragments: Feminism and the making of Socialism*, Merlin 1979

104 Alice, Gordon, Debbie and Mary, op. cit., 31-40

know of which is beyond the categories of sex (man and woman)'.[105] Wittig moves towards a view of culture that goes beyond gender, beyond 'biological dimorphism', and biology.

Lesbianism questions the prevalence of patriarchy and heterosexuality as the norms in a society. In her excellent essay "Compulsory Heterosexuality and Lesbian Existence", Adrienne Rich writes: 'for women heterosexuality may not be a 'preference' at all but something that has had to be imposed, managed, organized, propagandized, and maintained by force'.[106] Not all feminists agree about the revolutionary potential of lesbianism, if it is a lesbianism that keeps defining itself in terms of patriarchy. Elizabeth Mees reckons that 'lesbianism, as in hetero-relations, takes (its) place within the structure of the institution of heterosexuality. The lesbian is born of/ in it.'[107] There is no escape, it seems, from patriarchal and heterosexuality: the world is permeated with them. As Sheila Jeffreys wrote: '[e]very woman grows up in a heteropatriarchal world',[108] while Ann Barr Snitow writes:

> One of our culture's most intense myths, the ideal of an individual who is brave and complete in isolation, is for men only. Women are grounded, enmeshed in civilization, in social connection, in family and in love (a condition a feminist culture might well define as desirable) while all our culture's rich myths of individualism are essentially closed to them.[109]

In pornography, lesbian eroticism is often introduced, but always controlled by a patriarchal force. Typically, in a soft porn scenario, two bisexual women cavort on a bed overseen by a male ('I've always wanted to see ya with another woman' drools the boyfriend; or, frequently, 'I got back from work an' saw 'em writhin' on the bed'). Towards the end of the scene, the man makes

---

105 Wittig: "One is not born a woman", in Hoagland, op. cit., 446-7

106 Adrienne Rich: "Compulsory Heterosexuality and Lesbian Existence", 1980, in E. Abel & E.K. Abel, eds. *The Signs Reader: Women, Gender and Scholarship*, University of Chicago Press, Chicago 1983

107 Elizabeth Mees, in Karla Jay & Joanna Glasgow: *Lesbian Text and Contexts: Radical Revisions*, New York University Press, New York 1990, 82

108 Sheila Jeffreys: "The Censoring of Revolutionary Feminism", in Chester, 139

109 Ann Snitow: "Mass Market Romance: Pornography for Women is Different", *Radical History Review*, no. 20, Spring/ Summer 1979

love to both women. Why? Because they needed the phallus, they needed a man to be fulfilled ('women need my cock after all,' says the male in pornography, 'to satisfy 'em'). We find this theme occurring endlessly in pornography. The male presence (the phallus) is seen as necessary for the true satisfaction for women.

Lesbian or women's pornography, made by women for women, disappoints some feminists. Elizabeth Carola, who describes herself as a 'radical feminist lesbian', discusses magazines such as *On Our Backs, Bad Attitude, OW! – Outrageous Women: A Journal of Woman-to-Woman SM, Yellow Silk, The Power Exchange*:

> Like all porn, this new 'woman's' porn is neither about nor for women. Like all porn it is, in a most basic sense, *against* women and *about* male fantasy – the basic male fantasy of Woman as Wholly Sexual Object whose Purpose is To Be Fucked – which feeds men's egos, fuels their violence...

Other women writers are disappointed by the 'new women's pornography', such as the anti-censorship and liberal Tuppy Owens, who is the author of *The Sex Maniac's Diary* and organizer of The Sex Maniac's Ball, where there is 'a playpen for adult babies, and a tearoom for people who like messy cake fights',[110] and who participated in swinging orgies where she was 'in the middle of eleven bisexual men with everything being penetrated everywhere (heaven!...)' (ib., 117). Tuppy Owens writes:

> You may be curious to know what I think of porn, after all this time. Well, I still like it, but I'm disappointed that it hasn't moved very far. I really don't bother to look at it much. I think that porno is really only of interest when it deals with impossible things. It's rather like fantasy – no point in fantasizing about something if you can actually do it...
> It's been very interesting working on these new sex mags for women. I don't think that they've got the formula right and I hope that the magazines I'm about to edit will smash barriers, turn everything on its head and open up a new world. (ib., 124)

According to Elizabeth Carola, lesbian pornographic magazines are full of images and themes usually associated with male pornography:

---

110 Tuppy Owens: "Sex On My Mind", in Assister & Carol, 121

On Our Backs, in particular, is full of adverts for phalluses and endless verbiage about (and imagery of) extremely masculine 'Butches' introducing large objects – fists, bottles, phalluses – into the bodies of 'Femmes'… *On Our Backs* represents the 'middle range' of lesbian porn. The harder core publications like *The Power Exchange* feature half page adverts for surgical scalpels for 'unparalleled cutting and piercing' interspersed with litanies of young women being violently fist fucked, whipped and pierced and, of course, gratefully licking their 'mistresses' boots in return.[111]

If pornography is a contentious issue among feminists, then lesbian or 'women's' pornography is extremely controversial, and feminists are very divided about it.[112] As Sue George notes: '[f]or a feminist, therefore, to enjoy pornography is to feel doubly guilty.'[113] Writers such as Pat Califa, Lisa Henderson and Sheila Jeffreys argue that sadomasochistic pornography operating inside lesbian practice can be enriching.[114] For men it is clearly threatening, because it excludes them; it is made by women, for women: 'it is no longer for men alone to decide what is, or is not, exciting in pornography' as Linda Williams writes in her book *Hard Core*.[115]

111 Elizabeth Carola: "Women, Erotica, Pornography: – Learning to Play the Game", in Chester, 169-171; see S. Jeffreys: "Butch and femme: now and then", *Gossip 5, 1987*

112 See: the essays in Sally Munt's book; A. Koedt: *Radical Feminism*, Quadrangle, New York 1973;

113 Sue George, in Chester, op. cit., 111

114 Pat Califa: "Feminism and Sadomasochism", *Heresies*, 12, 1981, *The Lesbian S/M Safety Manual*, Alyson, Boston 1990, and "Unravelling the Sexual Fringe: A Secret Side of Lesbian Sexuality", *The Advocate*, 27 December 1979; also: Lisa Henderson: "Lesbian Pornography: Cultural Transgression and Sexual Demystification", in Sally Munt, ed, 173-191; Sheila Jeffreys: "Sadomasochism: the erotic cult of fascism", in *Lesbian Ethics*, 2, 1, 65-82; M. Sulter: "Reviewing lesbian erotica", *Spare Rib*, no. 219, 1990-1, 42-4; see also, on sadomasochism: R.R. Linden *et al*, eds. *Against Sadomasochism*, Frog in the Well, East Palo Alto, California 1982; Justine Jones: "Why I liked screwing? Or, is heterosexual enjoyment based on sexual violence?", in Onlywomen, eds. *Love your Enemy?*, Onlywomen Press 1981; Katherine Davis *et al*, eds. *Coming to Power, Writings and Graphics on Lesbian S/M*, Alyson Publications, Boston 1983

115 Linda Williams: *Hard Core: Power, Pleasure, and the 'Frenzy of the visible'*, Pandora, 1990, 264; see also Andrew Ross: "The Popularity of Pornography", in *No Respect: Intellectuals and Popular Culture*, Routledge 1989, 171-208

Men are excluded from lesbian pornography: '[p]ornography for lesbians is unique in that it presumes a *female* gaze, and a lesbian one at that,' writes Barbara Smith. But although 'lesbian' and 'women's' pornography is for made for and by women, it still works within patriarchy, within male-made structures and attitudes, just as lesbianism itself, according to some feminists, is not truly 'outside' of heterosexuality and patriarchy. The view is that '[l]esbians who engage in consensual S/M are thus merely imitating and even colluding in patriarchal structures,' writes Clare Whatling.[116] Sheila Jeffreys claims that '[s]m practice comes from nowhere more mysterious than the history of our very real oppression.'[117] Clare Whatling suggests that lesbian S/M practice can parody and subvert patriarchal values and systems. She writes:

> S/M is never *intrinsically* revolutionary. Like all sexual practice, it is a product of its time and context. As with other sexual practices, it may be oppositional under certain conditions, but it is never always so... S/M is constructed in relation to the society in which it is played out and cannot be understood without reference to the structures that exist there... Where S/M does perhaps differ from more conventional sexual practices is in the self-consciousness it brings to encounters. For S/M as a practice does much to foreground the constructedness of all sexuality.[118]

As Barbara Smith writes: '[i]f heterosexual women fuck the enemy, then SM dykes fuck *like* the enemy.'[119]

Everyone has a line to sell in censorship debates, something to sell, and something to protect, to keep a deep secret. DO NOT PUBLISH FOR AT LEAST FIFTY YEARS. Carole Vance, commenting on the way the Meese Commission was handled, writes that

> witnesses provided by women's antipornography groups proved more useful than social scientists. They were eager to cast their personal experiences of incest, childhood, sexual abuse, rape and sexual coercion in terms of the 'harm' and 'degradation' caused by pornography. Some were wiling to understate, and most to omit

116 Clare Whatling: "Who's read *Macho Sluts*", in Judith Still & Michael Worton, eds., 193
117 Sheila Jeffreys: "Sado-masochism", op.cit., 68
118 Clare Whatling, op.cit., 194
119 Barbara Smith: "Sappho Was a Right-*Off* Woman', in Chester, 182-4. On sadomasochism, see Thomas S. Weinberg & G.W. Levi Kamel: *S and M: Studies in Sadomasochism*, Prometheus Books, Buffalo, New York 1983;

mentioning, their support for those cranky feminist demands so offensive to conservative ears: abortion, birth control, lesbian and gay rights. Other feminist groups, including COYOTE, the US Prostitutes collective, the ACLU Women's Rights Project and the Feminist Anti Censorship Task Force… criticized the panel's simple-minded attempt to link violence against women with sexual images.[120]

One of the most contentious and fiercely debated aspects of pornography is the issue of 'obscenity' and censorship. Throughout the history of art and pornography, various individuals or groups of people have sought to defend certain territories, whether moral, psychological, emotional, spiritual, religious, philosophical, political or ideological. There is always some line between the 'acceptable' and the 'obscene'. The history of censorship is long and complex. This century there have been many confrontations between artists and the 'establishment': with Lawrence's *Lady Chatterley's Lover*, with *Last Tango in Paris*, *The Killing of Sister George*, *Performance*, *Trash*, *A Clockwork Orange* and any number of films, with Senator Jesse Helms trying to stop NEA tax payers' money funding 'obscene' work, with reference to the photographer Robert Mapplethorpe (whose photos have created much 'controversy'), and so on.[121] The many debates concerning various Obscene Publications Acts and bills, the First Amendment of the American constitution, various regulatory groups, and all manner of 'intellectuals' and artists, have been heated, complex and often a shambles. The confusions and ambiguities are at the centre of Western society. Pornography debates produce, very quickly, all manner of confusions, of a moral, religious,

120 Vance: "The Meese Commission On the Road", in Chester, 90
121 See Dunne Dominick: "Robert Mapplethorpe's Proud Finale", *Vanity Fair*, February 1989; "Robert Mapplethorpe: Aestheticizing the Perverse", *Artscribe International*, Nov/ Dec 1988; Jorge Ribalta: "Decorative Heroism, The Death of Mapplethorpe", *Lapiz*, April 1989; Peter Schjeldhal: "The Mainstreaming of Mapplethorpe: Taste and Hunger", *7 Days*, 10 August 1988; Robert Rooney: "The unambiguous stare of Mapplethorpe's lens", *Australian*, 25 February 1986; Mark Schoofs: "Robert Mapplethorpe: Exquisite Subversions", *Windy City Times*, 16 March 1989; Hilton Kramer: "Mapplethorpe Show at the Whitney: A Big, Glossy, Offensive Exhibit", *The New York Observer*, 22 August 1988; Arthur C. Danto: *Encounters & Reflections*, Farrar Straus Giroux, New York 1990; Elizabeth Kastor & Carla Hall: "Mapplethorpe Aftermath", *Washington Post*, 23 June 1989; Todd Allan Yasui: "The Mapplethorpe Bonanza", *Washington Post*, 21 August 1989

psychological, social and ideological nature.[122] For some, though, the censorship debate is 'in fact, a little internal quibble between sections of the bourgeois community' (writes Suzanne Kappeler).

Pornography goes to the heart of what people hold dear: their identities, their feelings, their philosophic and political views, their view of the 'quality of life'. Pornography unsettles these notions and structures. The fervour and uncertainty of the various attempts at legislation and policing show how problematic pornography is. In a case of recent years, five 'homosexual sado-masochists' were convicted in 1990 of inflicting 'injuries on each another's genitals during ritual sex' which involved 'cutting each other's genitals with surgical scalpels, sandpapering scrotums and pushing hooks into penises'. Their appeal was rejected by the courts.[123]

For law-abiding citizens, it seems, the 'line' has to be 'drawn' somewhere. Somewhere between public and private, between sex and love, between visible and invisible, between freedom and control, between secrecy and publicity, between availability and censorship. Indeed, Walter Kendrick says the only definition of pornography is in terms of its forbidden or secret nature.[124]

Pornography brings the secret life of people out into the open. What the Western world holds most dear – the primacy and holiness of the individual, and the primacy and holiness of (hetero-sexual) love – is cast into doubt by pornography.

Hard core pornography, in particular, tries to make everything as clear and as visible as possible. There are, thus, many close-ups of genitals in hard core pornography. Sex is ecstatic, so pornography has to show this ecstasy. It does this by focussing on the genitals.

One 'mystery' of sublime pleasure is the orgasm. Cameras look at the body from the outside, so to show orgasm they get as close as possible, to show writhing genitals, to achieve the 'come shot',

---

122 See *Art in America*, May 1990; C.H. Rolph: *The Trial of Lady Chatterley*, Penguin 1961; Geoffrey Robertson: *Obscenity: an Account of Censorship Laws and Their Enforcements in England and Wales*, Weidenfeld & Nicolson 1979; *The Attorney General's Commission on Pornography – the Meese Commission – Final Report*, US Government Printing Office, Washington DC 1986; L. Lederer, ed, op. cit.

123 Ian MacKinnon: "Lords reject appeals by sado-masochists", *The Independent*, 12 March 1993

124 Walter Kendrick: *The Secret Museum: Pornography in Modern Culture*, Viking, New York 1987

the ejaculation.[125] Or, in films, a lot of groaning and gasping makes the bliss of the orgasm clear. Typically, it is the woman who gasps loudest, for she is, as Virginia Woolf said, a mirror that enlarges what men do, that mythicizes their acts. Sexologists (Krafft-Ebing, Freud, Reich) have always emphasized the materiality of the orgasm, describing it in Newtonian, mechanistic terms, as it were something a machine does. Wilhelm Reich, for instance, describes orgasm as electrical energy: '[t]he orgasm formula which directs sex-economic research is as follows: MECHANICAL TENSION › BIOELECTRICAL CHARGE › BIOELECTRICAL DISCHARGE › MECHANICAL RELAXATION'.[126]

It's also worth noting how humourless some pornography is, how dour and unsmiling and serious. Sex is taken very seriously by masculine culture: 'when one is making love,' writes P. Piobb, 'one does not laugh; perhaps one may just smile. During the spasm one is as serious as death.'[127] Isn't this typical: during the greatest of pleasures known to 'humanity', one is not allowed to laugh. Typical of the patriarchal view of lovemaking. Solemn to the last gasp.

At times the anti-pornography lobby can seem to be ridiculously alarmist, and reactionary. For, after all, it's only sex, isn't it? After all, say some feminists and pornographers, most of pornography is soft and merely depicts people having sex and so what is offensive about that?[128] Just because some piece of art or media shows people having sex, does that mean it should be banned? Or as Julienne Dickey puts it:

> It *is* important that we distinguish between how pornographic material makes us (women) *feel* and how it makes them (men) *act*. There can be no doubt that many women *feel* offended by media sexism and pornography... But because we feel offended by certain

---

125 The come shot or money shot might just be another part of fashion: popular in porn in the 1980s-2000s, the come shot might be just another element that'll be supplanted by summat else. First it was a glimpse of the ankle, then the thigh, remarked porn actress Brandy Alexandre, then it was nudity, then fucking, and then ejaculation. (Quoted in L. O'Toole, 73).
126 Reich: *The Function of the Orgasm*, London 1983, 9
127 P. Piobb: *Venus, la déesse magique de la chair*, Paris, 1909, 80
128 Jane Juffer reckoned that the anti-porn feminists 'conflate reality and fantasy, take pornography literally, ignore the complexities and uncertainties of interpretation' (23).

material, is this sufficient reason to have it removed?[129]

Why is lovemaking so offensive to some people, the anti-censorship feminists ask, for pornography just depicts people enjoying themselves, as Avedon Carol writes: 'most pornography is just about men and women enjoying sex together'.[130] Even as it is expressed, sexuality in culture is also denied and suppressed. Simultaneous desire and negation is the ambiguous cultural norm. Christobel Mackenzie writes:

> We aren't supposed to be really sexual, and we are discouraged from admitting we have positive feelings about being sexual. We are somehow seen as 'dirty' or 'bad' if we have sexual experience or if we admit we like sex.[131]

What happens is the women who use their sexuality openly and positively are regarded as 'dirty', as whores – we see this in the media time and time again (in the figures of, say, Marilyn Monroe and the pop star Madonna, or 'mistresses' of ministers and presidents). Christobel Mackenzie writes:

> And 'respectable' women [non-prostitutes] (again, including feminists), hate the women who say they like sex – especially the women who like sex with men… It is frightening to see so many feminists who want so desperately to believe that women can't enjoy sex, that every time we have sex with men, we are being victims. Why is it so necessary to see ourselves as poor little put-upon sufferers? …Why do we need to think that when men want to be with us, they only want to 'take advantage' of us? (in ib., 141-3)

Women who openly enjoy their sexuality are stereotyped and 'branded' by the media, time after time, as whores. It's important for some feminists that women who openly celebrate their

---

129 Dickey: "Snakes and Ladders", in Chester, 164
130 Carol: "Snuff: Believing the Worst", in Assister & Carol, 129
131 Christobel Mackenzie: "The Anti-sexism Campaign Invites you to fight Sexism, Not Sex", in Assister & Carol, 140

sexuality are not seen as 'victims'.[132]

The female orgasm is 'anatomically invisible', as far as pornography is concerned. So the 'history of pornography...is the history of visual strategies to overcome the anatomical invisibility of the female orgasm'.[133] In pornography, female orgasm is regarded with confusion and ambivalence. What actually is it? pornographers ask. Thus the controversy over clitoral and vaginal orgasm, over female 'ejaculation', over 'multiple' orgasms. Female 'ejaculation' is 'visible evidence' of orgasm, yet it is censored by pornographers themselves at times.[134]

Pornography is the culture of eroticism in the West. There is sex on TV, in fiction, in blockbusters, but it is in pornography that erotic feelings are most frequently communicated. Yet pornography is commodified sex, materialist sex, sex manufactured into particular types, genres, roles and modes. There are standard pornographic encounters, standard pornographic camera angles, standard pornographic orgasms. Eroticism, as Sigmund Freud knew, is powerful, whether emotionally, psychologically, culturally or politically. Pornography, then, deals with really wild eroticism by categorizing it, putting into particular genres or narratives. The visual aspect of pornography helps to deal with the wildness and passion of erotic feeling. Pornography produces images and representations, which are easier to deal with than the real thing. Jane Gallop writes that the 'visual mode produces representations as a way of mastering what is otherwise too intense'.[135] Experiences such as orgasm and erotic desire can be too powerful to be communicated in words. Putting these experiences into visual representations enables them to be controlled,

---

132 Christobel Mackenzie says: '[i]f women like sex, we are not always the perfect victims of violent or coercive males. If women like sex, then sex isn't the 'price' of the things women 'get' from men (home, marriage, love, security, etc.). Most of all, if some women like sex, then the women who have only endured sex for the sake of their relationships have been lying to themselves, selling themselves for no good reason.' ib., 142

133 Lynda Nead, 98; See also Linda Williams: *Hard Core*, Pandora 1990

134 see Shannon Bell: "Feminist Ejaculations", in Arthur and Marilouise Kroker, eds. *The Hysterical Male: New Feminist Theory*, St Martin's Press, New York, 155-169; also Chris Straayer: "The Seduction of Boundaries: Feminist Fluidity in Annie Sprinkle's Art/ Education/ Sex", in Gibsons, ed, 168f

135 Jane Gallop: *The Daughter's Seduction: Feminism and Psychoanalysis*, Cornell University Press, New York, 1982, 35

packaged, commodified. For, as many have noted, there are some experiences for which there are no words. Ludwig Wittgenstein, Paul Valéry, Samuel Beckett, Karl Krauss, Lawrence Durrell and T.S. Eliot are among those who have spoken of the limitations of words. Andrea Dworkin writes:

> We all of us got the consolation that nobody remembers the worst things. They're gone; brain just burns them away. And there's no words for the worst things so ain't no one going to tell you the worst things; they can't. You can pick up any book and know for sure the worst things ain't in it... I am telling you you have never read the worst. It has never been uttered by anyone ever' (*Mercy*, 157-8).

Pornography is *fantasy*, as well as, for some feminists, religious groups and the pro-censorship lobby, violence and extremism and materialism and women-hating. Pornography does not offer the consumer real people, but images, narratives, ideas, suggestions. The visual dimension of pornography helps to evoke certain kinds of representations of erotic feelings which the consumer can deal with, because they are communicated in recognizable forms. Ah, thinks the consumer, here we are in an S/M narrative; or, ah, here we in the narrative where a sexually frustrated male picks up a female hitchhiker; or, ah, here we are in the 'bored housewife' scenario: sex-starved, she humps the plumber over the washing machine. The consumer knows where s/he is with pornography.

Pornography delivers the goods.

A typical view is that pornography is *sex*, but art is *love*. Pornography trades in loveless sex, while art trades in sexy love. Each era, each generation, redefines what sex and love are, what is acceptable and what is not. But 'love', as feminists say, is largely about power relations between people – relations that are dependent on and controlled by an array of factors: enculturation, social and economic pressures, political agendas, racial issues, classism, etc.

The general view is that pornography is depersonalized, dehumanized, unemotional, saccharine, synthetic, 'obscene' or 'dirty'. Art, meanwhile, is personalized, special, emotional, 'real' and sane. Yet art and pornography are interchangeable in many ways.

One of the most contentious of issues is the link between pornography and violence, where, according to Robin Morgan and many second wave feminists, 'pornography is the theory, and rape is the practice'. Morgan says: '[w]e have met the enemy and he's our friend. And dangerous.'[136] For some people, pornography is criminal by its very existence. It invades the private sphere, as the Williams Committee of 1979 claimed,[137] and sex, the ultimate private 'act', becomes very public. Alison King has some useful observations to make in her survey of the pornography-violence surveys: '[a]lmost every major researcher has found that soft-core pornography can *inhibit* aggression in individuals',[138] and King concludes her survey:

> Time and time again, soft-core pornography far more explicit than that available in Britain has been shown to lower aggression levels.[139]

What all the debates around pornography demonstrate is that most people regard pornography as amazingly powerful. Whatever their views on pornography, most people seem to agree that it has a massive influence, whether or not this influence

136 Robin Morgan: "Goodbye to All That", in *Going Too Far*, Random House, New York 122

137 *Report of the Committee on Obscenity and Film Censorship*, Chairman, Bernard Williams, Her Majesty's Stationery Office, 1979, para. 7.6; see also, A.W. B. Simpson: *Pornography and Politics: The Williams Committee in Retrospect*, Waterlow 1983; Kate Ellis *et al*, eds. *Caught Looking: Feminism, Pornography and Censorship*, 1987; Beverly Brown: "Private Faces in Public Places", *Ideology and Consciousness: Technologies of the Human Sciences*, 7, Autumn 1980, 3-16

138 Alison King: "Mystery and Imagination: the Case of Pornography Effects Studies", in Assister & Carol, 73, referring to: R.A. Baron: "The Aggression-Inhibiting Influences of Heightened Sexual Arousal", *Journal of Personality and Social Psychology*, 30, 3, 1974; R.A. Baron & P.A. Bell: "Effects of Heightened Sexual Arousal on Physical Aggression", American Psychological Association, Proceedings, 8, 1973; E. Donnerstein et al: "Erotic Stimuli and Aggression Facilitation or inhabitation?", *Journal of Personality and Social Psychology*, 32, 1975; L.A. White: "Erotica and Aggression: the influence of Sexual Arousal, Positive Effects and Negative Effects on Aggressive Behavior", *Journal of Personality and Social Psychology*, 34, 1979; A. Frodi: "Sexual Arousal, Situational Restrictiveness and Aggressive Behaviour", *Journal of Research in Personality*, 11 1977; D. Zillmann & B. Sapolsky: "What Mediates the Effect of Mild Erotica on Annoyance and Hostile behavior in males?", *Journal of Personality and Social Psychology*, 35, 1977

139 King, ib., 86

manifests itself later as violence. Pornography, it seems, is the most powerful communication type of any communication type. Whatever form it takes – painting, video, photograph, prose, performance – pornography seems to be the most powerful kind of communication. The debates, about obscenity, censorship, regulation, policing, decency, etc, all acknowledge the power of pornography. Some feminists have made the point that if you agree that pornography is influential and powerful, then you must also look at all other art, whether high art (the nude painting) or 'low art' (TV ads, billboards, tabloids, etc). Even unlikely candidates such as President Nixon realized this point. He comments on the American congressional report of the Commission on Obscenity and Pornography of 1970:

> The commission contends that the proliferation of filthy books and plays has no lasting harmful effect on a man's character. If that be true, it must also be true that great books, great paintings and great plays have no ennobling effect on a man's conduct. Centuries of civilization and ten minutes of common sense tell us otherwise.[140]

What follows from this is that, by extension, if you police pornography you have to police all areas of artistic expression, all of culture. Andrea Dworkin's stance on this issue is firm: '[w]e will know that we are free when the pornography no longer exists' (*Pornography*, 224). Feminists ask, is it simply pornography that is the problem? Or is it the other institutions, such as education, or marriage? Is it not the whole of heterosexuality that is the problem? Or patriarchy, the whole of Western culture? These questions are endlessly debated. Stephen Heath asks some of the basic questions:

> Is all pornography violent and offensive? Are there connections between pornography and sexual liberation that are important, progressive? Are men's and women's pleasures in sexual imagery bound up with or separate – separable – from pornographic representations and how? Are pornographic images for male arousal necessarily the reproduction of domination? What should be done about pornography and how?[141]

---

140 Richard Nixon, *New York Times*, 25 October 1970, 71
141 Stephen Heath: "Male Feminism", *the Dalhousie Review*, and in Alice Jardine and Paul Smith, eds. *Men in Feminism*, Methuen, New York 1987

There are pertinent questions asked by feminists concerning pornography. For instance, Rosalind Coward asks, does male sexuality always have a violent component? 'Is it true that *any* public representation of sex is *only* for male sexuality and therefore male domination? Is it true that pornography is about violence against women or *necessarily* sustains violence against women?' she asks.[142] Is all pornography an incitement to violence? feminists wonder. Elizabeth Sidney questions the involvement of women in pornography: '[w]hy do women help to create these materials?'[143] Some male feminists have explored their sexuality, debunking 'myths' about male ejaculation, orgasm, lovemaking, etc[144] while other anti-sexist men have claimed that in pornography, men are shown, ultimately, in an inferior way to women: '[m]en might set the rules, but women are shown to come out 'enjoying it most'', writes Andy Moye.[145] Catherine MacKinnon suggests that pornography helps to encode power relations between men and women by making the power relations seem 'sexy': 'male and female are created through the eroticization of submission and dominance'.[146] The submission is made 'sexy', as is the objectification of women that occurs in pornography. So much of culture follows on from this eroticization. The world of fashion and 'style', for instance, seems to come straight out of the eroticization of women in pornography. Karen Myers writes that, though 'the fashion image and the pornographic image are in the first instance produced within quite distinct sets of social and economic circumstances', 'notions of hard-core pornography as mediated through auteuristic eroticism affect the form and presentation of certain up-market fashion images.'[147] Myers is referring to those

---

142 Rosalind Coward: "Sexual Violence and Sexuality", in *Feminist Review*, eds., 309

143 Elizabeth Sidney: "Liberals, Feminism and the Media", in Chester, 208

144 See John Stoltenberg: "Refusing to be a Man", in J. Snodgrass, ed. *A Book of Readings for Men Against Sexism*, Times Change Press, New York 1977; Jack Litewka: "The Socialised Penis", in Snodgrass, op. cit.; H. Brod, ed. *The Making of Masculinities*, Allen & Unwin 1987

145 Andy Moye, "Pornography", in A. Metcalf & M. Humphries, eds. *The Sexuality of Men*, Pluto Press 1985, 58

146 Catherine MacKinnon: "Feminism, Marxism, method and the state: towards feminist jurisprudence", in S. Harding, ed. *Feminism and Methodology*, Indiana University Press, Indiana 1987, 136

147 Karen Myers: "Passion 'n' Fashion: A Working Paper", *Screen*, vol. 23, no. 3/4, 1983

auteurs of high fashion photography, David Bailey and Helmut Newton and their ilk. Their images take up the sadomasochistic and highly fetishized motifs of pornography and transplant them into the high fashion spreads of the glossy fashion magazines. Because these images are set in high fashion contexts, they are regarded as 'art' rather than pornography.

The economics of pornography are straightforward: pornography operates on the basis of maximum capitalism, maximum 'market economy' and exploitation.[148] Ann Snitow writes that pornography 'is exploitation of *everything*'.[149] Pornographers pay very well for the 'services' of women models – hundreds and thousands of dollars per photo or video shoot. Pornography is big business. It is a bigger business than the film and pop industries combined – a four and a half billion dollar business in the USA, according to Dworkin and Itzin in the early 1980s (actually, Forbes have estimated that porn in 2001 was worth $2.6-3.9 billion, much less than previously thought; meanwhile *Newsweek* in 1997 reckoned that about $8 billion was spent on porn in the USA, a figure which included live performances, cable TV, sex toys, the internet, as well as magazines and videos).[150] Elizabeth Sidney offers the following facts as an indication of the mass consumption of pornography:

> In America, according to NAPCRO the (U.S.A.) National Anti-Pornography Civil Rights Organisation, over 2 million households now subscribe to cable pornography and the magazines *Playboy, Penthouse* and *Hustler* each have a larger readership than *Time* and *Newsweek* combined.[151]

Catherine Itzin writes: 'pornography *is* violence. Against women by men. The violence is institutionalized and it is internalised (by women, which accounts in part for their 'tolerance'

---

148 Porn actor Nicholas White reckoned that exploitation didn't come into it: 'the whole idea of "exploitation" is meaningless where consenting adults are concerned' (quoted in L. O'Toole, 323).

149 Ann Snitow: "Mass market romance: pornography for women is different", in Snitow et al, eds. *Powers of Desire: the politics of sexuality*, Monthly Review Press, New York 1983, 1983, 269

150 Andrea Dworkin: *Pornography*, 10, Catherine Itzin, in Chester, 39. E. Schlosser: :The Business of Pornography", *Newsweek*, Feb 10, 1997.

151 Elizabeth Sidney, writing in 1988, the early years of cable and satellite consumption, so the figures must be greater now, in Chester, 206

and sometimes 'participation' in it.)'[152] Annie Blue of Women Against Violence Against Women says in a blanket statement: '[w]e see all pornography as violence against women'.[153]

Women are involved in pornography for a number of reasons, many of them social, economic and political. For anti-porn activists, the involvement of women in pornography reveals again the power relations that operate within patriarchy and heterosexuality. The economics of pornography, like the economics of all of society, favour men. That is clear from any clutch of statistics (such as the comparison of salaries of men and women: women are always paid less).

In pornographic production companies, whether of videos, magazines, goods, etc, men often do the 'important' jobs – editor, art director, writer, manager, proprietor, photographer, camera person, etc, while women are the models, the skivvies, the cleaners, the 'assistants' and secretaries. The hierarchical organization of pornographic production emulates that of society as a whole, just as the ethics and attitudes and values of pornographic products emulate those of society as a whole. The economy of pornography is not confined to sexism, to male-against-female issues, it can also be classist, and racist. Feminists note that despite so-called 'improvements' in race relations, it is still black people who are at the bottom of the societal pile, who do the menial jobs, such as cleaning. The economics of black labour helps institutions such as pornography – and medicine, education, government, etc – to thrive.[154]

For Alison Assister, people who work in pornography are not automatically 'victims'. Discussing Andrea Dworkin, she writes:

> Pornography, for her, becomes a Foucauldian discourse of power. Similarly, in the work of constructivists – and Andrea Dworkin falls into this camp on this issue – women working in the sex industry lose all agency. They become 'victims' of the power-knowledge complex:

152 Itzin, in Chester, 43

153 Quoted in Sarah Baxter: "Women Against Porn", *Time Out*, London, 23 March 1988

154 See La Frances Rodgers, ed. *The Black Woman*, Sage, Beverly Hills 1989; G.T. Hull et al, eds. *All the Women Are White, All the Blacks Are Men, But Some of Us Are Brave: Black Women's Studies*, Feminist Press, New York 1982; B. Bryan et al, eds. *The Heart of the Race: Black Women's Lives in Britain*, Virago 1985; Anima Mama: "Black Women, the Economic Crisis and the British State", *Feminist Review*, 17, 1984

pornography. Their ability to choose what they do is lost. In fact, neither rapists, on the one hand, nor sex workers, on the other, are victims; rather, both are agents actively choosing what they do.[155]

Working in pornography is not automatically 'wrong', as feminists have pointed out. Carol Avedon and Nettie Pollard write

Many hard-core porn models can be perceived as playing a particularly exploited role only if the viewer assumes that only men can enjoy sexual activity. However, that pernicious assumption pervades society to the extent that even some feminists claim that all pornography shows women performing acts that we could never enjoy.

Which is rubbish. Carol and Pollard continue their discussion:

Some feminist authors have written whole books to this effect, maintaining that every aspect of the sexual acts portrayed in pornography represents sexual interests and approaches that are unique to male psychology and contradict the true female personality, in which all such acts are unpleasant and abhorrent. It has even been asserted that all pornography is made by force or coercion, as no woman would willingly perform these acts.[156]

Pornography creates paradoxes all the time, effortlessly, it seems. The questions pornography raise are not simply resolvable. For instance, is *all* 'violent' sex bad, is sadomasochism 'bad'? Is painful sex 'wrong'? Is S/M wrong because it's 'violent', and what is the definition of S/M 'violence'? Gayle Rubin writes of Dworkin's civil rights bill:

The notion of harm embodied in the MacKinnon/ Dworkin approach is based on a fundamental confusion between the content of an image and the conditions of its production. The fact that an image does not appeal to a viewer does not mean that the actors or models experienced revulsion while making it. The fact that an image depicts coercion does not mean that the action or models were forced into making it.[157]

---

155 Assister: "Essentially Sex: A New Look", in Assister, ed, 103
156 Avedon and Pollard, in Assister, 55
157 Gayle Rubin: "Misguided, Dangerous and Wrong: an Analysis of Anti-Pornography Politics", in Assister & Carol, eds., 32

For the feminists who are against censorship (though not always pro-pornography), working in pornography is not *automatically* 'degrading' or 'wrong'; indeed, some feminists say that any menial, low-paid job is as 'degrading' as being photographed for a porn magazine: the Feminists Against Censorship write:

> The working-class women who make up a substantial part of the sex industry are not deeply moved by the suggestion that being pushed around and demoralized for 40 hours a week is so much better than posing for pornography for a few hours and making a lot more money at it. Nor are they thrilled to hear than feminists want to make them criminals and throw them in jail. Do anti-pornography feminists really imagine that sexual harassment happens *only* in relation to porn, or never occurs in any other industry? Do they think that working in a factory, or standing at a counter, is so much more desirable than being a 'page three' girl?[158]

These are good questions, which hit to the heart of the pornography debate: for Andrea Dworkin, Catherine MacKinnon and other anti-pornography feminists, anyone working in the pornography industry is colluding with the enemy – literally 'sleeping with the enemy', or fucking the enemy – that is, men. Yet as a mode of labour, working in pornography is perhaps not as 'degrading' or 'demeaning' as working at a supermarket check-out for hours on end – now that really is slavery. But *all* labour is slavery, for the woman working at a check-out is literally, physically, *there*. She cannot move, her *body* is *there*. She is being paid, like the prostitute, for her body, for her 'manual' labour, for her body being there. So, finally, *all* labour in capitalism is prostitution, on one level, on a very simplistic level, perhaps, but all labour is about working with one's body for someone else, the exchange of use and value in the culture of 'commodity fetishism'. As Claudia, 'author of *I, Claudia, Love Lies Bleeding* and other Class Whore Productions', writes on this issue of working in pornography as unfeminist and morally 'wrong':

> It is apparently 'OK' for a woman to get a job as a waitress or a secretary, however. Work is an exchange of degradation for money... Anti-pornography feminists are quite comfortable with the degradation of the female (and male) labour force; many are

---

158 Feminists Against Censorship: "The Wages of Anti-censorship Campaigning", in Assister & Carol, eds., 148

employers themselves. They remain as millions of women wear out their mental and physical health – that is 'OK' so long as there are no topless calendars on the canteen walls.[159]

The hypocrisy of the anti-pornography position is brought into focus on this issue of work and production, where it's OK for feminists to complain about the people who work in pornography, the anti-anti-pornography feminists suggest, but it's not OK for women to work in porn which may be not as 'degrading', finally, as other forms of work, including housework. The anti-censorship feminists would agree with the anti-pornography feminists, though, about the sexualized nature of labour, how much of labour is founded on sexual economies, as Sheila Jeffreys writes: '[t]he foundation of the family in which men are served emotionally, economically and through domestic labour, is sexual intercourse'.[160]

Alison Assister and Avedon Carol suggest that Jeffreys and Dworkin are mistaken about the relation between politics and sexuality: '[n]owadays, Andrea Dworkin and Sheila Jeffreys both seem to place intercourse and the phallus at the centre of oppression, as if reproduction and child-care had nothing to do with it'. And they continue:

> both Dworkin and Jeffreys seem to believe that the purpose of heterosexism and sexism in general is a male conspiracy to get women to provide the maximum amount of sexual pleasure to males – but this hardly explains why society deliberately limits female willingness to become involved in sex, nor why fellatio, male voyeurism, female exhibitionism, 'hand jobs' and the like are stigmatized. (If Jeffreys is correct, why aren't girls trained from birth to suck cock?) No, it's clear that our society has fetishized reproduction to the point that even where sex is clearly when conception is not desired, we still fear to acknowledge outright that we're not in it for the babies. (in ib., 154-5)

Gayle Rubin, 'a veteran of the feminist sex wars', who lives in San Francisco, finds Andrea Dworkin's depiction of prostitutes offensive:

159 Claudia: "Fear of Pornography", in Assister & Carol, 136
160 Sheila Jeffreys: "The Censoring of Revolutionary Feminism", in Chester, 138

Throughout her book, *Pornography*, Dworkin uses the stigma of prostitution to convey her opprobrium and make her argument against pornography. She says, '[c]ontemporary pornography strictly and literally conforms to the word's root meaning: the graphic depiction of *vile whores*, or in our language, *sluts*, *cows* (as in: *sexual cattle, sexual chattel*), *cunts*.' [page 200 of Dworkin's *Pornography*, Rubin's emphasis] This is a degrading and insulting description of prostitutes. Feminists should be working to remove stigma from prostitution, not exploiting it for rhetorical gain.[161]

Gayle Rubin is opposed to the Dworkin-MacKinnon ordinance, as many are many feminists, claiming that Dworkin/MacKinnon's 'new category of 'pornography' would have codified a feminist anti-porn description into law', something anti-censorship feminists find dangerous. Censorship, says Wendy Moore,[162] is 'like freedom an entirely subjective term' (in ib., 26). For Claudia, Dworkin and MacKinnon rely too much on the assumed decency of the people in government to carry out their bill:

The implicit message, of safety through vulnerability, is broadcast by all those from Ms Cartland to Dworkin and MacKinnon who believe in the readiness of the 'decent chaps' in the government and police departments to protect them from the misogynist bad guys.[163]

But the problem is, as the anti-pornography feminists put it, is, how can you be anti-pornography *and* anti-censorship? Or, putting it another way, how can you be liberal or radical and for the non-censorship of all art, yet, at same time, you want to police pornography and set limits on what people can and cannot consume? This is the question that critics of Andrea Dworkin, Catherine MacKinnon, Susan Griffin and the anti-porn feminists ask. Both sides of the argument are very solid, and very eloquently argued. For these discussions go the quick of our lives, to the quiddity of what we value in life, and what we value in art, and how art relates to life – and to love, for that matter – and to sexuality.

The policing of the Dworkin-MacKinnon bill is problematic, as

---

161 Rubin, op.cit., in Assister & Carol, 34
162 Moore: "There should Be a Law Against It… Shouldn't There?", in Chester, 140
163 Claudia, in Assister & Carol, 136

Annie Blue of Women Against Violence Against Women acknowledges:

> We'd like a law that uses this radical feminist definition of its function
> in society. It's a double-edged sword, because it would give more
> power to the police and state, but in this present climate, it's the best
> of two evils. What else have we got?[164]

In feminism, the privileged person is white, middle class, First
World, Anglo-Saxon, Protestant/ Christian – and male. Whoever
may make pornography, pornography privileges a white, middle
class, Anglo-Saxon, North American and European male viewpoint. Whoever the producers may be, pornography, as a text, is
firmly located within white, middle class, Christian, masculine
discourse. Whoever the authors are, pornography ends up,
textually, and contextually, as a white, middle class, Anglo-Saxon,
Christian, male discourse. And at the bottom of the hierarchy of
power are not white women, but black women.[165] The texts of
pornography, as well as the contexts, are white, middle class,
Anglo Saxon and male. Or, in short, patriarchal, the term used as a
shorthand in feminist theory for all that is masculine, aggressive,
heterosexual, white, bourgeois and First World.

We must always remember, feminists say, the racial as well as
the sexist implications of pornography. Not only it is produced by
and for men, it is produced by white, bourgeois, Anglo Saxon,
Christian men, but is 'for' anybody who will buy it. As Barbara
Smith writes:

> 'Lesbian' pornography is not for or about lesbians and lesbian
> sexuality, so 'black' porn is not for black people, and 'kiddie' porn is
> not for children. Pornography does not describe sexuality, it describes
> sexual *acts*. It solidifies white, male, heterosexual fantasies, and the
> commoditises them.[166]

Pornography can be seen as simply another genre or mode of
consumerism, in which the 'commodity' is desire and fantasy, a
commodity that exists, like television programmes, in that strange
non-material realm that we call 'culture'. Pornography seems at

---

164 Quoted in Sarah Baxter: "Women Against Porn", *Time Out*, London, 23
March 1988
165 See Alice Walker: "Coming apart", in L. Lederer, ed. *Take Back the
Night: Women on Pornography*, Bantam, New York 1982, 84-93
166 Barbara Smith: "Sappho Was a Right-*Off* Woman", in Chester, 179

first to trade in fake flesh of one sort or another, but really it trades in commodities, consumerism, economics, ideologies, social and psychic power relations, fantasies and desires.

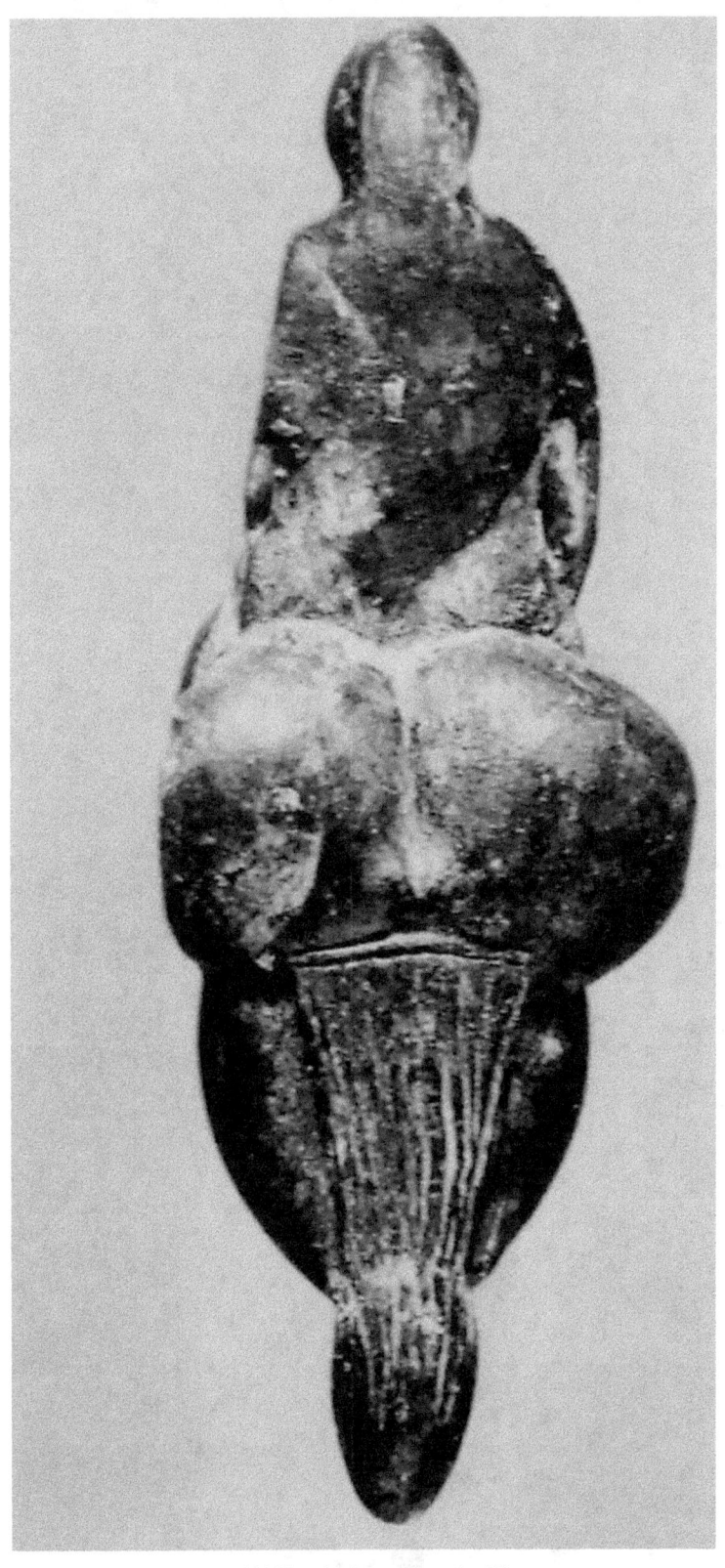

Venus of Willendorf, prehistoric, Vienna

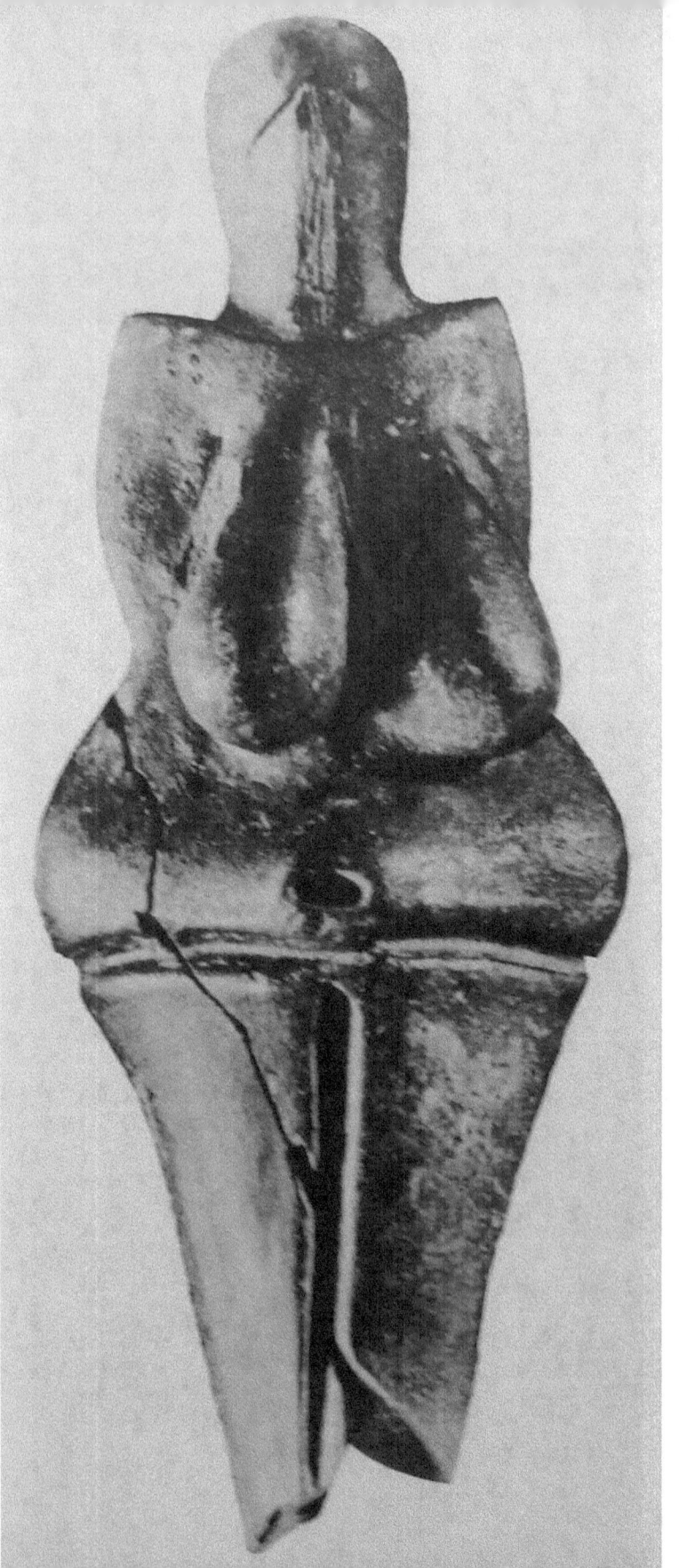

Stone Venus,
prehistoric.

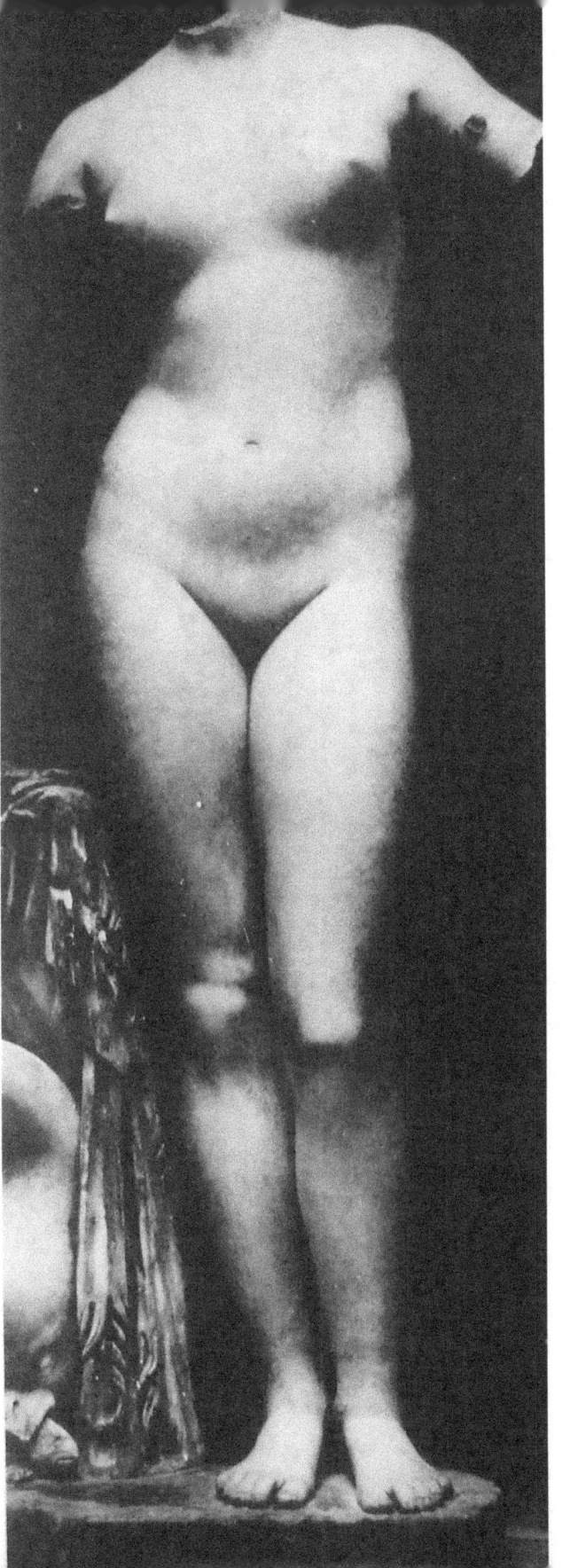

Aphrodite of Cyrene

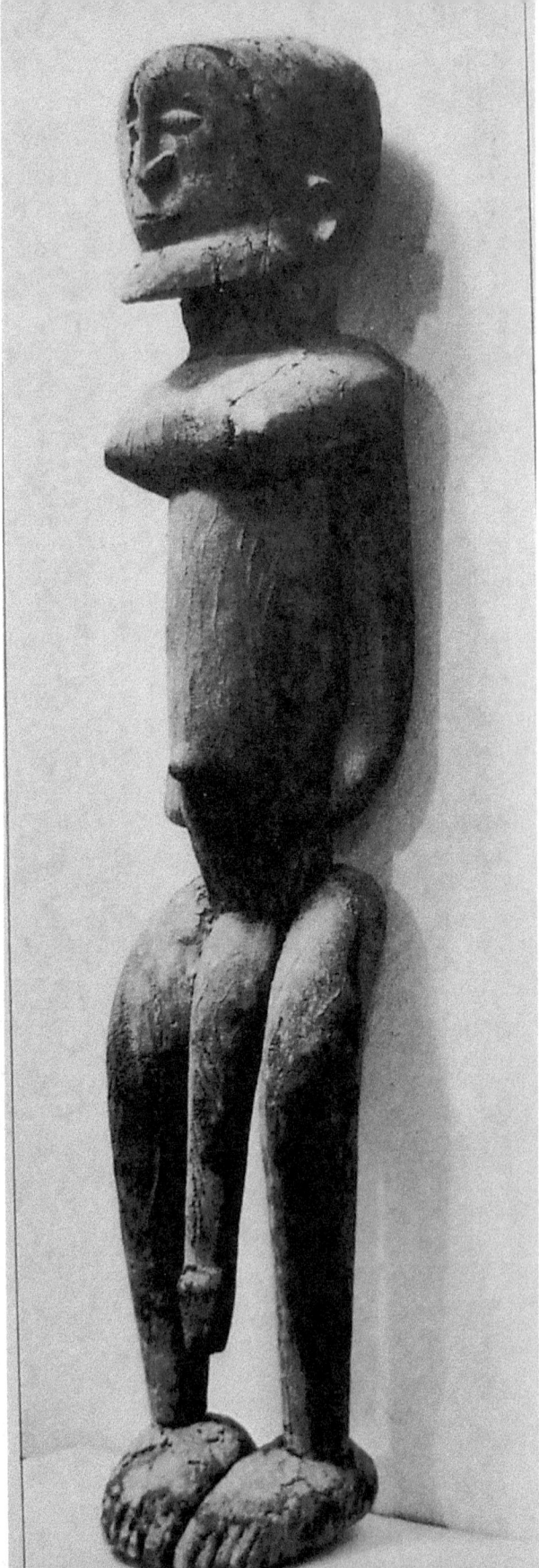

Wood figure, Ivory
Coast

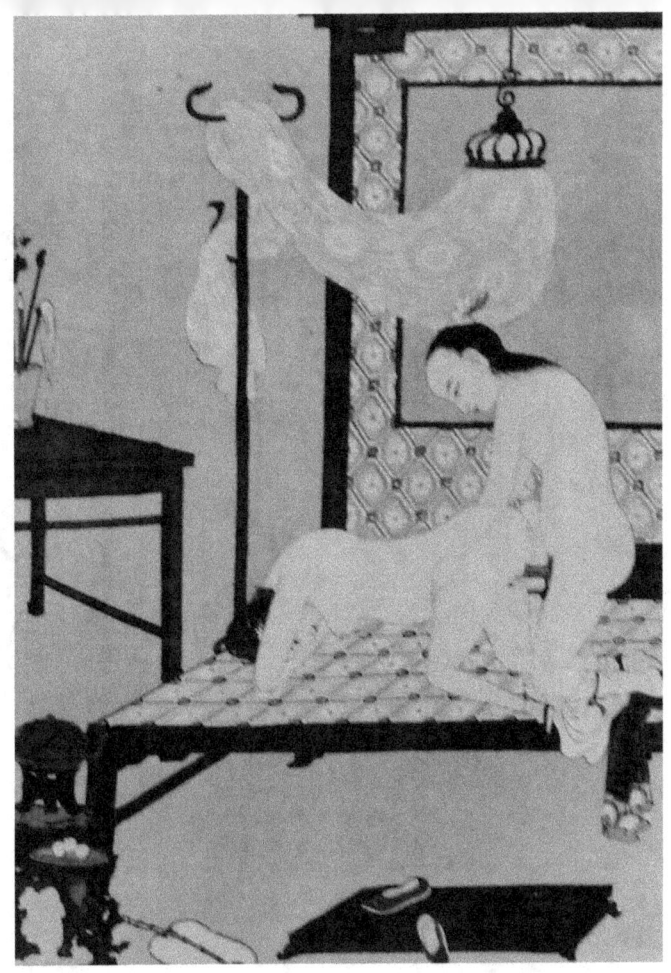

Chinese erotic art: erotic album, above.
Painted scroll, ukiyo-e school, c. 1640, below

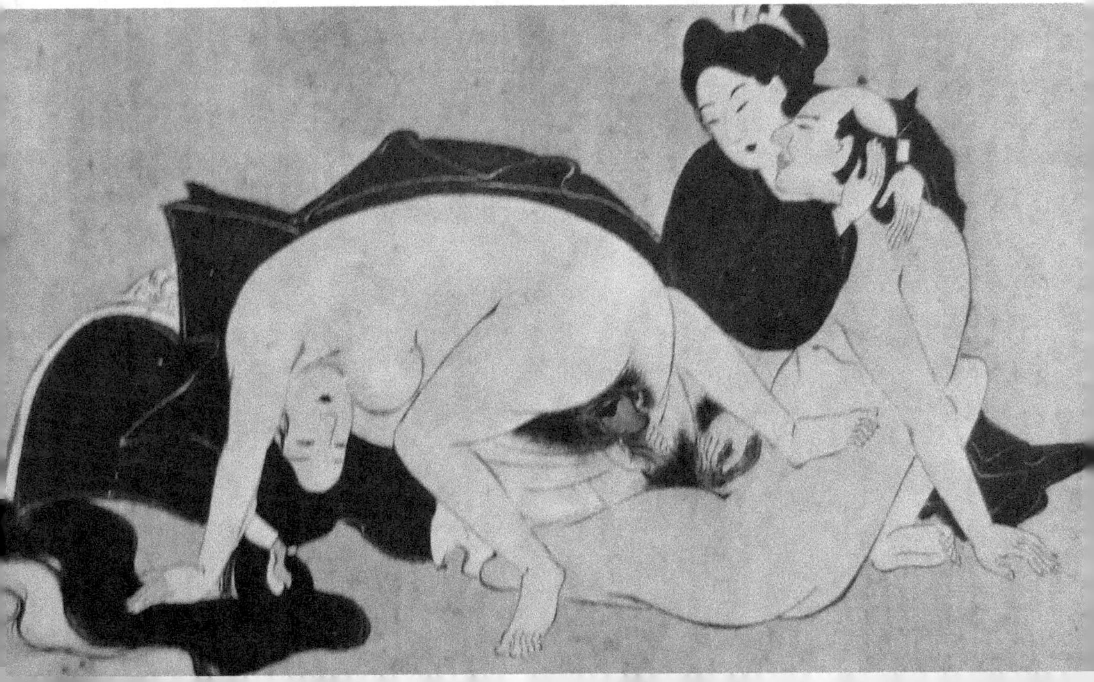

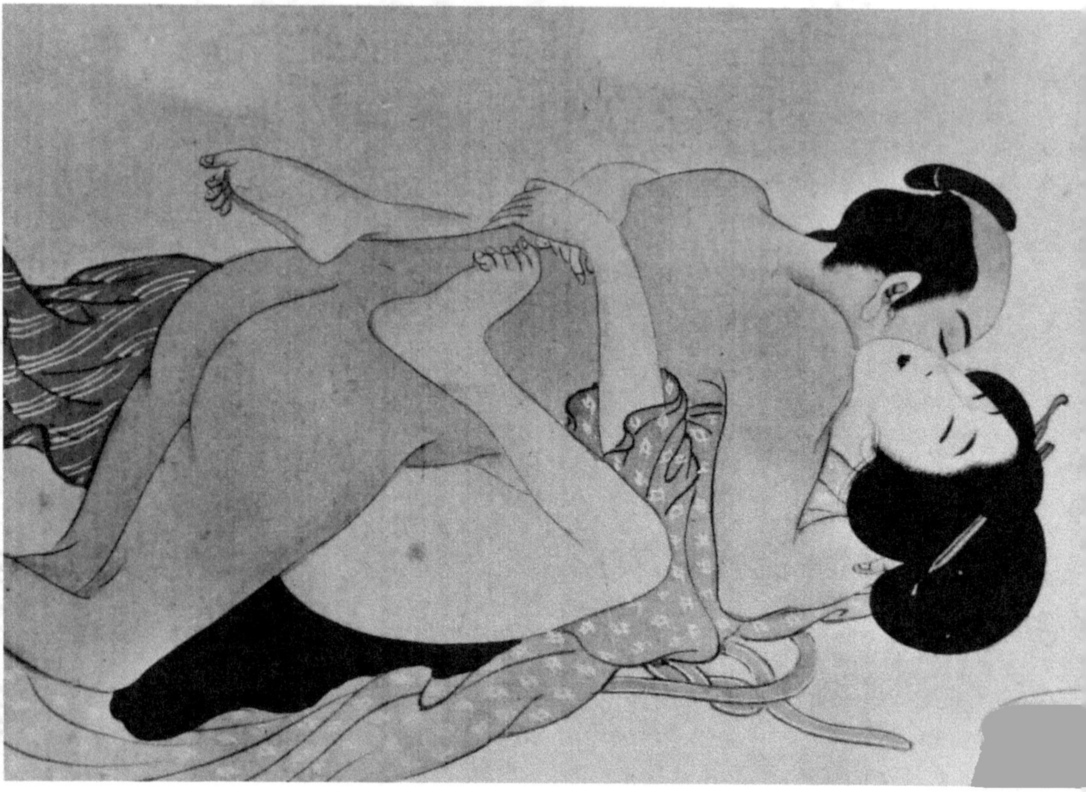

Two Hokusai school pictures: woodblock, 19th century, below.
Hokusai school, c. 1830, above.

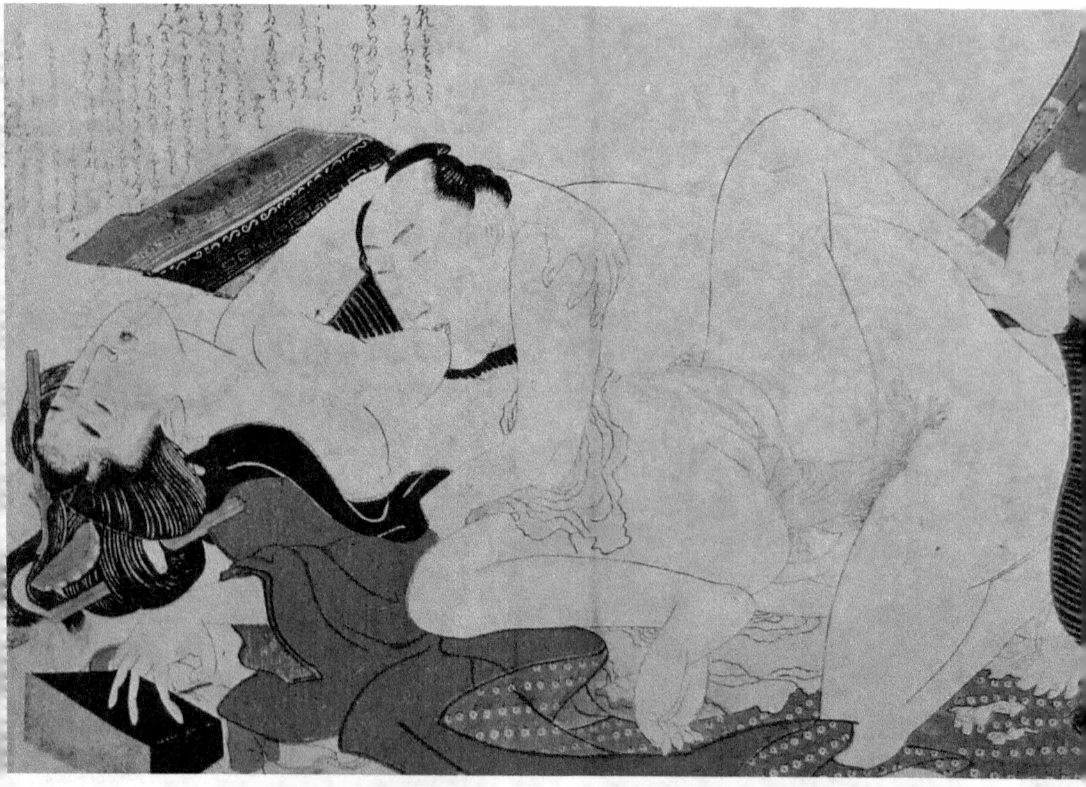

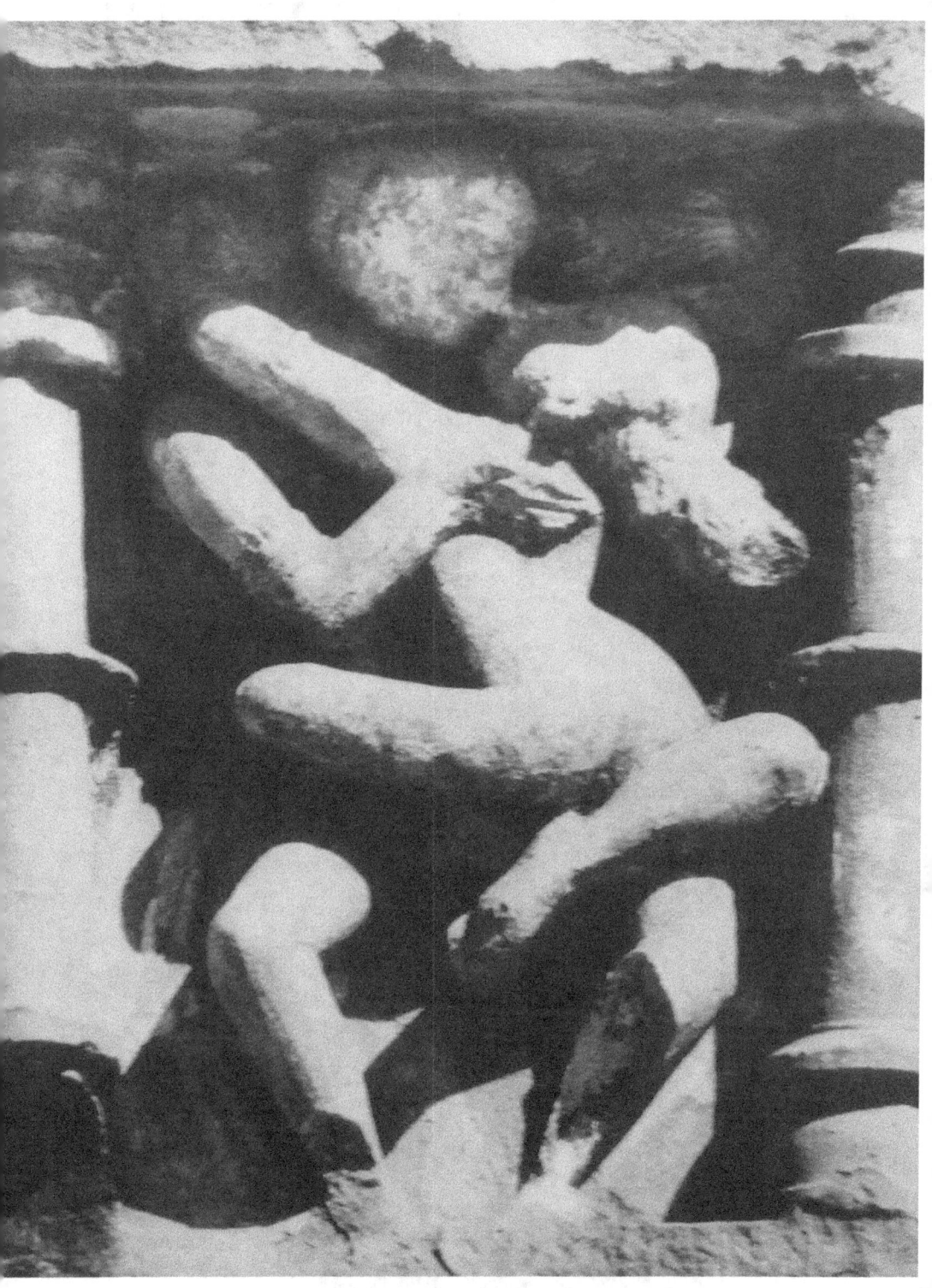

Khajuraho temple, 9th-11th century, North India

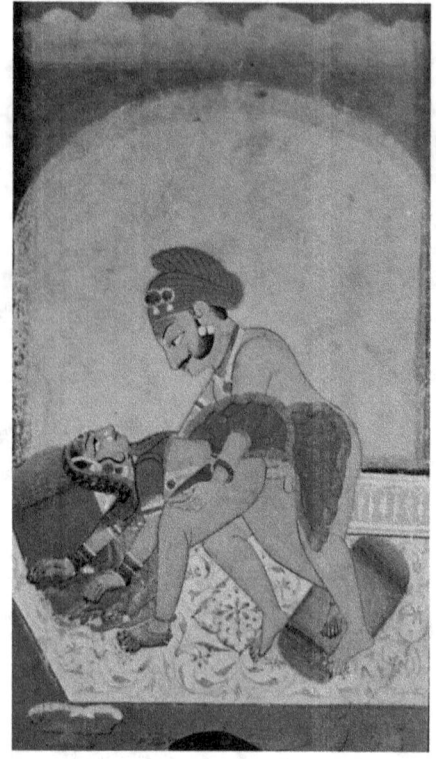

Indian erotic art:
Rajput, late 18th century, above.
Mogul style, 18th century, below.

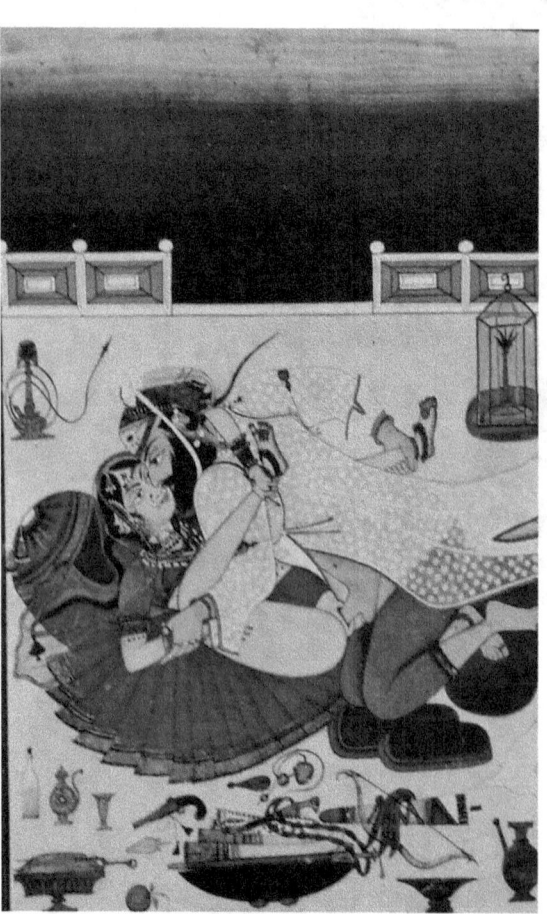

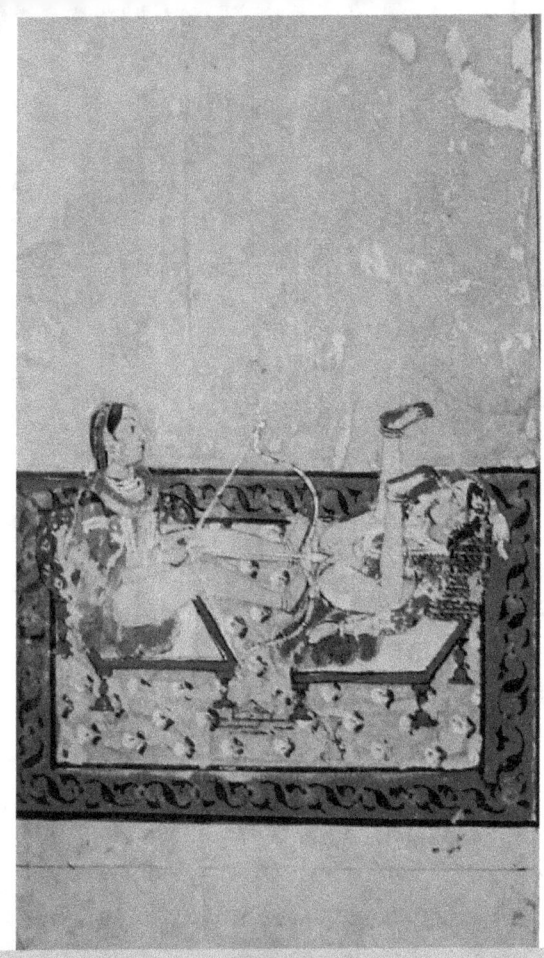

Indian erotic art:
mid-18th century, below.
Rajput miniature, 17th
century, above

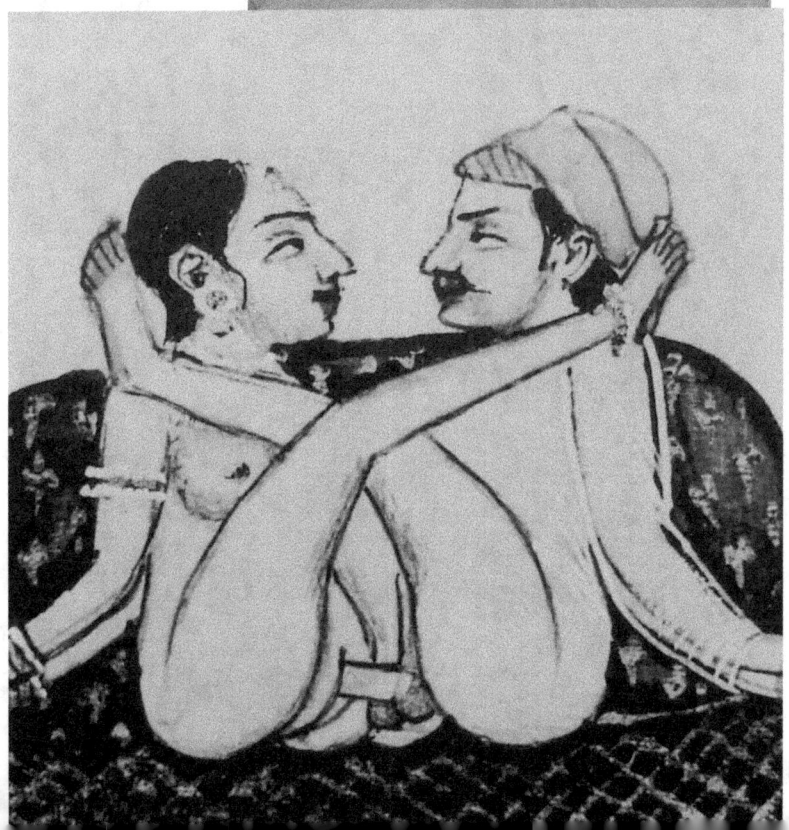

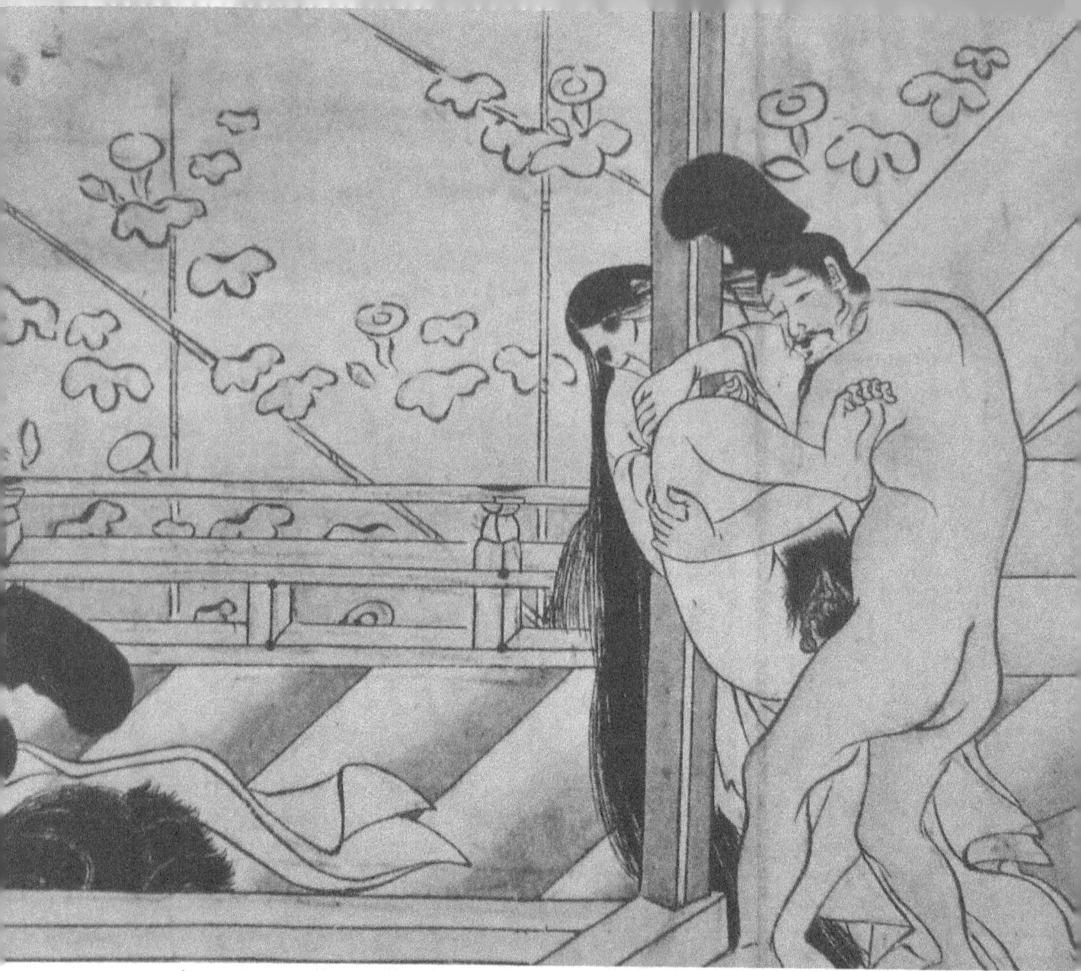

Japanese erotic art. Brushwood fence scroll, 1800s, above. Woodblock, below

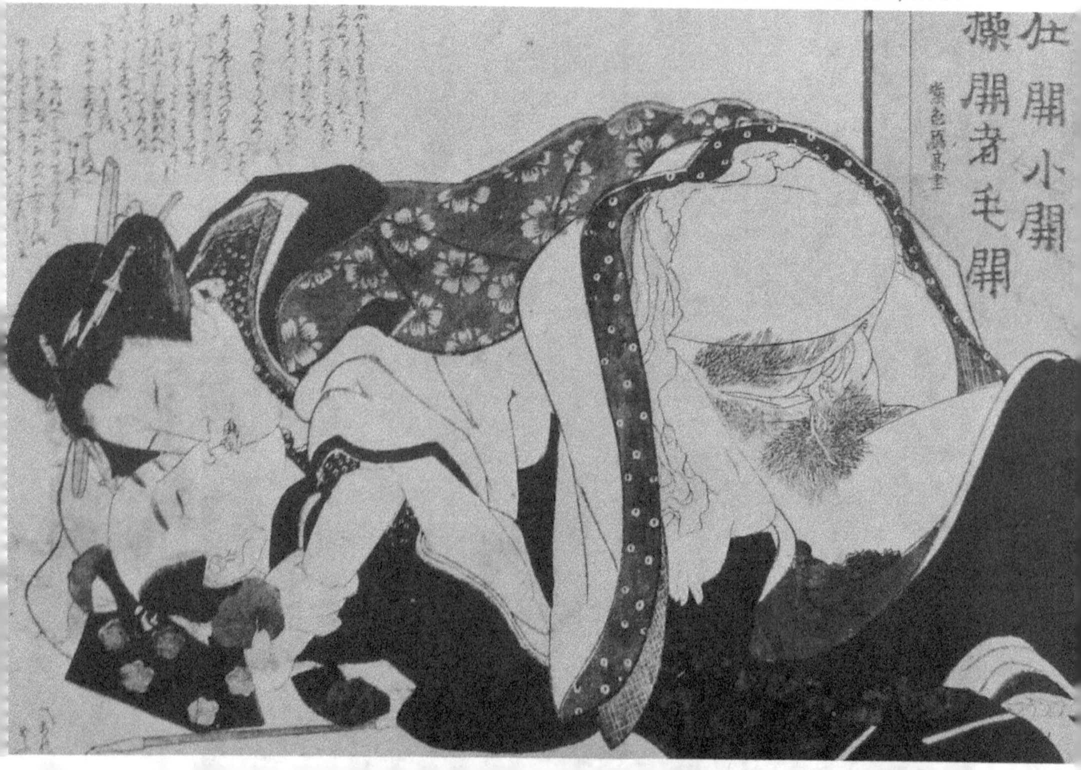

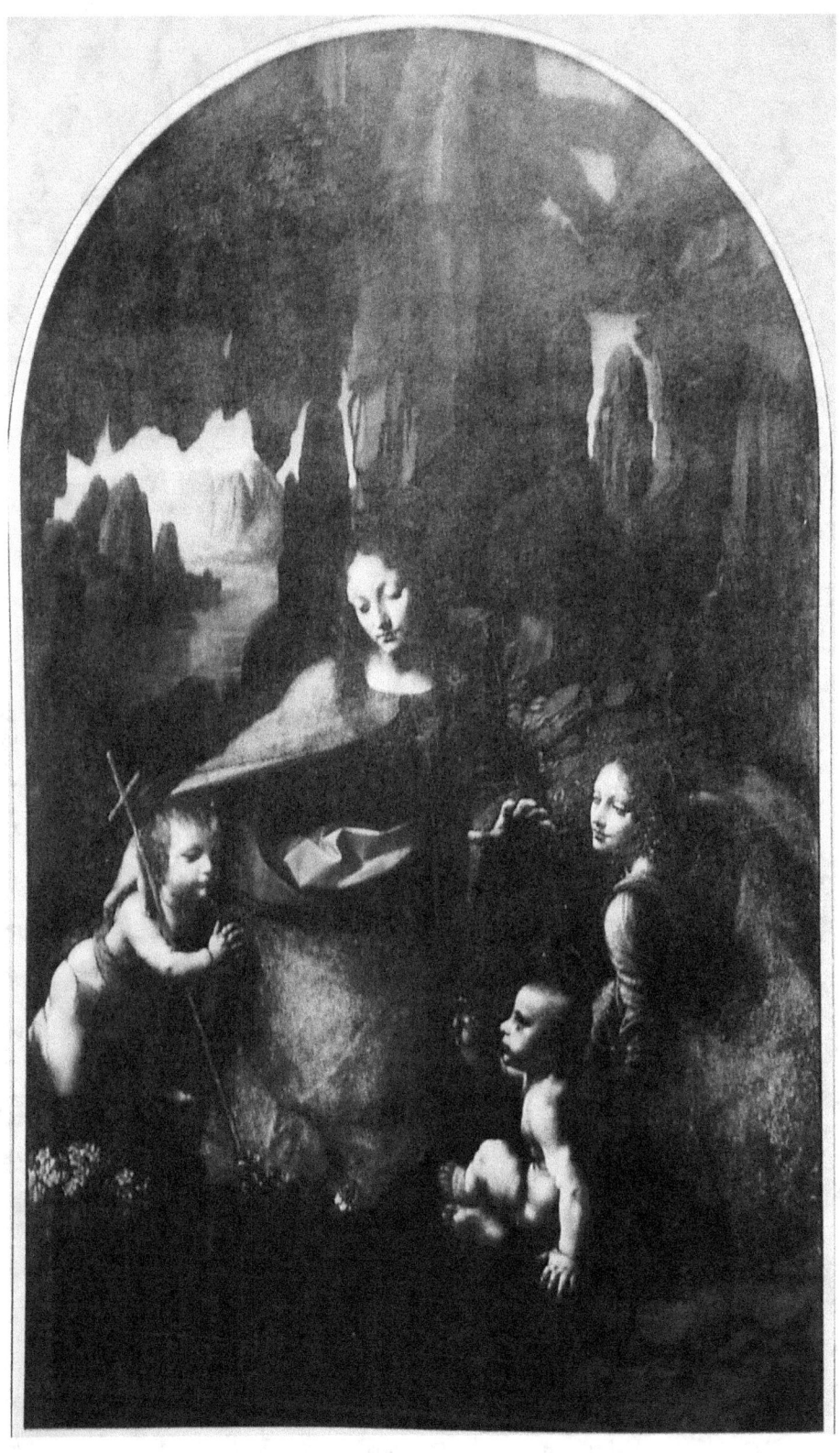

Leonardo da Vinci, The Madonna of the Rocks, London

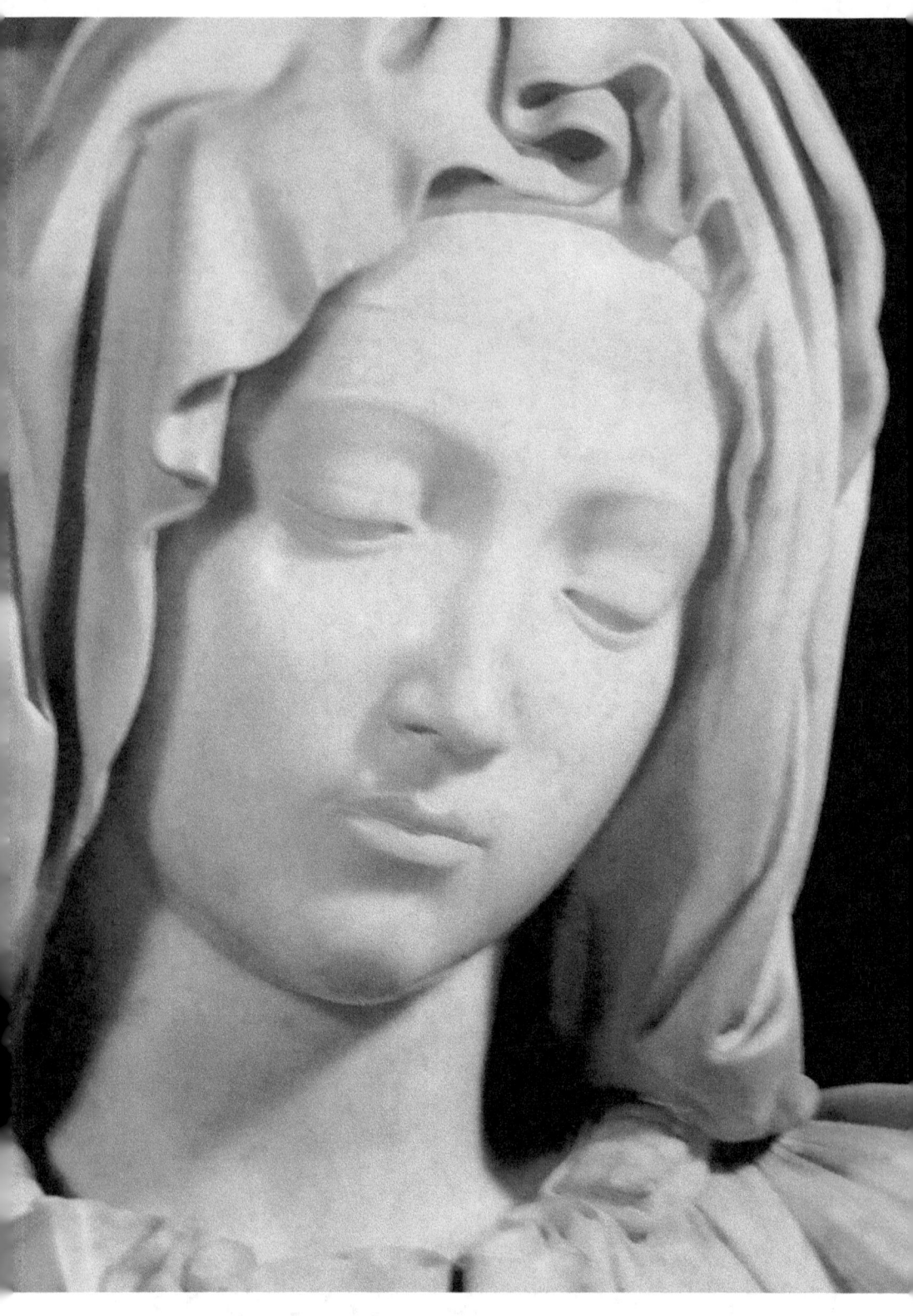

Michelangelo, Pietà, detail, Vatican, Rome

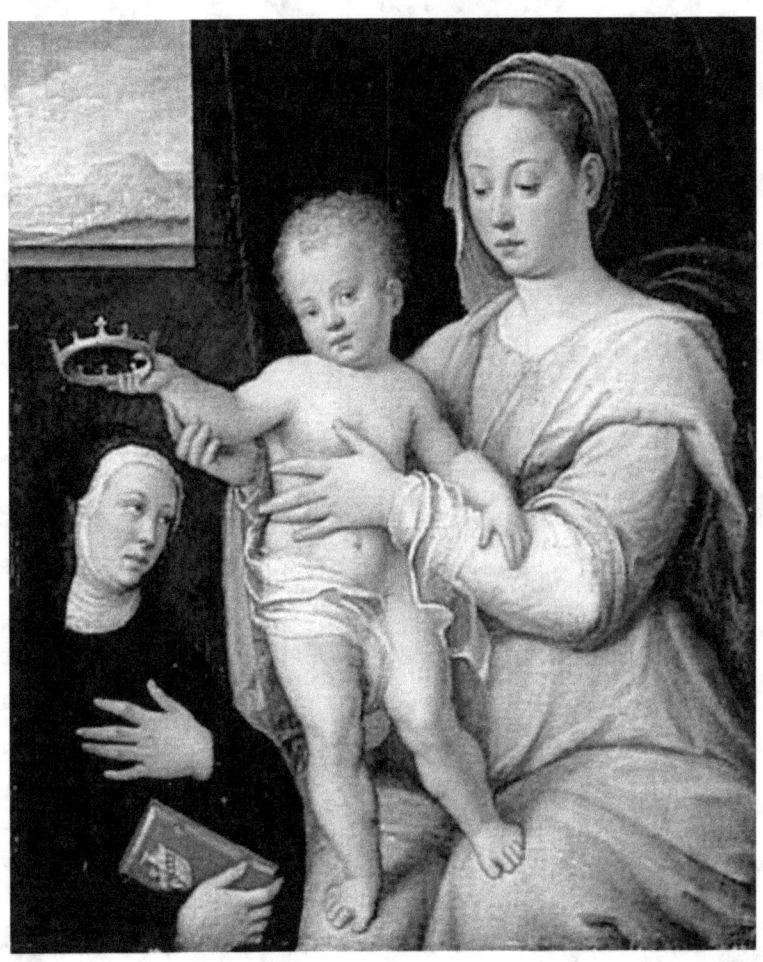

Barbara Longhi, Madonna and Child

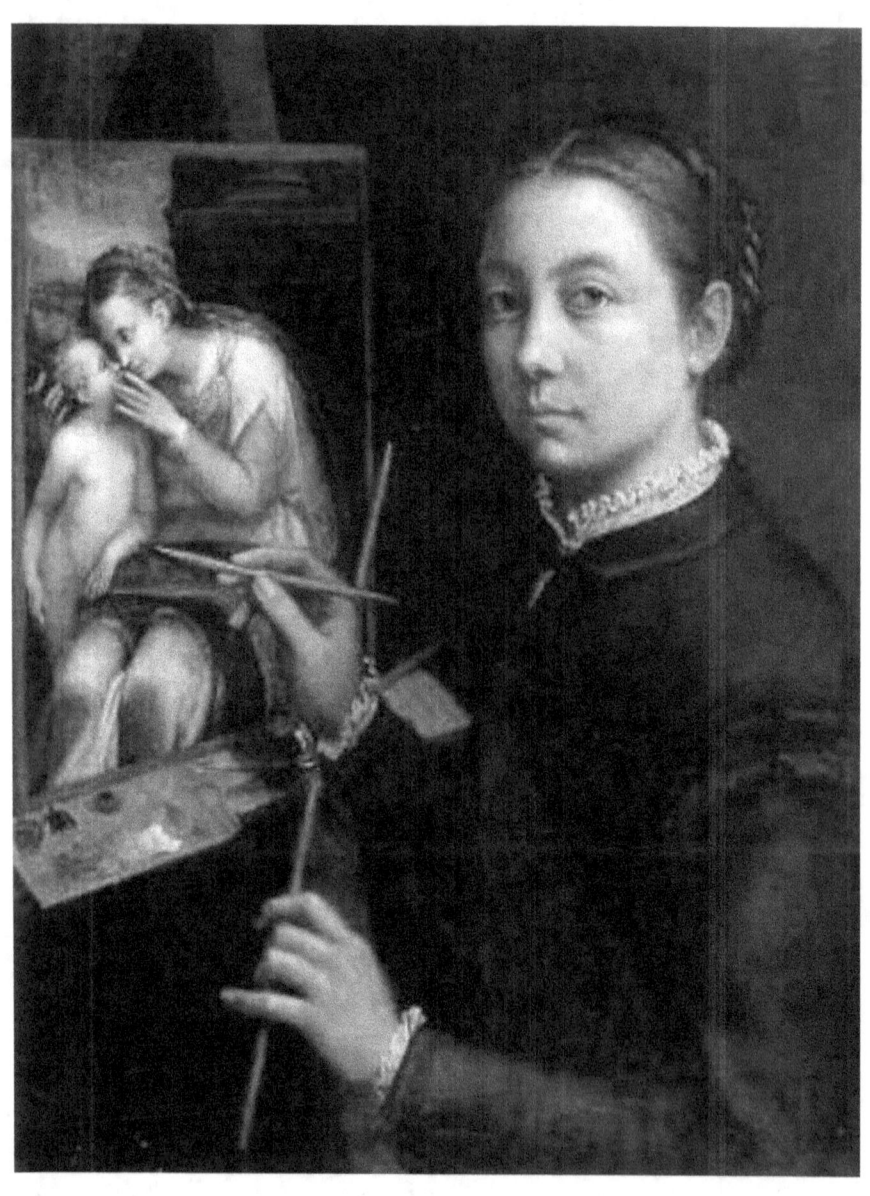

Sofonisba Anguissola, Self-Portrait, 1556, Lancut Museum, Poland

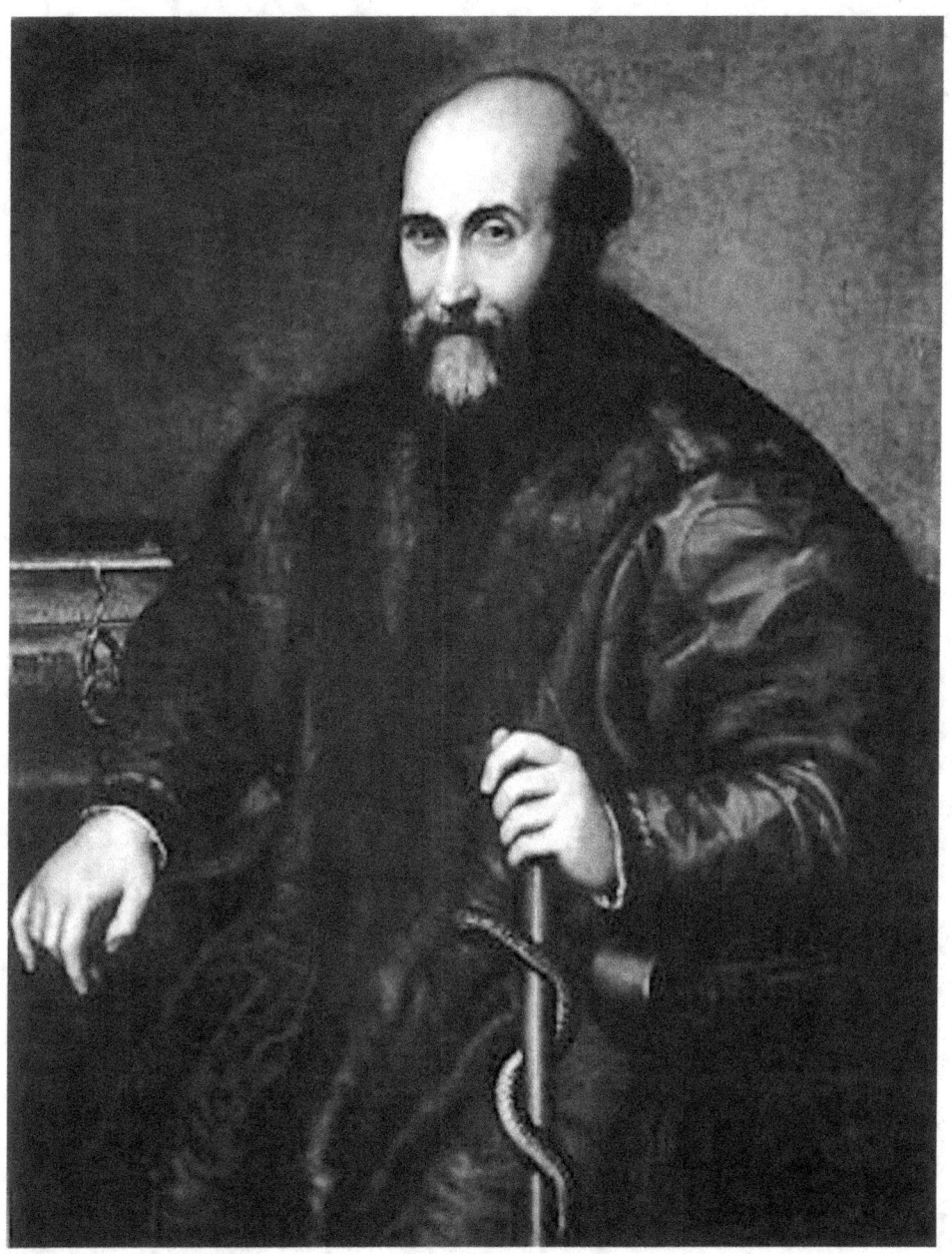

Lucia Anguissola, Pietro Maria, Doctor of Cremona, 1560, Museo del Prado, Madrid

Artemisia Gentileshi, Self-Portrait as a Martyr, 1615

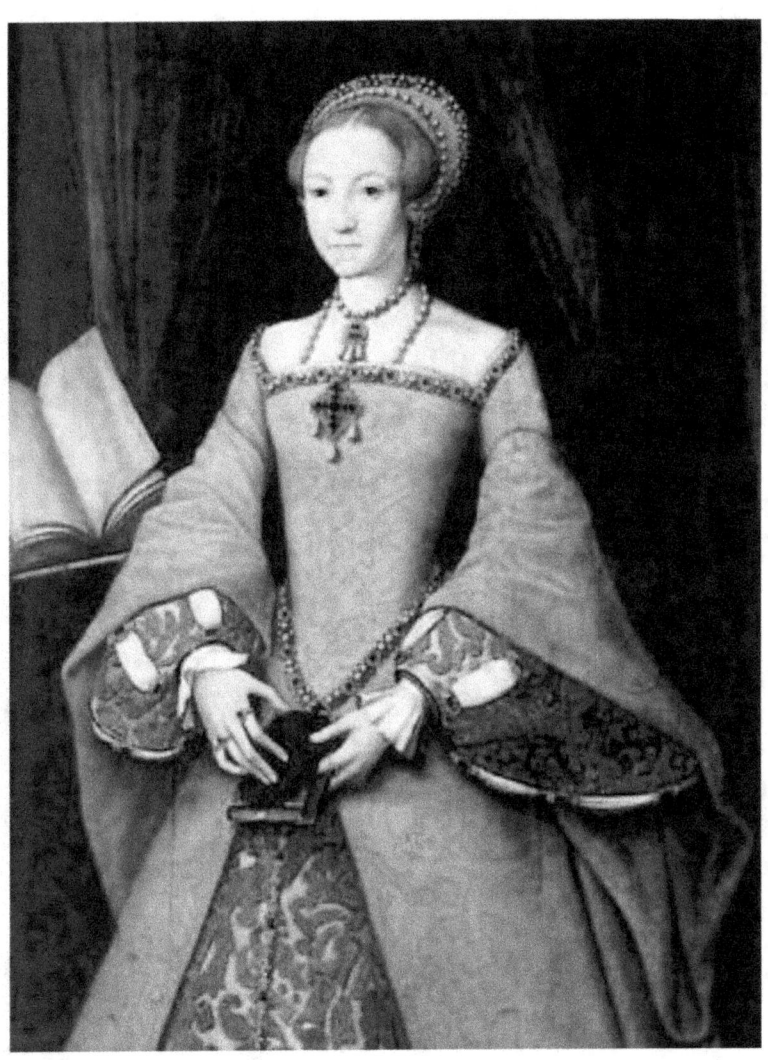

Levina Teerline (a Flemish painter)

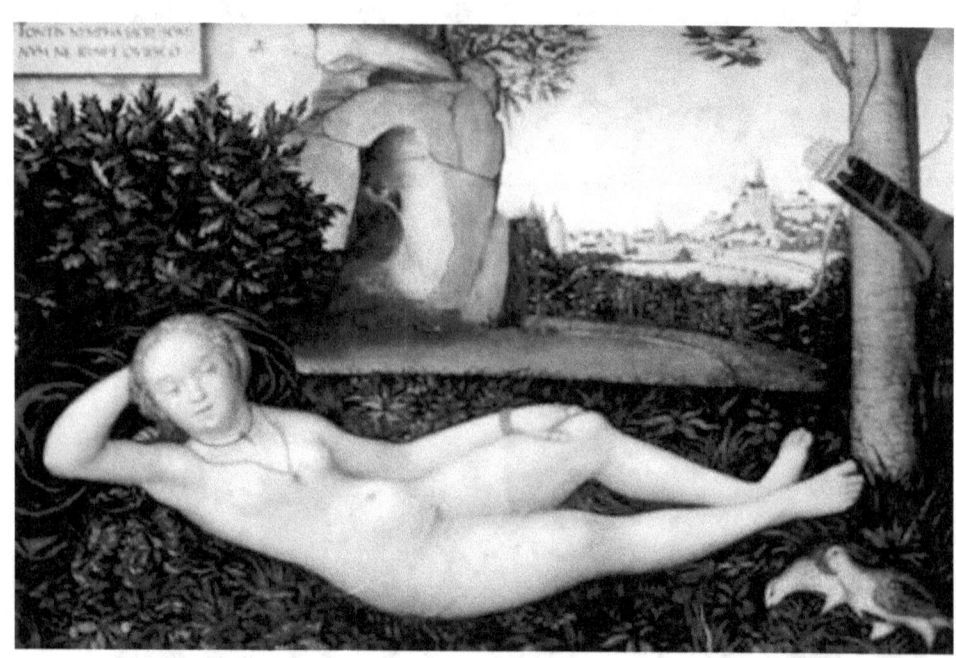

Lucas Cranach, Nymph of the Spring, 1537,
National Gallery of Art, Washington, DC

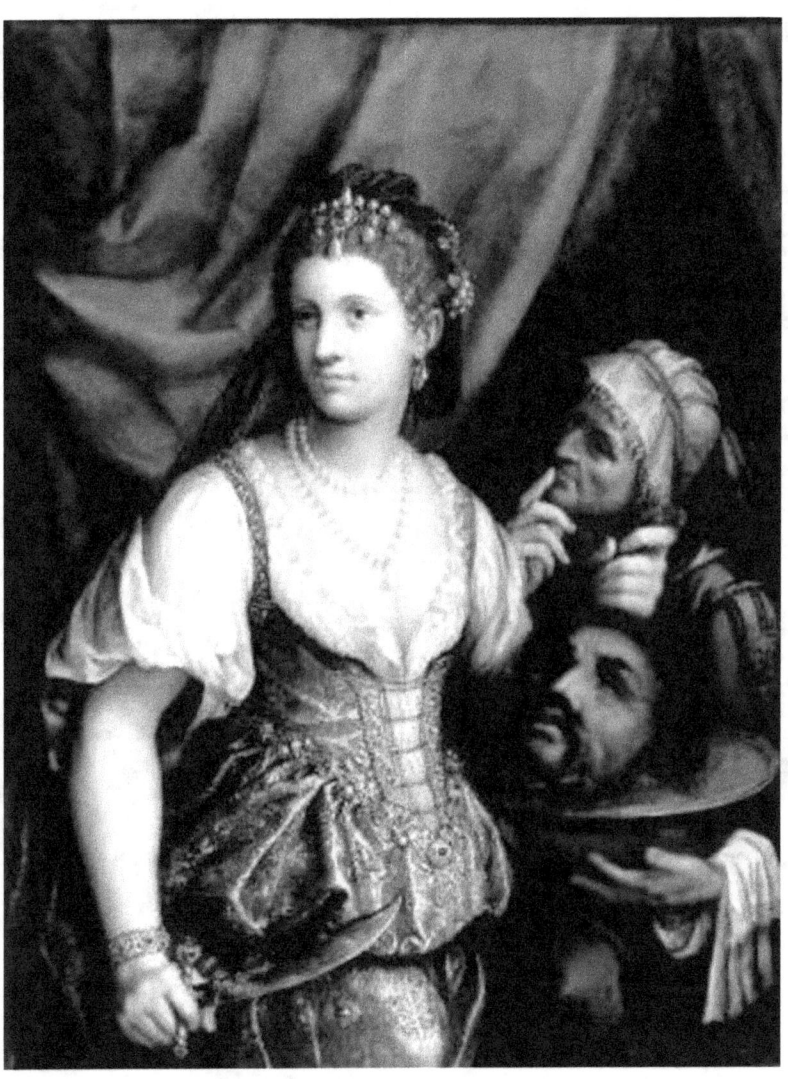

Fede Galizia, Judith with the Head of Holofernes,
Museum of Art, Sarasota, Florida

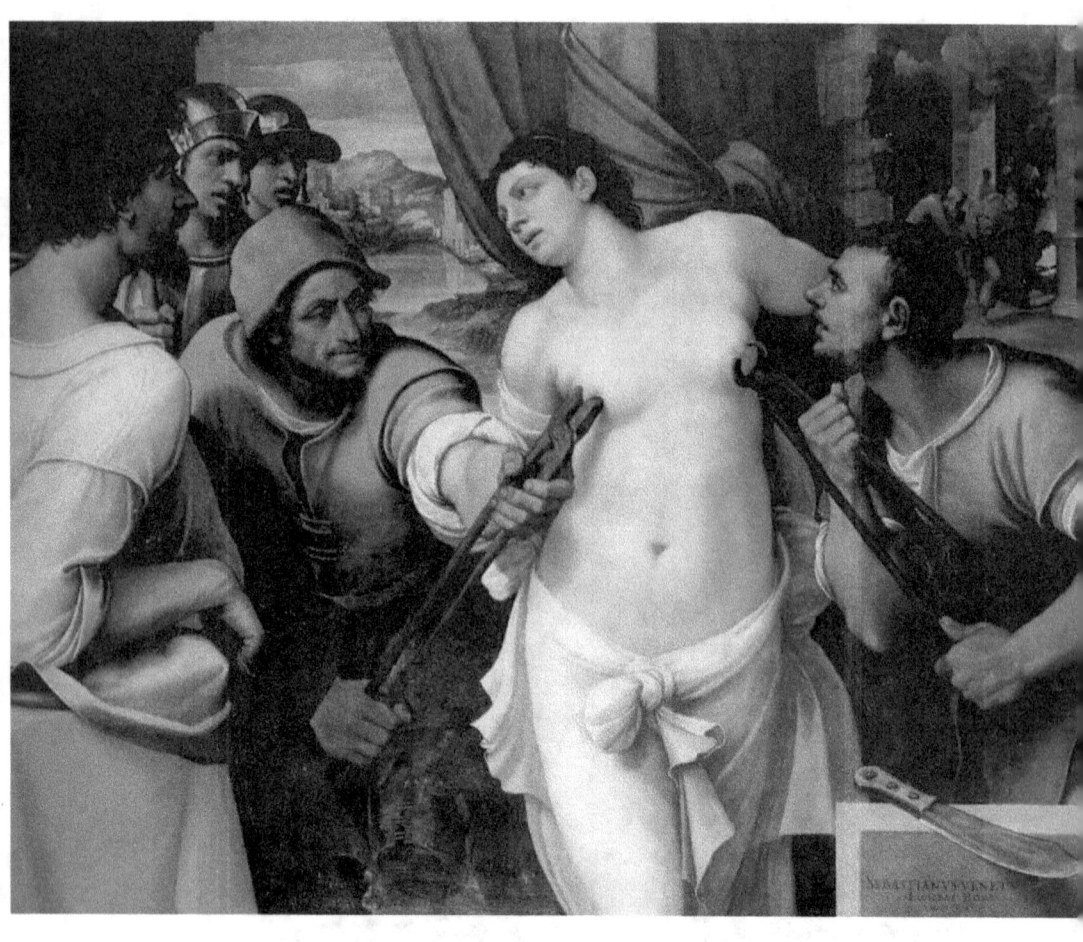

Sebastiano del Piombo, The Martyrdom of St Agatha, 1520,
Pitti Palace, Florence

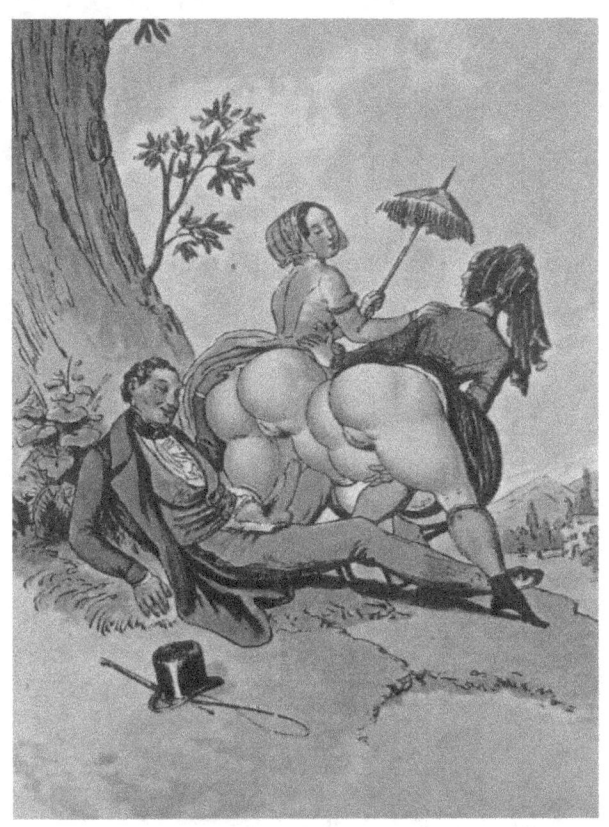

Peter Fendi, above.
Thomas Rowlandson, below.

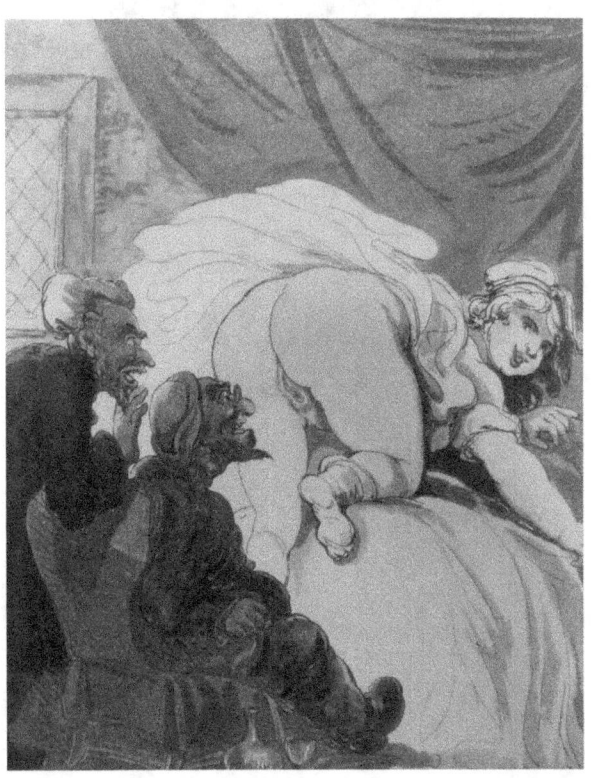

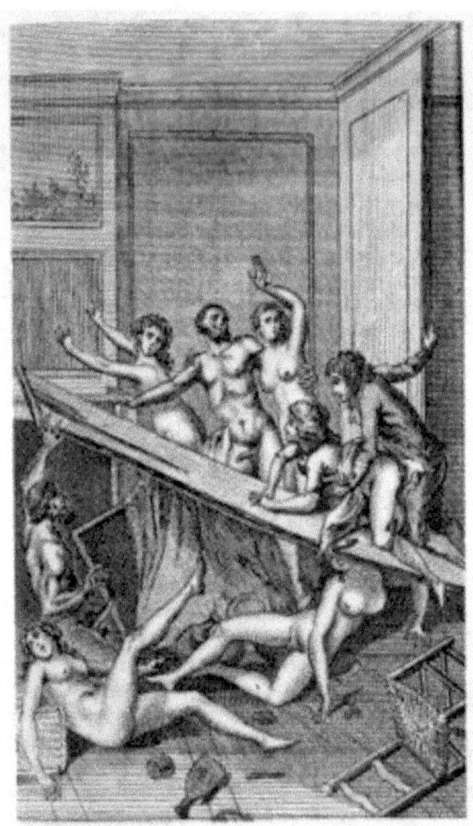

Illustration from Histoire de Juliette,
Marquis de Sade, 1797

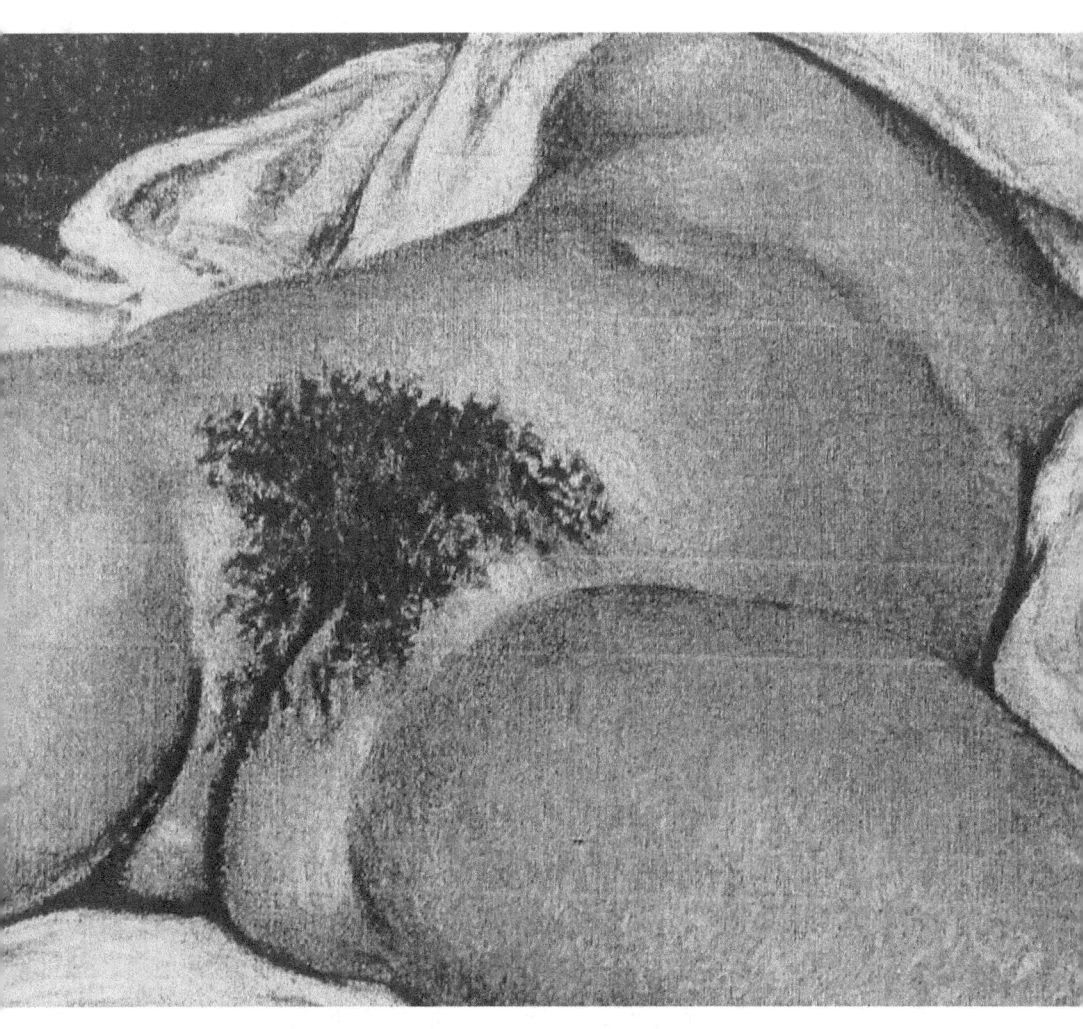

Gustave Courbet, The Creation of the World

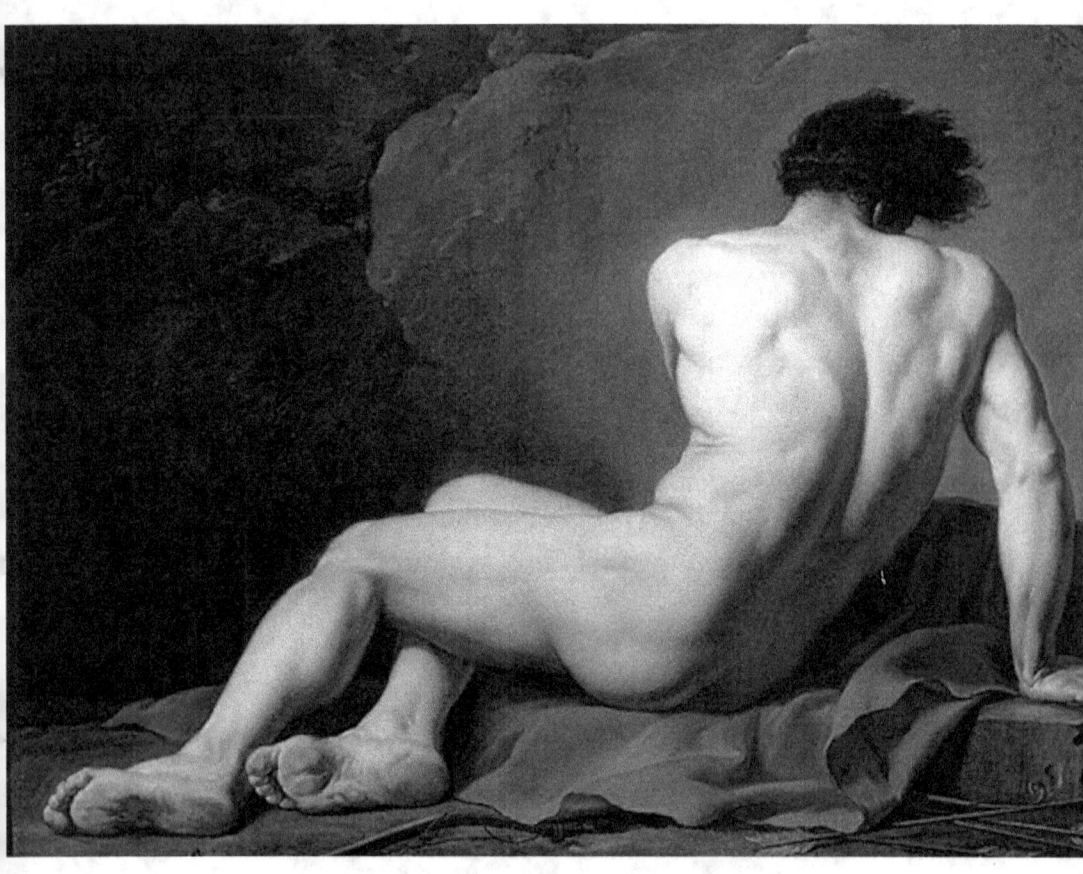

A classical French male nude painting
by Jacques-Louis David (known as Patrocles)

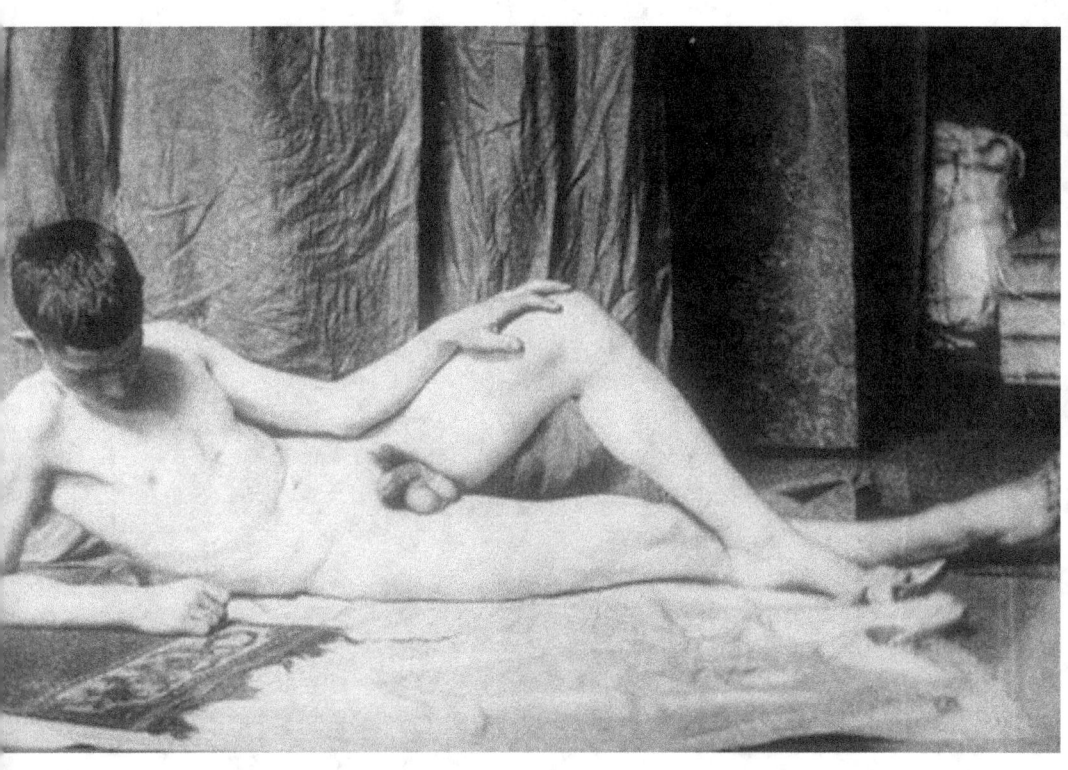

Reclining Male Nude, 1887–92,
Thomas Eakins, platinum print

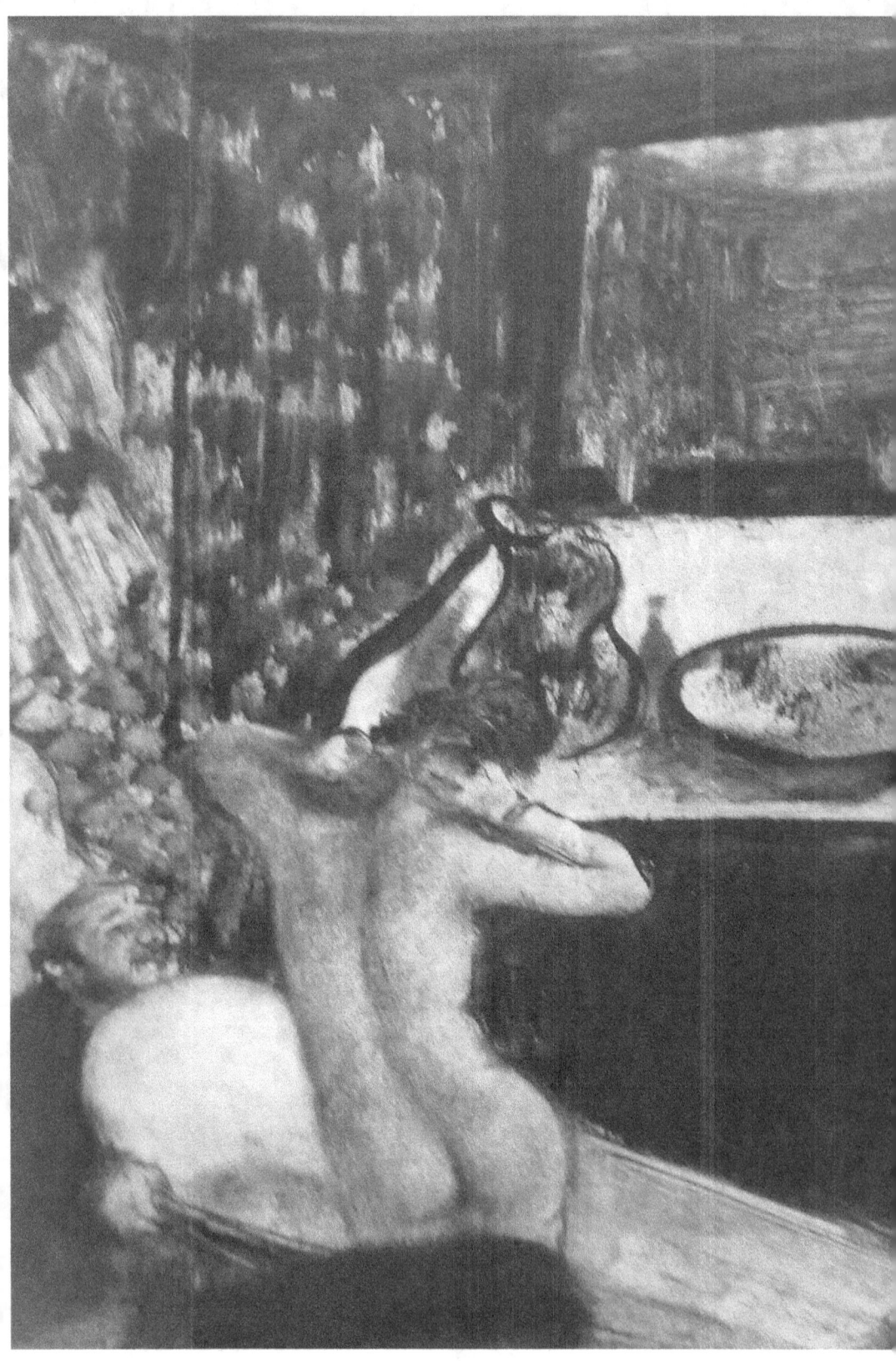

Edgar Degas, The Bath

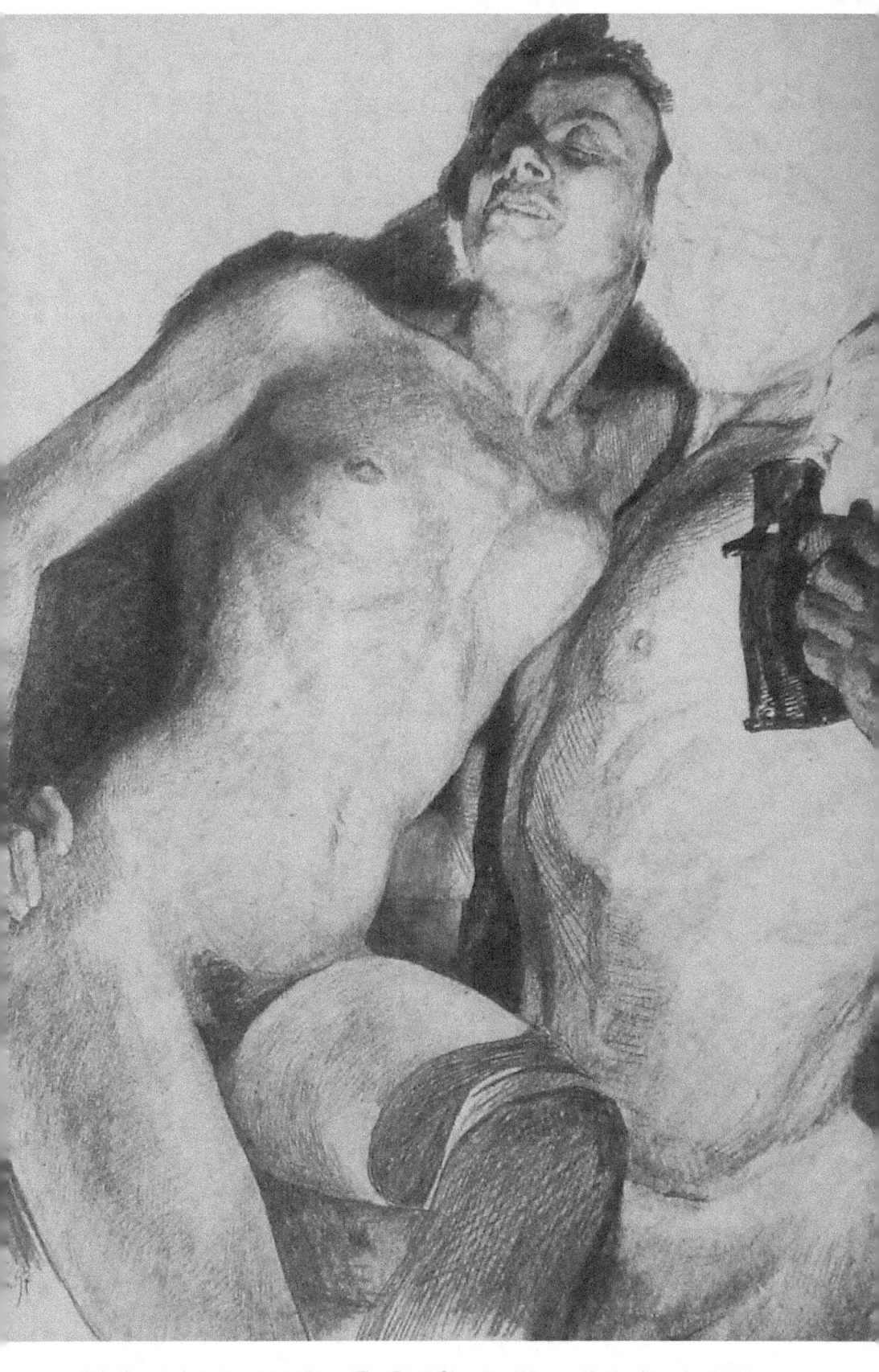

Otto Grenier's truly extraordinary The Devil Showing Woman To the People, 1897

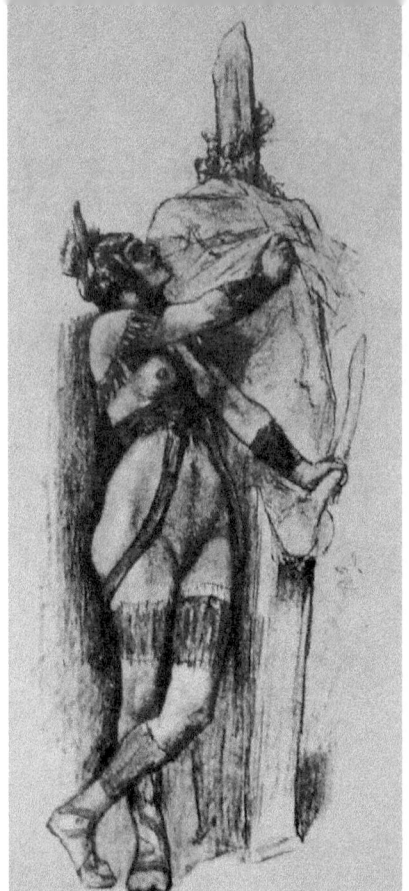

The inimitable Félicien
Rops, French fin-de-siècle
Decadence at its most
extreme.

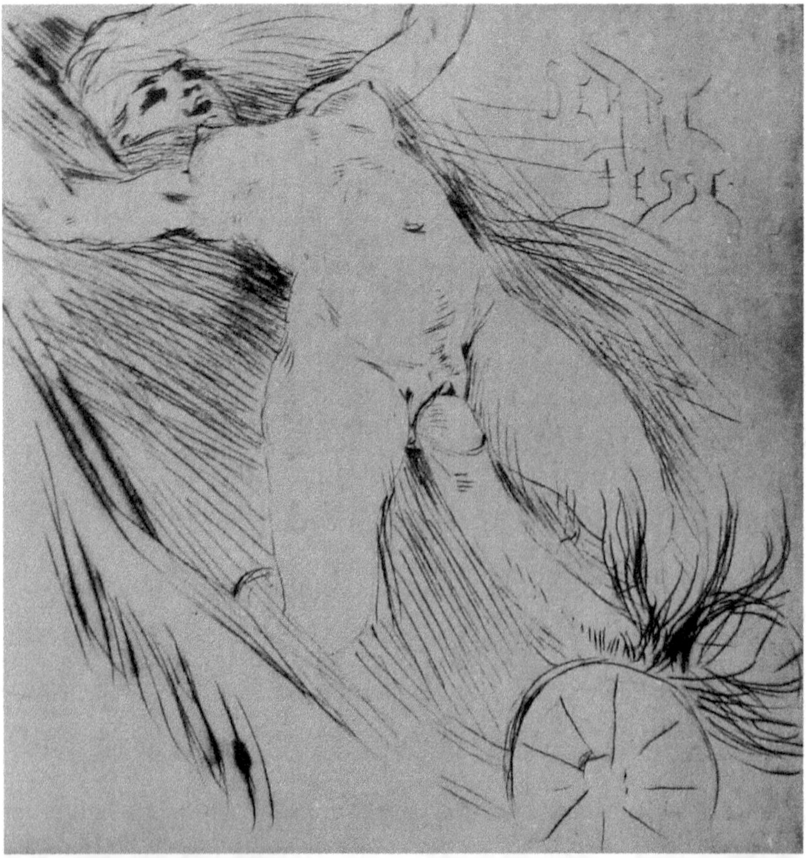

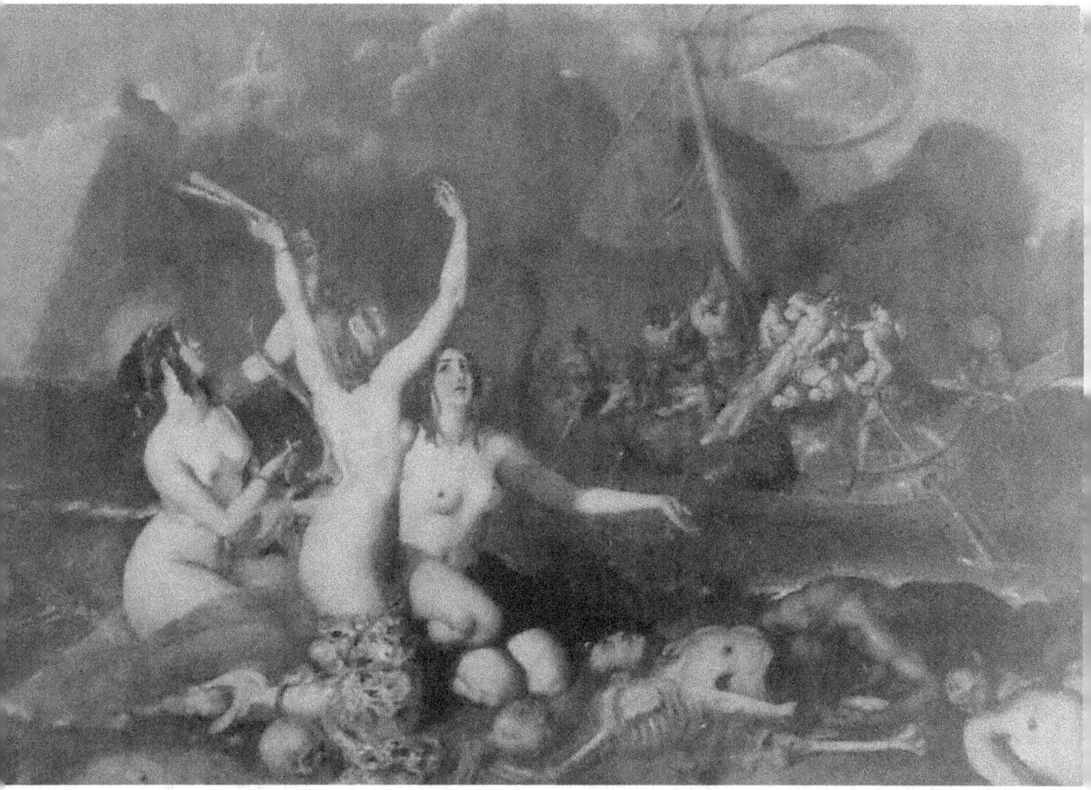

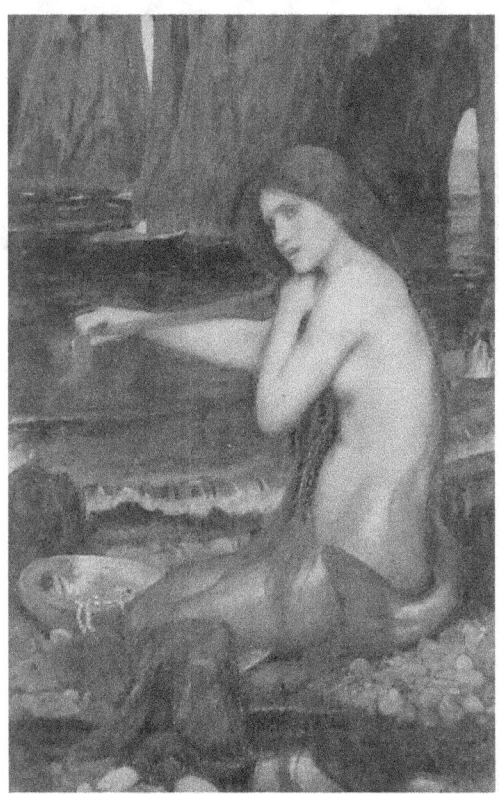

A favourite theme in 19th century painting: sex, death, nudity and the sea.
William Etty's The Sirens and Ulysses, 1837, Manchester. above.

J.W. Waterhouse,
A Mermaid, 1901, Royal Academy, London, below.

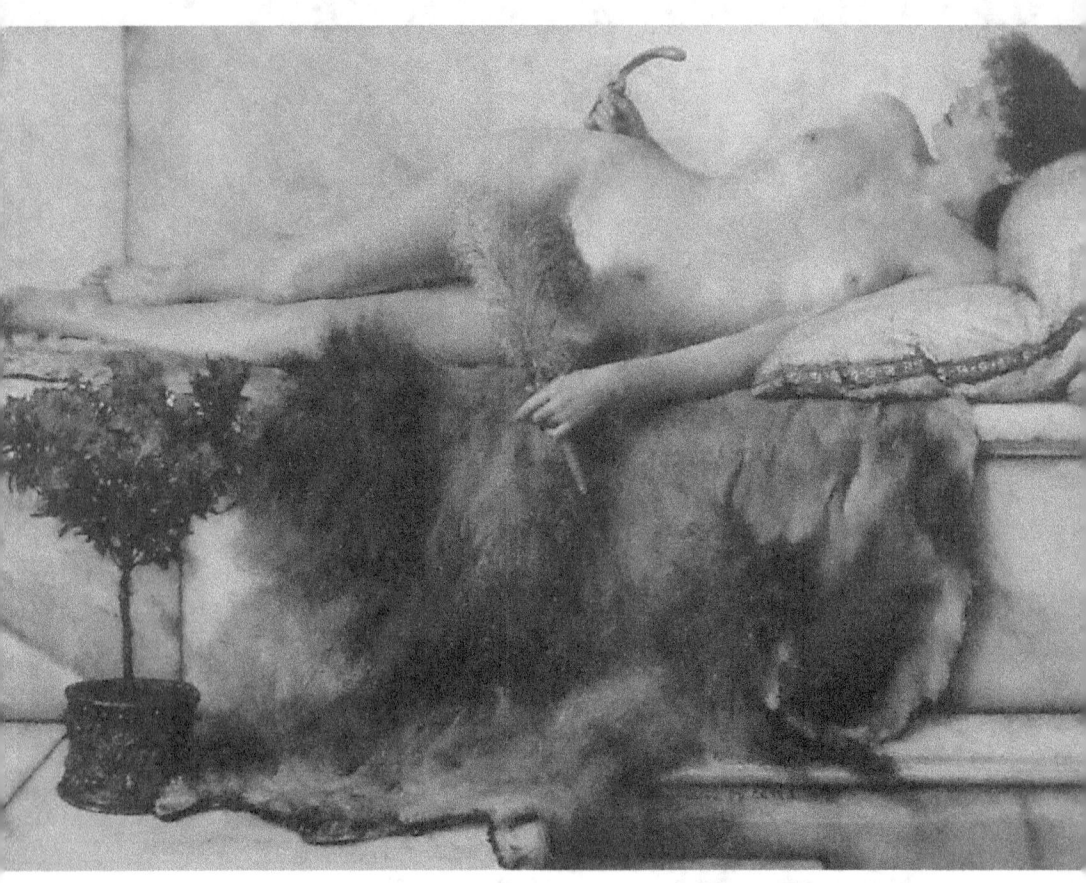

Lawrence Aldma-Tadema, In the Tepidarium, 1881, Lady Lever Art Gallery,
Liverpool

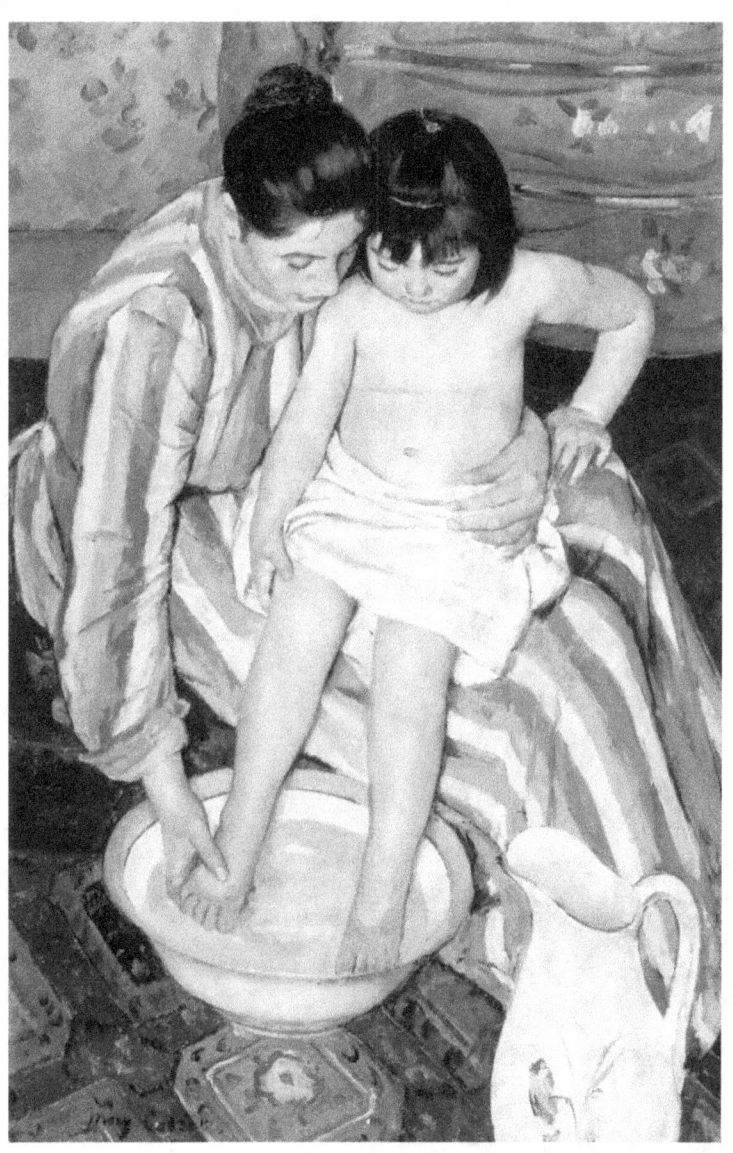

Mary Cassatt, The Bath, 1891

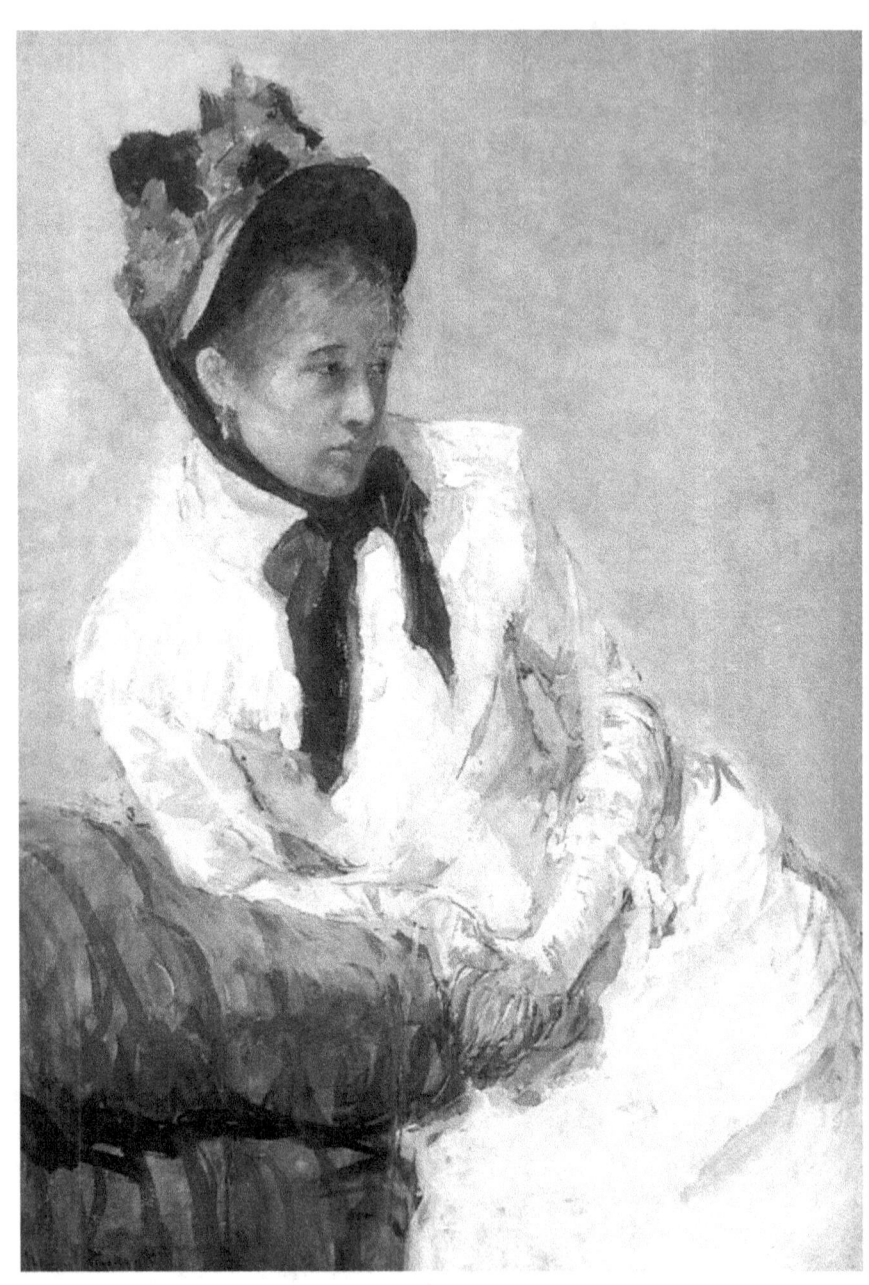

Mary Cassatt, Self-Portrait, 1878,
Metropolitan Museum of Art, New York City

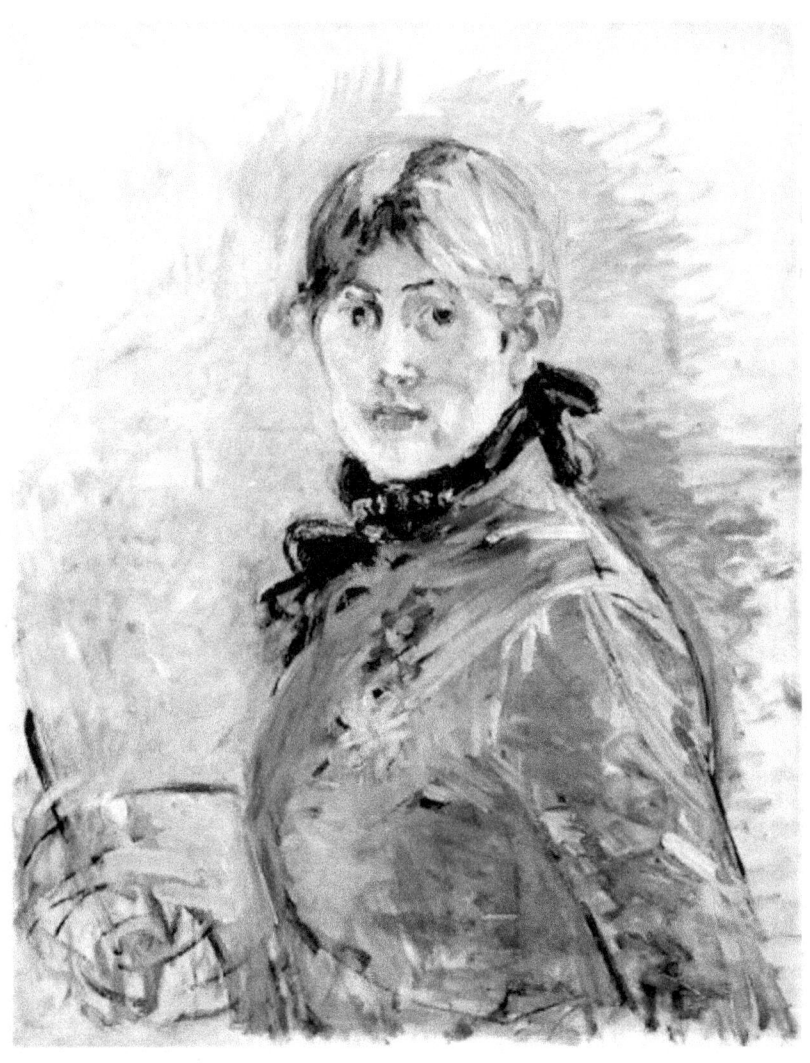

Berthe Morisot, Self-Portrait, 1885

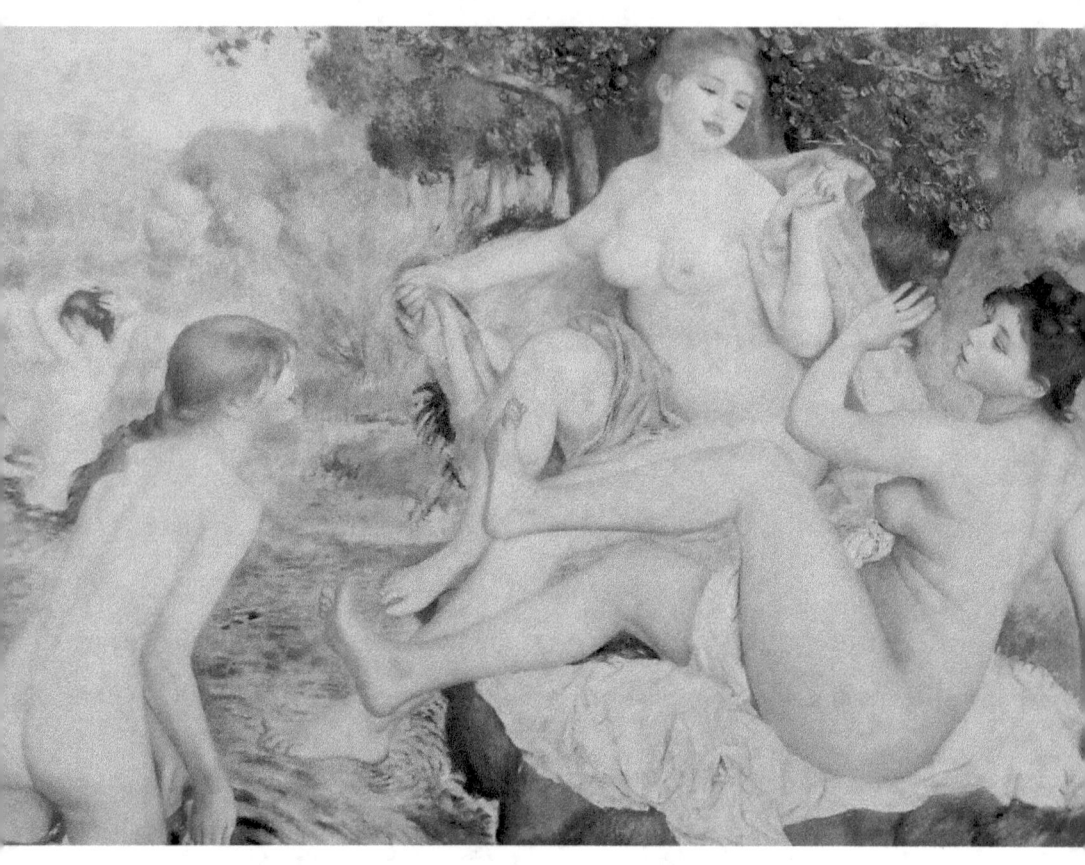

Pierre Renoir, The Bathers, 1887, Philadelphia

2

ART / SEXUALITY / PORNOGRAPHY

The age-old debate between art and pornography revolves around tired old questions: is art pornography? Is pornography art? Is consuming art therefore consuming pornography? Is there a set of attitudes, values, ethics and morals ascribed to art but not pornography? Is pornography any different, æsthetically, psychologically, physically, politically and morally from art? What is the 'boundary' between art and pornography?

These questions, for feminists, become irrelevant beside debates of race, class, economics, political oppression, poverty, exploitation, war and violence. The art/ pornography debate is the game of bourgeois people, some feminists claim, who have nothing better to do. Instead of concentrating on pornography, what about looking at other forms of oppression – racial, economic, political, ideological, heterosexual, familial, psychological, etc. This is the question some feminists ask. B. Ruby Rich writes:

> If an analysis of porn were to confront its basic origin in the power relations between men and women, then it would have to drop the whole eroticism-versus-pornography debate and take on a far more complex and threatening target: the institution of heterosexuality.[1]

---

1 B. Ruby Rich: "Anti-Porn: Soft issue, Hard World", in Chester, 348

We know the male/ patriarchal view of the art versus pornography debate. Eroticism is justified and good because it is 'high art', it is superbly crafted, it is a 'work of art'. Thus the Kronhausens, the organizers of a major exhibition of 'erotic art',[2] write: 'one can perhaps distinguish between pornography and art. The criterion would be that the more a picture contains evidence of interpretative, creative elaboration, the closer it is to art.'[3] For the Kronhausen's, as for so many artists and philosophers and intellectuals, erotic art is art because it is done well. Pornography is simply bad art.

Many guardians of æsthetics, many professors of art history and dons of 'the beautiful' go along with this view. Kenneth Clark is a typical establishment critic who puts forward the patriarchal view: nudes are OK provided they are æsthetically pleasing, provided they remain 'in the realm of contemplation' as he put it.[4]

The establishment art historical view of erotic art and pornography is that true erotic or high art engenders quiet contemplation, a detached ravishing of the senses, a meditation on Platonic, Aristotlean and Kantian ideas of 'beauty' and æsthetics. 'High art', which is legitimate art, art which justifies itself by its 'genius' or obvious 'greatness', is about distance and disinterested pleasure. The high art nude, in painting or sculpture, in the patriarchal view, justifies its existence by the brilliance of its production, the sumptuousness of its colour and form, the marvel of its human touches, the grandeur of its design, the loftiness of its ambition, the dynamism of its structures, and so on. As that producer of exquisite bodies, Jean Auguste Dominique Ingres, wrote: '[t]here are not two arts, there is only one: it is the one which has as its foundation the beautiful, which is eternal and natural.'[5]

The 'sublime' qualities of high art, to use one popular adjective of art criticism, are crucial to its success, as Carol M. Armstrong notes in her essay on Edgar Degas:

---

2 The 'first international exhibition of erotic art' was at the Museum of Art, Lund, Sweden, and Aarhus, Denmark, in 1968

3 Phyllis & Eberhard Kronhausen: *Erotic Art: A survey of erotic fact and fancy in the fine arts*, W.H. Allen, 1971, 3

4 Quoted in Lord Longford: *Pornography: The Longford Report*, Coronet, 1972, 99f

5 Ingres, quoted in Goldwater, 216

One of the things any painted object does is to resist signification at some level because of its very objecthood. And the female nude – because of *its* objecthood may be seen as almost emblematic of that level of resistance. In fact, the female nude has been linked to that stratum of painting most in tension with the work of signification – the stratum we connect to what we call, inadequately, "abstraction"; facture, the handling of paint per se, foregrounded as an obvious fact of the painting. Femaleness and facture, facture and the female nude, they go together somehow. One need only think of Titian, the first great painter of the female nude in the Western tradition.[6]

Much as worshippers properly gaze at an icon or an image of a deity with wonder, the art critic and historian kneels before 'great art' and worships it.[7] The female nude is the highest form of non-religious art, and it confers a religious awe in its consumers. The emphasis is on Neoplatonic terms such as 'purity', 'beauty', 'form' and 'symmetry'. As Aristotle puts it: '[t]he chief forms of beauty are order and symmetry and definiteness.'[8]

In the Neoplatonic, Aristotlean, Renaissance view of the fine art establishment, there is good art and bad art, there is the art of 'taste', 'decency', 'refinement', 'purity' and 'civilization', and there is the vulgar, the uncouth, the disrespectful, the unornamental, the unlearned. Pornography falls into the latter category. In mediæval culture, there is Sacred and Profane love, drawn from Plato's *Symposium*, and the Venus Vulgaris (Earthly Venus) and Venus Coelestis (Heavenly Venus). The Celestial Venus is the one to aspire to, even though the Earthly Venus may be much more exciting. These dichotomies are found throughout art. There is the chaste, passive, motherly Virgin Mary and the sexual, active, lascivious Mary Magdalene.[9] There is good and evil. There is Heaven and Hell. There is male and female. Throughout the history of Western culture we come across the same dualities, in one form or another. The female is clearly on

6 Carol M. Armstrong; "Edgar Degas and the Representation of the Female Body", in Suleiman, 223
7 See Pierre Bourdieu: *Distinction: A Social Critique of the Judgment of Taste*, tr. Richard Nice, Routledge & Kegan Paul, New York 1984
8 Aristotle: *Metaphysics*, book XIII, in Albert Hofstadter & Richard Kuhns, eds. *Philosophies of Art and Beauty: Selected Readings in Aesthetics From Plato to Heidegger*, Random House, New York 1964, 96
9 See Marina Warner: *Monuments and Maidens*; Kenneth Clark: *The Nude*; Lynda Nead, 19;

the 'left' side, on the wrong side of the 'right' way. Women are the 'second sex', 'second class citizens': Sherry Ortner writes there is an opposition between culture and nature, and women are lower down in the male-made hierarchy: 'my thesis is that woman is being identified with – or, if you will, seems to be a symbol of – something that every culture devalues, something that every culture defines as being of a lower order of existence than itself'.[10]

Women are imprisoned, as Hélène Cixous notes, in masculine binary logic, which is the 'classical vision of sexual opposition between men and women', as Verena Conley writes in her book on Cixous.[11] For Luce Irigaray, this duality is called 'the recto-verso structure that shores up common sense'. (*The Irigaray Reader*, 127)

A list of these oppositions is useful, because they can be applied to every area of culture, from colonialism and racism, to science and medicine, from legislation of any kind to art of any kind;

male	female
right	left
Heaven	Hell
positive	negative
speaking	silence
good	evil
us	them
rationality	irrationality
reason	intuition
science	religion
patriarchy	matriarchy
self	other
capitalism	communism
precision	imprecision
active	passive
subject	object
viewer	observed
high art	low art
bourgeoisie	proletariat
mind/ soul	body

10 Sherry B. Ortner: "Is Female to Male as Nature is to Culture", in M. Evans, ed. *The Woman Question*, Fontana 1982
11 Verena Andermatt Conley: *Hélène Cixous: Writing the Feminine*, University of Nebraska Press, Lincoln, 1984, 129

It's no exaggeration to say that by and large men have created the æsthetics of art throughout Western culture. It is men, largely, or masculinist culture, who have defined what is and is not 'acceptable', what is to be applauded and what is to be ignored, outlawed or suppressed. And the producers of art that have been acknowledged publicly are (mostly) male. The artists of the West, like the pornographers, are mainly men. This fact explains a lot. The basic fact of Western art, which we shall keep returning to, is that, as Mary Ann Caws notes, 'the woman's body has been presented for the man's erotic pleasure'.[12] Throughout Western art, it seems, the scenario has been: man looking, woman being looked at; man creating representations of women to be looked at; men creating the economies and modes of representations within which everyone must operate.

Depictions of the female nude and of erotic gestures or 'acts' or whatever are problematic. The female body, for instance, is already 'objectified' even before it is painted or represented. Once painted, it becomes a cultural artifact, a mass of codes, meanings, signs and values, none of them fixed, all of them dependent on the context of consumption, dependent on the socio-political make-up of the viewer, and so on.

Context is crucial in matters of eroticism and pornography. An image that is seen as 'erotic' in one context can easily be seen as 'pornographic' in another context. Take an image out of context, and soon a new, often ironic set of meanings are put in motion. Jacques Derrida has shown that a text may have many contexts, and is not fixed in one context forever.[13]

Feminist artists have explored meanings and contexts, by placing traditional images in new contexts. Meanings are constantly in a state of flux. Nothing is fixed anymore. As Catherine Belsey writes: 'meanings circulate between text, ideology and reader' (144). Roland Barthes wrote that '[a]ll images are polysemous... they imply, underlying their signifiers, a floating chain of signifieds'. The consumer has the ability to 'choose some and ignore others'.[14] For Barthes, the link between

---

12 Mary Ann Caws: "Ladies Shot and Painted: Female Embodiment in Surrealist Art", in Suleiman, ed. 267-8; see also Linda Nochlin, ed. *Woman as Sex Object: Studies in Erotic Art 1730-1970*, Newsweek, New York 1973
13 Jacques Derrida: *Eperons. Les styles de Nietzsche*, Flammarion, Paris 1978, 103f
14 Roland Barthes: *Image-Music-Text*, Hill & Wang, New York 1977, 39

text and 'real world' is not direct, but was a convention: thus, reality too, like the literary text, was itself inseparable from the language and discourse which shaped it' writes Leslie Hill.[15] The cultural environment, socialization, economy, power relations, education, any number of factors can influence the meanings drawn from an image. With the female nude, in painting or pornography, the meanings are contextualized as erotic. As Anne Hollander notes, the nude always has a sexual dimension to it.

For instance, men can 'possess' and yet never 'possess' a female nude painting. It remains an image. The 'possession' or consumption is of a cerebral order, which is why critics and professors such as Kenneth Clark, Bernard Berenson, Jacob Burckhardt, Walter Pater, John Ruskin, Aby Warburg, Roger Fry, Ernst Gombrich and other art critics emphasize the *intellectual* nature of enjoying art. Art for the head, not the body, art for the eyes, not the full five senses. Françoise Parturier writes:

> With sex now subject to the exercises of thought, sexuality can no longer be sublimated in love, but rather in eroticism, which in the West is much more a philosophy, a cerebral enterprise, than an art of pleasure. Because it is founded on the theorem that woman is an object, that love and pleasure are two distinct realities which are naturally harmful, eroticism can only be misogynous.[16]

The establishment view of art and pornography, then, is full of ambiguities, which many intellectuals have tried to resolve. Art critics, for instance, find themselves sinking in philosophical quagmires when they start to rave about depictions of the body, because they start to reveal their erotic arousal, their sexual identity; their lust, in short. There is always the chance that in talking of the eroticism of an artwork the critic will move unconsciously into pornography. It is a slip many art critics are aware of, but many, despite themselves, do it. They do not like to admit the amount of sex there is in art, the amount of erotic energy there is in creativity. The (male) critics don't like to acknowledge what (male) artists know, that sex, for man men, is primary. As Carol Duncan writes: '[m]ore than any other theme, the nude could demonstrate that art originates in and is sustained

15 Leslie Hill: "Julia Kristeva: Theorizing the Avant-Garde?", in Fletcher & Benjamin, 141

16 Françoise Parturier: *Lettre ouverte aux hommes*, tr. Elissa Gelfand, Albin Michel 1968, in E. Marks, 63

by male erotic energy.'[17]

The female nude is the apotheosis of 'high art', yet it constantly wavers around the borderline between art and pornography. The female nude is erotic *and* obscene, in the male system, both desired and loathed, both representable and unrepresentable.

With the rise of cultural or postmodern theory, which sees artworks as 'texts', the body has become a 'text'. The body, that thing that people thought was fixed and always in one place, is in motion. It is as fluid as emotions. For centuries, (male) critics and artists thought the nude was either a model in a studio or in a painting on a gallery wall. Not so. Feminism has shown that the body itself is a site of social, racial, moral, æsthetic and political debates. The body, in fact, is central to feminism, as much as sex is. Elizabeth Grosz writes that the body's

> form, capacities, behaviour, gestures, movements, potential are
> primary objects of political contestation. As a *political* object, the body
> is not inert or fixed. It is pliable and plastical material, which is
> capable of being formed and organized in other, quite different ways
> or according to different classificatory schema than our binarised
> models.[18]

When feminists speak of 'rewriting the body', or of 'reclaiming' the body, they do not mean simply physically reclaiming the body, they mean reclaiming it politically, ideologically, psychologically, morally and artistically. The body is where everything happens: acts, thoughts, experiences, desires, they are all sited in the body. So feminism has to address the body and body politics, because the body is crucial. Similarly, pornography is powerful (partly) because it so powerfully deals with the body.

---

17 Carol Duncan: "Virility and Domination in Early Twentieth-Century Vanguard Painting", in N. Broude & M.D. Garrard, eds. *Feminism and Art History: Questioning the Litany*, Harper & Row, New York, 306
18 Elizabeth Grosz: "Corporreal Feminism", in *Australian Feminist Studies*, 5, Summer 1987, 3; also "The Body of Significance", in John Fletcher & Andrew Benjamin, eds. *Abjection, Melancholia and Love: The Work of Julia Kristeva*, Routledge 1990, 80-103

Lynda Nead writes in *The Female Nude* (71):

> The body is, therefore, central in the formation of individual identity and is the site of the subject's desires and fantasies, actions and behaviour. Once one rejects the perception of the body as a biologically determined and pre-cultural given and moves towards the conception of 'embodied' subjects, the way is opened for feminist interventions within the definition of the female body.

In art and pornography, in fashion and manufacture, down the ages, the female body has been defined largely by men. If not by men, then by male-made ideas, male notions of what is 'beautiful', what is desirable, what is erotic, what is *de rigeur*. Feminism seeks to rewrite men's definitions of the body and eroticism.

The art-pornography debate centres around power, politics, acceptability, philosophy and pleasure. The proper response to high culture is a detached enjoyment; pornography is disruptive, disturbing, debasing. Looking at a piece of high art, the pornographic response is lust while the high art response is rarefied contemplation. When pornographic responses to high art occur, the result is indignation from the art establishment. There are famous incidences of the 'debasing' of high art, as when a youth was so obsessed with a statue of Aphrodite of Cnidos that he masturbated on it, leaving a stain, as recorded in Pliny's *Natural History*; then there is the myth of Pygmalion, later reworked by William Shakespeare in *The Winter's Tale*, where the statue is sensually responsive; then there was Henry George Quinn who sneaked into the Uffizi to 'fervently kiss' the Medici Venus all over.[19]

Throughout history, female nudes of the high art type have been made for clients and connoisseurs – Titian painted many nudes for such private, privileged consumption. Pornography too has been manufactured for the same clients and connoisseurs. When does a refined, rarefied enjoyment of erotic art become the vulgar, debased gratification of pornography? When does the connoisseur become the pornographic consumer? Erotic art may defined as simply 'æstheticized sexual representation' (Nead,

19 Nicholas Penny: "Goddesses and Girls", in *London Review of Books*, 2-29, December 1982, 20; Simon Wilson: "Short History of Western Erotic Art", in Robert Melville: *Erotic Art of the West*, Weidenfeld & Nicolson 1973, 16

103), that is, erotic feelings processed through the mechanisms of 'high culture'.

For some feminists, there is no doubt that the enjoyment of the female nude is pornographic, and is largely inseparable from the lustful consumption of pornography. The boundaries between 'art' and 'pornography' are being constantly blurred, constantly reset and rewritten. For instance, Louise O'Murphy, the model for Francois Boucher's famous nude *Mademoiselle O'Murphy*, became King Louis XV's personal prostitute (his 'mistress', as critics call them) after the King saw Boucher's painting. The high art 'possession' or pleasure of the female nude in Boucher's painting became the real 'possession' of Louise O'Murphy's body. Clearly, kings can 'buy' what they like: they can have the best art, and 'have' the best women.

The high art nude, then, is a site of political and economic manipulation, an expression of the power relations between patron and painter, between connoisseur, artist and model. In the trinity of people linked by the painting – patron, painter and model – the model is clearly at the bottom of the pile. She is dependent on both painter and patron. She has to please both of them to be successful. The relation of artist to model thus is another manifestation, for feminists, like that of husband and wife, of male power, of patriarchal culture in action, of the sexual economics which are at work everywhere in the world, and everywhere in history.

For Andrea Dworkin, 'erotic art' is simply high class pornography:

> ...erotica is simply high-class pornography: better produced, better conceived, better executed, better packaged, designed for a better class of consumer... Intellectuals, especially, call what they themselves produce or like "erotica," which means simply that a very bright person made or likes whatever it is. (*Pornography*, 10)

Dworkin is spot-on here. This is an accurate reading of the situation. This view can be proved by many examples from the history of art. (Male) power and money buys high class pornography. The Emperor Tiberius had pornography hung on his walls at his villa at Capri, while the Emperor Nero had his Golden Palace decorated with pornography. Power and pornography have always gone together. Pornographic images themselves are expressions of power relations – social, political, racial, classist, economic and sexist power.

'High class' pornography (a.k.a. 'erotic art') is thought to be 'revolutionary' and 'rebellious'. But it is not. Benoîte Groult writes, voicing the opinions of many feminists:

> I'm sick and tired of these same old obsessions that never change, even in "modern style" without punctuation. I'm sick and tired of the way eminent philosophers and sociologists put forth as "free," "new," and "revolutionary" those same old perverse scripts which do nothing but try, unsuccessfully, to stage the little sadist's timeless repertory in a new way: the same old shit, pus, blood, sperm (oh! come on!), whips, and chains are dressed in smart new clothes... That's revolution? That's subversion? To be precise, it's an extension of the bourgeois world, that world in which a few males obsessed with virile violence and convinced they are prophets shit on women, rip apart their vaginas, and kill them while fucking them – all because they hate women so for being desirable.[20]

Context, then, is crucial, as Julia Kristeva notes. If pornography is displayed in certain contexts it can seem to be 'erotica', or high art. If it is consumed in other contexts, it can seem to be nothing but pornography.[21] Discussing pornography on a platform at a feminist conference gives pornographic material one context, not necessarily anti-porn, but often pro-porn; discussing pornographic material in a porn shop, surrounded by shelves of the stuff, will give pornography another context. Anti-porn feelings expressed inside a porn shop would be laughed at: but it depends who is speaking and why they are there: to be consume or to criticize? Also, pornography debates depend on any number of other factors: the status, race, gender and economy of the people involved, the intentions of the people involved in the discussion, and their socio-political background. In other words, discussing pornography without first precisely contextualizing the discussion renders much of what is said too generalized. This is what the anti-pornography lobby does, all the time: Andrea Dworkin does it: she generalizes about so much of pornography. She acknowledges the genres of 'kiddie porn', of soft core and hard core, of 'snuff' porn and 'black' or 'Asian' porn. But within

20 Benoîte Groult: "Les portiers de nuit", in E. Marks, 72
21 See also Rosalind Coward: "Porn: what's in it for women?", *New Statesman*, 13 June 1986

each of these categories or genres there is a huge range of material. Pornography cannot be lumped altogether, unless one is making extremely generalized statements. The most notorious category of pornography is the so-called 'snuff' movies. For a start, only one or two feminists have actually seen them, and the particular one that was made was a joke, a simulation. Avedon Carol writes:

> Feminist hyperbole about the violence of pornography, along with an insistence from some that there is no difference between consensual sex and rape, reached such a peak by the mid-1970s that it had nearly become impossible, in discussion, to distinguish real violence from ordinary sex.[22]

Clearly, not all the sexual representations are violent in pornography, but anti-pornography feminists continually portray pornography as 'violence'.

Taking pornography out of context throws light on it, but, at the same time, may distort it too much. Context is crucial: a small Jan Vermeer painting set on its own on the wall of a museum in the capital of a Western nation will be regarded reverently by some as exquisite 'high art'. Put it in a glossy magazine, and it'll be another commodity to acquire.

People consume pornography for a variety of reasons, not all of them to do with jerking off. Further, the *meanings* that pornography generates are not, as the anti-porn lobby contend, confined to sadomasochism, subordination of women and orgasmic pleasure. Pornography generates an infinity of meanings, like any other art. And pornography is consumed in any number of contexts, so you cannot simply reduce pornography to one set of meanings, to one context, to one intention, to one form of ideology, and so on.

'What some call 'erotica' others call 'pornography',' as Lizbeth Goodman writes.[23] While Joanna Russ writes: '[m]aybe Gloria Steinem can tell the difference between pornography and erotica at a single glance. I can't'.[24] Pornography is what *other* people do or consume, it seems.

22 Carol: "Snuff: Believing the Worst", in Assister & Carol, 126
23 Goodman: "The Pornography Problem", in Bonner, 279
24 Joanna Russ: "Being against Pornography", in C. Kramarae, re.
Steinem: "Erotica and pornography: a clear and present difference", also in Kramarae

It's a question of levels, areas, boundaries. The 'acceptable' becomes nothing more than the 'consensus' but, as any study of the media shows, 'consensus' is created not by a nation or a mass of people, but by a very small group of particular sorts of people (in UK broadcasting, for instance, mainly white Oxbridge middle-aged males).

The context of consumption of art, the media, pornography and any kind of communication determines much. For instance, both pornography and art are consumed in particular socio-political environments. For pornography, like art, is expensive, and requires a certain amount of money to be able to be consumed, whether this means buying magazines, or possessing a satellite dish and decoder, etc, at a banal, materialistic level; at a deeper level, the consumption of art and pornography is determined very much by the strictures of class, race, economy, privilege, place and politics.

'Art' is, typically, for the 'privileged', for the select few, while pornography is mass culture. As Joel Jovel wrote: 'pornography is the captivity of the erotic within mass culture.'[25]

Artists continually defend their 'right' to make 'erotic' art. There must be no censorship whatsoever, say artists (and many feminists agree with them. There are feminists groups who are anti-censorship, such as Feminists Against Censorship, Feminist Anti-Censorship Task Force, Campaign Against Pornography and Censorship). Censorship of/ in pornography will not, feminists believe, lead to a better, freer culture:

> Lack of censorship against pornography is therefore highly unlikely to lead to lack of censorship against other areas of publication. Instead, it is the publication of oppressive material, such as pornography, which is likely to increase.' (Marianne Hester, 70)

André Masson said: 'censorship enforces a sort of involuntary hypocrisy of the artist'. The artist censors her/ himself, says Masson: s/he knows there are certain images that cannot be shown in a gallery.[26] A familiar argument, which allows for total subjectivity, the individual's 'rights' of 'freedom of expression'. The view is backed up by any number of artists. One of the most

25 Joel Kovel: "The Antididactic of Pornography", in Michael Kimmel, ed. *Men Confront Pornography*, Crown Publishers, New York, 1989
26 André Mason, quoted in Phyllis & Eberhard Kronhausen, op. cit., 42

consistently pornographic of modern artists, Hans Bellmer, said: '[t]he idea of eroticism is an essential part of life, so it's right that artists like me should devote themselves to exploring that idea.'[27] The argument is also used by film directors when asked about violence in the cinema. Life is violent, they say, so we have to reflect that in our movies.

The 'erotic' is a part of life, say artists, so we must be erotic in our works. What happens with pornography is that sex becomes everything, and everything is subsumed to sex. The protagonists of pornography tumble into bed at every opportunity. There are none of the usual structures of the traditional novel or fiction in pornography. The aim is simply to create as much sex as possible. Every other consideration – of personalities, of feelings, of social, political and economic obligations, of familial and societal respons- ibilities, etc – are mostly forgotten. The protagonists simply get on with sex, and nothing but sex. Everything else is padding in pornography. If there's no sex occurring, or desire being evoked, porn has failed: there must always be sex, and lots of it.

It is the same with erotic and pornographic visual art and sculpture. Nothing else must get in the way of the sexual aspects. Thus, the female nude is not a part of some larger picture, of a city, a landscape, a group portrait, a political statement (although it is this also), it is simply a nude, in the foreground, on some couch, openly displaying, even if coyly, her body. Some female nude paintings do include landscapes, cities or background interest, as in Lucas Cranach's *Nymph of the Spring*, but the real point of the picture is the nude, which dominates it.[28] The female nude is, simply, right in front of the viewer, despite the distantiation of the mechanics and politics of representation. There's the nude, right in front of the viewer, much as in pornography, there is the 'sex act', right on page one.

Pornography, like art, pivots around *desire*. And desire, as Hélène Cixous notes, is something that never dies: '[d]esire never dies' she says.[29] Pornography is about 'having' something *now*. Not in ten minutes, not next year, but *now*. 'Erotic art' is about anticipation, about desire, about longing for 'the moment', the

27 interview, 1972, in Peter Webb, 369

28 Lucas Cranach: *Nymph of the Spring*, c. 1525, oil on wood, 107 x 136cm, National Gallery of Art, Washington DC

29 Cixous and Catherine Clément: *The Newly Born Woman*, University of Manchester Press 1985

moment of pleasure. Pornography clears away all that stuff, and presents the Freudian primal scene now. Right now.

If some work is erotic – a scene on TV, a photo, a sculpture, a dance – it's because, in the opinion of some people, you don't 'see' everything. Something is hidden. The 'erotic' in art is about anticipation, waiting, yearning. It's about potential and possibility, hidden but not hidden, partially clothed. As the photographer Grace Lau, who has made many pictures of fetishism, wrote: 'I prefer images that conceal, rather than those that reveal all.'[30]

Pornography, meanwhile, has people doing it now. They undress, and get freaky immediately. There's nothing to get in the way, not contraception, not fear, not aversions, not menstruation, not impotence, not interruptions, not anything. People leap into bed immediately, for pornography is fantasy, unalloyed by negativity.

Pornography turns 'what if?' into a reality. What if somebody took their clothes off in this train carriage and started having sex? is a typical question that erotic art suggests but pornography answers. In pornography, people *do* rip their clothes and start tupping.

Pornography presents as a normal, everyday occurrence what is hidden away, what is desired but unspoken. Pornography is the ultimate in fantasy, for in the fairy tale world of pornography, every dream comes true. Worse, it is not only 'true', it is 'real'. Worse, it is not only 'true' and 'real', it can hurt. For pain can be a large part of pornography. As Andrea Dworkin writes: '[p]enetration was never meant to be kind. In pornography, scissors, razors, knives, and daggers are poised at the entrance to the vagina, cuts evident on the delicate skin of the pubic area, often shaved...' (*Intercourse*, 223) But pain is also a large part of Western culture.

Pain is good, because it means you are fully alive. This is the view of patriarchal culture. 'Sensual pleasure is agony in the strictest meaning of the word', says C. Mauclair in a Freudian tone.[31] Suffering is holy, in the Christianity tradition. The journey from martyrdom to sainthood and beatification is swift. The West exalts pain. Christ *suffered*, say theologians, so he must have been right, holy, a hero, he must have lived hard, because he died

---

30 Grace Lau: "Confessions of a Complete Scopophiliac", in Gibbons, 195
31 C. Mauclair: *Magie de l'amour*, 145, quoted in Julius Evola, 84

hard. Death becomes heroic. Death transfigures people. Suicide is even better, if you can manage it. Hence Marilyn Monroe, Vincent van Gogh, Johann Wolfgang von Goethe's Werther, and Virginia Woolf. Die young, and become famous (many artists have adhered to this equation: Egon Schiele, Fréderic Chopin, Wolfgang Amadeus Mozart, Georges Seurat, James Dean, Paula Modersohn-Becker, D.H. Lawrence, Jimmy Hendrix, Jim Morrison, Arthur Rimbaud, Raphael, John Keats, Percy Shelley, Novalis).

In the patriarchal system, sex and death are entwined. Further, death and the feminine, death and women are combined. Further, pain and sex are combined. Painful sex must be good sex, according to the male system. 'If it hurts, it works' is a typical adage often bandied about. Pain is good, because it cuts through everything and makes acute the transitoriness and bliss of the human condition, according to the (male) Existential view.

A lot of art of any kind comes out of pain, according to men. Love poetry flows from the emotional pain of being left by the lover. Thus, love poetry, from Sappho to the latest pop song, is a cry of pain from a bereft soul. Love songs come from loss, from losing the object of bliss, the beloved. Like babies, love poets sob forlornly. Love is pain, death, sin, vice and fornication in the Christian view. Love poets transform the pain into art, as do creators of erotic art. There is a masochism at the heart of Western art, as there is at the core of Christianity. Christ on the Cross is the supreme example of masochistic agony in the West, and is the most painted image, apart from the Madonna and Child, in the West. There is a link here: the Crucifixion is the end of life, the painful letting go, while the child in the Madonna's arms is the beginning of life, swathed in the softness and care of the mother figure. The two images, Virgin and Child and the Crucifixion, form the twin poles of Western art. Both images are dominated by the feminine, for the Cross in the Crucifixion is the Mother, the Goddess, the Cross being part of the Earth from which Christ is later reborn – the second, spiritual birth echoing his first, earthly birth, depicted in so many Nativity scenes and Madonna and Child images.

It is noble to suffer, say male poets and artists and theologians and philosophers. As Joseph Campbell put it (in *The Power of Myth*, 205):

Love is the burning point of life, and since all life is sorrowful, so is
love. The stronger the love, the more the pain... Love itself is a pain,
you might say – the pain of being truly alive.

In pornography, you simply change the word 'love' for 'sex'.
Thus, to rewrite Joseph Campbell: 'the stronger the sex, the more
the pain'. Good sex, in patriarchy, is often painful sex. The
greater the pain, the better the sex. This is the formula behind
much of pornography not only exemplified by sadomasochistic
sex, but also by soft core pornography, and by bourgeois
conceptions of love and marriage.

The patriarchal equation is sex = pain = life. Notions of
'woman' and the 'feminine' are bound up in this formula. Indeed,
they make carrying out the formula possible. The emphasis in
culture on pain in sex comes from any number of sources. De
Sade is a famous one. He inaugurates the modern age of
pornography, and the age of intellectual sex, mental or head sex,
sex without touching, sex for pornographers, the philosophical sex
as espoused by Georges Bataille, Charles Baudelaire, Guillaume
Apollinaire, Friedrich Nietzsche, Henry Miller, Sigmund Freud
and Jean-Paul Sartre.

The Marquis de Sade's *œuvre* is quite astonishing. As Andrea
Dworkin writes: 'Sade's work is nearly indescribable. In sheer
quantity of horror, it is unparalleled in the history of writing.'
(*Pornography*, 92) De Sade is the high priest of metaphysical
eroticism, as championed by Charles Baudelaire, Jean Cocteau,
the Surrealists, Algernon Charles Swinburne, Lautréamont,
Fyodor Dostoievsky and John Cowper Powys. Among visual
artists, the inheritors of the Sadeian pornographic ethic include
Pablo Picasso, Hans Bellmer, Jean Cocteau, Max Ernst, Allen
Jones, David Salle, etc. The Sadeian philosophy of sex is fiercely
heterosexual and heterosexist, with woman definitely the object of
male lust. The history of the arts is also Sadeian and
pornographic. Look at the poems of William Shakespeare, Dante
Alighieri, Francesco Petrarch, Paul Éluard, Robert Graves,
Maurice Scève, Torquato Tasso, John Donne, John Skelton, etc.
'Woman' is the object of male desire in these poems. The poets
emphasize the *pain* of love, the agony of desire. How I suffer for
love of you! they cry, so many times – in Petrarch's *Rime Sparse*,
Dante's *Vita Nuova*, Shakespeare's *Sonnets* or Robert Graves'
Collected Poems. Some male poets tried to stylize the pain of love,

but agony is inescapably a part of their form of erotic desire, as Dante shows time and time again in his *Divina Commedia*, as this extract from the *Paradiso* shows:

> Then Beatrice looked at me, her eyes
> sparkling with love and burning so divine,
> my strength of sight surrendered to her power –
>
> with eyes cast down, I was about to faint.[32]

In the male, Sadeian view, only painful sex is authentic. This view is found in the 'major' works of high class or literary pornography: *The Story of the Eye, The Story of O, The Image, Tropic of Cancer, Lady Chatterley's Lover, The 120 Days of Sodom,* etc. Bataille's *The Story of the Eye,* acclaimed by intellectual luminaries such as Jean-Paul Sartre, Susan Sontag, Michel Foucault and Peter Brook, is typical amongst intellectual pornography. The ethics it proposes – not secretly, not between the lines, not in the silences and spaces of the text, but upfront, in every sentence – are explained accurately by Andrea Dworkin: '[d]eath is the stunning essence of sex. The violence of death is the violence of sex and the beauty of death is the beauty of sex and the meaning of life is only revealed in the meaning of sex which is death.' (ib, 174-5). In 'high class' pornography, sex leads to death. The orgasm is the 'little death' (*petit mort*) and the most blissful way to die is at orgasm, where sex and death fuse rapturously and most poetically of all. The '*raptus*' of sex, the 'spasm', as men insist on calling the orgasm, is the experience that 'kills', and people 'die' in orgasm. As Dworkin explains, the stylization and so-called lyricism of high class pornography hides the real violence underneath. It is already about power – power over other people, and the ultimate expression of power is killing someone (as countless films show). Dworkin writes:

> What matters is the poetry that is the violence leading to death that is the ecstasy. The language stylizes the violence and denies its fundamental meaning to women, who do in fact end up dead because men believe what Bataille believes and makes pretty: that death is the dirty secret of sex. (ib., 176)

---

32 Dante: *The Divine Comedy: Paradiso,* tr. Mark Musa, Penguin 1986, IV: 139-142

The metaphysics of pain and sex and death and love are not confined to pornography or erotic art. It is at the heart of Christianity, and Christianity is the most sacred of the Western world's institutions according to some people. Pain is glorified in Christianity – in Christ dying on the Cross. The West does not exalt Christ's Resurrection, his glorious rebirth. No, it exalts the awful suicide on the Cross. Jesus does not die with a bullet, instantly or 'humanely', to use that ridiculous term when applied to people sentenced to death (to die 'humanely'). No, Jesus dies a lengthy and extremely painful death. All the better to ram the message home: that suffering = glorification, that martyrdom is wonderful, that the ultimate sacrifice is also the ultimate beatification.[33]

---

33 Lawrence Durrell took a dim view of Christianity, which he expressed in one of his late poetry books, *The Red Limbo Lingo*: 'the extraordinary blood-spattered figure of a man nailed to a wooden cross, like an expiring frog' (*The Red Limbo Lingo: A Poetry Notebook*, Faber, 1971, 10-11).

3

THE HISTORY OF PORNOGRAPHY

The history of pornography, then, is also the history of attitudes, values, ideologies, morals and politics in the West (I'm focussing mainly on porn in the West here). The history of pornography is also the history of art. Pornography and art go together. They both contain the same tenets of sex, pain, control and death, of male power being exerted over 'victims' or inferiors, of whatever race, class, age, economy or nationality. The history of pornography is largely the history of power.

The emphasis on pain or control in this chapter is not the whole story in porn, though. There's lots of fun, fantasy, and light-hearted fooling around too. In this chapter, I'm deliberately emphasizing the more extreme aspects of porn to make some points, particularly about how feminism has viewed porn over the past forty years.

Pornography, like art, is born in the West from a white, middle class, Christian, First World experience. Pornography's religious background, like that of Western art, is Judæo-Christian. Religious imagery itself features in pornography (nuns, monks, the bishop and the actress, Regan in the film *The Exorcist* masturbating with a crucifix, Mary Magdalene masturbating in front of a crucified penis in Félicien Rops' drawing, etc).

In the patriarchal view, religion is sexy, and sex is religious. Artists such as Eric Gill, Félicien Rops, Gustav Klimt, Gustave Moreau and Egon Schiele have combined sexual and religious imagery. Art, like pornography, comes out of the Judæo-Christian insistence on sin, death, vice, fornication, dirt and suppression. The 'father' of Christianity is not Jesus but St Paul. Jesus wrote nothing; St Paul wrote everything, setting down the crazier views of Christianity in the fanatical prose in the *Corinthians* a n d *Galatians*. And *Romans*, which gets so many things wrong about 'flesh' and 'spirit' and 'marriage'. Michael Foucault writes of some of the strictures of Christianity:

> Christianity associated it ['the sexual act'] with evil, sin, the Fall, and death, whereas antiquity invested it with positive symbolic values.[34]

In Christianity, women are the 'gateway to Hell' as the early Christian theologian Tertullian (3rd century A.D.) poetically put it; women are evil, sinful, lustful ('the Devil is a woman' is a common theme in mediæval philosophy as well as pop songs). From Eve in the Old Testament to the Virgin and Magdalene in the New, women are definitely second class citizens in the eyes of Western religion. Women-hating is startling in its violent manifestations – not just in wife-beating, which occurs everywhere and, one supposes, at every moment of human history, but also in mass movements, such as the fight against 'witchcraft' in the Middle Ages and later, when, armed with the *Malleus Maleficarum*, the Witchfinder Generals hunted down and tortured and killed hundreds or thousands of women.

In Christianity, chastity, abstinence, purity, virginity, monogamy, negation and suppression are exalted. Pornography reverses Christianity's strictures, it turns them upside down, it lets chaos loose, as in the Dionysian orgies, in the Greek bacchanales, in the Roman Saturnalia or 'time of chaos', a Twelfth Night of the senses, in which a Trickster God, Pan or Dionysius, usurps the norms and lets wild desire rage forth. Pornography subverts the laws of Christianity, but it is based on the same laws. Pornography comes out of the same world as Christianity. Not only is there much of Christianity in pornography, there is much of pornography in Christianity. For instance, Christian history is a catalogue of sadomasochistic events and acts, some really horrific scenes of torture and oppression. More acts of terror have been carried out in the name of God than in the name of 'freedom' or 'truth' or 'honour'.

---

34 Foucault: *The Use of Pleasure*, 14

Painters throughout Western history have reflected the violent acts of Christianity, portraying them as heroic gestures: Sandro Botticelli painted the massacre of the Innocents; Nicolas Poussin depicted St Erasmus having his entrails pulled out by a winch, many painters portrayed St Sebastian full of arrows (Andrea Mantegna, Antonello Messina, Pietro Vanucci Perugino, Henrick Terbruggen, and, this century, Eric Gill and Egon Schiele), Francisco de Zurbarán painted a saint being crucified upside down.[35] A good bout of flagellation goes down well with Christians too, and many Renaissance painters painted Christ being whipped or tortured by the guards, and being crowned with thorns. Examples include Titian's two *Christ Crowned with Thorns* paintings, which make suffering a sublime, heroic experience,[36] or the ritualized whipping in Piero della Francesca's *The Flagellation of Christ*, a much-discussed Renaissance painting, or Luca Signorelli's more staid approach to the torture.[37] Not to be outdone, Vittore Carpaccio painted a bizarre picture: the crucified Jesus sitting on a throne, dead, with his eyes closed, with two semi-naked old men sitting on either side of him. The title is *Meditation on the Passion of Christ*.[38] There's the Saviour, looking very dead, on a throne, in a ruined landscape, while two old men sit right next to him and muse upon his suicide. Bizarre.

Sebastiano del Piombo goes even further: his *The Martyrdom of St Agatha* depicts the saint, nude of course, being tortured by a

---

35 Nicholas Poussin: *The Martyrdom of St Erasmus*, 1628, Pinacoteca Vaticana, Vatican, Rome; Hendrick Terbrugghen: *St Sebastian Tended by St Irene and the Maid*, 1625, Allen Memorial Art Museum, Oberlin College, Oberlin, Ohio; Antonello da Messina: *St Sebastian*, c. 1475, oil on panel, 67.4 x 33.5in, State Picture Gallery, Dresden; Andrea Mantegna: *St Sebastian*, c. 1470, tempera on canvas, 101.2 x 55.8in, Louvre, Paris, Pietro Perugino: *St Sebastian*, c. 1495, panel, 170 x 117cm, Louvre, Paris; Zurbaran: *The Apostle Peter Appearing to St Peter Nolasco*, 1629, oil on canvas, 5ft 11 x 7ft 4in, Prado, Madrid
36 Titian: *Christ Crowned with Thorns*, mid-1450s, panel, 303 x 180cm, Louvre, Paris; *Christ Crowned with Thorns*, c. 1570-6, canvas, 280 x 181cm, Alte Pinakothek, Munich
37 Piero: *The Flagellation of Christ*, c. 1450, panel, 59 x 81.5cm, Ducal, Urbino; Signoreli: *Flagellation*, c. 1480, canvas, 80 x 60cm, Brera, Milan
38 Carpaccio: *Meditation on the Passion of Christ*, c. 1505, panel, 70 x 86cm, Metropolitan Museum of Art, New York

bunch of men, fully clothed of course.[39] They are applying gigantic metal pliers to her nipples. This is a depiction of sadism (in Christianity the euphemism is 'martyrdom'). Naturally, it seems, this is *sexual* torture, painted in such a straightforward fashion, the woman centre frame, the men surrounding her intent on brutalizing her. The rape, which must follow this torture, is not shown, and it is never shown in Renaissance art, and rarely in Western art. When rape occurs, as it must have done millions of times through the Christian era, men dragging away women are shown, or Jupiter as a swan screwing Leda, but not the rape itself

Not all of Christianity is suppression and chastity. In Christian mysticism there is wildness and ecstasy, in mystics such as Jan van Ruysbroeck, St Theresa, Meister Eckhart, Richard Rolle, Richard of St Victor, Catherine of Siena, John of the Cross, etc. Mysticism is the centre of religion. It is the record of moments of revelations. Mystics speak of the amazing bliss which is surely the goal of religion. Yet religion constantly moves mysticism to the fringes. Hence many of those wonderful ecstasies of the mystics – of any religion – are regarded with suspicion by the establishment, and are suppressed.

One such ecstasy in Christianity, of St Teresa, was the subject of Gian Lorenzo Bernini's famous statue.[40] More than a few commentators have noted that Bernini's saint is in orgasm. Lacan writes that 'you only have to go and look at the Bernini statue in Rome to understand immediately she (St Teresa) is coming'.[41]

Parts of Christianity are pornographic, then, just as parts of Western culture are pornographic. There is nothing new about this view. The central image and meditation of Christianity, Christ on the Cross, is a pornographic image in itself. The pain Christ experiences is both fleshy and spiritual, both masochistic and glorified. Like religion, pornography makes a cult out of pain, makes pain an essential ingredient in authentic living. Philosophies such as Existentialism bear this out. What this means is that the creators of philosophy, religion, politics, art and culture

---

39 Sebastiano del Piombo: *The Martyrdom of St Agatha*, 1520, 31 x 175cm, Pitti Palace, Florence

40 Giovanni Lorenzo Bernini: *The Ecstasy of St Theresa*, 1645-52, S. Maria della Vittoria, Rome

41 Jacques Lacan in *Feminine Sexuality*; also Mervyn Levy, 32; also Président des Brosses, quoted in Howard Hibbard: *Bernini*, 1965, 241-2: 'If this is divine love, I know what it is'.

see pain as an essential component in life. Life without pain is not quite an authentic life, in the male view. In the realm of sexuality, of which pornography and art are expressions, pain is also regarded as important. This is where things get controversial. Saying that pain is essential in art or pornography or culture is one thing, saying it is essential in people's lives and in their sexuality is another. Some radical feminists make the connection between theory and practice, between representations and realities, between culture and people, so that what happens in pornography happens in real life. Andrea Dworkin writes:

> Pornography reveals that male pleasure is inextricably tied to victimizing, hurting, exploiting; that sexual fun and sexual passion in the privacy of the male imagination are inseparable from the brutality of male history. The private world of sexual dominance that men demand as their right and their freedom is the mirror image of the public world of sadism and atrocity that men consistently and self-righteously deplore. (*Pornography*, 69)

Dworkin touches on one of the major hypocrisies surrounding pornography; that, while publicly deploring it, people secretly consume it. Pornography is consumed by the very people who would legislate against it: lawyers, police, judges, doctors, teachers. There is one rule for the public domain, but another for the private realm. In second wave (1960s-1970s) feminism, the personal is political, private and public are identical. Patriarchal people, however, like to keep the public and the private quite separate. Thus, while voting for political parties which deplore pornography, people in private consume it. After all, somebody must be consuming pornography somewhere. If the pornography industry is bigger than the movie or record industry, as some claim, then there must be a *lot* of people consuming it.

Art and pornography alike, then, are founded on patriarchal, white, bourgeois, First World, Imperialist and male tenets. Whoever the audience of pornography is – gay, straight, bi, feminist, Marxist, capitalist, communist, A, B, C1, C2, D, E, bourgeois, proletariat, etc – the content and views of pornography are white, bourgeois, First World, and male. Pornography is founded, like art and religion, on the tenets of patriarchy, where heterosexual sex is both a metaphor and a method of enforcing male power over others, for feminists. 'The foundation of the family in which men are served emotionally, economically and through domestic , is sexual intercourse' writes Sheila Jeffreys.[42] For feminists, the 'sex act' is an expression of power, one of the methods which men use to assert their supremacy over others. In violent situations, sex is clearly a weapon: the invading forces of many an army in history, up to and beyond Vietnam, have raped the women after slaughtering the men. Rape is one of the hidden, suppressed elements of contemporary society. Susan Brownmiller writes: '[r]ape became not only a male prerogative, but man's basic weapon of force against woman, the principal agent of his will and her fear';[43]

In violent situations, it is easy to see where the power lies. In psychological or cultural realms, it is more difficult. But products such as pornography clearly reflect what people are thinking. Other forms of communication, such as newspapers and TV, reflect what people are thinking and feeling, but pornography shows vividly the desires of people. And the desires that abound in pornography revolve around power, around sex without any strings attached, around objectification and control.

42 Sheila Jeffreys: "The Censoring of Revolutionary Feminism", in Chester, 138
43 Brownmiller: *Against Our Will*, 5

4

IN BETWEEN SEXUALITY, ART AND PORNOGRAPHY

What is the 'erotic' element that art and pornography claim to describe? What is sexuality? What is the relation of sexual feelings to their representation in art and pornography? Sexual feelings *seem* to be very subjective, something experienced by individuals in their own way. Cultural theorists and feminists have shown that sexual feelings, which form part of sexual identities, are shaped, influenced and controlled by cultural and political forces, as well as by personalities and personal experiences. How we think about our bodies and our sexuality, say feminists, is very much dependent on our cultural environment, as well as by our experiences in childhood. As Gayle Rubin wrote: '[s]ex as we know it – gender identity, sexual desire and fantasy, concepts of childhood – is itself a social product.'[44] This is a crucial point. It means that sexual feelings and fantasies are not to be considered in isolation, like specimens of a meteorite fallen to Earth, examined in some top secret scientific laboratory. Rather, they are part of a cultural and psychological continuum. According to the cultural theorists, analyses of sexual experiences and fantasies and identities which do not take social, political and cultural dimensions into consideration can never be authentic or really

44 Gayle Rubin: "The Traffic in Women: Notes on the "Political Economy" of Sex", in M.Z. Rosaldo & L. Lamphere, eds. *Women, Culture and Society*, Stanford University Press, Stanford 1974

useful. This relation of sexuality to, for instance, race, or to economy, means that the traditional views of sexuality have to be completely reworked. For feminists, rape is not a private, individual matter, between raper and rapist and close friends and family. It is something that involves *the whole of society,* all people everywhere.

Further, there is no 'fixed' kind of sexuality: sexual identities of people are always changing, as the cultural environment changes. The personal is political, so what happens in the sociopolitical world affects the individual's sexuality directly, according to some feminists.

If Gillian Rodgerson and Linda Semple are right when they define the Dworkin-MacKinnon ordinance against pornography as being based on a view that 'basically any depiction of women in a sexual situation' was wrong or bad, then somebody is very mistaken here.[45] Dworkin and MacKinnon are not against *every* depiction of women as sexual beings. Dworkin is not 'against' sexual feelings. Rather, she despises those representations that damage, terrorize, debase and exploit women. Sheila Jeffreys concords with Dworkin's view of the damaging effects of patriarchy and pornography:

> Another reason for women's opposition is that we have all, as women, been trained to eroticise our own subordination and to call that pleasure and freedom. The sexual liberals argue that if we have a sexual response to anything then that must be good and positive. This is clearly not true, since women can orgasm during rape and sexual abuse, and men do so when torturing and killing women, as in Vietnam.[46]

The interpretation of the Dworkin-MacKinnon Bill is problematic, and would vary from judge to judge, from court to court, as Pratibha Parmar notes: '[a] second problem is that Dworkin's definition of what is pornographic can be interpreted in a variety of ways, depending on who is doing the interpreting.'[47] To put an anti-porn law into action requires tremendous legal, civil and social knowledge and skill, and the attempts of Dworkin and

---

45 Gillian Rodgerson and Linda Semple: "Who watches the watchwomen?: Feminists against censorship", *Feminist Review*, no 36, Autumn 1990
46 Jeffreys, : "The censorship of revolutionary feminism", in Chester, 138
47 Parmar, in Chester, 128

MacKinnon and Catherine Itzin have simply been too crude. Their bills and laws fall apart, for the realities of each situation are complex.

One must do something, though, some feminists claim, rather than simply leave things in the patriarchal order as they are. Andrea Dworkin's point is that the patriarchal system is made by people, and so can be changed by people. In "Feminism: An Agenda", Dworkin writes:

> The women's movement is like other political movements in one important way. Every political movement is committed to the belief that there are certain kinds of pain that people should not endure. They are unnecessary. They are gratuitous. They are not part of the God-given order. They are not biologically inevitable. They are acts of human will. They are acts done by some human beings to other human beings.[48]

Catherine Itzin is with Dworkin and MacKinnon in some ways: Itzin, for example, see no conflict between being against censorship and for the censoring of pornography – as Itzin puts it:

> I have now had an insight into the *meaning* of pornography... I can see now that the 'freedom' of pornography is posited on the 'censorship' of women: that the price of the 'freedom' given to those who publish and purchase pornography (men) is freedom denied to its objects.[49]

And, then of course, there is the eternal question, who watches the watchdogs? As is clear, watchdogs themselves are very dubious. Pratibha Parmar writes:

> The Dworkin/ MacKinnon ordinance, which seeks to enable anyone to bring a civil suit against anything deemed to be 'offensive' and hence pornographic', poses several problems. What puzzles me is how women who have defined all men as the enemy can ask the 'patriarchal state' to intervene on their behalf and pass laws in the interests of women. Expecting the state to behave in a benevolent manner is naive.[50]

---

48 Dworkin, "Feminism: An Agenda", *Letters*, 134
49 Itzin: "Sex and Censorship: The Political Implications", in Chester, 42
50 Pratibha Parmar "Rage and Desire: Confronting Pornography", in Chester, 126

Some feminists have noted that talking about pornography positions the critic in an ambivalent relation with pornography itself, because pornography breaks down distance and introduces a new, ambivalent kind of relationship and subjectivity. As Liz Kotz writes:

> ...pornography represents a place where distance breaks down, where subjectivity is insistently engaged, even uncomfortably so. Even its incorporation into a project of critique is notoriously unstable, since even the most determined efforts to reframe pornographic representations as objects of a politically motivated examination can go deeply awry, subverting authorial intention in fascinating if problematical ways'.[51]

Perhaps any mention of pornography sets up an involvement and semantic circularity between critic and subject, so that there can never be a 'distanced', cool, detached, 'objective' reading of pornography.

When anybody tries to define or describe their sexuality, things can get very confused. For a start, there are areas or causes which people seek to advertise or defend. Christians have their view of sex, while Marxists have another view. Lumping all Christians or all Marxists together is plainly ridiculous. Yet debates on sexuality are full of such problems of generalizing and stereotyping. The problem of language, of naming and describing, is central to any debates on sexuality. People can't agree on what colour something is, or what something smells like, so they have no hope of communicating their differences, because there is no really sophisticated language of colour or smell. If people can't even describe colours fully, there seems little hope of them really describing their sexual feelings.

Many people have tried, however, to describe sex. Most of the known examples are by men. So we know what men feel during sex. All we get in mainstream culture is men's descriptions of sexuality.

You can find men's depictions of sexuality throughout Western culture. It is men, for instance, who invent terms such as 'the sex act'. It is actions that patriarchal culture exalts, not states of being. As Valerie Traub puts it: '[e]roticism itself is increasingly being defined less as a fixed identity dependent on the gender of

---

51 Liz Kotz, op.cit., 107

one's partner, and more as a dynamic mode based on the sum of one's erotic *practice*.'[52] Sexuality is therefore not what you *are*, but what you *do*. It is not *who* is fucking *whom*, but *how*.[53] The question is *how is this fucking being done?* Never *why*, always *how*.

For patriarchal people, of either sex, it seems it is essential to know *who* is speaking about sex. Is the author male or female? What is her/ his sexual identity? Patriarchal people are disturbed when their expectations of gender are disrupted. When, say, a male author writes of lesbian sexuality as if from the 'inside', as if in the 'character' of a lesbian. For example, who is the speaker and who is the subject of this poem: '[f]irst, I want to make you come in my hand/ while I watch you and kiss you… I want to make you come/ in my mouth like a storm'.[54] It seems the speaker is female and she is describing lesbian sex. But the words could just as well apply to heterosexual or homosexual eroticism. Only when various parts of the body are mentioned – clitoris, nipples, penis, breasts – is it possible to decipher the gender of speaker, text or subject, and sometimes not even then.

Knowing what male sexuality is like – *aggressive, quick, painful, superficial, self-centred* are some of the adjectives some feminists employ – we might look at some descriptions of female sexuality. Many feminists and women artists speak of 'female' sexuality as wild, terrifying, shocking, open, transgressive, fatal. For some feminists, female sexuality is beyond description, because it is beyond patriarchal language, which is the only language around. Men cannot control female sexuality, feminists claim, so they try to suppress it. They mystify it, they ignore it, they mock it. Men, say feminists, are scared of women and their sexuality, so they suppress women and their thoughts, feelings and acts. Or they get violent. Hélène Cixous writes:

> Men say that there are two unrepresentable things: death and the feminine sex. That's because they need femininity to be associated with death; it's the jitters that give them a hard-on! for themselves! They need to be afraid of us.[55]

---

52 Valerie Traub: "Desire and the Difference It Makes", in Valerie Wayne, 88
53 See Valerie Traub, in Wayne, 83
54 Marilyn Hacker: 'Noces', from *Love, Death and the Changing of the Seasons*, Arbor House 1986
55 Cixous: "The Laugh of the Medusa", in E. Marks, 255

Luce Irigaray in her famous description of women's sexuality says women have an all-over eroticism, a total body sensuality, where the whole of the skin is alive to touches. 'The whole of my body is sexuate. My sexuality isn't restricted to my sex and to the sexual act (in the narrow sense)' writes Luce Irigaray (*Je, tu, nous*, 53). Critics of Irigaray's view of women's eroticism as two lips continually embracing say: '[a]ll that 'is' woman comes to [Irigaray] in the last instances from her anatomical sex, which touches itself all the time. Poor woman.'[56] While other feminists see the emphasis on just one form of female sexuality a distinctly reductive and inauthentic kind of feminism:

> If we define female subjectivity through universal biological/ libidinal givens [writes Ann Rosalind Jones], what happens to the project of changing the world in feminist directions? Further, is women's sexuality so monolithic that shared, typical femininity does justice to it? What about variations in class, in race, and in culture among women? about changes over time in *one* woman's sexuality? (with men, with women, by herself?) How can one libidinal voice – or the two vulval lips so startlingly presented by Irigaray – speak for all women?[57]

Some feminists (such as Anais Nin) argue for multiple sexualities, for a plurality of sexualities, as against the standard, traditional notions of heterosexuality, homosexuality, lesbianism and bisexuality. Some feminists argue for the use of erotic feeling as a political weapon. Instead of denying eroticism, some feminists propound an ethics of glorifying sexuality. The body becomes then the centre, the subject, instead of being merely the object of male lust. Eroticism then becomes a source of power, as Audre Lorde explains; '[t]he erotic is a resource within each of us that lies in a deeply female and spiritual plane, firmly rooted in the power of our unexpressed or unrecognized feeling.'[58]

Women speak of their eroticism in fiction and fantasy as being multi-sensual, not simply a matter of the visual or haptic senses, but of every sense, and more, in a synæsthetic experience. 'In those early mornings it all tasted of sex after a few moments... The

56 Monique Plaza: ""Phallomorphic power" and the psychology of "woman""", *Ideology and Consciousness*, 4, Autumn 1978, 32
57 Jones: "Writing the Body", in Showalter, ed, 369
58 Audre Lorde: *Sister Outsider*, Crossing Press, New York 1984, and in Humm 1992, 283

whole room seemed full of our commingled, complicated smells. And over and over again I'd come, sometimes still nearly asleep', writes Sue Miller,[59] while Summer Brenner writes: 'our bodies made light in a soft room'.[60] Susan Griffin has written powerfully of lesbian eroticism:

> ...my most profound longings and desires, for intimacy, to know, to touch and be inside the body and soul of another, becoming and separating from, devouring and being devoured, that wild, large, amazing, frightening territory of lovemaking belongs for me not with men, but with women.[61]

Nancy Friday has collected women's fantasies in a number of books: *My Secret Garden, Women On Top* and *Forbidden Flowers*. The fantasies involve lesbianism, group sex, sex with animals, sex with pop and movie stars, rape, anal sex, domination, S/M and all manner of erotic activities. Women's fantasies, like their fictions, are, some feminists believe, wilder, larger, more amazing and more frightening, to use Susan Griffin's words, than male fantasies and fictions. The books of erotic fiction and fantasy by women[62] demonstrate something of the erotic ecstasy of women which, as Xavière Gauthier writes 'is so violent, so transgressive, so open, so fatal, that men have not yet recovered.'[63] Incredible though women's sexual fantasies may be, they are always defined in terms of male fantasies, often in terms of difference. Camille Paglia has written of a new form of sexuality which is not afraid of being extraordinary:

---

59 Sue Miller: *The Good Mother*, Harper & Row, New York 1986
60 Summer Brenner: *The Soft Room*, Figures 1978
61 Susan Griffin: *Viyella*, in Laura Chester, ed. *Deep Down*, 326
62 See, for instance, Lonnie Barbach, ed. *Pleasures: Women Write Erotica*, Doubleday, New York 1984; Laura Duesing: *Three West Coast Women*, Five Fingers Poetry, 1987; Clayton Eshleman, ed. *Caterpillar Anthology*, Anchor 1971; Summer Brenner: *The Soft Room*, The Figures 1978; Lynne Tillman: *Weird Fucks*, 1980; Jane Hirshfield: *Of Gravity and Angels*, Wesleyan University Press 1988; Jayne Anne Phillips: *Black Tickets*, Delacorte Press 1979; Marilyn Hacker: *Love, Death and the Changing of the Seasons*, Arbor House 1986; Nancy Friday: *Forbidden Flowers: More Women's Sexual Fantasies*, Arrow 1993
63 Xavière Gauthier: "Pourquoi Sorcières?", in *Sorcières*,1, 1976, in E. Marks, 201-2

Neo-Sexism, or the New Sexism [is] a progressive feminism that
embraces and celebrates all historical depictions of women,
including the most luridly pornographic. It wants mythology without
sentimentality and every archetype, from mother to witch and whore,
without censorship... The New Sexism puts sensuality at the centre of
our responsiveness to life and art.[64]

One aspect of art, the media, sexuality and pornography is
common to all of them: looking. In cultural/ postmodern/ post-
Lacanian theory there is a politics and a psychology of looking. It
is central to art and pornography. In the Lacanian system, desire,
loss, seeing, language, expression and early psychosexual conflicts
are all bound up together. Art and pornography are founded on
wanting to 'have' something, but the object remains 'other' and
unattainable. In art, you can repossess something that was lost –
some memory, or feeling. Lacan explains how desire is based on
loss:

Desire is that which is manifested in the interval that demand
hollows within itself, in as much as the subject, in articulating the
signifying chain, brings to light the want-to-be, together with the
appeal to receive the complement from the Other, if the other, the locus
of speech, is also the locus of this want, this lack.[65]

For French feminists such as Hélène Cixous, this philosophy
of 'the lack' is ridiculous. As she writes in "The Laugh of the
Medusa": '[w]hat's a desire originating from a lack? A pretty
meagre desire' (in E. Marks, 262). And Luce Irigaray and other
feminists have criticized the Freudian-Lacanian emphasis on the
phallus as the 'transcendental signifier', as the measure of
authentic sexual pleasure.[66]

The Lacanian Look emphasizes eroticism. Seeing is erotic, the
eye becomes a kind of phallus, caressing the obscure object of
desire, which it can never 'possess'. As the poet Rainer Maria

---

64 Camille Paglia: "New Sexism for women", *The Guardian*, 30 September
1993

65 Lacan: *Ecrits: A Selection*, tr. Alan Sheridan, Tavistock 1977, 263

177 Luce Irigaray: *Speculum of the Other Woman*, tr. Gillian C. Gill, and
This Sex which Is Not One, tr. Catherine Porter, both Cornell University
Press, New York 1985; see also: Dorothy Leland: "Lacanian
psychoanalysis and French feminism: toward an adequate political
psychology", *Hypatia*, 3 (3), Winter 1989, 81-103

Rilke wrote '[g]azing is a wonderful thing.'[67] The act of looking eroticizes the object. Jack Zipes explains:

> For [Lacan], seeing is desire, and the eye functions as a kind of phallus. However, the eye cannot clearly see its object of desire, and in the case of male desire, the female object of desire is an illusion created by the male unconscious. Or, in other words, the male desire for woman expressed in the gaze is auto-erotic and involves the male's desire to have his own identity reconfirmed in a mirror image.[68]

The Look is an assertion of male power and sexuality. For the gaze is male, and feminists have grappled with the notion of a 'female' gaze.[69] 'Male desire is presented as a response to female beauty', writes Andrea Dworkin.[70] Margaret Whitford describes Luce Irigaray's work thus:

> Western systems of representation privilege *seeing*: what can be seen (presence) is privileged over what cannot be seen (absence) and guarantees Being, hence the privilege of the penis which is elevated to the status of the Phallus.[71]

In the Jungian system, Beatrice, Laura, Cleopatra, Isolde, Eurydice, Ariadne and all those women of myth, poetry and legend, are incarnations of the *anima*, which is, as Carl Jung explains, something all males possess: '[e]very man carries with him the eternal image of woman, not the image of this or that particular woman, but a definitive feminine image.'[72] The *anima* is 'a personification of the unconscious in a man, which appears as a woman or a goddess in dreams, visions and creative fantasies',

---

67 Rilke, letter to Clara Rilke, 8 March 1907, in *Gesammalte Briefe 1892-1926*, Insel Verlag, Leipzig 1940, II, 279f
68 Jack Zipes: *Don't Bet on the Prince: Contemporary Feminist Fairy Tales in North America and England*, Gower, Aldershot 1986, 258
69 Maggie Humm: "Is the gaze feminist? Pornography, film and feminism", in G. Day, 1988; L. Gamran, 1988; E.D. Pribram, ed. *Female Spectators: looking at film and television*, Verso, 1988
70 Dworkin: *Intercourse*, 114
71 Marget Whitford: *Luce Irigaray: Philosophy in the Feminine*, 1991, 1990, 30
72 Jung: *The Development of Personality*, vol. 17, Routledge, 1954, 198; Marie-Louise von Franz: *The Psychological Meaning of Redemption Motifs in Fairy Tales*, Inner City Books, Toronto 1980, 39f

write Emma Jung and Marie-Louise von Franz.[73] Male painters throughout history have depicted their version of the *anima*, it seems. Each (male) painter has a version of the 'inner feminine figure' as Jung calls her.[74] For painters, this idealized *anima* figure seems to be another manifestation of that obscure object of desire, the eroticized woman, a mirror for male lust. The equation is: the more sublime and voluptuous the woman is painted, the more sublime and voluptuous is the artist's desire. The artist's model, then, can be seen as a Jungian *anima*, heavily eroticized, a Lacanian phallic mirror.

In Lacanian psychology, desire, which is the foundation of the system, is enmeshed with speaking, with creativity and art. The œdipal crisis and the repression of the desire for the mother occurs with the entry into the Symbolic Order, and the entry into language. As Toril Moi crystallizes Lacan's thought so concisely: '[t]o speak as a subject is therefore the same as to represent the existence of repressed desire.'[75] The links between seeing and erotic pleasure, between the eye and the phallus, are found in much of Western 'high culture': not only in the history of painting, but also in the great works of poets such as Dante Alighieri, Francesco Petrarch, William Shakespeare and the troubadours. In the 'classic' of pornography, Bataille's *The Story of the Eye*, there are eyes placed in mouths, vulvas and anuses. Bataille takes the Sadeian ethic of the pornographic Look to its logical, literal extreme.

Men gaze at women and manipulate them into erotic poses. Larysa Mykyta writes:

> The sexual triumph of the male passes through the eye, through the contemplation of the woman. Seeing the women ensures the satisfaction of wanting to be seen, of having one's desire recognized, and thus comes back to the original aim of the scopic drive. Woman is repressed as subject and desired as object in order to efface the gaze of the Other, the gaze that would destroy the illusion of reciprocity and oneness that the process of seeing usually supports. The female object does not look, does not have it own point of view; rather it is

73 Emma Jung & Marie-Louise von Franz: *The Grail Legend*, tr. Andrea Dykes, Sigo Press, Boston, Mass., 1980, 64
74 Jung: *Memories, Dreams, Reflections*, Collins 1967, 210-1
75 Moi, *Sexual/ Textual Politics*, 99-100

erected as an image of the phallus sustaining male desire.[76]

The pleasure of the text, whether the text is a painting, film, magazine, photograph, piece of theatre, etc, comes, according to Roland Barthes, when the Look of the spectator is aligned with that of the author.[77] What feminist criticism has done is to question the masculine 'pleasure of the text', arguing for a feminist reading of the traditional masculine or patriarchal view of texts. For some feminists, however, there can be no true 'feminist gaze', because the Look is always masculine, ultimately. If the spectator is a 'gendered object', suggests Annette Kuhn, then 'masculine subjectivity [is] the only subjectivity available'.[78] The politics of representation, which are central to the consumption of pornography and art, are weighted firmly in favour of men and patriarchy. As John Berger writes: 'men act and women appear'.[79] As Catherine King notes: 'most images in masculine visual ideology are created to empower men as spectators – that is, to see themselves as endlessly important with things laid out for their desire'.[80]

Clearly, pornography is a series of texts or representations that maximizes the pleasure of the male spectator. The female nude painting does the same.

---

76 Larysa Mykyta: "Lacan, Literature and the Look", *SubStance* (39), 1983, 54

77 See Laura Mulvey: "Visual pleasure and narrative cinema", *Screen*, vol 16, no.3, 1975, 6-19

78 Annette Kuhn, 1982, 63

79 John Berger: *Ways of Seeing,* 1972, 47

80 Catherine King: "The Politics of Representation: A Democracy of the Gaze", in F. Bonner, 136

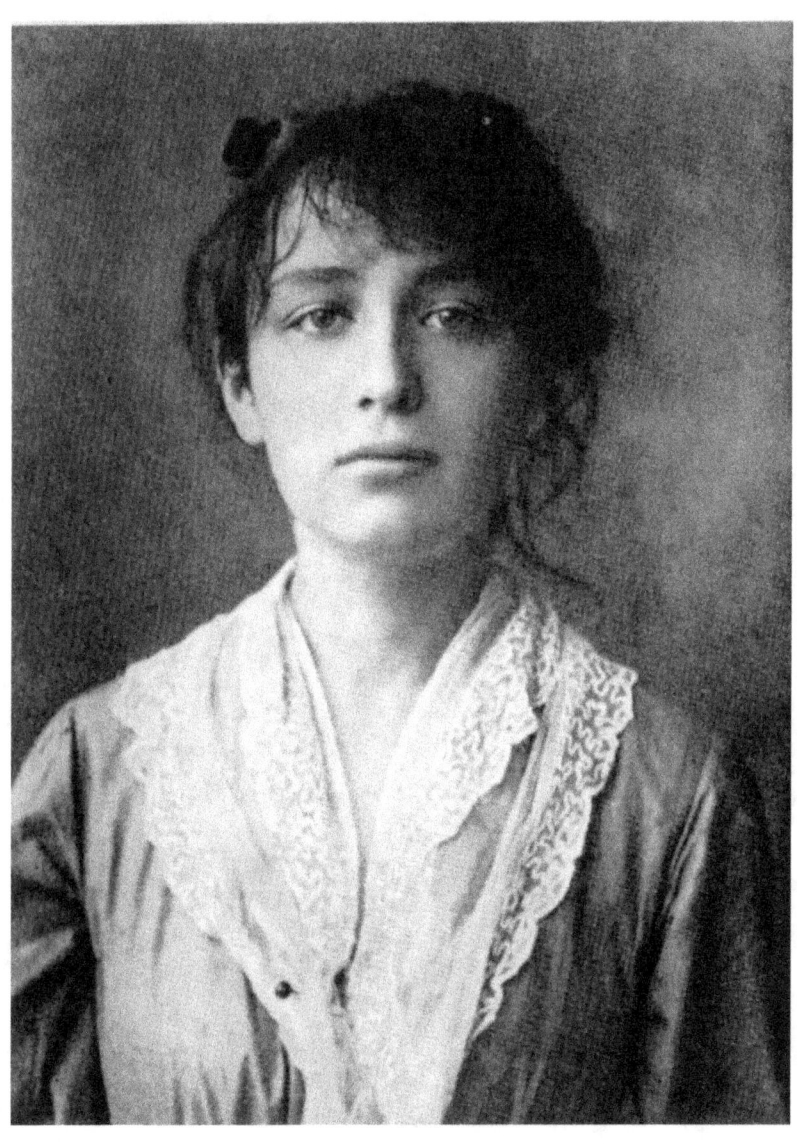

Camille Claudel

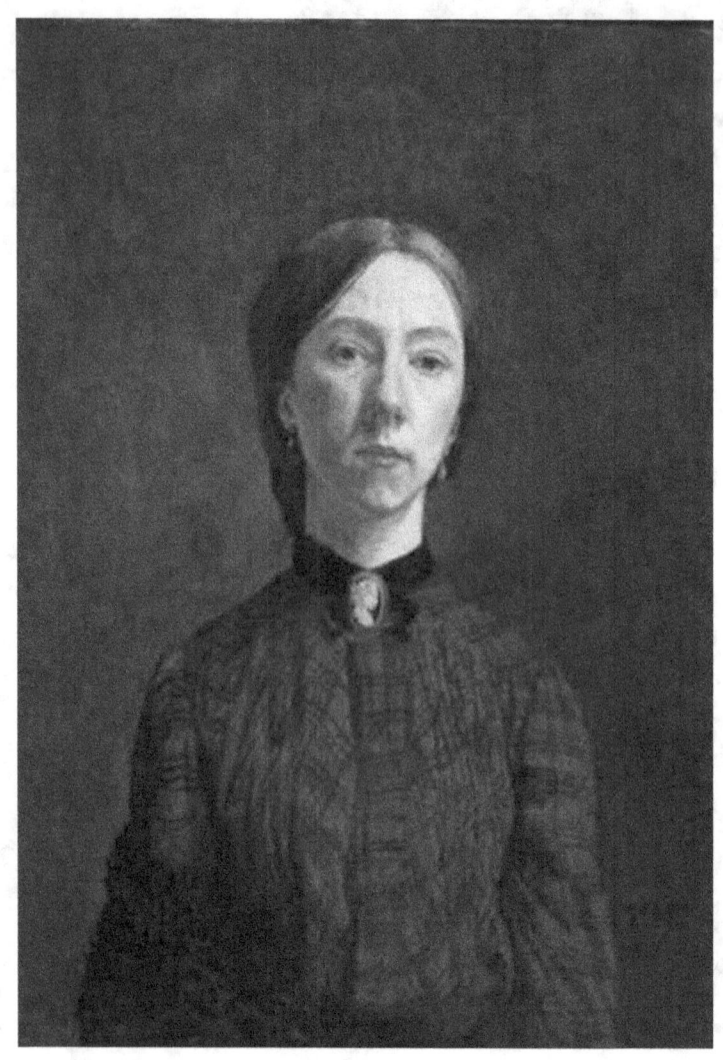

Gwen John, Self-Portrait, National Portrait Gallery, London

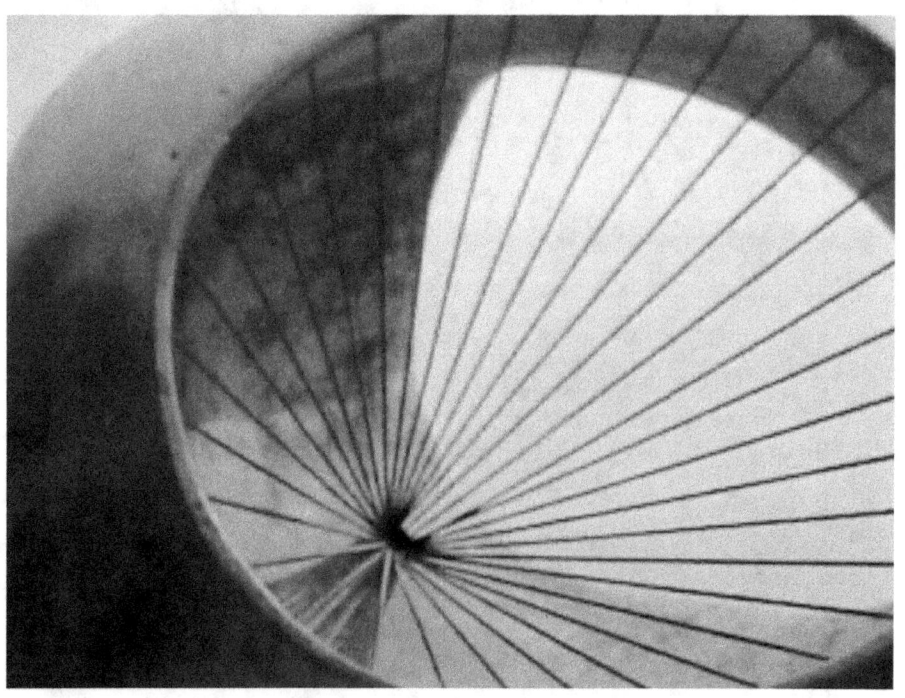

Barbara Hepworth, Sculpture with Colour and String, 1939-61

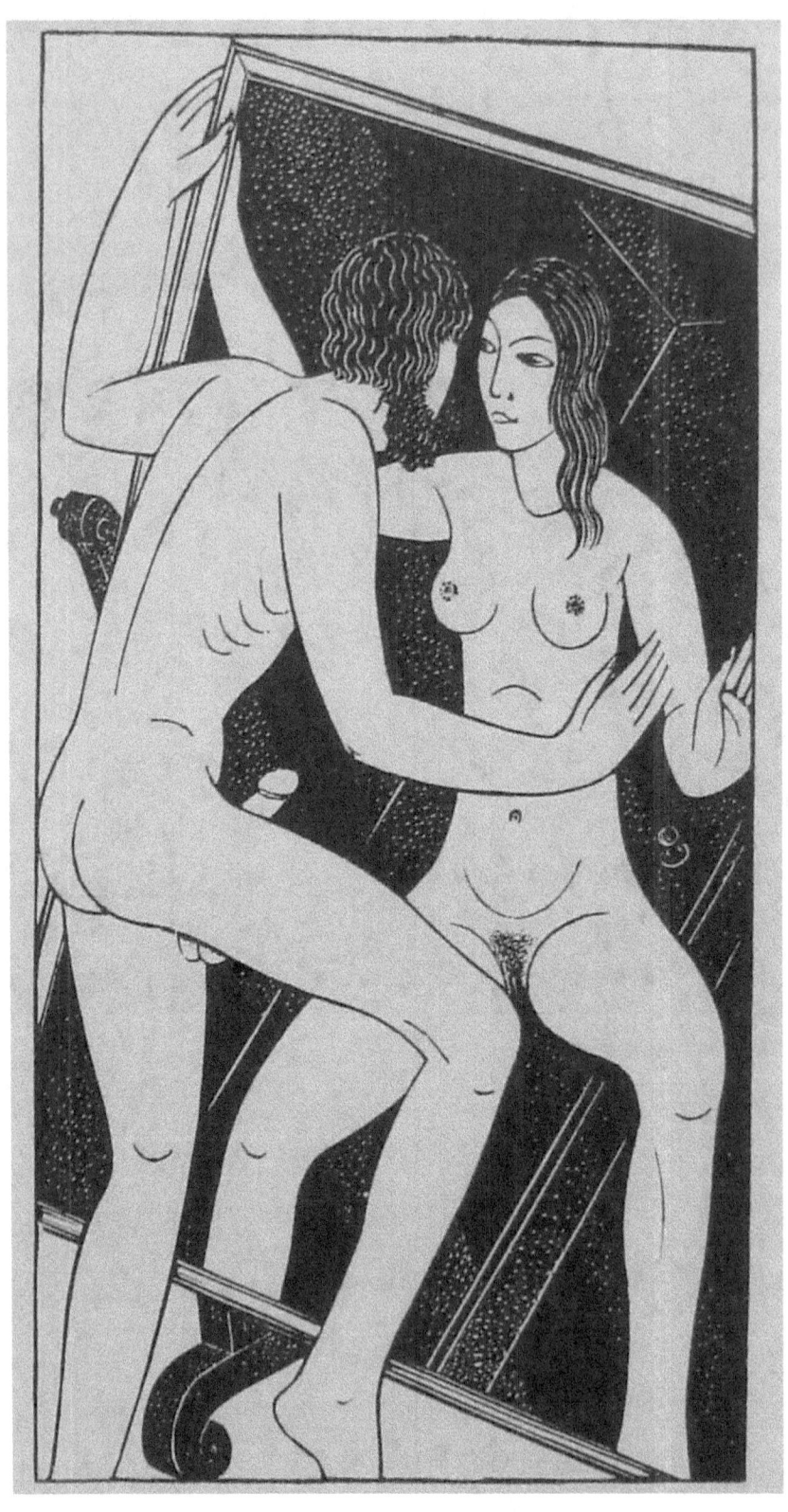

Eric Gill, Artist and Mirror, 1932

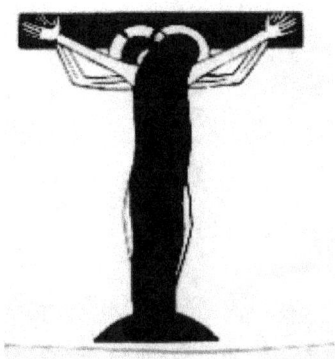

Eric Gill's Nuptials of God, 1922.

An extraordinary image, by any standards,
it depicts Mary Magdalene making love
to Christ on the Cross.

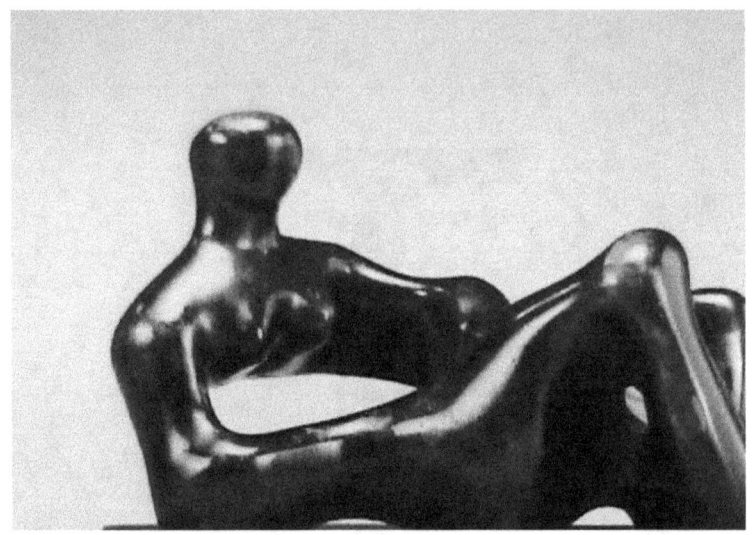

Henry Moore, Maquette For Recumbent Figure, 1938

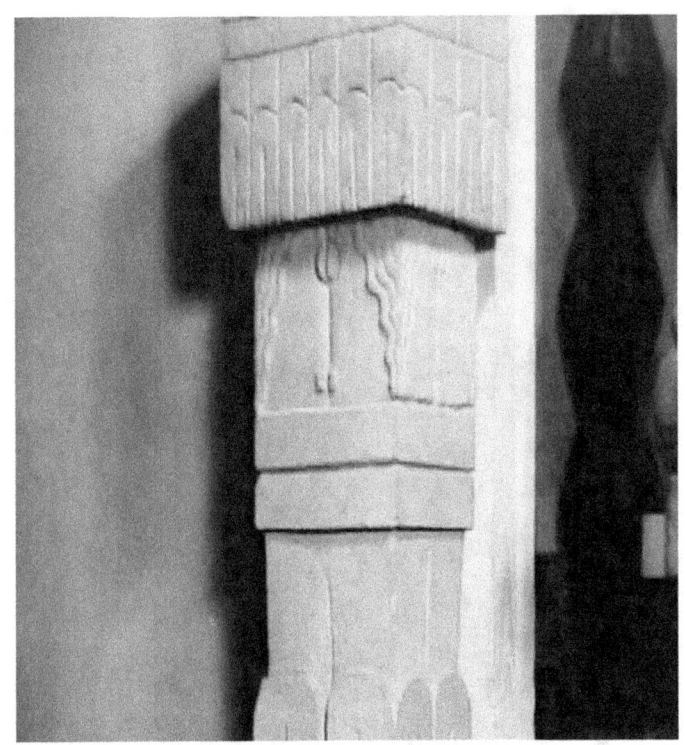

Versions of Constantin Brancusi's The Kiss

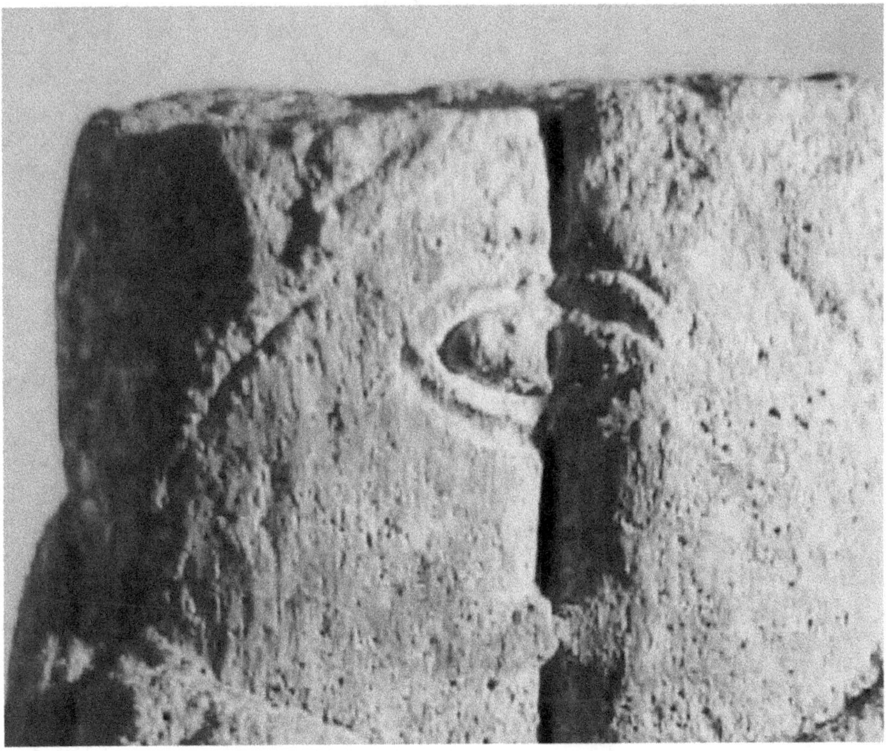

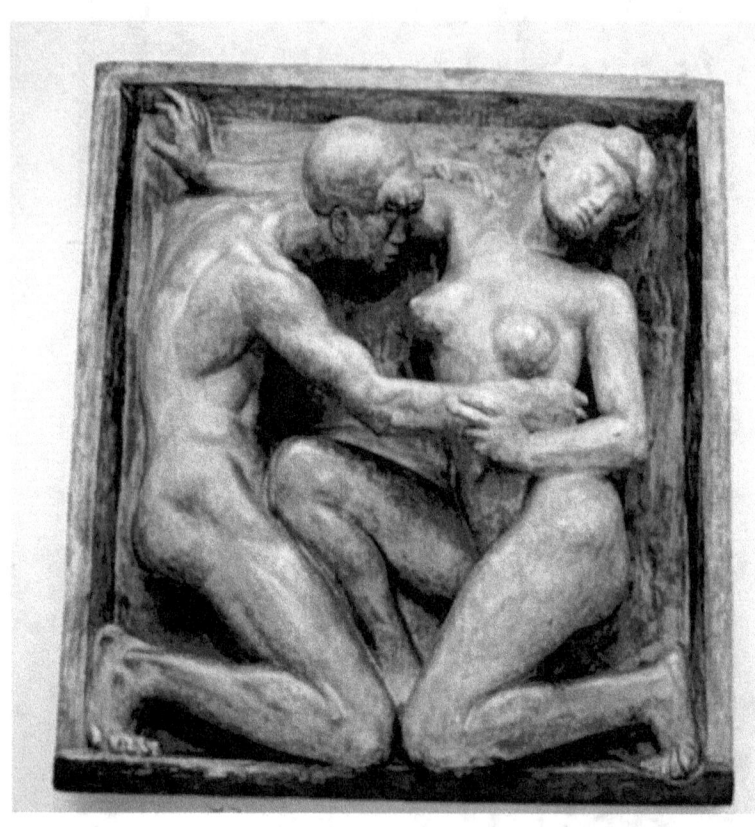

Aristide Maillol, Desire, 1908

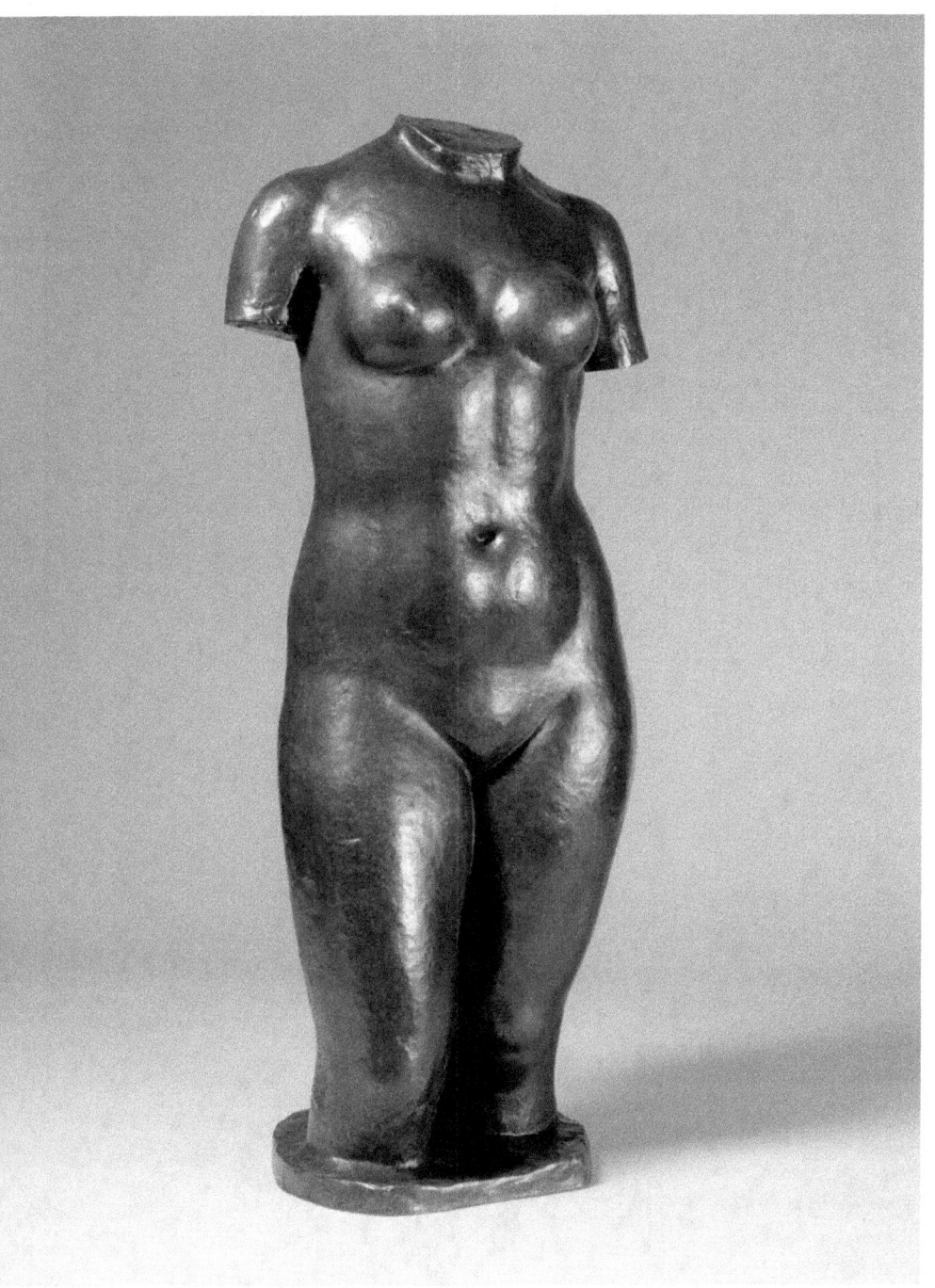

Aristide Maillol, Torso of a Young Woman, 1935,
Montreal Museum of Fine Arts

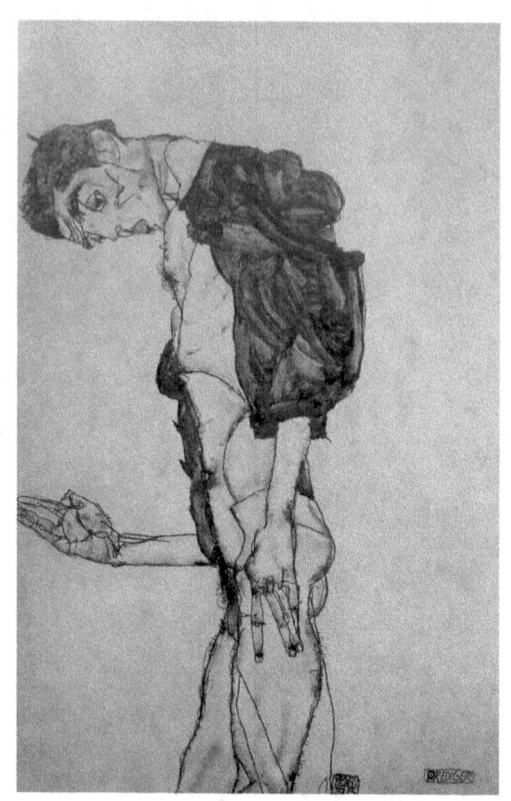

Two Egon Schiele
figures:
Preacher, 1913,
above.
And Standing Nude
Girl With Stockings
1914, below.

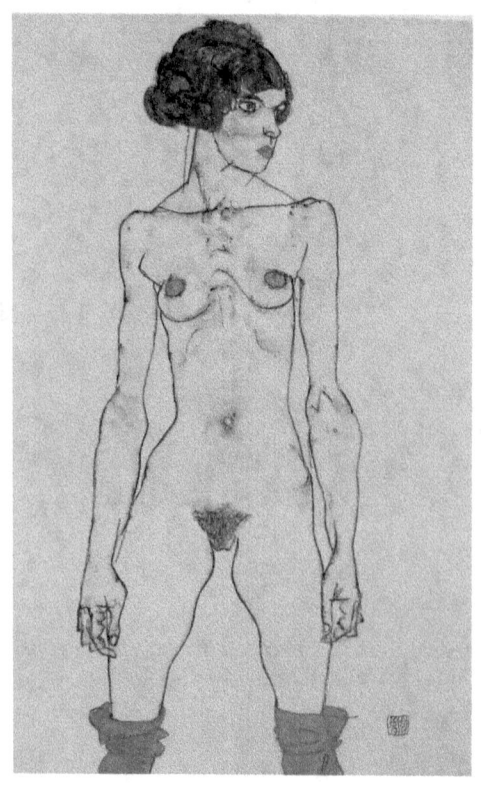

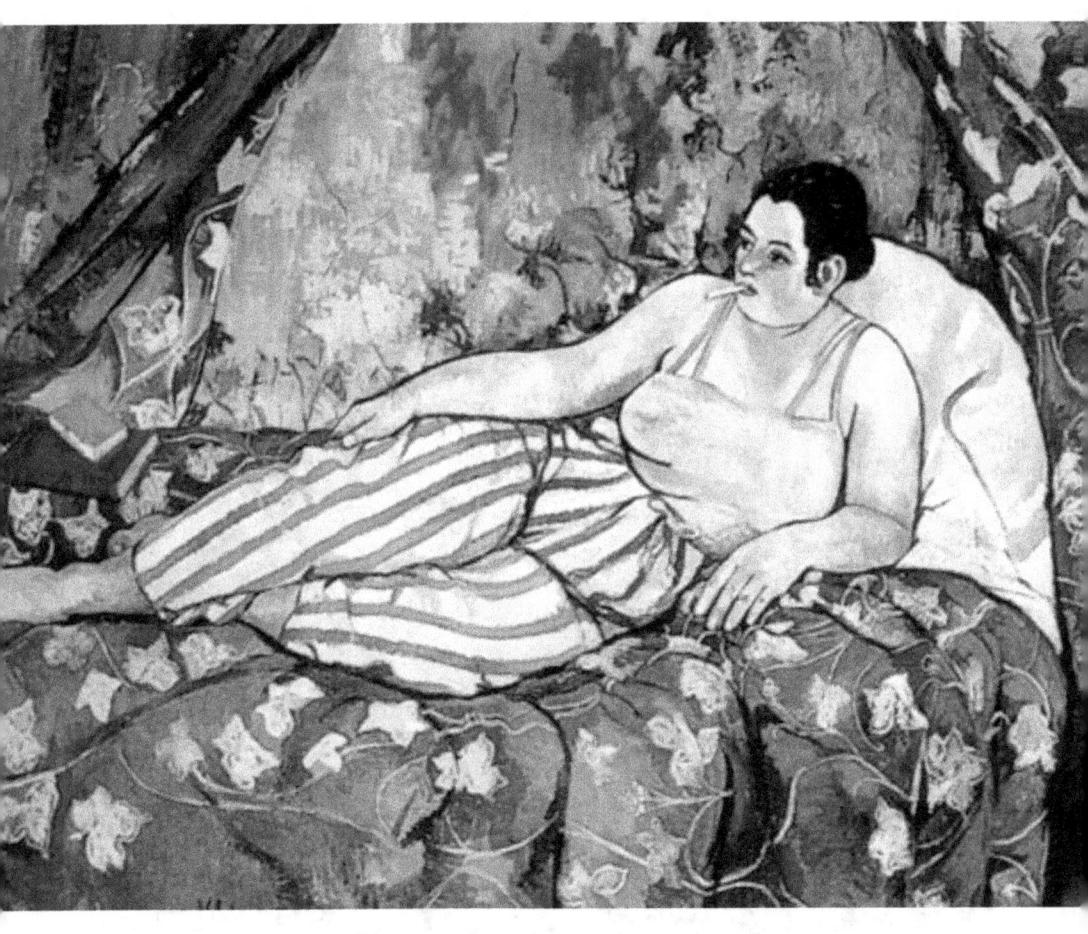

Suzanne Valadon, The Blue Room, 1923

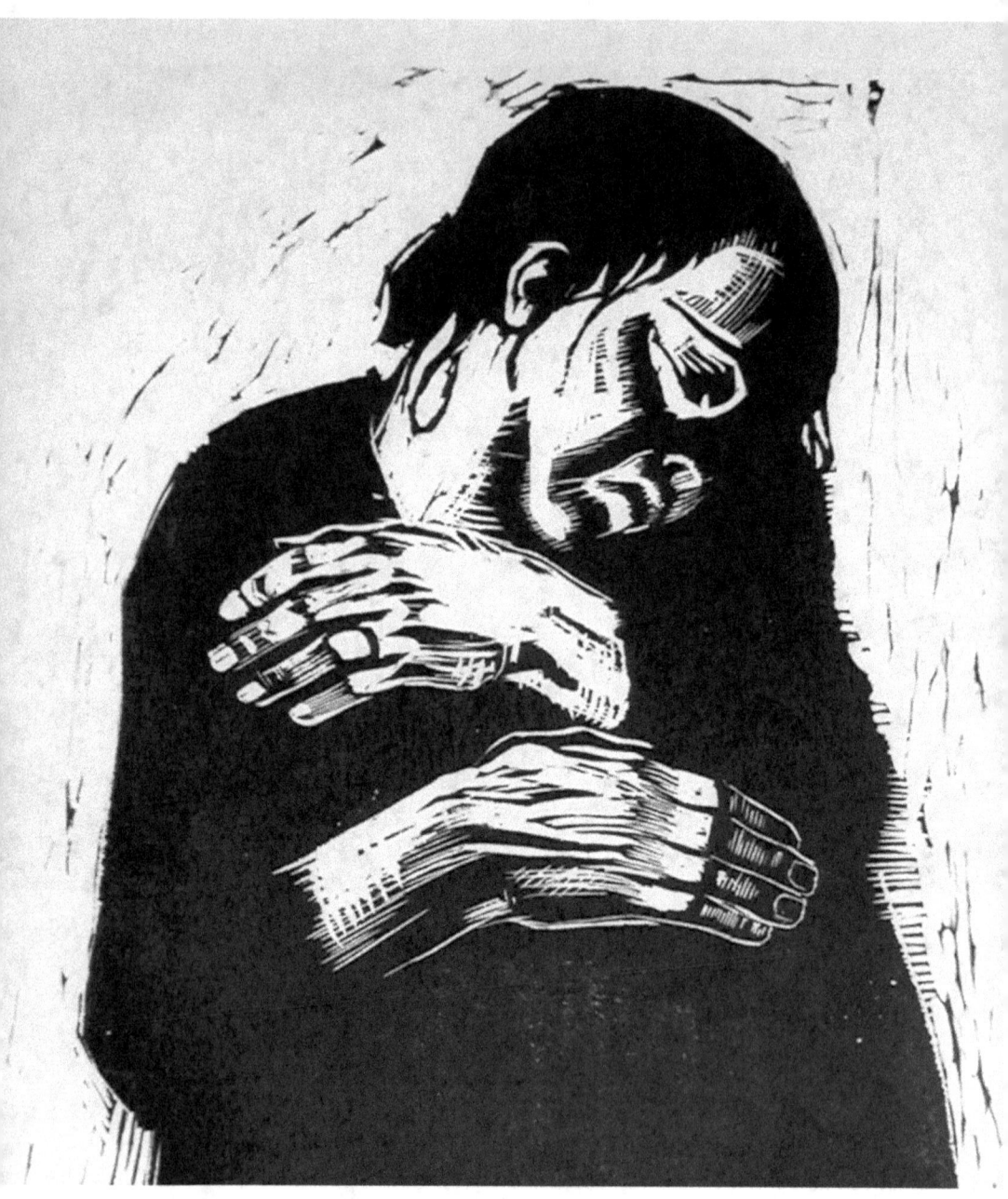

Käthe Kollwitz, The Widow, 1922

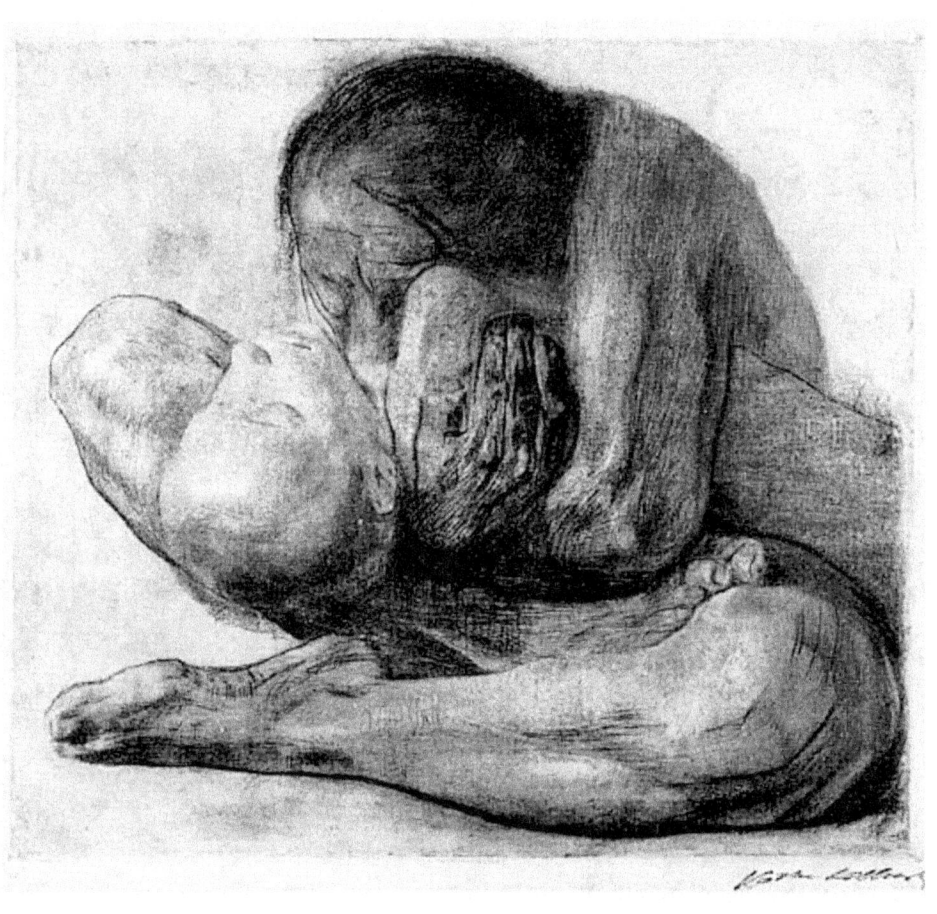

Käthe Kollwitz, Woman With Dead Child, 1903

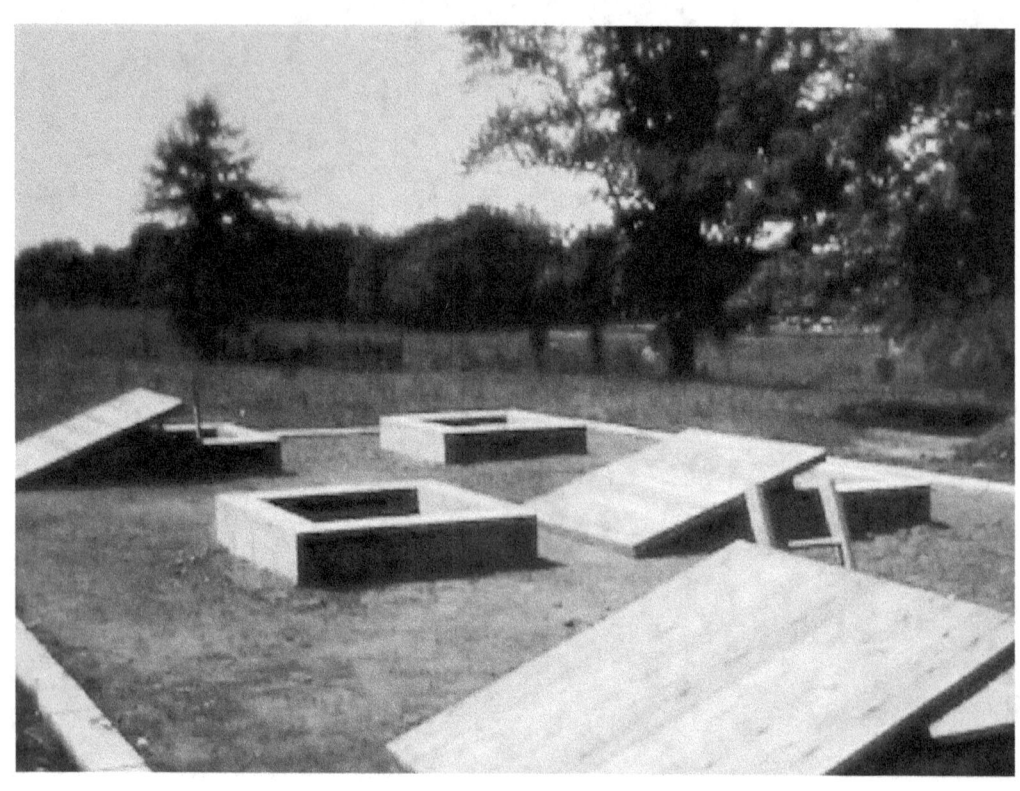

Alice Aycock, A Simple Network of Underground
Walls and Tunnels, 1975

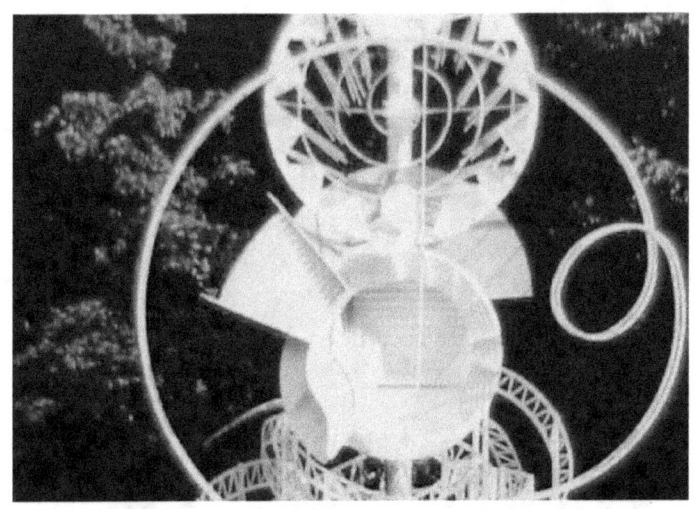

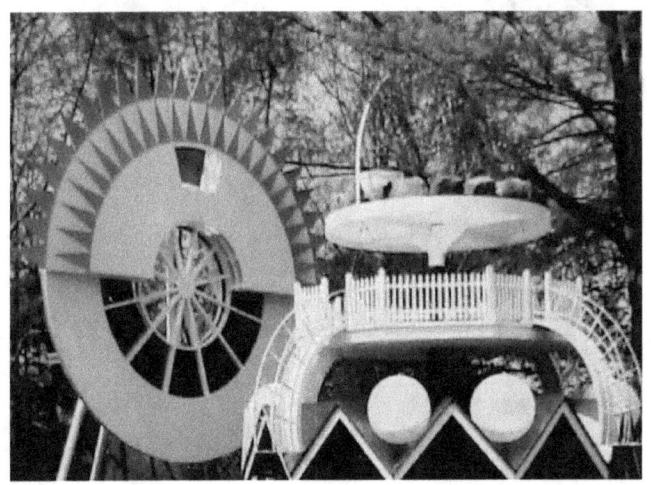

Alice Aycock

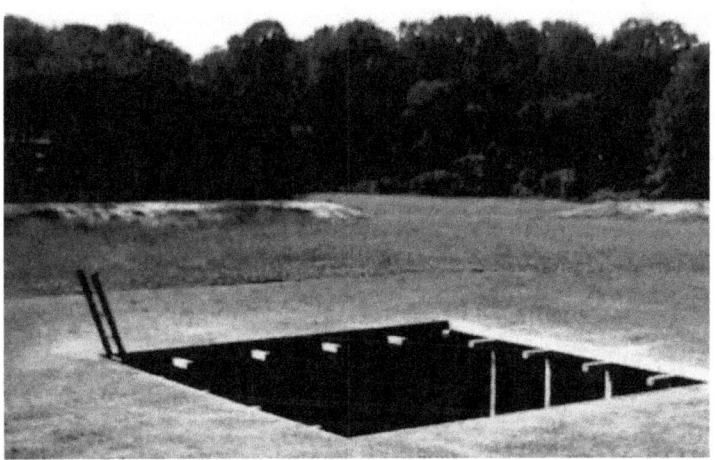

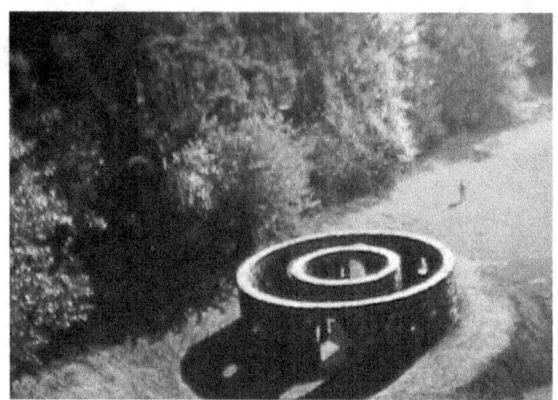

Nancy Holt, Stone Enclosure - Rock Rings, 1977-78

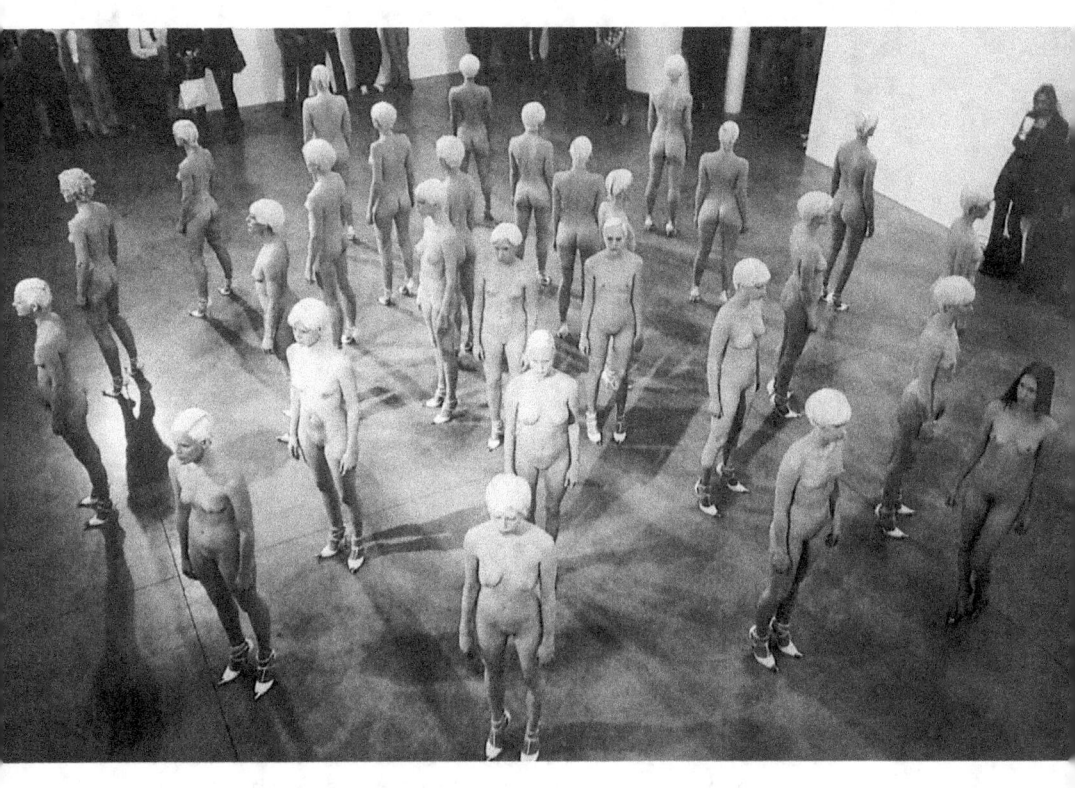

Vanessa Beecroft, VB45.026.ali, 2001

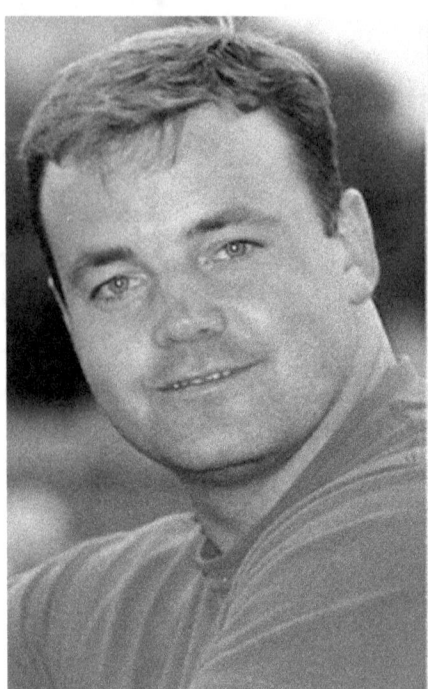
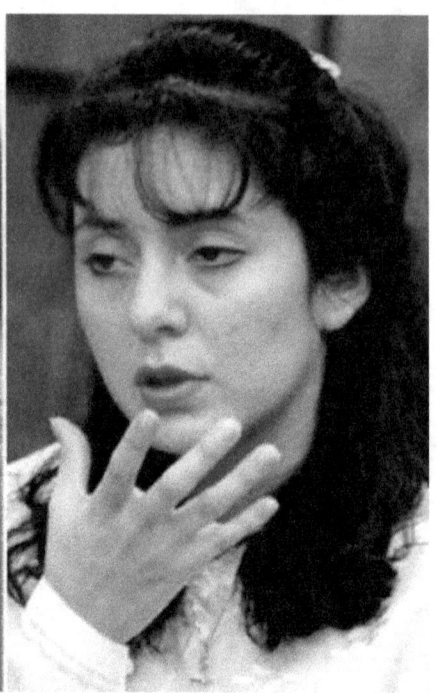

The Bobbitt case, where a woman cut off her husband's penis, reveals some of the powergaming and goals of the media and how it reports sexual violence. The dick-chopping case caught the imagination of America: a newspaper report describes the merchandize that people cooked up to cash in on the incident:

Other T-shirts were for sale among the satellite trucks and live cameras set up from around the world. If you wanted a commemorative slogan you could choose from "You snooze, you lose", "He lost that loving feeling", "Hung jury", "What's up with you?" and "Clean-cut kind of guy". One enterprising vendor was hawking $10 gift packs of chocolate penises complete with knife. A prospective purchaser complained that the penises were broken. 'They're not broken, sir, they're sliced," was the reply. [...] Inside court, the debate boiled down to its essence. "A sleeping man's penis was amputated," stated the state persecutor (a man). "What we have, ladies and gentlemen," claimed the defence lawyer (a woman), "is Lorena Bobbitt's life juxtaposed against John Wayne Bobbitt's penis." The husband was the first witness to take the stand and his penis was an early exhibit. A photograph of what the police described as "the appendage" was quickly produced (prompting cheers, applause and roars of approval among reporters watching the trial in a nearby room). The photograph was not shown in close-up on national television. "It was just too gross," said Stephen Johnson, executive producer of Court TV.

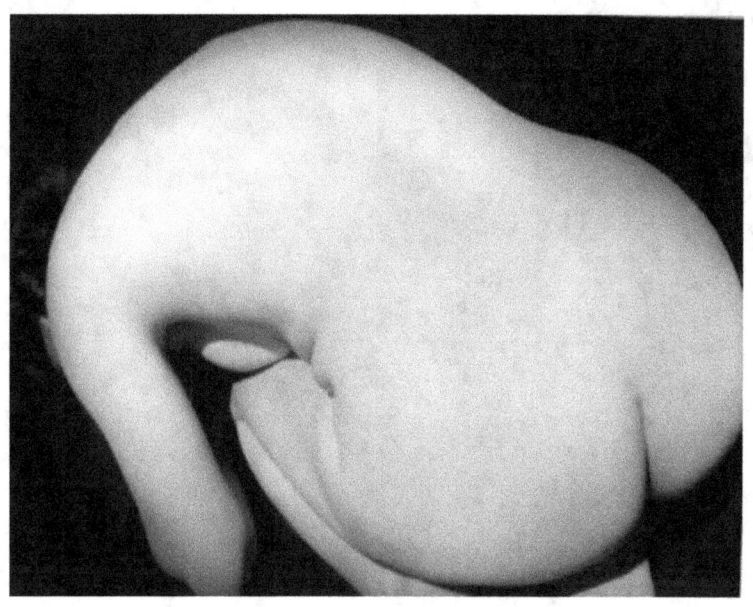

Imogen Cunningham, Nude, 1932 (above).
Imogen Cunningham and Twinka, 1974, by Judy Dater (below).

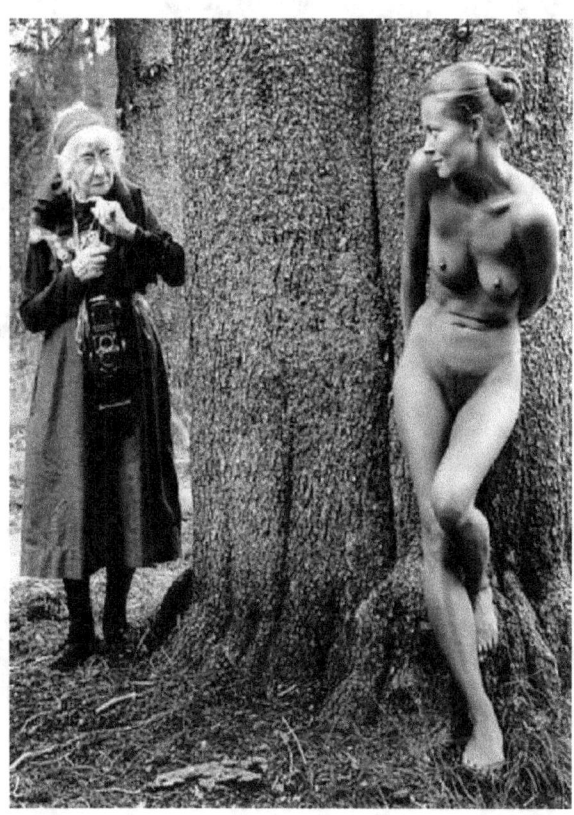

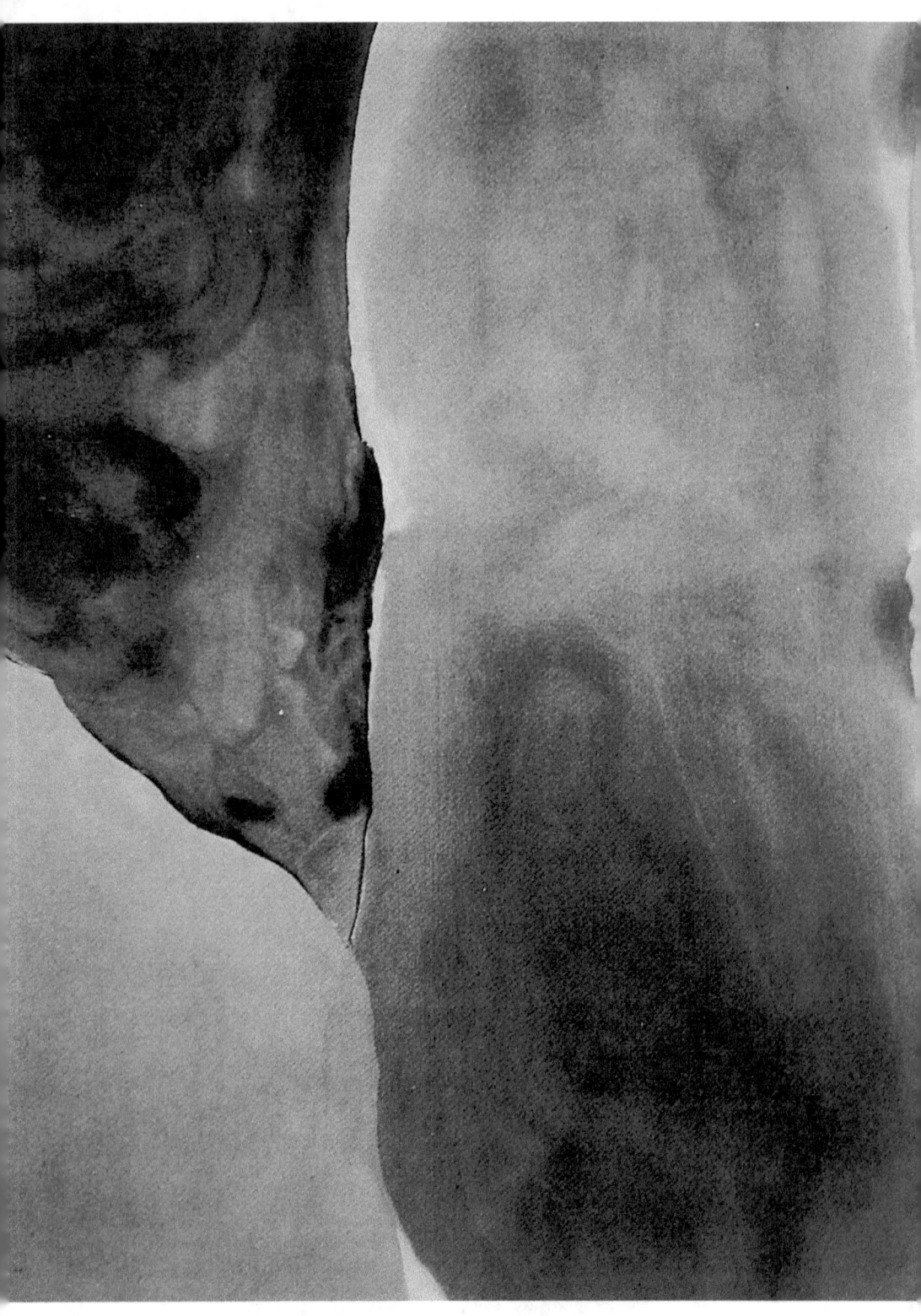

Helen Frankenthaler, Gambit, 1969

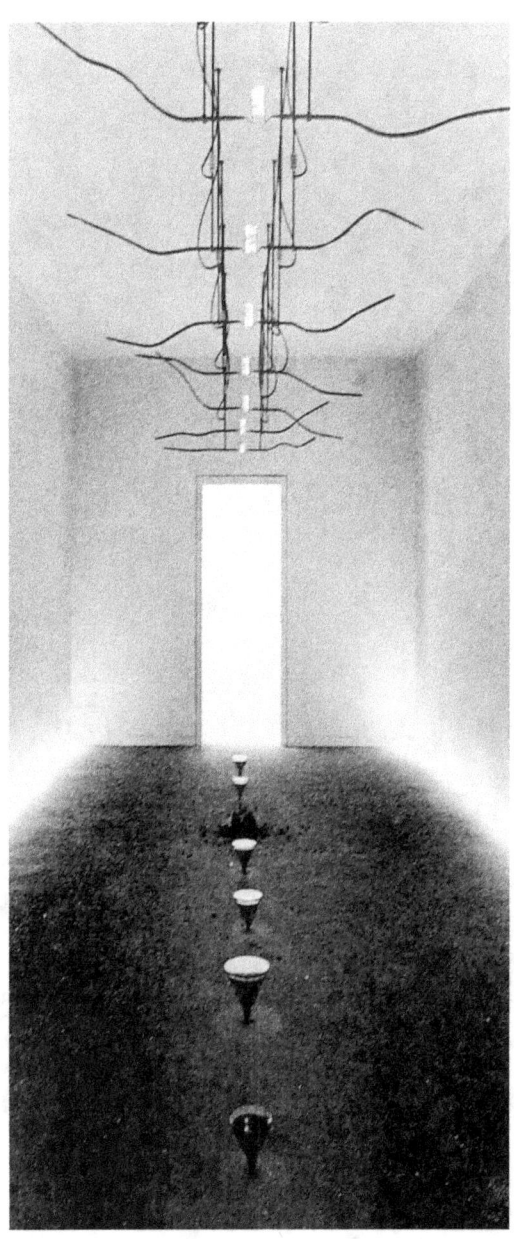

Rebecca Horn

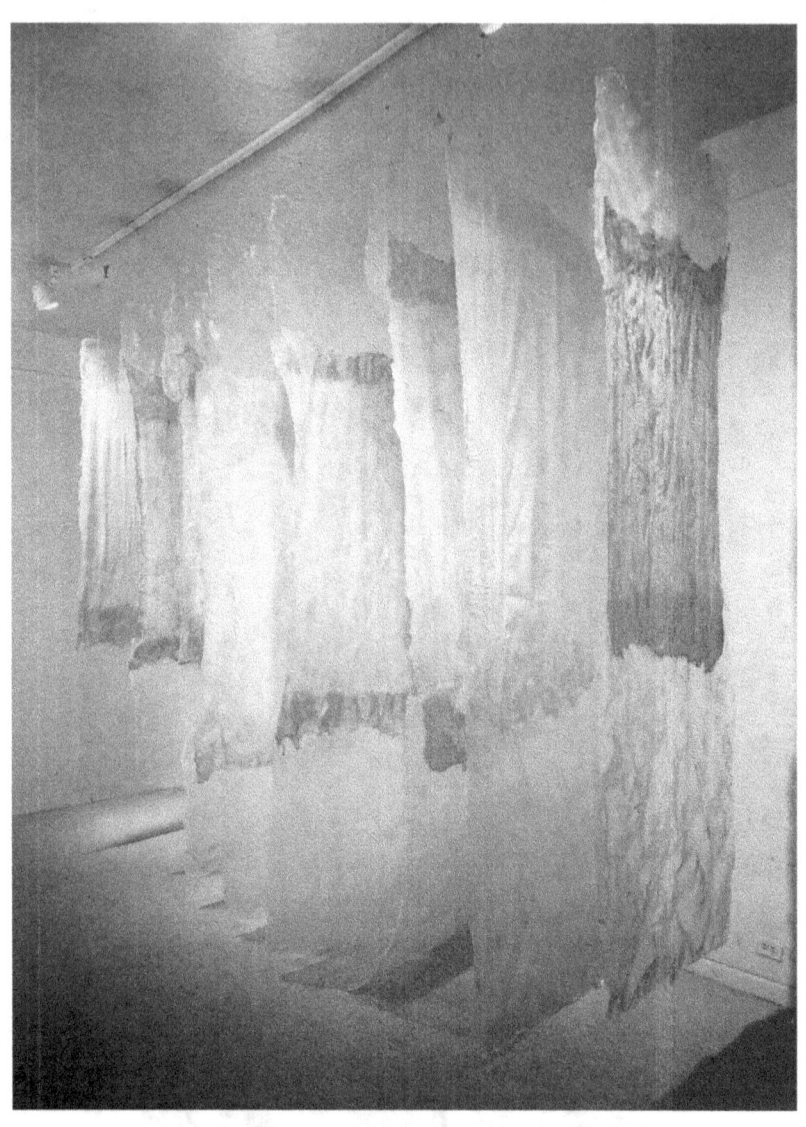

Eva Hesse, Contingent, 1969

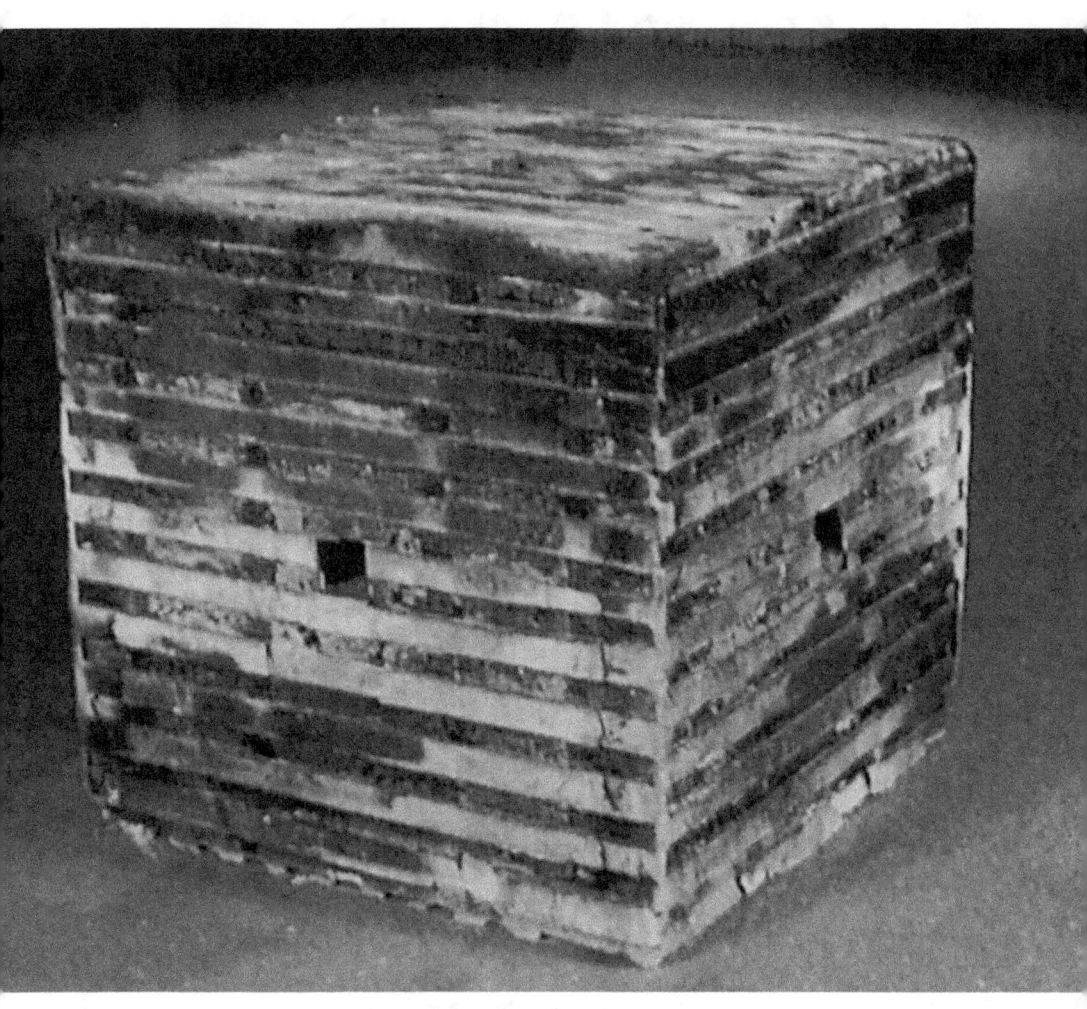

Jackie Winsor, Burnt Piece, 1977

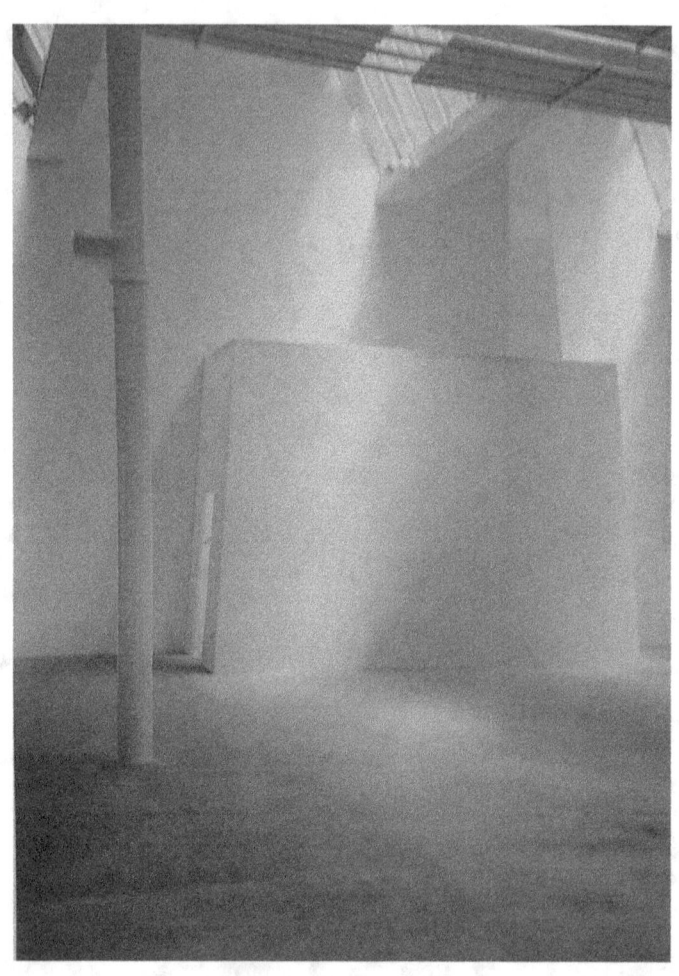

Alison Wilding, Pulse, 1991

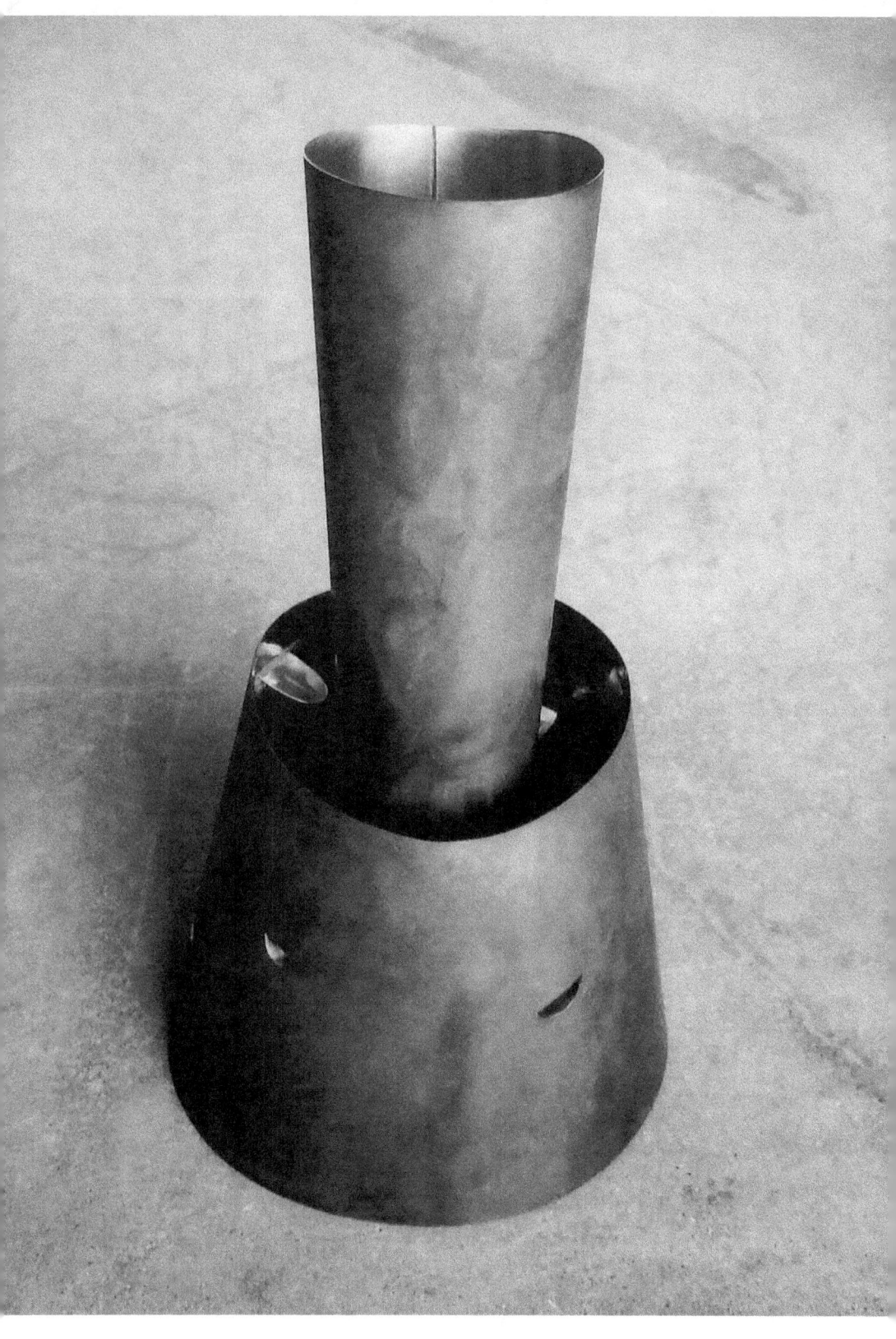

Alison Wilding, Immersion, 1988

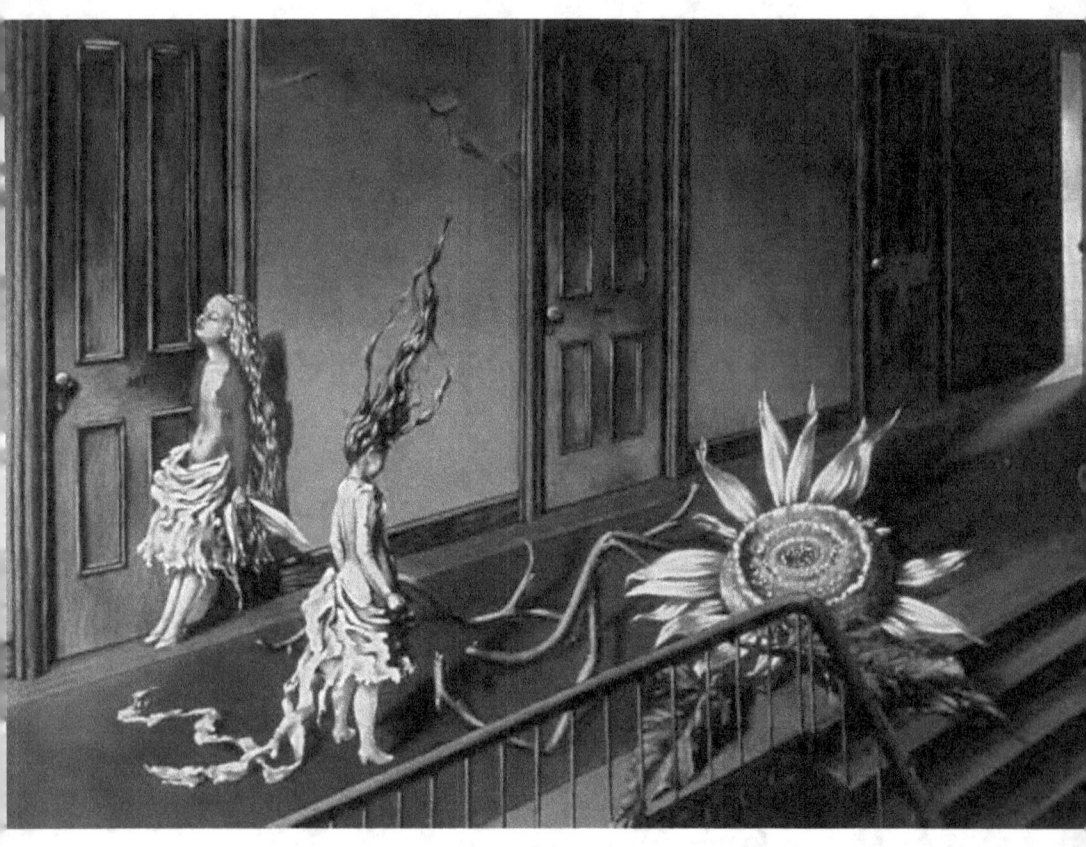

Dorothea Tanning, A Little Night Music, 1946

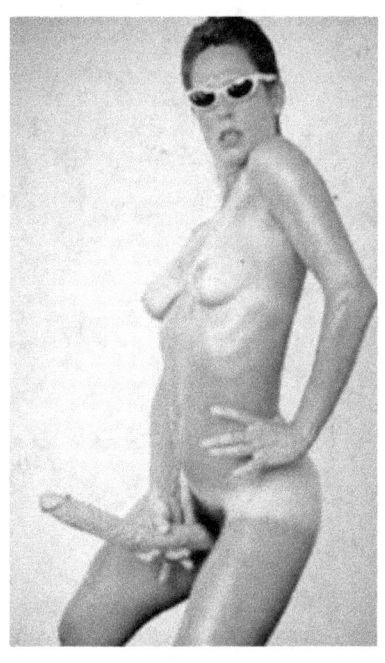

Lynda Benglis, Self-Portrait,
in Artforum, 1974 (left).

Karen Finley (below).

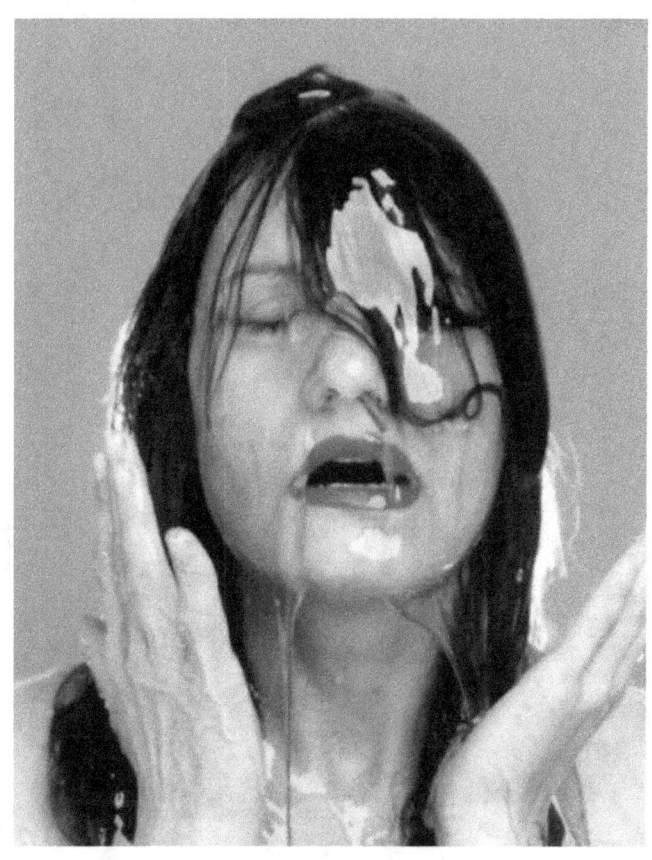

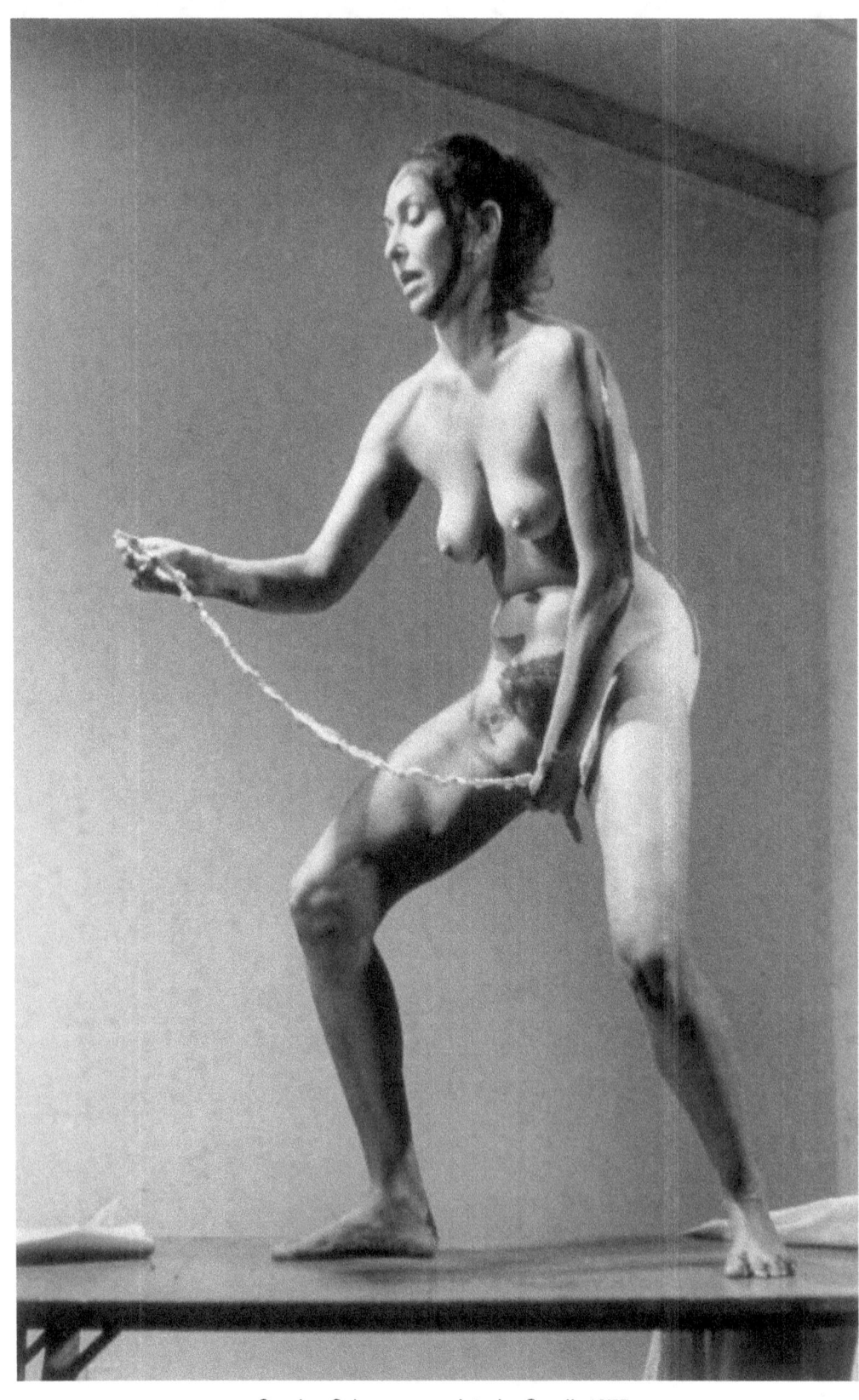

Carolee Scheenmann, Interior Scroll, 1975

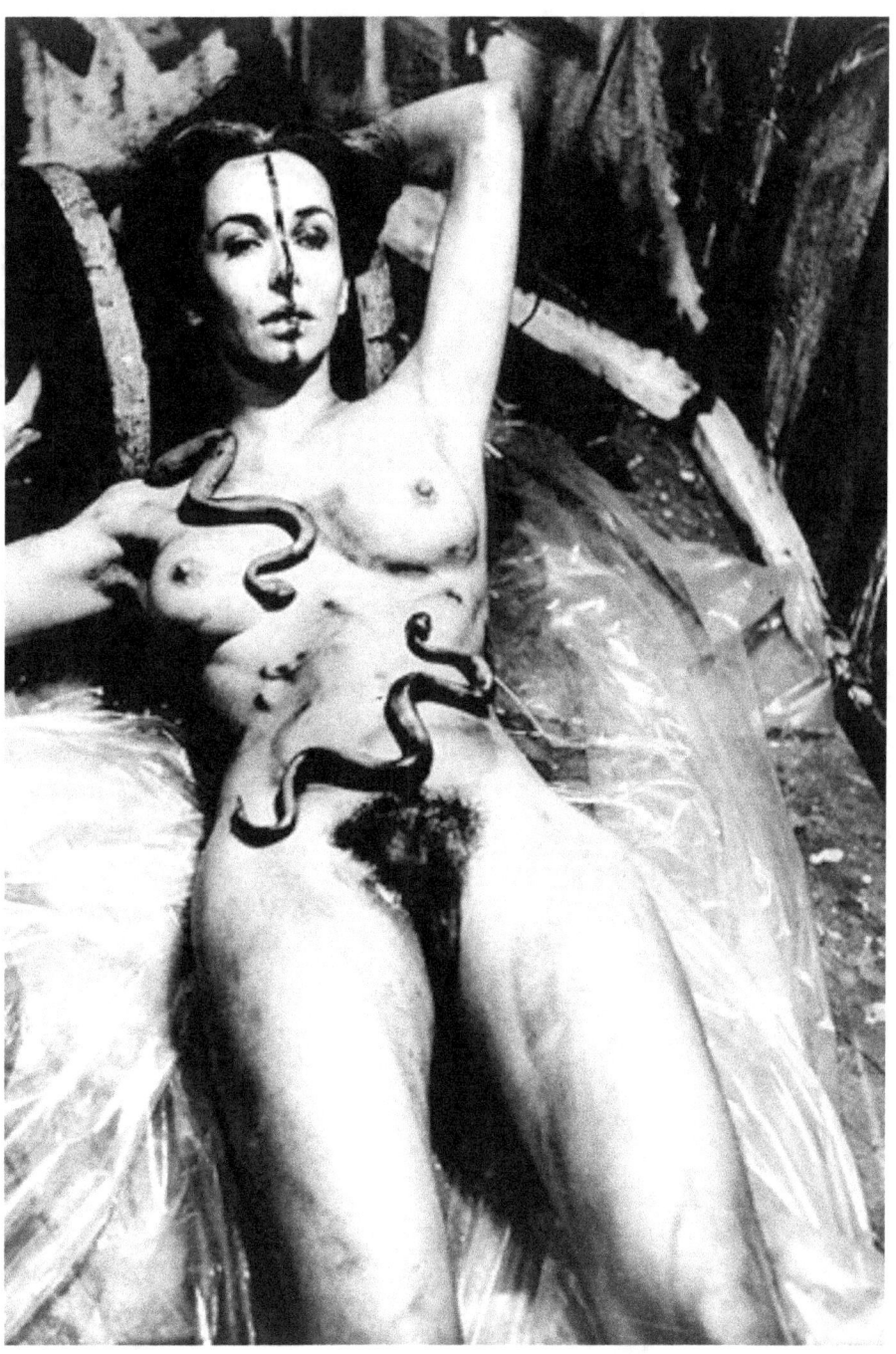

Carolee Schneemann, Eye-Body, 1963

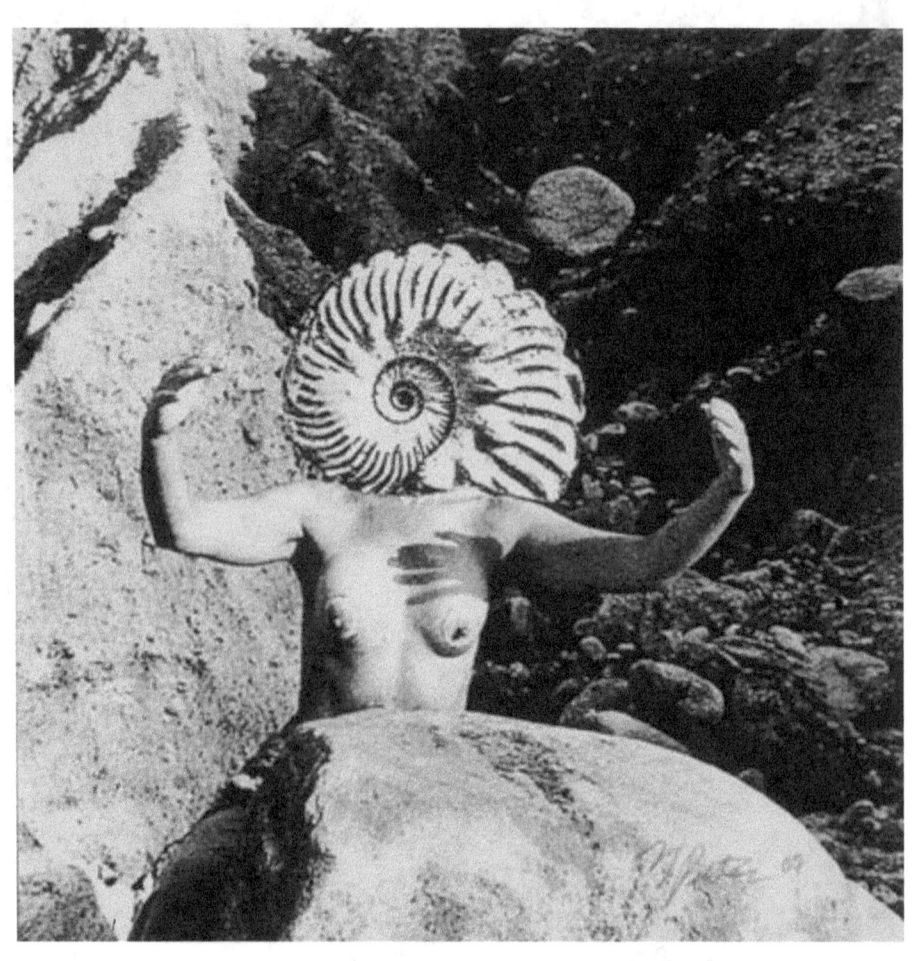

Mary Beth Edelson, Godless Head, 1975

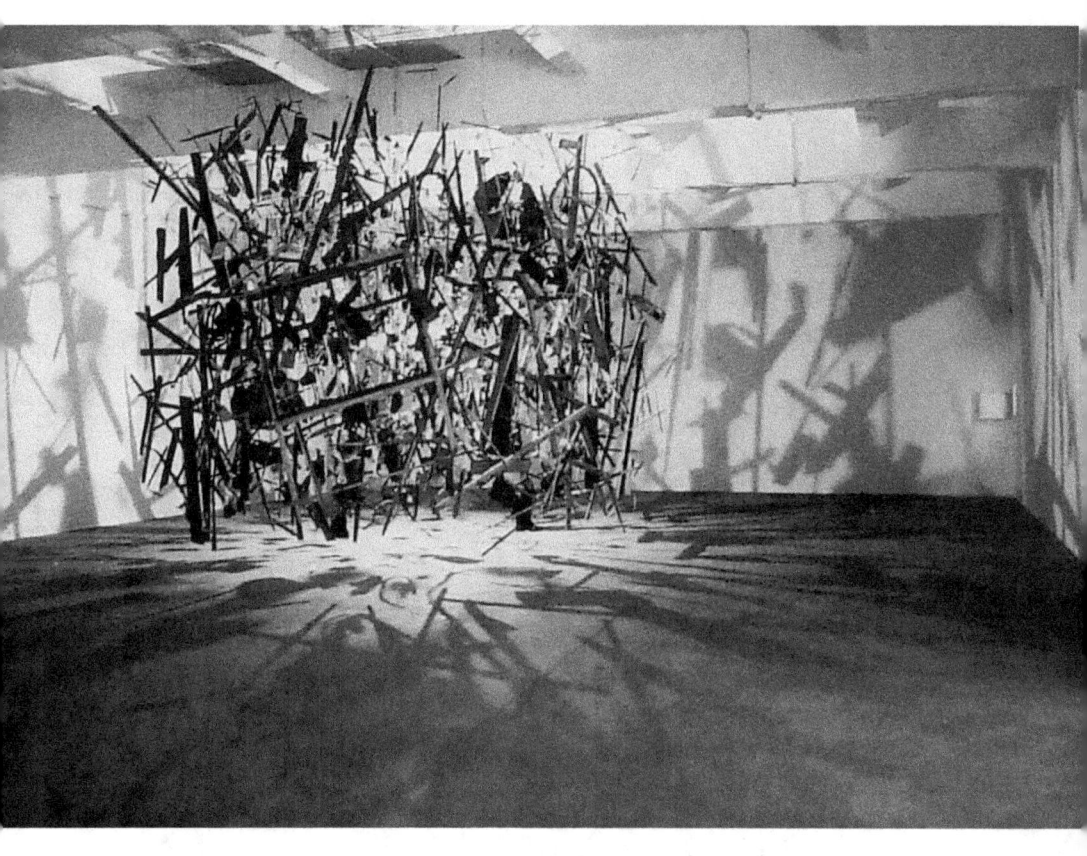

Cornelia Parker, Cold Dark Matter, 1991

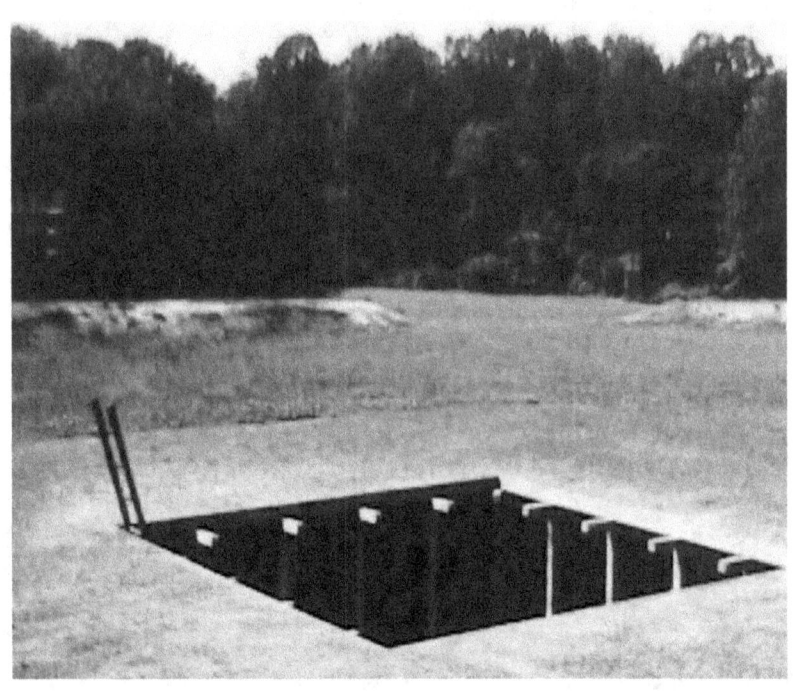

Mary Miss, Perimeters/ Pavilion/ Decoys. 1978

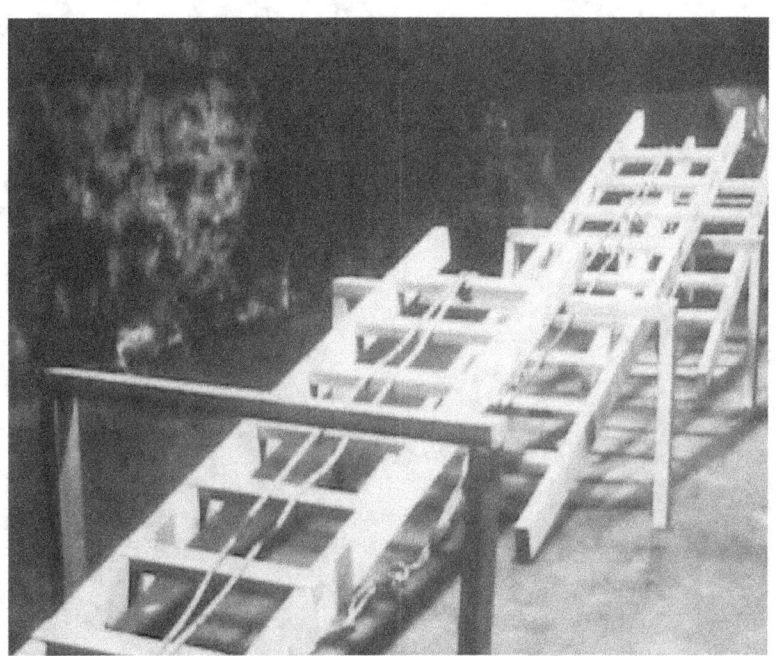

Mary Miss, Ladders and Hurdles

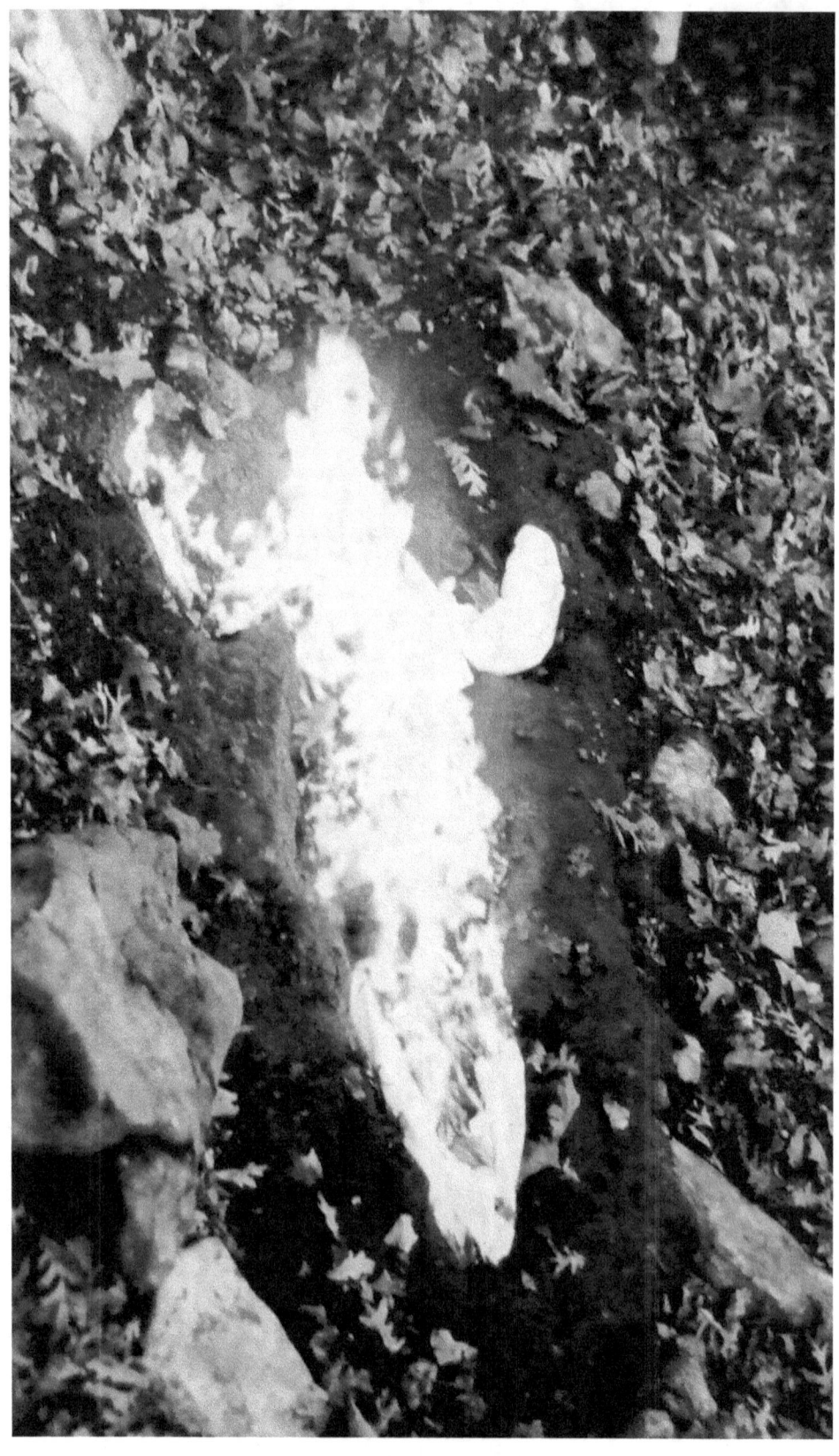

Ana Mendieta, Soul Silhouette On Fire, 1975

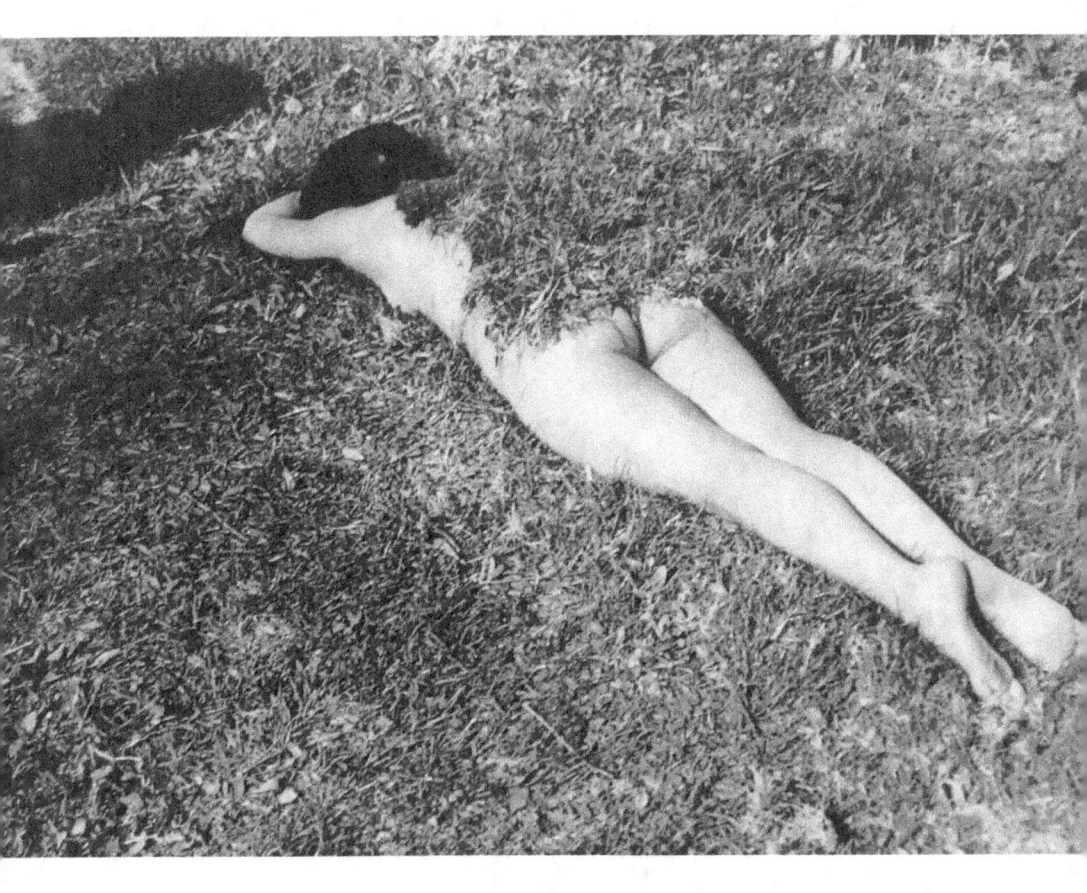

Ana Mendieta, Untitled (Grass On Woman), 1972

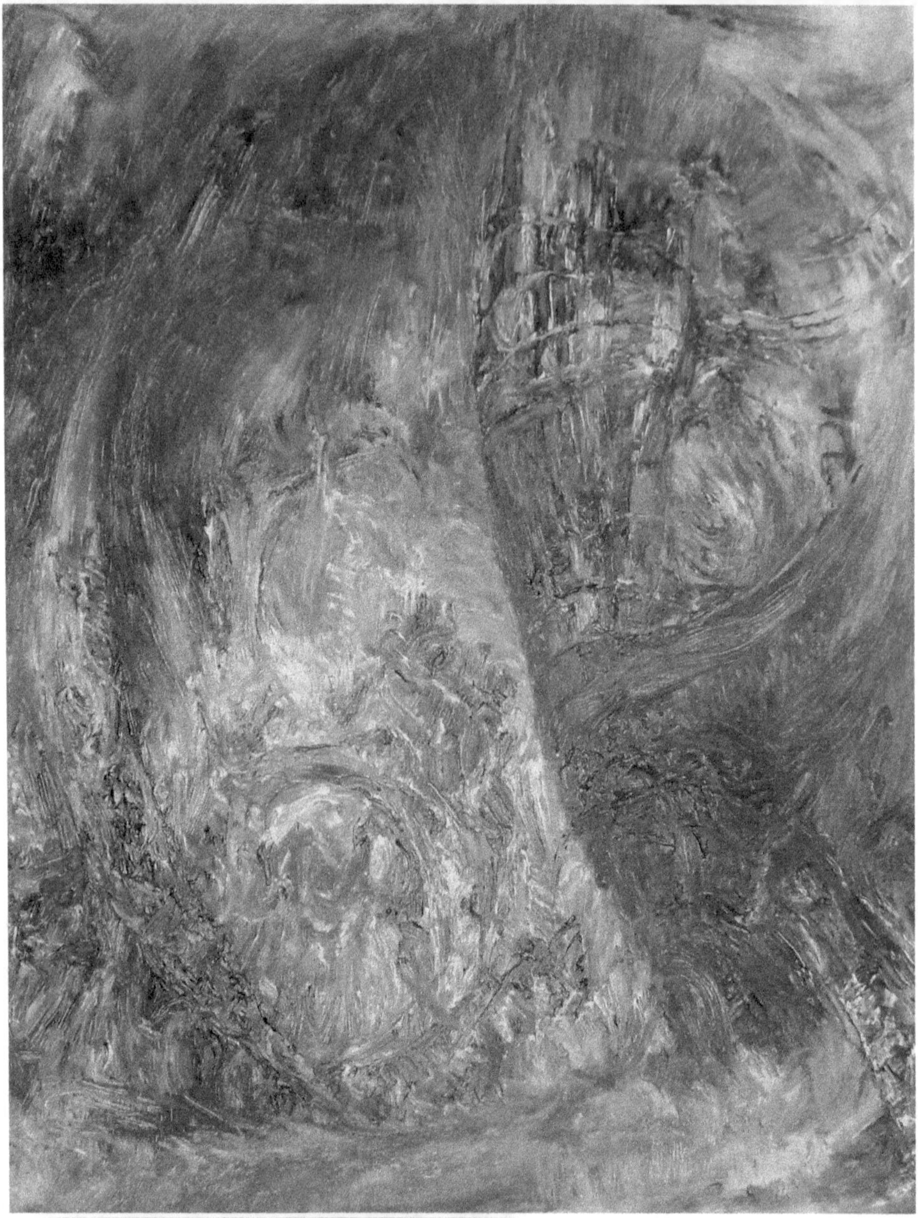

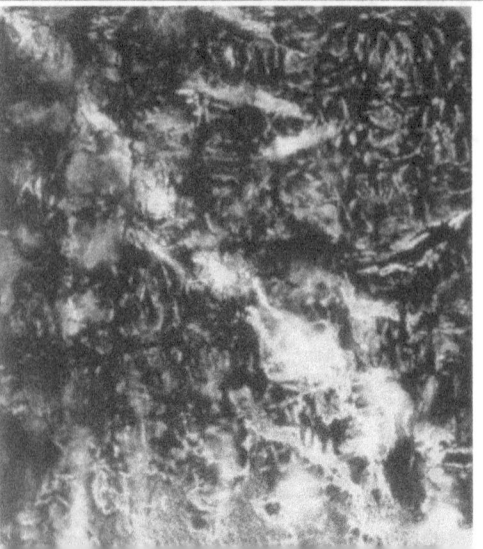

Thérèse Oulton, Hermetic Definition No. 2
1985 (above).
Undoings (left).

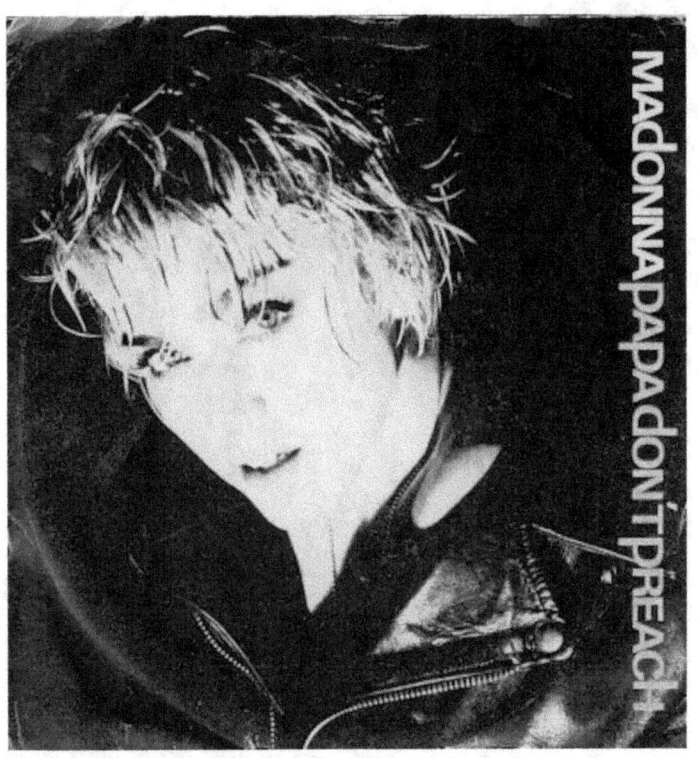

The pop star Madonna fused the sensuality of pop icon Marilyn Monroe with the untouchableness and sanctity of the Virgin Mary. She danced in a wedding dress in the video for Like a Prayer, and wrote the song Papa Don't Preach, mocking male authority figures, and her products Erotica and the book Sex flirted playfully with pornographic images.

That was the late 1980s and early 1990s. More recently, in the 2000s, that rebellious element in Madonna's output seems to have fizzled out.

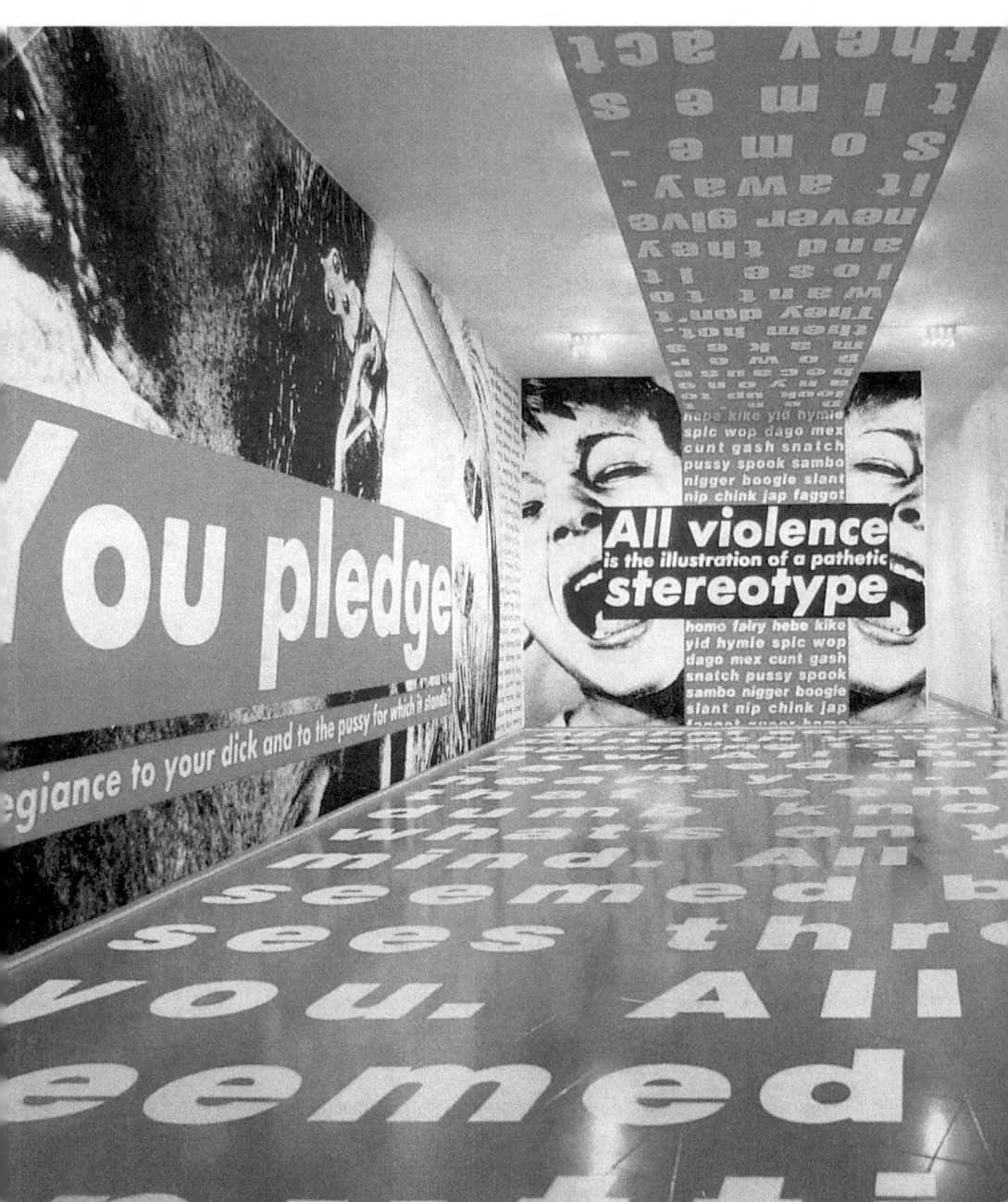

Barbara Kruger, Untitled, 1991

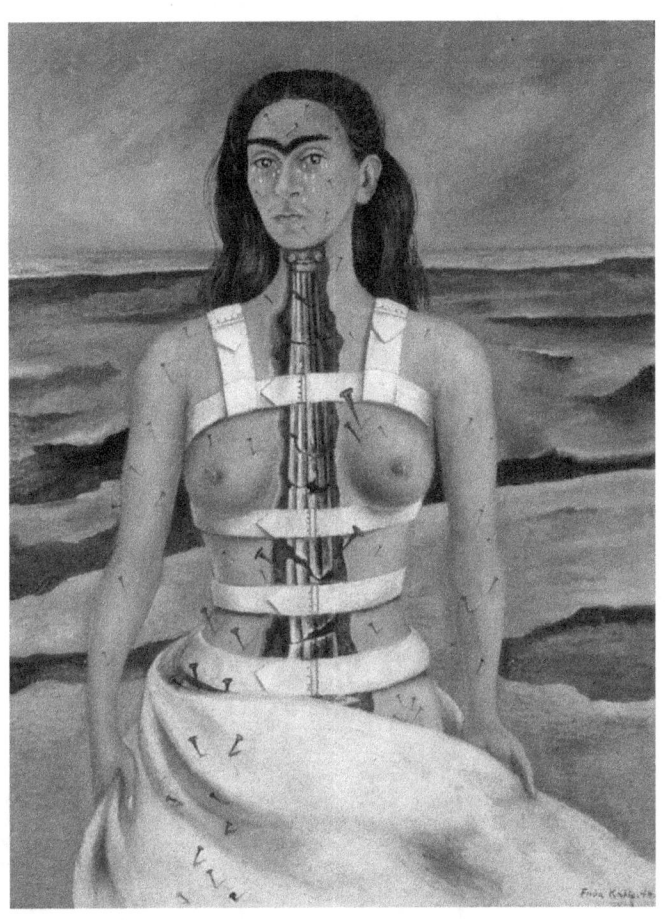

Frida Kahlo, The Broken Column, 1944,
Museo Dolores Olmedo Patino, Mexico City

5

WOMEN'S ART

Many feminists and commentators have studied the history of
women's art and women artists. Where are the 'great' women
painters, feminists ask, the artists who can stand alongside
Edouard Manet, Michelangelo Buonaroti, Sandro Botticelli and
Peter Rubens? So feminists have been discovering, rediscovering,
excavating and rewriting the past of art history. It turns out there
have been many, many brilliant women artists: Artemisia
Gentileschi, Sofonisba Anguissola, Gwen John, Mary Cassatt,
Berthe Morisot, Ana Mendieta, Suzanne Valadon, Käthe Kollwitz,
Frida Kahlo, Paula Modersohn-Becker, Ch'en Shu, Barbara
Longhi, Natalia Goncharova, Gabriele Münter, Nancy Holt,
Dorothea Lange, Julia Margaret Cameron, Harriet Hosmer, Ma
Shou-Chen, Anna Bilinska, Elisabeth Vigée-Lebrun, Françoise
Duparc, Rosalba Carriera, Angelica Kauffmann, Donna Dennis,
Georgia O'Keeffe, Diane Arbus, Judith Leyster, Sonia Delaunay,
Kuan Tao-Sheng, Ts'ao Miao-Ch'ing, Alice Aycock, Clara Peeters,
Catharina van Hemessen, and a host of postwar and
contemporary artists: Miriam Schapiro, Leonor Fini, Niki de Sant-
Phalle, Judy Chicago, Mary Beth Edelson, Barbara Hepworth,
Helen Frankenthaler, Cindy Sherman, Jennifer Bartlett, Elizabeth
Catlett, Alison Wilding, Barbara Kruger, Mary Duffy, Jo Spence,
Lyn Malcolm, Agnes Martin, Elizabeth Murray, Judy Rifka,
Louise Bourgeois, Nancy Graves, Katherine Porter, Susan
Rothenberg, Eva Hesse, Louise Nevelson, Lynda Benglis, Lee

Bontecou, Sherrie Levine, Rebecca Horn, Magdalena Abakan-owicz, Mary Miss, Judy Pfaff, Pat Steir, Catherine Murphy and Audrey Flack.

Many images made by women artists have become widely celebrated: Gentileschi's marvellous *Judiths*, and her luminous *Self-Portrait*; Käthe Kollwitz's emotionally-charged sculptures; Georgia O'Keeffe's vulva-shaped flowers; Barbara Hepworth's abstract holed forms; Mary Cassatt's independent form of Impressionism; Elisabeth Vigée-Lebrun's royal portraits, and so on. These works by women, though, are still not as highly regarded by the art world as, say, Jasper Johns' *American Flag* or Eugène Delacroix's *Sardanapale*.

One of the problems that feminists have addressed with regard to women's art is: can there be a truly 'female' or 'feminine' or 'women's' art? Is art made by women (women's art) ever completely free of patriarchal influences, structures, forms? Can there be a women's art that exists in its own 'female' space, away from patriarchy and masculinist ideas and experiences? Julia Kristeva is pessimistic on this contentious issue. For her, there has been no 'female writing' thus far in our culture. She says:

> If we confine ourselves to the *radical* nature of what is today called 'writing', that is, if we submit meaning and the speaking subject in language to a radical examination and then reconstitute them in a more polyvalent than fragile manner, there is nothing in either past or recent publications by women that permits us to claim that a specifically female writing exists.[1]

For Hélène Cixous, most writing, by men or women, is masculine. She writes: '[m]ost women are like this; they do someone else's – man's – writing, and in their innocence sustain it and give it voice, and end up producing writing that's in effect masculine.'[2] The notion of '*écriture féminine*' of Luce Irigaray and

---

1 "A partir de *Polylogue*", interview with Françoise van Rossum-Guyon, *Revue des sciences humaines*, vol. XLIV, no. 168, tr. Seán Hand, Oct-Dec 2977, 495f
2 Cixous: "Castration or Decapitation?", *Signs*, 7, 1, 52

Hélène Cixous is much discussed in feminist literary criticism.[3] It is rejected by Monique Wittig. Wittig also rejects the notion of 'man' and 'woman'. For her, 'woman' is a historical, political, ideological and cultural construct. She writes that "woman' has meaning only in heterosexual systems of thought and hetero-sexual economic systems'.[4]

Camille Paglia, one of the more outspoken of feminist critics, is not so optimistic about female artists:

> One of the many lies of women's studies is that European art history was written by white males and that feminism has conclusively rewritten that history by discovering and restoring major female artists excluded from the pantheon by patriarchal conspiracy. But European art history was not just written but created by white males. We may lament the limitations placed on women's training and professional access in the past, but what is done cannot be undone. The last 20 years of scholarship have brought many forgotten women artists to attention, but too often their presentation has been marred by anachronistic feminist rhetoric: feminism has not found a single major female painter or sculptor to add to the canon.[5]

The discussion of women's art and women artists is, though, many feminists feel, crucial to feminism. After all, *we know what male artists are like,* and we are utterly familiar with male art. We are surrounded, embedded, drenched, choked, smothered by patriarchal art and culture, by male-orientated, even if not specifically male-*made*, culture. Male projections, often onto women, have become dogma. Masculinist fear of the body, and sexuality, have been projected onto women, so that the vagina becomes a hell hole, the 'gateway to Hell'. As Luce Irigaray

3 Arleen B. Dallery: "The politics of the body: *écriture féminine*", in Alison M. Jaggar & Susan R. Bordo, eds. *Gender/ Body/ Knowledge: feminist reconstruction of being and knowing,* Rutgers University Press, New Brunswick, 1989; Deborah Cameron, 1990; Jan Montefiore: *Feminism and Poetry: Language, Experience, Identity in Women's Writing,* Pandora 1987; Andrea Nye: "The voice of the serpent: French feminism and the philosophy of language", in Ann Garry & Marilyn Pearsal, eds. *Women, Knowledge and Reality: explorations in feminist philosophy,* Unwin Hyman 1989

4 Wittig: "The Straight Mind, *Feminist Issues,* I:1, 110

5 Camille Paglia: "New Sexism for women", *The Guardian,* 30 September 30, 1993

writes: men's *'fantasies lay down the law'*.[6]

Feminists have, rightly, a lot to complain about. Look at any art history book: nearly all the names, either of artists or critics, are male. Books such as *Techniques of the World's Great Painters* are typical. *All* the fifty painters featured in this book male. Published in 1980, i.e. in the age of second wave feminism, around the time of Griselda Pollock and Rozsika Parker's *Old Mistresses: Woman, Art and Ideology* and Karen Petersen and J.J. Wilson's *Women Artists* were published, books such as *Techniques of the World's Great Painters* should have known better.

There are hundreds of art books which feature the same roll-call of male artists: in Robert Goldwater and Marco Treves' anthology *Artists on Art From the 14th to the 20th Century*, there are no women artists in amongst the quotes from one hundred and forty-one male artists. In Waldemar Januszczak's book, we find the usual litany of holy male artists: Giotto, Duccio, van Eyck, Piero, Leonardo, Bosch, Titian, Caravaggio, El Greco, Velásquez, Rubens, Rembrandt, Vermeer, Watteau, Reynolds, Constable, Ingres, Delacroix, Turner, Millet, Courbet, Manet, Monet, Renoir, Degas, van Gogh, Munch, Cézanne, Gauguin, Matisse, Picasso, Kandinsky, Bonnard, Hopper, Dali, Klee, Mondrian, Ernst, Pollock, Johns, Stella, Lichenstein, Hockney. These are the 'great' names, the 'great' surnames, of Art. They form a religion of art, a cult which decisively excludes women and the female voice. 'High art' is distinctly a male preserve, an area presided over and fiercely guarded by men and male ideology.

Of course, the reasons why there are so few exalted women artists in the art world are many and complex, having to do with economy, power, politics, law, ideology, sexuality, identity, etc. The guardians of 'high art' are also male: the critics and reviewers. The 'great' critics have always been male: Giorgio Vasari, Bruce Berenson, Jacob Burckhardt, Kenneth Clark, John Ruskin, Walter Pater, Friedrich Nietzsche, Leon Battista Alberti, Benvenuto Cellini.

Is there a true 'women's art'? Is there feminist art? What is the relation of feminist to masculinist art? Does 'feminist art' have to be made by women? These questions go to the heart of feminist and feminist cultural criticism. Feminist art is not simply all women's art, all women's 'experience' in/ of art, some feminists

---

6 Luce Irigaray: *Parler n'est jamais neutre*, tr. David Macey, in *The Irigaray Reader*, 94

state: '[f]eminist art is not the same as any art which emphasizes women's experience.'[7] Shoshana Felman has criticized Luce Irigaray's writings on 'women's' art and feminist æsthetics:

> Is [Irigaray] speaking *as* a woman, or *in the place of* the (silent) woman, *for* the woman, *in the name of* the woman? Is 'speaking as a woman' a fact determined by some biological *condition* or by a strategic, theoretical *position*, by anatomy or by culture? What if 'speaking as a woman' were not a simple 'natural' fact, could not be taken for granted?[8]

There are many feminists who advocate the exaltation of all manner of women artists, who argue for a 'women's art' based on women artists, who want us to look at women artists. There are other feminists who deny the primacy of the author, who say that the work – the text – is primary, who deny the transparency of the text. Toril Moi and many other feminists have questioned the humanist notion of 'realism' or 'authenticity' where a text is seen to reflect the actual experience of the one who created it. Humanist criticism sees a direct relation between author and text, assuming that the artwork is a 'direct expression' of the artist's experience. Artists, however, know that very often the artwork ends up being far away from what they intended to 'express' or 'communicate'.

The artwork, whether painting, sculpture, magazine, installation, dance, performance, etc – is not a 'person' or an individual, but a series of gestures, surfaces, motions, materials, signs, and so on. The link between artist/ author and artwork/ text is often very tenuous. As Toril Moi writes: '[w]hen the text no longer offers an individual grasped as the transcendental origin of language and experience, humanist feminism must lay down its arms.'[9] The artwork in cultural theory is not a direct extension of the artist, even though it is manufactured by and from her body, however indirectly. When the text is primary, the notion of an artist/ author dies. Roland Barthes writes:

---

7 Michele Barrett: "Feminism and the Definition of Cultural Politics", *Feminism, Culture and Politics*, ed. Rosalind Brunt & Caroline Rowan, and in Eagleton, ed, 163
8 Shoshana Felman: "The critical phallacy", *Diacritics*, Winter 1975, 3
9 *Sexual/ Textual Politics*, 80

> Once the Author is removed, the claim to decipher a text becomes quite
> futile. To give a text an Author is to impose a limit on that text, to
> furnish it with a final signified, to close the writing.[10]

But if the 'author' is dead, as Barthes contests, then there is no
one to 'blame' for producing pornography. When the anti-
pornography people point the finger at the producers of
pornographers and say, look, you've produced this shit, you're
being prosecuted under the Obscene Publications Act, or some
similar law, or the Dworkin-MacKinnon's anti-porn legislation,
the pornographers can turn round and say, 'sorry, we didn't
produce it. The 'author', you see, is dead.' If the 'author' is dead
and there are simply all manner of texts left, with readers/
viewers/ consumers consuming them.

There is no 'final' and definitive reading of any text, then, but
only endless openness, endless permutations of readings, which
shift continually, dependent upon a variety of factors, among
them: politics, ideology, identity, power, economy, class, race,
sex, etc. Sue Warrick Doederlein writes:

> New insights in linguistics and anthropology have surely given the lie
> to any view of autonomous works of art whose sanctity we must not
> violate and whose space we only enter (in our abject objectivity) 'to
> provide a reliable reading'. Feminist critics can (carefully) take
> certain postulates from current masculinist-endorsed hypotheses that
> will allow us never to apologize for 'misreading' or 'misinterpreting'
> a text again.[11]

But if there is an infinity of readings, then any reading of
pornography is possible. If people are consuming texts in an
infinity of readings, then there is no legislation that can fight
pornography, or any kind of art. No censorship would be
possible, because any reading would be possible. An infinity of
readings means an infinity of 'get-out clauses'. Say some child
pornographers are attacked by people who tell them: 'you are
producing degenerate, obscene, violent filth'. The pornographers
can turn round and say: 'no, sorry, you are mistaken. We are
producing scientific explorations of humanity complete with close-
up photographs'. Or the pornographers could reply: 'no, sorry,
you are wrong. We are producing incisive materialist critiques of

---

10 Barthes: *Image Music Text*, tr. Stephen Heath, Fontana 1977, 147
11 Sue Warrick Doederlein: "Comment on Jehlen", *Signs*, 8, 1, 1982, 165

capitalist ideology complete with detailed close-up photographs'. Or the pornographers could reply: 'no, sorry, you are utterly mistaken in your view of our product. This is random non-determinist multi-dimensional situationist stochastic art, complete with close-up illustrations of children's genitals.

If the 'author' is dead, there is perhaps no one to prosecute.

There are many problems, then, in creating a philosophy of feminist criticism, in looking at women authors and artists, in producing a tradition of 'feminine art'. Many feminist critics have addressed the matter of 'women's' or feminist art.[12] Focusing on women artists – Jane Austen, Emily Brontë, George Eliot, Emily Dickinson, Virginia Woolf and Gertrude Stein in writing, or Artemisia Gentileschi, Mary Cassatt, Gwen John, Berthe Morisot, Georgia O'Keeffe, Käthe Kollwitz and Suzanne Valadon among visual artists – is absolutely crucial. But what is the relation of the 'feminine' qualities of the woman artist to her work? Is not all art, of any kind, produced *within* patriarchal culture? Is it possible to make art that is utterly outside of patriarchy? Is the 'female tradition' of women artists simply patriarchal art made by women? If men, or masculine culture, has defined everything in culture, how can there by a truly 'feminine art'? These are important questions, that require much debate and analysis.

'Feminist art', then, aims to question all manner of notions of æsthetics, attitudes, assumptions, traditions, representations, meanings and mythologies. 'Feminist æsthetics' aims to rewrite, recreate, and rework received, established notions of art. 'Feminist art' remakes art from the foundations upwards. It seems

12 See H. Robinson, ed. *Visibly Female: feminism and art today*, Camden Press 1987; J.P.Stanley & S.J. Wolfe: "Toward a feminist æsthetic", *Chrysalis*, no. 6, 57-71; P. Palmer: *Contemporary Women's Fiction: narrative practice and feminist theory*, Harvester Wheatsheaf 1989; L. Nochlin: "Why are there no great women artists?", in V. Gornick & B. Moran, eds. *Women in Sexist Society*, 1971; R. Betterton, ed. *Looking On: Images of femininity in the visual arts and media*, Pandora Press 1987; D. Butturuff & E.L. Epstein, eds. *Women's Language and Style*, University of Akron, Akron 1978; Griselda Pollock: "A Politics of Art or an Aesthetics for Women?", *Feminist Art News*, 1981, no.5; Maggie Humm: *Feminist Criticism*, 1986; Barbara Smith: *Toward a Black Feminist Criticism*, Crossing Press, New York 1980; I.J. Nicholson, ed. *Feminism/ Postmodernism*, Routledge 1990; C. Belsey & J. Moore: *The Feminist Reader: Essays in the Politics of Literary Criticism*, Macmillan 1989; Gisela Ecker: *Feminist Aesthetics*, Women's Press 1985; Susan Santoro: *Towards a New Expression*, Rome 1974

to be an impossible task, but it has to be attempted. As Gisela Ecker writes: '[w]e have to be aware of the paradox that there cannot be any certainty about what is feminine in art but that we have to go looking out for it.'[13]

It is crucial to make art, to write, to create, as every feminist, of whatever political belief, agrees. You must write, because otherwise you get written. If you don't write, someone else will 'write' you. You'll be written over, written out, edited, selected, controlled, censored, cut up, packaged, suffocated. All feminists agree that, whatever one believes, and whatever one desires, whether emotionally, politically, or socially, writing and creating are absolutely essential. As Hélène Cixous states:

> And why don't you write? Write! Writing is for you, you are for you; your body is yours... Write, let no one hold you back, let nothing stop you... Women should break out of the snare of silence...[14]

You can 'read' creatively, if you don't write. Much of feminist theory is based on 'reading' texts as a woman, a feminist, a lesbian. If the author is 'dead', and the text is primary, then deeply engaging with texts is crucial. Hence the importance, too, of feminist æsthetic and philosophic criticism, which aims to interpret all manner of texts. The reader, at least, is 'real'. The reader, it would seem, is truly flesh and blood, not a linguistic abstraction. Even here, though, some feminists dispute the 'reality' or 'authenticity' of the body, for the body, like education or desire or the family, is culturally and socially conditioned. That is, there is no such thing as a 'pure' reality, a 'pure' experience, a 'pure' response to a text, a response that is not modulated by all manner of social, societal, familial, psychological, political, ideological and cultural influences. In feminism, the scenario is not simply a woman and a book, existing completely separately from everything else, in some utopian place. No, there is so much that gets in the way of the seemingly 'innocent' or 'pure' exchange between a woman and an artwork, a person and a text. But the personal response is crucial, and alive. Reading can be, in itself, radical and transformative.

Creating a 'feminist æsthetics' means writing/ rewriting language, art, culture, notions of knowledge and ontology, of

---

13 Gisela Ecker: *Feminist Aesthetics*, Women's Press 1985
14 H. Cixous: "The Laugh of the Medusa", in E. Marks, 246-7, 251

identity and politics, all manner of things. For Julia Kristeva, there is no 'other place' in language, for, as Ludwig Wittgenstein said, the world we live in is a world circumscribed by language. In effect, language 'writes' the world: to go beyond it is the quest for the 'wild zone', the utterly Other Place. For Kristeva, revolution must occur *within* symbolic (that is, patriarchal) language.[15] Women's writing or art becomes a literature of absence, of negative capability, revealing by what it does not reveal, forever outside yet also inside patriarchal discourse. As the Marxist-Feminist Literature Collective write:

> Women, who are speaking subjects but partially excluded from culture, find modes of expression which the hegemonic discourse cannot integrate. Whereas the eruptive word cannot make the culturally inaccessible, it can surely speak its absence.[16]

Julia Kristeva asks questions which are central to feminist æsthetics and 'women's' art. Will there be a visionary feminism which takes women's art (French feminists use the term 'writing' to cover cultural/ creative activities) into a new era?

> Or is it, on the contrary and as avant-garde feminists hope, that having started with the idea of difference, feminism will be able to break free of its belief in woman, Her power, her writing, so as to channel this demand for difference into each and every element of the female whole, and, finally, to bring out the singularity of each woman, and beyond this, her multiplicities, her plural languages, beyond the horizon, beyond sight, beyond faith itself?[17]

Kristeva is very positive, though, despite her insistence on absence. She is uncompromising; in "Freud and Love" she says she believes in the 'notion of emptiness, which is at the heart of the human psyche'.[18] Yet she is optimistic, too. Her philosophy is founded on absence, yet she often writes of the possibility that a

---

15 See Julia Kristeva: *Desire in Language,* 1980; *Révolution du language poétique,* Seuil, Paris 1974

16 Marxist-Feminist Literature Collective: "Women's Writing: *Jane Eyre, Shirley, Villette, Aurora Leigh*", in Francis Barker *et al,* eds. *1848: The Sociology of Literature,* in Eagleton, 1991, 197

17 J. Kristeva: *Women's Time,* in *The Kristeva Reader,* 208

18 J. Kristeva: *Histoires d'amour,* Denoël, Paris, 1983, and in *The Kristeva Reader,* 242

'wild zone' or otherness has been neglected, that there maybe a nighttime space, of the unconscious, of magic or otherness. In *Women's Time* she asks more questions:

> Is it because, faced with social norms, literature reveals a certain knowledge and sometimes the truth itself about an otherwise repressed nocturnal, secret and unconscious universe? Because it thus redoubles the social contract by exposing the unsaid, the uncanny? (*The Kristeva Reader*, 207)

And, again from *Women's Time*, Kristeva argues for aspects of female subjectivity that could exist outside of patriarchy:

> As for time, female subjectivity would seem to provide a specific measure that essentially retains *repetition* and *eternity* from among the multiple modulaties of time known through the history of civilizations. On the one hand, there are cycles, gestation, the eternal recurrence of a biological rhythm which conforms to that of nature and imposes a temporality whose stereotypes shock, but whose regularity and unison with what is experienced as extra-subjective time, cosmic time, occasion vertiginous visions and unnameable *jouissance*. On the other hand, and perhaps as a consequence, there is the massive presence of a monumental temporality, without cleavage or escape, which has so little to do with linear time (which passes) that the very word 'temporality' hardly fits: all-encompassing and infinite like imaginary space, this temporality reminds one of Kronos in Hesiod's mythology, the incestuous son whose massive presence covered all of Gaea in order to separate her from Ouranos, the father.[19]

Language is central to the creation of a 'feminist æsthetics'. Women are denied the place to really *speak*, as many feminists note. Luce Irigaray writes:

> When a girl begins to talk, she is already unable to speak of/ to herself. Being exiled in man's speech, she is already unable to auto-affect. Man's language separates her from her mother and from other women, and she speaks it without speaking in it.[20]

Mary Daly has written exuberantly of creating a new language, and her books – *Pure Lust*, *Gyn/ Ecology*, *Webster's First*

---

19 J. Kristeva: *Women's Time*, in *The Kristeva Reader*, 191
20 L. Irigaray: "The poverty of psychoanalysis", *The Irigaray Reader*, 101

New Intergalactic Wickedary of the English Language – are full of energetic incantations of a new 'women's' language:

> Our call of the wild is a call to dis-possess our Selves of the shrouds, the winding sheets of words. We eject, banish, dispose the possessing language – spoken and written words, body language, architectural language, technological language, the language of symbols and of institutional structures – by enspiriting our Selves. The Sister Selves are the only Selves who can bond together and con-quest beyond, before, beneath, and around the seductive pseudowords. (*Gyn/Ecology*, 345)

So far in our history, men have done most of the 'speaking', or male-made culture has. Language itself, as Dale Spender notes, is 'man-made'.[21] And everybody knows somebody who speaks as the person (the male) does in Xavière Gauthier's essay:

> the frightful masculine fashion of speaking always surprises me. Speaking in order to be right – how ridiculous! In fact, to put someone else in the wrong. Speaking to nail the listener's trap shut. Speaking to put her in her place: man's language, man's rod.[22]

It is not a simple act of substituting feminism for masculinism, women for men, female for male. Griselda Pollock writes:

> Feminism in culture cannot be reduced to substituting *women's* for men's subjectivities in an otherwise unchanged notion of art as self-expression. It is not, therefore, the fact that activities or representations are undertaken by *women* which renders them feminist. Their feminism is crucially a matter of *effect*. To be feminist at all work must be conceived within the framework of a structural, economic, political and ideological critique of the power relations of society and with a commitment to collective action for their radical transformation.[23]

The question we keep returning to is: can there be a 'female' of 'feminine' 'wild zone', an utterly non-patriarchal, non-male space? If it is true, as Andrea Dworkin maintains, that '[m]en have defined the parameters of every subject' (*Pornography*, 7), how can there be an extra-masculinist place? For Julia Kristeva,

21 Dale Spender, 1985, 12
22 Gauthier: "Why Witches?", in *Sorcières*, 1, 1976, in E. Marks,200
23 Griselda Pollock: "Feminism and Modernism", in R. Parker, 1987

the problem is not one, as in the feminism of Hélène Cixous and Luce Irigaray, of essence, but of positionality, a question of discourse and viewpoint, rather than biology and essentialism.

The problems stem, partly, from accepting and using systems and approaches of criticism, philosophy, psychology and politics that are male-made or masculinist. It's all very well, feminists comment, using the vulva or womb as a powerful image of the feminine, as artists such as Judy Chicago have done in many works (one of Chicago's ceramic pieces is entitled *The Cunt as Temple, Tomb, Cave and Flower*),[24] but this very notion plays into the hands of men and patriarchal attitudes, which so often reduce women to sex objects, so that the body becomes mere 'cunt'.[25] And a female artist such as Nancy Grossman, who employs the imagery of bondage, S/ M and fetish pornography, seems to be wholly phallic and patriarchal. Her images depict cult, kitsch gear, such as leather, zips, straps, chains, and guns in erotic contexts.[26] Her views on art are patriarchal and phallic, those of de Sade, Baudelaire, Bataille, Reich, Miller: she wishes to get rid of taboos: 'to have a head and no feelings, to have a vagina and not fill it, to have a penis and not stick it in – that is not living.'[27]

How is it possible, though, to employ strategic, radical, political and specifically feminist approaches to criticism, philosophy, psychology and politics, when the means and structures and approaches we have are shot through with masculinist notions? As Elaine Showalter says:

> One of the problems of the feminist critique is that it is male-orientated. If we study stereotypes of women, the sexism of male critics, and the limited roles women play in literary history, we are not learning what women have felt and experienced, but only what

24 Judy Chicago: *The Dinner Party*, 1975-9; *The Cunt as Temple, Tomb, Cave and Flower*, c. 1974, china pencil on porcelain, collection; the artist; *Female Rejection Drawing*, 1974, coloured pencil on paper, 30 x 40in, collection: the artist; *Earth Birth*, from *The Birth Project*, 1982-3, sprayed fabric paint and quilting, 152 x 365cm, ACA Gallery, New York
25 See Lisa Tickner: "The Body Politic: Female Sexuality and Women Artists since 1970", *Art History*, 1:2, June 1978, 236-51; also Lynda Nead: *The Female Nude*, 65f
26 Nancy Grossman: *Figure*, 1970, ink on paper, 45.5. x 34.5in, Princeton Art Museum, Princeton
27 Nancy Grossman, quoted in Tilly, 74

men have thought women should be.[28]

If there really is no non-patriarchal culture space, then feminism is going to end up somewhat limited in its scope and depth, and limited in its effects. Perhaps. If there is no true female 'wild zone', a place which is strange, terrifying, ecstatic and truly beyond men or, rather, beyond male culture, this is a depressing thought. As Toril Moi writes in *Sexual/ Textual Politics*: '[i]f there is no space uncontaminated by patriarchy from which women can speak, it follows that we really don't need a fulcrum at all: there is simply nowhere else to go.' (81)

Of course, it might be utopian to think there is a truly non-patriarchal, non-male place. But, after all, men have their own 'wild zone', their thoroughly male/ masculinist space. Why not women too?

Some of the problems of feminist poetics, and of feminism in general, is the constant reference to patriarchy and masculinist experiences and ideas. If men and patriarchy are always the measure of all things, the results will always be limited, some feminists claim. That is, being female is simply being 'not-male'. Being feminist always means being non or anti masculinist. As Luce Irigaray puts it: '[b]eing a woman is equated with not being a man.' (*Je, tu, nous*, 71)

This cannot be the case. It's not right to use men/ masculinity/ patriarchy as a guide or measure for feminist æsthetics and criticism. Because everything said will be referenced to men and male constructions. Far better to speak of *difference*, to state that women's creations, experiences and ideas are not the other side of the ontological coin from men's; they are different. Instead of saying all things female or feminine are simply the counterpart or companion, or opposite, of all things male and masculine, it is, perhaps, more fruitful to say all things female and feminine are *different* from all things male and masculine. Of course, a mythology or economy of *difference* has its

---

28 Elaine Showalter: "Towards a feminist poetics", in Mary Jacobus, 1979, 27

problems, as commentators acknowledge,[29] but it does free feminists up from always referring to men, masculinity and patriarchy.

The notion of 'difference' is controversial in feminist philosophy. There is cultural, psychological, political and emotional difference, but most problematic is sexual and biological difference, the culture of 'difference' based in sexuality and the body.

The figure of the lesbian and the culture of lesbianism becomes central to some approaches of feminism, because the lesbian stands outside of patriarchy, even as she is defined by heterosexuality and patriarchy. Men cannot control lesbian culture in the same way they can control heterosexual culture. As Alice, Gordon, Debbie and Mary say: '[l]esbians, by loving women and not men, pose a direct threat to the very basis of male supremacy.'[30] Feminism and lesbian culture can lead to separatism, where patriarchy is avoided – not only culturally, but physically. Janet Dixon writes that '[s]eparatism is to feminism what fundamentalism is to Christianity.'[31] The extreme of separatism is the creation of an all-woman state, a utopian female and feminine space. Utopian, separatist or lesbian feminism, then, looks towards a radical and revolutionary transformation of the world.. The opposers of radical separatism claim it is fascistic and racist, in its destruction of all things built, written and produced by men.

Part of lesbian culture seeks to get beyond patriarchy, and lesbian-orientated art is perhaps one way of producing non-patriarchal art. As Monique Wittig says of the lesbian: '[l]esbian is the only concept that I know of which is beyond the categories of sex (man and woman)'.[32]

Other feminist critics have said that lesbianism is not a culture

---

29 See Teresa de Lauretis: "The essence of the triangle or, taking the risk of essentialism seriously", *differences*, 1 (2), 1989, 3-37; Domna C. Stanton: "Difference on Trial: a critique of the maternal metaphor in Cixous, Irigaray and Kristeva", in N. Miller, 1986, 157-82; Rosi Braidotti: "The ethics of sexual difference: the case of Foucault and Irigaray", in *Australian Feminist Studies*, 3, 1986, 1-13

30 Alice, Gordon, Debbie and Mary: "Separatism", in Sarah Lucia Hoagland & Julia Penelope, eds. *For Lesbians Only: A Separatist Anthology*, Onlywomen Press 1988, 31-40

31 Janet Dixon: "Separatism", *Spare Rib*, 192 (1988), 6

32 Monique Wittig: "One is not born a woman", in Hoagland, op.cit., 440

that exists truly outside of patriarchy. In fact, says Elizabeth Meese, 'lesbian as an attack on hetero-relations, takes (its) place within the structure of the institution of heterosexuality. The lesbian is born of/ in it.'[33] Defined by heterosexual patriarchy, lesbianism may be limited in its potential for radically transforming society, say some feminist critics.[34] It's always going to be held back by aspects of patriarchal society. The feminist social movement totally away from patriarchal culture is all the more urgent, then, if the radical forms of feminism, lesbianism and separatism are to be realized.

---

33 Meese, in Karla Jay and Joanna Glasgow: *Lesbian Texts and Contexts: Radical Revisions*, New York University Press, New York 1990, 82

34 See Bonnie Zimmerman, and Sonya Andermahr's essays in Sally Munt, 4, 133, 151; Sally Miller Gearhart: *The Wanderground*, Persephone Press, Watertown 1978; Joanna Russ: *The Female Man*, Women's Press, 1976; S. Rowbotham: *Beyond the Fragments: Feminism and the Making of Socialism*, Merlin 1979; Adrienne Rich: "Toward a woman-centred university", in *On Lies, Secrets and Silence*, Novotony, New York 1979; C. Moraga & G. Amzaldue, eds. *This Bridge Called my Back: Writings by Radical Women of Color*, Persephone Press, Watertown 1981; Jill Johnston: *Lesbian Nation: The Feminist Solution*, Simon & Shuster, New York 1974; Radicalesbians: "The woman-identified woman", in A. Koedt, ed. *Radical Feminism*, Quadrangle, New York 1973; Adrienne Rich: "Compulsory heterosexuality and lesbian existence", *Signs*, vol. 5, no.4, 631-660

6

WOMEN SCULPTORS

Sculpture is a three dimensional projection of primitive feeling: touch, texture, size and scale, hardness and warmth, evocation and compulsion to move, live and love.

Barbara Hepworth[35]

Sculpture is of course supremely erotic in its sense of surface. The sense of touch is not crucial to all sculpture, but without it sculpture loses some of its *frisson*, its visceral effect. Painters too explore the eroticism of touch, its tactile element in paintings. Rebecca Purdun paints with her fingers. Her billowy, smeared canvases resound with the vibrancy of the touch of the human hand, the eloquence of the pure gesture.[36] She writes: '[t]he more you get physically into the paint, you lose, you forget yourself. You become the paint, you become the form, you become the structure.'[37] Tactile surfaces are found everywhere in modern sculpture – think of the felt in Dorthea Tanning's sculptures, or the fur in Meret Oppenheim's *Object* or wood in Louise Bourgeois'

35 Hepworth: quoted in A.M. Hammacher: *The Sculpture of Barbara Hepworth*, Abrams, New York 1968, 99
36 Rebecca Purdum: *In Threes*, 1985, oil on canvas, 210.2 x 204.5cm,
37 Purdun, in C. Jolles: *Rebecca Purdun: Abstract Painting*, Jack Tilton Gallery, catalogue, 1986

works.[38] Bourgeois explores the relations between form and eroticism, volume and psychology, shape and nature. Her forms are nearly always dealing with eroticism – her *Nature Study*, for instance, feature those bulbous volumes which are practically her trademark, echoing breasts, clitorises, vulvas, buttocks, heads, hands, knees, tongues, all the parts of the eroticized body.[39]

The works of contemporary sculptors such as Alison Wilding are distinctly erotic. Wilding's *Hemlock III*, for example, is, like her *Blueblack*, a wooden dish containing hemlock, lead, lime and beeswax, hinting at alchemical transmutations.[40] The dish with its dangerous substances is a kind of womb, a motif or experience that appears in much of modern sculpture, from Judy Chicago's *Dinner Table* to the womb interiors of Louise Bourgeois and others.

Alison Wilding's sculpture often features two elements, one is often large, the other, small.[41] These two elements are luscious and mysterious, beyond interpretation, though some interpret them as masculine and feminine elements, the twin poles of heterosexuality, which are involved in some arcane dance or dalliance.[42]

Sexuality in Alsion Wilding's art is immediately apparent, as in her sculpture *Minge* (1982). This is made from a left-over piece of metal, looking distinctly bird-like, with two pointed 'wings'. In the centre, though, the sensuality of the sculpture is made

38 Louise Bourgeois: *One and Others*, 1955, painted wood, 18 x 20 x 17in, Whitney Museum of American Art, New York. See Deborah Wye: *Louise Bourgeois*, MOMA, New York 1982, Carl R. Baldwin: "Louise Bourgeois: An Iconography of Abstraction", *Art in America*, April 1975, 82-3, Corrinne Robbins: "Louise Bourgeois: Primordial Environments", *Arts Magazine*, June 1976, 81-3, Paul Gardner: "The Discreet Charm of Louise Bourgeois", *Art News*, Feb 1980, 80-86; Robert Storr: *Louise Bourgeois*, Galerie Maeght Lelong, Zurich 1985
39 Bourgeois: *Nature Study*, 1984, bronze, 30 x 19 x 15in, Serpentine Gallery, London
40 Alison Wilding: *Hemlock III*, 1986, lime, hemlock, lead, beeswax, pigment, Karsten Schubert; *Blueblack*, 1984, lime & elm woods, wax, lead, 36 x 28 x 49cm, collection: the artist
41 See Alison Wilding's *Nature: Blue and Gold*, 1984, brass, ash, oil and pigment, 47 x 109 x 22cm, British Council Collection, and *Untitled*, 1980, Arts Council of Great Britain, London; *Locust*, 1983, wood, wax, copper, 208 x 71 x 46cm, collection: the artist
42 See Lynne Cooke: *Alison Wilding*, Arts Council 1985; L. Biggs: *Between Object and Image*, British Council 1986; Wendy Beckett, 116;Terry A. Neff, 43-5

apparent by a red triangle made with a wax crayon heated up. 'There is exuberance in the way it makes wings of legs, like a sexual cherub', wrote John McEwen.[43] Wings extending out from some core, globe or cylinder is a favourite Wilding motif. Sculptures such as *Meridian II* and *Hemlock II* feature little wings either side of a central node.

The sexual connotations are both obvious and limiting: the wings as labia and the nodule as a clitoris is an obvious parallel, and, in the case of *Minge*, it is deliberately meant. It is limiting, too, for Wilding's sculpture, like any sculpture, goes far beyond a genital or body-centred sensuality. The eroticism of Wilding's sculpture, like most sculpture, is not confined to vulvas, clitorises or penises; neither is it limited to any particular part of the body, or any particular sexual or gender identity; or any particular sort of sexuality; or any particular socio-political interpretation of sexuality. Thus, the work and title, *Minge*, like Wilding's other sculptures, is not feminist nor anti-feminist, not for this or that form of sexuality or sexual politics, not wholly representational nor wholly abstract.

Alison Wilding herself stresses the enigmatic nature of her work: '[t]he obverse of making is looking, not telling',[44] and she emphasizes, as so many artists do, the making of the sculpture: '[t]he making and doing processes...[are] always the mainspring of the work'.[45]

At the same time, however, touching is an exercise of power, as Andrea Dworkin reminds us: '[a]nyone whose legal status is that she exists to be touched, intimately, inside the boundaries of her own body, is controlled, made use of: a captive inside a legally constructed cage.' (*Intercourse*, 196) Sigmund Freud too recognized the power relation exercised in the mere act of touching: '[t]ouching is the first step towards obtaining any sort of control over, or attempting to make use of, a person or object.'[46]

The eroticism of sculpture is everywhere affirmed in 'high art' itself, and in 'high art' cultural criticism. Of course, a lot of this has to do with the eroticism of the nude human form, something

---

43 John McEwen: "Alison Wilding: *The Stuff of Metaphor*", in
Transformation; New Sculpture From Britain, British Council 1983, 57.
44 Wilding, quoted in Wendy Beckett, 116
45 Wilding, quoted in Terry A. Neff, 45
46 Freud: *Totem and Taboo and Other Works*, tr. James Strachey & Anna
Freud, *Standard Works*, vol 13, Hogarth Press 1955, 33-4

that thousands of sculptors have explored and exploited. Renaissance sculptors – Luca della Robbia, Lorenzo Ghiberti, Andrea del Verrocchio, Pietro Lombardo, Michel Colombe – systematically exaggerated the sexuality of the body. Donatello's famous *David*, for instance, is a highly camp, homoerotic boy, an icon of stylized homoeroticism.[47] (A similar eroticization occurs in Andrea del Verrocchio's *David*, Benvenuto Cellini's *Perseus*, Giovanni Bologna's *Mercury*.)[48] This Renaissance eroticization of the human form finds its apotheosis in, of course, Michelangelo Buonaroti, whose *Dawn*, *David*, early and late *Pietàs*, and of course the most voluptuous of all figurative statues, the *Dying Slave*. The heroic homoeroticism of Michelangelo's sculpture continues throughout post-Renaissance sculpture. In, for instance, the bombast and masculine power of Antonio Canova's *Hercules and Lichas*, or Gian Lorenzo Bernini's *David*.[49] And there is much homoeroticism in that most sinister of all forms of sculpture, fascist art: in, for instance, Josef Thorak's *Comradeship*, two monumental male nudes with the bodies of he-men, supermen, Nietzschean *Übermensch*, clasping each other by the hand. The statues were commissioned by the Nazi government.[50] Fascist sculpture typically presents an ascetic, aggressive but banal stance, where eroticism is suppressed but never completely erased, as so much of fascist art depicts naked people. See, for the apotheosis of violence and banality, Ferruccio Vecchi's statue of Benito Mussolini.[51]

The eroticism of celebrated statues of the ancient and Classical world, such as the *Venus de Milo*,[52] has been seen by some feminists as another manifestation of patriarchal culture's dismemberment of the female form. So many statues of the ancient world are headless or armless. For feminists, this fragmentation of the female body echoes that of pornography, where women's

47 Donatello: *David*, c. 1440-2, bronze, Museo Nazionale, Florence
48 Benvenuto Cellini: *Perseus with the Head of Medusa*, 1554, bronze, Loggia dei Lanzi, Florence; Giovanni da Bologna: *Mercury*, 1564, Museo Nazionale, Florence; Andrea del Verrocchio: *David*, c. 1475, bronze, Museo Nazionale, Florence
49 Canova: *Hercules and Lichas*, 1812-5, marble, 138in high, Gallery of Modern Art, Rome; Bernini: *David*, 1623-4, marble, Galleria Borghese, Rome
50 Josef Thorak: *Comradeship*, 1937
51 Ferruccio Vechi: *The Empire*, 1939-40
52 *Venus de Milo*, 2nd or 1st centuries BC, Parian marble, Louvre, Paris

bodies are cut up, sometimes literally (as in S/ M, 'snuff' porno-graphy, and the pornography of amputees). Any number of (mainly male) artists have depicted armless and/ or legless and/ or headless women (Gustave Courbet in his infamous 1866 torso of a woman, Eric Gill, Bill Brandt, Edvard Munch in his 'cruel' *Madonna*, etc).[53]

Other sexist and heterosexist depictions of people (i.e. women) in sculpture include Alberto Giacometti's *Spoon Woman*, a view of woman as Earth Mother, a totemic figure;[54] Gaston Lachaise's *Standing Woman*, one of those smooth, curvy Goddess types, also favoured by Aristide Maillol;[55] Hans Bellmer's bizarre *Dolls*, where the slit of a vulva is where the head would be, and set amidst exaggerated, bulbous forms;[56] Henri Gaudier-Brzeska's *Red Stone Dancer*, though it attempts a new way of depicting gesture and posture in space, is still sexist;[57] Elie Nadelman's *Dancer*, like Paul Manship's *Dancer and Gazelles*, and Edgar Degas' *Dancer* sculptures, is also sexist;[58] and Ernst Kirchner's *Standing Nude* is pornography masquerading as art, but then, most of his depictions of women are pornography.[59]

Contemporary women sculptors such as Alice Aycock, Mary Miss, Nancy Graves, Rebecca Horn, Eva Hesse, Alison Wilding and Louise Nevelson out-dazzle the painters. The bombastic, 'monumental', massive and brash 3-D art of contemporary sculpture was not made exclusively by male artists. Mary Miss

53 See Bill Brandt: *Nude: London 1977*, silver gelatin print, Estate of Bill Brandt; Eric Gill: *Life study of a woman*, 1927, pencil, Victoria & Albert Museum; and see Saunders, 75f

54 Giacometti: *Spoon Woman*, 1926, bronze, 57.2in high, Kunsthaus, Zurich

55 Gaston Lachaise: *Standing Woman*, 1912-27, bronze, 70in high, Whitney Museum of American Art, New York

56 Bellmer: *La Poupée*, 1936, painted bronze, 16.8in high, Musée National d'Art Moderne, Paris

57 Henri Gaudier-Breska: *Red Stone Dancer*, 1914, waxed stone, 33.5in high, Tate Gallery, London

58 Degas: *Dancer Putting On Her Stocking*, bronze, 17in high, Metropolitan Museum of Art, New York; Elie Nadelman: *Dancer*, c.1918, painted wood, 28.5in high, Robert Isaacson Gallery, New York; Paul Manship: *Dancer and Gazelles*, 1916, bronze, 32.2in high, Smithsonian Institute, Washington DC

59 Kirchner: *Standing Nude*, 1908-12, wood, painted yellow, 35.5in, Stedelijk Museum, Amsterdam

created a 5-acre scale work in Illinois, while Nancy Holt produced gigantic *Sun Tunnels*, 18ft long pipes that were 9 feet high with many holes punched in the side, to let light in.[60] Helen Escobedo has created some huge concrete and steel sculptures which 'attempt to fuse hard-edge geometric forms with nature's organic manifestations' as she puts it. Works such as *Snake* rise impressively from the Earth, celebrating the flux and movement of organic forms.[61]

Many of the products of contemporary sculpture celebrated by critics, however, have been made, predictably, by male artists: Donald Judd's 'specific objects', those blocks of aluminium and plexiglass that 'climb' gallery walls,[62] Tony Smith's monumental cubes with their *thereness*, the primacy of presence, not effect,[63] Dan Flavin's mesmeric fluorescent tubes,[64] Sol LeWitt's

---

60 Mary Miss: *Field Rotation*, 1981, wood, steel, gravel, earth, 5-acre site, central well 60 ft square and 7 feet deep, Governors' University, Park Forest South, Illinois; Nancy Holt: *Sun Tunnels*, 1973-6, concrete, each pipe 18 ft long, 9ft high, Great Basin Desert, near Lucin, Utah
61 Helen Escobedo: *Snake,* 1980-1, painted steel, 49ft high, National University of Mexico Cultural Centre
62 Donald Judd: *Untitled*, 1968, ten units, each 9 x 40in x 31in, height 14'3", Nelson A. Rockefeller Empire State Plaza Art Collection, New York. See Donald Judd: *Complete Writings, 1959-1975*; New York University Press, 1975, William Agee: "Unit, Series, Site: A Judd Lexicon", *Art in America*, May 1975, 40-49, P. Carlson: "Donald Judd's Equivocal Objects", *Art in America*, Jan 1984, 114-8; Donald Kuspit: "Donald Judd", *Artforum*, vol. 23, no.5, February 1985, Barbara Haskell: *Donald Judd*, Whitney Museum of American Art, New York, 1988, Brydon Smith: *Donald Judd*, National Gallery of Canada, Ottawa 1975
63 Tony Smith: *Die*, 1962, 72 x 72 x 72in, Paula Cooper Gallery, New York. See Lucy Lippard: *Tony Smith*, Thames & Hudson 1972, Gene Baro: "Toward Speculation in Pure Form", *Art International*, Summer 1967, 27-31, E. Greene: "Morphology of Tony Smith's Work", *Artforum*, April 1974, 54-9
64 Dan Flavin: *Untitled (to the "innovator" of Wheeling Peachblow)*, 1968, 96.5 x 96.5 x 5.7in, Museum of Modern Art, New York; *Untitled*, 1976, pink, blue, green fluorescent light, 96in high, Saatchi Collection, London. See Ira Licht: "Dan Flavin", *Artscanada*, Dec 1968, 50-57, William Wilson: "Dan Flavin: Fiat Lux", *Art News*, Jan 1970, 48-51; Jack Burnham: "A Dan Flavin Retrospective in Ottawa", *Artforum*, vol.8, no.4, December 1969, 48-55

Conceptual cubes, Richard Serra's huge 'walls' or slabs of steel,[65] Carl Andre's plates of steel, copper and zinc.[66] One of the most exciting developments of contemporary sculpture and art is the installation, the taking-over of a whole space or environment – the floor, walls and ceiling, as in Rebecca Horn's *Ballet of the Woodpecker*, a room full of mirrors, or Sylvia Stone's *Crystal Palace*.[67]

Among women artists, Eva Hesse is particularly powerful. Her artworks hang from ceilings, in rows, made of rubber, latex, cloth, wire, fibreglass, evoking organic forms in ambivalent, sensual ways.[68] Pieces such as *Ingeminate* offer up a mysterious affirmation of life in the form of two coils of cord connected by a long piece of surgical hose. *Sans II*, meanwhile, is a dozen rectangular 'compartments' made from fibreglass which hints at some obscure systematization of flesh and organic form. Hesse wrote: '[i]f I can

65 Richard Serra: *Clara-Clara*, 1983, Cor-Ten steel, installation, Jardin des Tuileries, Paris. See Rosalind E. Kraus: "Richard Serra: Sculpture Redrawn", *Artforum*, May 1972, 38-43, Douglas Crimp: "Richard Serra: Sculpture Exceeded", *October*, Fall 1981, 67-78
66 Carl Andre: *Lead Piece (144 Lead Plates)*, overall 75 x 144.8 x 145.5in, Museum of Modern Art, New York. See Kenneth Baker: "Andre in Retrospect", *Art in America*, April 1980, 88-94, Diane Waldman: "Holding the Floor", *Art News*, Oct 1970, 60-2, 75-9, Phyllis Tuchman: "Background of a Minimalist: Carl Andre", *Artforum*, March 1978, 29-33; Enno Develing: *Carl Andre*, Gemeentenmeuseum, The Hague 1969
67 Sylvia Stone: *Crystal Palace*, 1971-2, plexiglass, 6.5 x 14 x 16ft, Andre Emmerich Gallery, New York; Rebecca Horn; *Ballet of the Woodpecker*, 1986-7, room installation with mirrors, small hammers and a painting machine,330 x 230cm (4 mirrors), 330 x 125cm (4 mirrors), Eric Franck Gallery, Geneva; Red Grooms & Mimi Gross: *The City of Chicago*, 1967, mixed media, c. 12 x 25 x 25ft, Art Institute of Chicago
68 Eva Hesse: *Contingent*, 1969, reinforced fibreglass and latex over cheesecloth, each of 8 units, 9.5-14 x 3-4ft, Australian National Gallery, Caberra; *Aught*, 1968, double sheets of latex rubber, polyethylene plastic inside, 4 units, each 78in high, collection: the artist; *Ice Piece*, 1969, fibreglass and wire, 62 x 1in, Xavier Fourcade Gallery, New York; see Bill Barrette: *Eva Hesse's Sculpture*: Catalogue Raissonné, New York 1989, Rosalind Krauss & Eva Hesse: *Eva Hesse: Sculpture*, Whitechapel Art Gallery 1979; Cindy Nemser: "My Memories of Eva Hesse", *Feminist Art Journal*, Winter 1973, 12-3

name the content... it's the total absurdity of life.'[69]

Louise Nevelson produces huge reliefs or structures which are like Cubist or Constructionist altarpieces full of objects, various articles made of wood, all painted in one colour, black, white or gold: chair legs, railings, door knobs.[70] Her sculptures are like magical cupboards, vertical dreamscapes created from boxes stacked on top of each other.

In Barbara Hepworth's art, organic forms are not sexualized, as they are in so many other (male) sculptors. As with Brancusi, Hepworth's art hovers between subjectivity and objectivity, between natural form and æsthetic abstraction (as in her *Two Forms*, for example.)[71] Like Brancusi, Hepworth maintained that she always returned to nature, and took her inspiration from nature. For her, nature meant the (Cornish) landscape, and the human body. 'We return always to the human form – the human form in landscape', she said.[72] Her sculpture stems from emotion and expression, from feeling: 'I rarely draw what I see – I draw what I feel in my body', she remarked.[73] Hepworth's distinctive forms, with their smooth curves and holes, are clearly sensual objects.[74] Hepworth acknowledged the sensuality of sculptural forms (see the quote, above). In 1969 Elizabeth Catlett took the holed form of Hepworth and suppressed the erotic dimension to produce a political work that celebrated 'the struggle for liberation by black women in this country and everywhere' (Petersen & Wilson, 142).

Käthe Kollwitz's monumental pieces are heavy with life, heavy with grave feelings, the weight of life on one's shoulders. This emotional gravity is apparent in powerful sculptures such as her *Pietà*, where Christ lays in his mother's lap, as in Sandro

---

69 Cindy Nemser: "An interview with Eva Hesse", *Artforum*, May 1970, 62

70 Louise Nevelson: *Royal Tide IV*, 1960, wood, 1 x 14ft, Ludwig Museum, Cologne; *Sky Cathedral – Moon Garden Plus One*, 1957-60, black painted wood, 9.1 x 10.1 x 1.6ft, collection: A. & M. Glimcher, New York

71 Hepworth: *Two Forms*, 1937, marble, 26in high, private collection

72 Barbara Hepworth: *Pictorial Autobiography*, Praeger, New York, 50-3

73 Quoted in Hammacher, op.cit., 98

74 Barbara Hepworth: *Porthmeor: Sea Form*, 1958, bronze, 30.5in high, Hirshhorn Museum and Sculpture Garden, Washington DC; *Pendour*, 1947, painted wood, 10 x 27 x 9in, Hirshhorn Museum and Sculpture Garden, Washington DC, *Forms in Movement*, 1956, Barbara Hepworth Museum and Sculpture Garden, St Ives, Cornwall

Botticelli's *Pietàs*, or those of the Flemish school.[75] Her body encircles the dead Christ, like the *Madonna della Misericordia* of Piero della Francesca. Here, the Mother encircles the Son. The Madonna, though, is brooding on her fate, not just the death of her child, but on the whole meaning of the cycle of events which brought her from being the 'handmaiden of the Lord', as a young woman, to this final, terrible point, with her grown child dead on her lap. Köllwitz's *Pietà* is unusual among *Pietàs*, if one thinks of those of Michelangelo, Botticelli and Roger van der Weyden, in that instead of gut-wrenching pain and anguish, which is usual in *Pietàs*, Kollwitz depicts a sombre, contemplative Mother, musing upon the ravages of time and age. Similar deeply parental feelings are expressed in sculptures such as *Twins* where, again, the mother passionately enfolds her offspring.[76]

Among contemporary women sculptors who are producing work right now, special mentions must be made of Alison Wilding and Rebecca Horn. Alison Wilding directly embraces the potential for sculpture to be supremely sensual. Her abstract forms hint at alchemical transformations, intimate experiences, investigations of sexuality and the relations between space, imagination, fantasy and the body.[77] Rebecca Horn's sculptures are based on natural forms, but also on movement, dance, time and environments. Horn's wonderful *Peacock Machine* is an exuberant activator of space, one of those pieces that aims for the essence of a natural form and captures it: a peacock's magnificent tail.[78] Lila Katzen sets alive public spaces with her flowing, curling forms.[79]

Alice Aycock, using science as her Muse, has produced some wonderfully fantastical machines, such as *The Angels Continue Turning the Wheels of the Universe*, or the marvellous, massive piece *The Miraculous Machine in the Garden (Tower of the Winds)*,

75 Köllwitz: *Pietà*, 1937, bronze, Staatliche Museen, Berlin
76 Köllwitz: *Twins*, 1935, bronze, Staatliche Museen, Berlin
77 Alison Wilding: *Bare*, 1989-90, Newlyn Art Gallery, *Into the Dark*, 1986, limewood, lead and pigment, Newlyn Art Gallery; see also Hilary Gresty: *Bare*, Newlyn Art Gallery 1993
78 Rebecca Horn: *Peacock Machine*, 1982, installation at Documenta 7, Kassel. See Mina Roustayi: "Getting Under the Skin: Rebecca Horn's Sensibility Machines", *Arts*, May 1989, 58-68; Michael Kimmelman: "A Sculptural Circus of Whips and Suspense", *New York Times*, 23 Sept 1988, C29
79 Lila Katzen: *Guardian*, 1979, bronze, 35 x 15 x 3ft, private collection, Saudi Collection

which features 268 antenna and bells ringing in a vacuum.[80] Many of Alice Aycock's land sculptures involve underground passages and spaces. In 1972 she constructed a series of underground spaces in *Low Building Made with Dirt Roof (For Mary)* in Pennsylvania. The spectator entered the 20 by 12 feet work through a doorway thirty inches high. The work was experienced by crawling through it. Aycock's intention was to evoke an experience of claustrophia, of being in a cellar.

Alice Aycock wants viewers to be confused, even frightened, by her underground passages and mazes. Aycock did not wish the viewer to be able to get out of her labyrinth easily (it was partially based on a circular Egyptian labyrinth (designed as a prison), the Zulu *kraal* and the Amerindian stockade. Aycock also cited a circular Greek temple at Epidarus, a 'Place of Sacrifice').

Aycock has spoken of the relations between her art and her own childhood dreams and fears. Her works recreate disturbing moments from her childhood, such as when she was trapped in a revolving barrel at an amusement park. Aycock's works deal with such moments of fear, confusion, strangeness and risk. Aycock also remarked that her structures were inspired by visits to the Pyramids in 1970 and the Greek tombs at Mycenae, and fantasies of being buried alive.

With Aycock's bewildering and unsettling catacombs and mazes one had to move 'one's body through them', a process which also involved descending back through time and memory. Confronted with the subterranean passage or the *Circular Building with Narrow Ledge for Walking* it is soon apparent to the spectator that one is not dealing simply with an art object to be admired for its formal characteristics alone. Aycock wants the spectator to become physically involved in the sculpture: the physical actions of climbing and scrabbling over and through the sculpture trigger an exploration of one's own psychology and memory. The physicality of the body as a tool for exploration in Aycock's works soon becomes a pretext or an inspiration for an exploration of personal psychology. Spectators are invited to risk themselves in exploring her works. Her land/ site art offers seductive as well as potentially dangerous spaces. Aycock wants the spectator to enter,

---

80 Alice Aycock: *One Thousand and One Nights in the Mansion of Bliss*, 1983, mixed media, private collection; *The Miraculous Machine in the Garden (Tower of the Winds)*, 1983, mixed media, 16ft high, private collection

but then confronts her/ him with a door that opens onto a wall, or a tiny passage to crawl through, or a ledge over a precipice, or a pit to vault over. Such devices go straight back to childhood, to acts of dare and bravado (such as walking along a high brick wall, egged on by other children).

Land artists, such as Beverly Pepper or Nancy Holt, might also be seen as producing Goddess-orientated art. Pepper's large, curving mirrored slabs of wood buried in sandy beaches might be seen as a type of 'Earth Mother art', art which worships and works with the Earth, rather than, as in so much of male land art, cutting or penetrating it, phallically (like Michael Heizer, Robert Smithson and Waler de Maria).[81]

Nancy Holt's art, with its large, heavy landscaping gestures (such as her *Dark Star Park*), is comparable with the male land artists, with their large, heavy landscaping gestures (such as her *Dark Star Park*).[82] The globes and pools of water, though, are traditionally seen as 'feminine' volumes, but here given a new, monumental turn. Holt's art concerns the movements of the heavens. Her sculptures focus the viewer on the motions of the earth, moon, sun and stars. Holt's art is concerned with the notion of time, in particular with geological time, the relation between time and the Earth.

Nancy Holt has said she is interested in 'conjuring up a sense of time that is longer than the built-in obsolescence we have all around us.' Hence she uses long-lasting materials, such as steel and rocks. Using enduring materials does not stem from a sense of vanity, of wanting one's works to last forever, but rather because Holt wants to create a sense of time that extends beyond the human lifespan.[83]

One of Holt's biggest projects was the *Sky Mound*, begun in the late 1980s (the first phase cost $11 million). Situated in amongst Amtrack and NJ Transit train tracks, highways, bridges, the Pulaski Skyway, the New Jersey turnpike, and metropolitan New Jersey and New York, with views over Newark and Manhattan, *Sky Mound* was a converted landfill which Holt turned

81 Beverly Pepper: *Sand Dunes*, 1985, Mylar over wood, approximately 100ft long, temporary installation for the Atlantic Center for the Arts, New Smyrna Beach, Florida
82 Nancy Holt: *Dark Star Park*, 1979-84, concrete, steel, water, earth, .67 of an acre, Rosslyn, Virginia
83 In T. Castle. "Nancy Holt, Siteseer", *Art in America*, Mch, 1982, 88.

into an observatory to mark solstices, equinoxes, and the stars Vega and Sirius.

Mary Miss's 1978 work *Perimeters/ Pavilion/ Decoys* was constructed in Roslyn, New York, in a field that was part of the Nassau County Museum's ground. *Perimeters/ Pavillion/ Decoys* consists of three wooden towers, which look like tree houses with four platforms on stilts, two mounds of earth, and an underground space which's accessed by a ladder. The wooden towers are not for climbing on, but for viewing. The tallest is 18 by 10 by 10 feet. The subterranean atrium was for exploring. It was a 16 ft^2 pit with a seven foot hole acting as an entrance; visitors climbed down a ladder to explore the various underground spaces, some with wooden, others with soil walls.

Perimeters/ Pavillion/ Decoys was related to Pueblo Indian structures, Pompeiian and Mexican courtyards, and Mesopotamian brick complexes. The site explored the physical and psychological aspects of 'inside/ outside, above/ below, light/ dark, open/ closed, nature/ artifice'.[84] Miss's works are often large, spreading over a wide area of ground. In Illinois she created a 5-acre scale work.[85]

Donna Dennis took the vernacular architecture of New York City as her starting-point in her 1970s works: *Tunnel Tower* was based on the entrance building to the Holland Tunnel. Later, nostalgic works, such as *Deep Station* (1981-85), recreated the shadowy recesses of subway stations (in full-scale, something like a movie set or an installation).

Patricia Johanson's most well-known work is probably the large water park she fashioned in Dallas, Texas, between 1981 and 1986. *Fair Park Lagoon* comprised a series of interlacing walkways above the pool in an 'organic', Gaudiesque manner, and cost over $2 million.

Miriam Schapiro has taken up materials branded 'feminine' by patriarchy (cotton, taffeta, burlap, wool, sequins, buttons, thread) and has created artworks (she calls them 'femmages') that

84 R. Onoratio. "Illusive Spaces: The Art of Mary Miss", *Artforum*, Dec, 1978, 32. See See also R. Onoratio: *Mary Miss – Perimeters/ Pavilions/ Decoys*, Nassau County Museum, 1979, and K. Linker: "Mary Miss", *Mary Miss*, ICA, 1983.
85 See L. Anderson. "Mary Miss", *Artforum*, Nov, 1973; M. Miss. *Mary Miss: Interior Works*, Bell Gallery, University of Rhode Island, Autumn, 1981.

deal with notions of the home, feminist iconography, abstraction and the æsthetics of 'Pattern and Decoration'.[86] Schapiro says: 'I wanted to explore and express a part of my life which I had always dismissed – my homemaking, my nesting'.[87] A number of male artists have explored traditionally 'feminine' notions of pattern, decoration and colour, among them Robert Zakanitch, Lucas Samaras, Robert Kushner, Rodney Ripps, Kim MacConnel, Frank Stella and Ned Smyth. The male-made pieces, such as by Rodney Ripps,[88] occasionally approach the flamboyance and intricacy of artworks made by women, such as by Joyce Kozloff, or Valerie Jaudon.[89]

The 'traditional' 'women's' arts and crafts of textiles, pattern, sewing, decoration, pottery, etc, are bound up with the economies of labour, race, class, identity, patriarchy, politics and finance. They are modes of production and art that are regarded as secondary by patriarchal culture, not as 'high art', such as painting or sculpture. Feminist artists, then, have to tackle not only the images of themselves, whether of patriarchy, the body, or whatever, but also the *production* of the images. The economics of artistic production are embedded with patriarchal slants, just as much as the images themselves. The piece of textiles, the decorative tile, the pot, then, are objects that in the patriarchal system speak of their second-rate mode of production. To make a pot, tile or blanket and to hold it up as a serious artwork, like a painting or a sculpture, the feminist artist has to grapple with the scorn of 'high art' critics, who demean such work. As Catherine King writes, '[m]edia associated with 'malestream' codes, like bronze, marble, or oil, have been regarded with suspicion' by women artists.[90] The field of sculpture is just one area in which women artists often far excel male artists.

American land artists, such as Walter de Maria and Michael Heizer, are the most patriarchal and phallic of modern sculptors.

86 Miriam Schapiro: *Heartland*, 1985, acrylic, fabric and glitter on canvas, 7.1 x 7.8ft, Bernice Steinbaum Gallery, New York
87 Quoted in Wheeler, 285
88 Rodney Ripps: *Gay Princess*, 1980, oil, wax and cloth on wood, 52 x 51 x 8in, Holly Solomon Gallery, New York
89 Valerie Jaudon: *Caile*, 1985, oil on canvas, 48 x 40in, Sidney James Gallery, New York; Joyce Kozloff: *New England Decorative Arts*, 1985, tile mural, 8 x 83 feet overall, Harvard Square subway station, Cambridge, Mass.
90 Catherine King: "Feminist Arts", in Frances Bonner *et al*, eds., 185

Walter de Maria made a deep wound in the Earth when he cut a 4.5 mile long scar in the desert in Nevada. The ultimate in ithyphallic, male land art must be Walter de Maria *Vertical Earth Kilometer*. At a cost of $500,000, de Maria sunk a 1-kilometre brass rod into the planet. Nothing can be seen of it except a 2 inch brass disc on the ground.

Not all of land or earth art is phallic and bombastic. Some land artists employ so-called 'feminine' emblems and characteristics. The circle motif, one of the primæval symbols of femininity, eternity, cycles, time, rebirth, etc, is employed throughout the work of Richard Long. Long's circles, made from slate, timber or by walking in a circle, are gentler, more eco-friendly kinds of sculpture.[91] The circle shape itself speaks of organic forms, and, in some religions, speaks of the feminine and the Goddess. Not a few sculptors and land artists have made the circle crucial to their works: Richard Long, Andy Goldsworthy, Robert Morris and Dennis Oppenheim.

Robert Morris has produced gigantic circular works, such as his *Observatory*, which is a huge earthwork recalling the megalithic structures of ancient times, such as Avebury stone circle, while his *Labyrinth* is a maze-size sculpture, the kind of maze one finds in theme parks and country houses, except that Morris' *Labyrinth* uses the ancient pattern of the Cretan labyrinth, itself a motif some see as distinctly feminine, speaking of Goddess mysteries. Some artists have produced stone circles which look very much like Stonehenge, such as Nancy Holt's monumental *Stone Enclosure: Rock Rings*.[92] Wolfgang Laib dusts the Earth with

---

91 Richard Long: *Circle in Alaska*, driftwood on the Arctic Circle, Bering Strait 1977; *Untitled*, 1987, mud on paper, Anthony d'Offay Gallery, London; *Mountain Lake Powder Snow*, 1985, Lapland. See J. Poinsot: "Richard Long: To Build the Landscape", *Art Press*, Nov 1981, 9-11, Michael Compton: *Some Notes on the Work of Richard Long*, British Council 1976, Gabriella Jeppson: *Richard Long*, Fogg Art Museum, Cambridge, Mass., 1980, Nancy Foote: "Long Walks", *Artforum*, Summer 1980, 42-7, Simon Field: "Touching the Earth", *Art and Artists*, April 1973, 14-19, John T. Paoletti: "Richard Long", *Arts Magazine*, Dec 1982, 3; Richard Long: "Richard Long replies to a critic", *Art Monthly*, 68, July 1983, 20-21; Rudi H. Fuchs: "Memories of Passing: A Note on Richard Long", *Studio International*, 1987, 965, April 1974, 172-3;
92 Nancy Holt: *Stone Enclosure: Rock Rings*, 1977-8, hand-quarried schist, outer ring 40 feet, inner ring 2 feet across, ring walls 10 feet high, Western Washington University, Bellingham

pollen, to form an enormous square layer of brilliant yellow.[93]
Andy Goldsworthy and Laib collect leaves, berries, pollen, honey
and other natural elements and weave sensuous artifacts that are
ephemeral and intricate.

Richard Long speaks in poetic, religious terms of his art – 'art
should be a religious experience'.[94] Although his sculptures alter
the world – no *object* can avoid altering the world – he maintains
that he takes his cue from the landscape, instead of imposing on it
'from outside', as it were: 'I use the world as I find it'.[95] Bill
Woodrow, a contemporary of Long's, also 'uses' the world as he
finds it: he trawls the world for materials with which to make
sculptures:

> My choice of objects is dictated, I think in the first instance by what is
> available, what I come across in the streets, on dumps... What I find
> more interesting about the work, is that these items are material for
> me that is found in my environments...[96]

Andy Goldsworthy seems particularly gentle and sensitive in
his handling of materials: he stitches together leaves to forms
lines, often placed in water, or makes circular slabs of snow, or
entwines twigs in an arc.[97] He creates a delicate spiral of chestnut
leaves, called *Autumn Horn*; he pins bright yellow dandelions on
willowherb stalks in a circle, on bluebells; he makes lines and
cairns, like Richard Long, of pebbles; he makes hollow, circular
structures, like igloos, from slate, leaves, driftwood and bracken;
he makes long wavy ridges in Arizona desert sand; he makes
arches, globes, hollow spheres, slabs, spires, spirals and star-

---

93 Wolfgang Laib: *Hazelnut Pollen*, Dokumenta 8

94 Quoted in Wheeler, 264

95 Long: *Five, six, pick up sticks/ Seven, eight, lay them straight*, 1980,
Anthony d'Offay Gallery, September 1980

96 Woodrow, quoted in *Objects and Sculpture*, Institute of Contemporary
Arts, 1981, 37

97 Andy Goldsworthy: *Japanese maple leaves stitched together to make a
floating chain*, 21 November 1987, Ouchiyama-mura, Japan; *Slate Stack*,
1988, Scaur Water Valley, Penpont, Dumfriesshire, Scotland; *Circular
stalks in a lake*, 29 April 1987, Yorkshire Sculpture Park

shapes out of snow and ice.[98] Very impressive it all is. The sculptures made of sticks, for instance, stuck together in an arch, or a line, reflected in the mirror-like water of Derwent Water in Cumbria, are indeed wonderful.[9] Or the globe made from oak leaves in various states of autumnal decay, superb stuff.[99] Or the globe made out of snow, and perched amidst some young trees, or the slabs of snow, set up in a line with slits cut in them.[100] Or his most dramatic work, *Touching North*, four circular arches or tunnels made of snow, which is dramatic partly because its location, that space so thoroughly a masculine 'wild zone', the place of macho adventures, colonization and courage, the North Pole.[101]

Goldsworthy speaks in similar tones to feminist artists: he talks of '[r]hythms, cycles, seasons in nature working at different speeds'.[102] Mysticism is emphasized in his writing, as is in Long's would-be 'enigmatic' statements. Goldsworthy's æsthetics are luscious and those of a neo-pagan, shamanic, native Amerindian, pantheistic, nature worshipping kind, the sort of beliefs that other people call Goddess worship. The spiral and snake employed by so many land artists down the ages (in ancient Peru, or on the doors of Neolithic tombs, or in the mid-west of America) is associated with the Goddess and with the energies of life. The circles and spirals of Goldsworthy, Nash, Smithson and Long are clearly those of the Goddess, the ancient Earth Mother. The land

---

98 Goldsworthy: *Autumn Horn*, Nov 1986, chestnut leaves, Penpont, Dumfriesshire; *Dandelion Flowers*, 1 May 1987, 'flowers pinned to willowherb stalks laid in a ring held above bluebells with forked sticks', Yorkshire Sculpture Park, West Bretton; *Line and Carin* 31 May & 1 June 1985, pebbles, St Abbs, the Borders; [*Cairns*], made of plane leaves, 19 Oct 1988, Castres, France, slate, Summer 1987, Stonewood, Dumfriesshire, bracken, 13 February 1988, Borrowdale, Cumbria, driftwood, 29 November 1987, Kinagashima-cho, Japan; [*Waves of Sand*], 21 Nov 1989, 'fine dry sand', Arizona; *Ice Arch*, 1-2 Dec 1982, Brough, Cumbria; *Stacked Ice*, 28 Dec 1985, Hampstead Heath
99 [*Oak Globe*], 15 September 1985, branches and oak leaves, Jenny Noble's Gill, Dumfriesshire
100 Goldsworthy: *Slits cut into frozen snow*, 12 February 1988, Blencathra, Cumbria; *Snowball in Trees*, February 1980, Robert Hall Wood, Lancashire
101 Goldsworthy: *Touching North*, 24 April 1989, North Pole
102 Goldsworthy: *Touching North*, Fabian Carlsson Gallery, London 1989

artists, then, make marks upon Mother Earth, upon the surface or skin of the Goddess. Goldsworthy speaks inadvertently of phallic penetration when he says: 'I want to get under the surface... At its most successful, my 'touch' looks into the heart of nature.' Earth or land artists, then, penetrate or cut into nature, into the Goddess. The Earth, which is female, is penetrated – by Michael Heizer gouging vast chunks out of the American desert, by de Maria thrusting a kilometre-long brass rod into the earth (art's biggest penis, perhaps?), and Goldsworthy, seemingly so gentle, has cut trenches into the earth, or smashed slabs of slate or pebbles or leaves, to make lines of broken, shattered material on the earth. He has torn leaves apart to form a line, and has smashed pebbles, making a line, like a fault line in continental structures. These are violent gestures, destroying the organic make-up of the natural forms he so adores.[103] All land artists, all artists, must break up and re-form materials, but these cracks and holes look like scars on the the earth.

Even in Minimal sculpture, which's certainly austere – 'cool', as some people call it, the body is present. It is very cool, ascetic, restrained, flat, exact, with its smooth surfaces and precise square edges and angles. Body has been erased from this 'cool' Minimal art. There is no space for the body, and the spectator is also 'erased', in some way. The ruthless asceticism of Minimal art denies, like early Christianity, the body. Rosalind Krauss writes:

> The art of [Rodin and Brancusi] represented a relocation of the point
> of origin of the body's meaning – from its inner core to its surface – a
> radical act of decentring that would include the space to which the
> body appeared and the time of its appearing. What I have been
> arguing is that the sculpture of our time continues this project of
> decentring through a vocabulary of form that is radically abstract.
> The abstractness of Minimalism makes it less easy to recognize the
> human body in those works and therefore less easy to project
> ourselves into the space of that sculpture with all of our settled
> prejudices left intact. Yet our bodies and our experience of our bodies
> continue to be the subject of this sculpture – even when a work is made

103 Goldsworthy: *Leaves torn in two*, 2 Nov 1986, Glasgow Green; *Broken Pebbles*, 12 April 1987, Scaur Water, Dumfriesshire; *Trench*, 6-7 August 1987, 'trench edged with clay supported by sticks', West Bretton, Yorkshire Sculpture Park; *Slate Crack Line*, Feb 1988, Little Langdale, Cumbria

of several hundred tons of earth. (279)

One can see the body written into, say, Andy Goldsworthy's delicate leaf sculptures, or Constantin Brancusi's extraordinary egg shapes, but not, perhaps, in the giganticism of Michael Heizer's *Double Negative*. Yet, even here, the human body is present – if only by the way it is violently dwarfed by the scale of Heizer's earthwork.

One area of contemporary sculpture seems undoubtedly sexist. In the figures of realist or hyperrealist sculpture we see people frozen in often bizarre attitudes and poses, as in Duane Hanson's *The Tourists and other works*.[104] Hanson's figures are vicious and ironic, while George Segal's explore the alienation of 'modern life'. Anthony Donaldson has produced a truly horrible *Girl Sculpture*, a plastic red and gold model of a woman – naked, of course – set in a 'streamlined' mould, rather like those 3-D logos beloved of entertainment organizations, where the letters are drawn in exaggerated perspective.[105] John De Andrea also explores 'the resignation, emptiness and loneliness'[106] o f contemporary life, that emotional territory of Middle America that Raymond Carver so successfully explored in his many short stories. But De Andrea's nudes turn out to be just as pornographic as other 'high art' nudes.[107] Take his *Reclining Woman*,[108] which is a Superrealist version of the 'high art' reclining nude, a life-size and seeming 'life-like' rendition of a person. There are differences of æsthetic approaches in the Superrealist plastic doll-woman and the female nude of high art sculpture, but, essentially, both are works of pornography, and De Andrea's work is no different than sculptures such as Fritz Klimsch's *Eos*, a woman posing in voluptuous fashion, arms behind her head, hips thrown to one side, a pin-up sculpted nude.[109] But De Andrea's reclining woman

104 Duane Hanson: *The Tourists*, 1970, polyester resin, polychrome glass fibre, National Gallery of Scotland, Edinburgh; *Bunny*, 1970, fibreglass, life-size, O.K. Harris Gallery, New York
105 Anthony Donaldson: *Girl Sculpture "Red 'n' Gold"*, 1970, 75 x 448cm, Rowan Gallery, London
106 John De Andrea, quoted in Le Normand-Romain, 241
107 John De Andrea: *Couple*, 1971, acrylic on polyester and hair, man 5.7ft high, woman 5.1ft high, Musée d'Art Moderne, Paris
108 John De Andrea: *Reclining Woman*, 1970, life-size, David Bermant Collection
109 Fritz Klimsch: *Eos*, 1904

recalls the blow-ups doll of pornography, that cruel form of erotic objectification of women. Reg Butler's bronzes of women – naked, of course – are 'exquisitely crafted', to use terms typical of art criticism,[110] but in fact turn out to be very sexist representations of women.[111]

Tim Head's *State of the Art* is a collection of phallic objects, stacked up like a Louis Nevelson wall of sculpture: Head places a host of dildos and vibrators next to electronic calculators, model aircraft, tape players, computers, computer games, deodorants, hair sprays, all the panoply of consumerist items.

There is an intrinsic sexism in the Romanian sculptor Constantin Brancusi's treatment of male and female, masculine and feminine forms. His *Torso of a Young Woman III* is, typically, a softly rounded volume, like a vase, recalling the eternal and mythical association of women with vessels, of women as something to be filled – or fucked, as Andrea Dworkin would say.[112] Brancusi's *Torso of a Young Woman* is supremely stereotypical, sexist, misogynist. The male *Torso*, on the other hand, is, as you might expect, phallically upright. Indeed, it looks like a phallus.[113] Interestingly, however, Brancusi claimed that '[n]ude men in sculpture are not as beautiful as toads.'[114] Further sexism occurs in Brancusi's *Adam and Eve*, where people are reduced to genitals, once again. So Eve is a mouth and vagina, and Adam is a phallus and testicles.[115]

Much of Auguste Rodin's art pivots around eroticism. Rodin produced drawings of women masturbating, which influenced Gustav Klimt's images of masturbating women.[116] Rodin's *Oceanides*, like his *Gates of Hell*, depicts lovers entwining in a

110 Edward Lucie-Smith: *Sculpture Since 1945*, 33
111 Reg Butler: *Girl on Red Base*, 1968-72, painted bronze, 32 x 43 x 63.5in, Pierre Matisse Gallery, New York
112 Brancusi: *Torso of a Young Woman III*, 1925, onyx, 10.4in, Musée National d'Art Moderne, Paris
113 Brancusi :*Torso of a Young Man*, after 1924, bronze, 18.4 x 12 x 6.7in, Cleveland Museum of Art
114 Brancusi, quoted in *This Quarter*, op.cit.
115 Brancusi: *Adam and Eve*, 1916-21, chestnut and oak, 89in high, base of limestone, 5.2in, Guggenheim, New York
116 Rodin: *Reclining Female Nude*, c.1900, pencil, 12.2 x 8in, Musée Rodin, Paris

series of fluid lines and sensuous forms.[117] Rodin's depictions of *The Kiss* centre around the voluptuousness of eroticism, on the beauty of bodies clasped together in complex poses. Rodin's *The Kiss* is the apotheosis of modern figurative sculpture, Michelangelo made heterosexually erotic. Other sculptors produced similarly sensuous, entwined *Kisses*, with the man always on top, always bearing down onto the woman, always enveloping, always controlling the kiss (in M.L. Bégine's *The Embrace*, J. Dalou's *The Kiss*, E. Munch's *The Kiss*, Klimt's *The Kiss*, Félix Voulot's *The Kiss*, Picasso's *The Embrace*, William Zorach's *The Embrace* and Émile Derré's *La Grotte d'Amour*).[118]

---

117 Rodin: *Océanides*, 1905, marble, 22in high, Musée Rodin, Paris
118 E. Derré: *La Grotte d'Amour*, 1905; Jules Dalou: *The Kiss*, Giraudon; M.L. Béguine: *The Embrace*, 1906; Edvard Munch: *The Kiss*, 1895, private collection; Picasso: *The Embrace*, 1900; F. Vaoulot: *The Kiss*, 1905; William Zorach: *The Embrace*, 1933, bronze, 66in high, collection the Zorach children

7

CONTEMPORARY WOMEN'S ART

There are many brilliant women artists working at the moment. Most of the feminist art being produced is by women. Male artists have only made tentative steps in producing art that radically questions or rewrites patriarchal attitudes, values, ideas, experiences or laws. Much of feminist or 'women's' art celebrates the 'feminine', what is special to 'femininity' or 'womanhood', the being of 'woman' and women.

One aspect of feminist or 'women's' art is embodied by the figure of the Goddess, the ancient and primæval Great Mother of all, celebrated then – and now – as Isis, Ishtar, Demeter, Kali, etc. The Goddess is now variously interpreted as fact, experience, idea, æsthetic, cult, religion, pagan emblem and many other things by women artists. There are a host of artists who have made what we might call 'Goddess art', art that employs the figure of the Goddess as an embodiment of female being or experience: Judy Chicago, Mary Beth Edelson, Miriam Schapiro, Niki de Sant-Phalle, Louis Bourgeois, Ana Mendieta and Helen Chadwick. Mary Beth Edelson engages in the resurgence of the Goddess, in her *Great Goddess* series.[119] Edelson has also produced a piece on menstruation, entitled, appropriately, *Blood Mysteries*.[120] In a piece of performance art, Catherine Elwes sat in an enclosed

119 Mary Beth Edelson: *Great Goddess Series*, 1975, collection: the artist
120 Edelson: *Blood Mysteries*, 1973, drawing, 91 x 57 in, collection: the artist

studio space and menstruated.[121] Judy Chicago, already mentioned, looked to the flowers of Georgia O'Keeffe, which, she said, 'stand for femininity'.[122]

The Goddess is a symbol and experience of a new spiritual consciousness that also embraces eroticism. Catholic feminists, such as Meinrad Craighead, have spoken of the need for Christians to embrace eroticism as well as spirituality.[123] Sutapa Biswas depicts women as incarnations of the Goddess Kali, who beheads men.[124]

Feminist artists and writers have been putting the erotic dimension back into the Goddess, after thousands of years of desexed deities such as the Virgin Mary. Images such as Piero della Francesca's *Madonna del Parto* are taken up by feminists because here is a depiction of a pregnant Goddess.[125] Goddess art is full of images of menstruation, pregnancy, childbirth, all those things termed by some 'women's mysteries'. Niki de Sant-Phalle has produced exuberant Goddesses, such as her *Black Venus*, or her marvellous *Pink Childbirth*, a Great Mother Goddess made from dolls, toys, tissues and various items collected together like a totem of the prehistoric world, while Sant-Phalle's *Un Ensemble de "Les Nanas"* is an effervescent – and multicoloured – represent-ation of female forms, dancing, cavorting, balancing.[126] Helen Chadwick has made a *Madonna and Child* image with a female

121 Catherine Elwes: "Floating femininity: a look at performance art by women", in S. Kent & J. Morreau, eds. *Women's Images of Men*, Pandora Press, 1985, 182

122 Quoted in Lucy Lippard, 219; see also Lucy Lippard: "Dinner Party", *Art in America*, April 1980, 122

123 See Mary Giles, ed. *The Feminist Mystic*

124 Sutapa Biswas, interview with Yasmin Kureishi, *Spare Rib*, no. 173, December 1986;

125 Piero della Francesca: *Madonna del Parto*, c. 1450-5, fresco, 260 x 203cm, Cemetery Chapel, Monterchi, Arezzo

126 Niki de Sant-Phalle: *Black Venus*, 1967, painted polyester, 110 x 35 x 24in, Whitney Museum of Art, New York; *Pink Childbirth*, 1964, painted relief, 86.24in high, Moderner Museet, Stockholm; *Un Ensemble de "Les Nanas"*, 1965, Archives Galerie Alexandre Iolas, New York. See David Bourdon *et al*: *Niki de Sant-Phalle: Fantastic Vision*, Nassau County Museum of Fine Art, Rosyln, New York 1987; Jean-Yves Mock: *Niki de Sant-Phalle: Exposition Retrospective*, CGP 1980

Christ Child, complete with labia, placenta and birthcord.[127] Louis Bourgeois has investigated the 'female form' in many works, using, as so many feminist artists have done, the female body as the site of feminist explorations.[128] Feminist artists have rewritten, recreated, reviewed the female body. Many feminist artists have used their own bodies as artworks, challenging radically traditional notions of fine and art criticism.

Lynda Benglis appeared in *Artforum* in 1974 nude, holding a giant phallus between her legs.[129] Cindy Sherman's photographs investigate the female body, often naked, in ever more complex and ironic ways. Her richly coloured photographs quote from films and create narratives which hover between fear and desire, clarity and ambivalence. Sherman takes the bland furniture and gestures of life and imbues them with a narrative strangeness that engages the spectator in an exploration of æsthetic expectation, identity, perception and tradition. Cindy Sherman has also used a Hans Bellmer-like doll, or plastic parts of the (female) body in ironic ways, in works that are, typically, titled *Untitled*.[130]

Feminist artists are using the body to explore political, erotic, pornographic, æsthetic and philosophical discourses. As Lisa Tickner writes: '[l]iving *in* a female body is different from looking *at* it, as a man. Even the Venus of Urbino menstruated, as women know and men forget.'[131] The female nude, for so long the model and image and object of lust in so many 'high art' paintings, has usurped the power relation between artist and art object, and between artwork and spectator. The woman is no longer content to be looked at and lusted after: she is making her own art, employing her body in a radical, challenging way. The 'Old Master/ *Playboy* tradition', as Tickner calls it, has been smashed. Feminists and feminist artists must make sure that the 'Old

127 Helen Chadwick: *One Flesh*, 1986, photocopies, 160 x 107cm, Victoria & Albert Museum, London
128 Louis Bourgeois: *Fragile Goddess*, c. 1970, clay, 10in high, Robert Miller Gallery, New York; *Femme Couteau*, 1982, black marble, 14 x 77.5 x 20.3cm, Robert Miller Gallery, New York
129 Benglis: *Self-portrait*, 1974, advert in *Artforum*
130 Cindy Sherman: *Untitled*, 1985, two colour photographs, both 72.5 x 49.5in; and see Laura Mulvey: "A Phantasmagoria of the Female Body: The Work of Cindy Sherman", *New Left Review*, 188, July/ August 1991, 136-150; P. Schjeldahl: *Cindy Sherman*, Pantheon Books 1984
131 Lisa Tickner: "Body Politic", op.cit., 239

Master/ *Playboy* tradition' never assumes dominance again.[132]

Feminist body and performance art is a way of repossessing the body, sexuality, identity, power, it is a way of 'rewriting the body'. It can be an act of transgression and subversion, which usurps the power relation between spectator and artwork, so that the (male) viewer's 'cloak of invisibility has been stripped away and his spectatorship becomes an issue within the work', as Catherine Elwes puts it (op. cit., 172) Displaying the female body, though, can also make it available for being appropriated by men, as some feminists have cautioned.[133] Women artists have to make sure they are not titillating their audience in that way so familiar in pornography. The issues raised by feminist body and performance art are many and complex, basically pivoting around whether body art is truly subversive, or whether it plays into the grasping hands of patriarchy.[134] As the Editorial Collective of *Questions féministes* write, 'it is also dangerous to place the body at the centre of a search for female identity.'[135]

Carole Schneemann pulls a scroll from her vagina and reads from it, in a famous performance piece.[136] Schneemann's most famous happening, though, was *Meat Joy* (1964), a kind of orgy which now looks like a bunch of people larking about. Chila Kumari Burman makes 'body prints'. Karen Finley pours 'a can

132 See T. Gouma-Peterson & P. Matthews: "The feminist critique of art history", *The Art Bulletin*, LXIX, 1987, 326-57
133 See Lynda Nead, 67; Lucy Lippard: "The Pain and Pleasures of Rebirth: European and American Women's Body Art", in *From the Center*, op.cit., 125
134 See Henry M. Sayre: *The Object of Performance: the American Avant-garde Since 1970*, University of Chicago Press 1989; Sally Potter: "Our Shows", *About Time: Video, Performance and Installation by 21 Women Artists*, ICA, 1980; Jeannie Forte: "Women's Performance Art: Feminism and Postmodernism", *Theatre Journal*, 40:2, May 1988, 217-35; Elinor Fuchs: "Staging the Obscene Body", *The Drama Review*, 33:1, Spring 1989, 33-58; Janet Wolff: "Reinstating Corporeality: Feminism and Body Politics", *Feminine Sentences: Essays on women and culture*, Polity Press, Cambridge 1990; Claudette Johnson: "Issues Surrounding the Representation of the Naked Body of a Woman", *Feminist Art News*, 3:8, 1991
135 "Variations on Common Themes", *Question féministes*, no.1, November 1977, quoted in E. Marks, 218
136 See Carolee Schneemann: *Interior Scroll*, 1975; *More than Meat Joy: Complete Performance Works and Selected Writings*, ed. Bruce MacPherson, Documentext, New York 1979

of yams over her naked buttocks'; she is 'a frightening and rare presence'.[137] In her *Cut Off Balls* she castrates Wall Street bankers.[138] Mary Duffy displays her disabled body in performance and photographic sequences;[139] Jo Spence has photographed the 'unhealthy and ageing female body'.[140]

Ana Mendieta (1948-85) produced a combination of Goddess art, performance art and environmental art. For *The Tree of Life* series (1977). made in Old Man's Creek, Iowa) she covered herself in mud (while nude) and stood against a tree, and left the outline of her body in leaves on a tree trunk. In the *Silueta* series (1979), Mendieta imprinted her body in the snow in Amana, Iowa, and in mud on a riverbank, or set the form on fire in the earth, or made a silhouette from flowers.

Mendieta's art has an undisguised ideological, spiritual and ecological agenda; some of Mendieta's works are explicit performance explorations of rapes, and Mendieta was also exploring her Cuban and Latin American heritage.

In some pieces Mendieta remodelled the entrance of a cave and a ravine into her Goddess shape. She also buried herself under turf – a literal Earth-Goddess mound, and had herself

---

137 C. Carr: "Unspeakable Practices, Unnatural Acts", *Village Voice*, 24 June 1986

138 See Anthony Adler: "Dangerous Woman: Karen Finley", *Chicago Reader*, 26 October 1990; Richard Lacayo: "Talented Toiletmouth", *Time*, 4 June 1990; Miranda Joseph: "Further Finley", *The Drama Review*, Winter 1990, 13; Kay Larson: "Censor Deprivation", *New York*, 6 August 1990; Catherine Schuler: "Spectator Response and Comprehensions: The Problems of Karen Finley's *Constant State of Desire*", *The Drama Review*, Spring 1990, 131-145; Clive Barnes: "Finley's Fury", *New York Post*, 24 July 1990; Tim Page: "Karen Finley's Tantrum, Amid Chocolate", *New York Newsday*, 24 July 1990

139 Mary Duffy: *Cutting the Ties that Bind*, 1987; *Stories of a Body*, 1990; see Hilary Robinson: "The Subtle Abyss: Sexuality and Body Image in Contemporary Feminist Art", unpublished dissertation, RCA 1987; Mary Duffy: "Cutting the Ties that Bind", *Feminist Art News*, 2:10, 1989, 6-7; Mary Duffy: "Redressing the Balance", *Feminist Art News*, 3:8, 1991

140 Jo Spence and Tim Sheard: *Narratives of Dis-ease*; see Jo Spence: *Putting Myself in the Picture: A Political, Personal and Photographic Autobiography*, Camden Press 1986; Patricia Holland, Jo Spence and Simon Watney, eds. *Photography/ Politics: Two*, Commedia 1986; Darcy Grimaldo Grigsby: "Dilemmas of Visibility: Contemporary Women Artists' Representations of Female Bodies", *Michigan Quarterly Review*, XXIX: 4, Autumn 1990, 584-618

photographed in an ancient Mexican stone grave.[2] Mendieta also lit fires in sculptures (such as *Volcano,* 1979), like Chris Drury and David Nash, and lit candles and fireworks in the shape of a woman.

Ana Mendieta was married to the Conceptual sculptor Carl Andre, and their relationship ended tragically when Mendieta fell to her death from a skyscraper in New York City. It was one of the more notorious incidents in contemporary art, and, like Robert Smithson's early death, a great loss to the art world.

The women Surrealists have been celebrated by some feminists and art critics as a crucial element not only in male/ patriarchal Surrealism, but also in 'high art' generally. There are some startling women artists who made Surrealist art, or art that has affinities with André Breton, Marcel Duchamp, Yves Tanguy, René Magritte, Salvador Dali, Max Ernst, Man Ray and the other oh so wonderful Surrealists.

Leonor Fini creates exquisite dream scenes,[141] such as *Red Vision,* which may be about the menstrual cycle: a white girl (ovulation, domesticity) meets in an empty room a floating red girl (menstruation, wildness), or her *Compositions with Figures on a Terrace,* where extraordinary women, dressed fabulously, stare off into space, or her highly potent *Chthonian Divinity Watching Over the Sleep of a Young Man,* where the woman, a dark sphinx behind the young Adonis, is clearly a Black Goddess of marvellous eroticism.[142]

Like Fini, Leonora Carrington paints the clean, empty rooms of the unconscious, populated by bizarre items, bizarre partly for their juxtapositioning with other objects,[143] such as in her *Self-*

141 See Xavière Gauthier: *Léonor Fini,* Paris 1973; Constantin Jelenski: *Léonor Fini* Lausanne 1972; *Léonor Fini,* Galleria Civica d'Arte Moderna, Ferrara 1983; Silvio Gaggi: "Léonor Fini: A Mythology of the Feminine", *Art International,* 23, Sept 1979, 34-38

142 Leonor Fini: *Red Vision,* 1984, oil on canvas, 17.2 x 20.6in, private collection; *Chthonian Divinity Watching Over the Sleep of a Young Man,* 1947, oil on canvas, 13 x 21.8in, private collection; *Composition with Figures on a Terrace,* 1939, oil on canvas, 38.8 x 31.2in, collection: Edward James Foundation, Sussex

143 See Juan Garcia Ponce & Leonora Carrington: *Leonora Carrington,* Mexico City 1974; Edward James, intr, *Leonora Carrington,* Center for Inter-American Relations, New York 1975; Gloria Orenstein: "Leonora Carrington's Visionary Art for the New Age", *Chrysalis,* 4, 1978, 65-77

Portrait.[144] Dorothea Tanning, for so long known simply as 'the wife of a famous artist' (Max Ernst), which has been (and is) the fate of so many women artists, also painted fantastic dreamscapes.[145] She paints places where shapes merge into shapes in flowing streams of energy, such as in her visionary *Guardian Angels*, or where young women, again, as in Fini and Carrington, with long, wild hair, encounter gigantic yellow sunflowers on mysterious hotel landings, as in *Eine Kleine Nachtmusik*.[146]

For strangeness, the images of women Surrealists far surpass those of many of the male artists. This is not only because the women's images are not so well known – indeed, are hardly featured in many art history books – but because they are actually often far stranger. Take the work of Remedios Varo, who, again, like Fini, Carrington and Tanning, creates the rooms of dreams, those spacious spaces that haunt the viewer with their extraordinary perspectives and contents.[147] In Remedios Varo's *Creation of the Birds* we see a bird woman (a female shaman) making birds with the aid of the light of a distant star focused through a prism, a machine which looks like two eggs on top of each that dispenses paint, and a paint brush connected to a violin. The painting fuses the magic of light, music and colour in an alchemical fantasy of creation, as in *Harmony*, where a poet, aided by supernatural Muses, composes art on a luminous, three dimensional musical stave.[148] Remedios Varo's paintings are based on an alchemical view of the world, where all things are related in a holistic continuum. 'Varo believed in magic. She had an animistic faith in the power of objects and in the interrelatedness of plant, animal, human, and mechanical worlds,'

144 Carrington: *Self-Portrait*, 1936-7, oil on canvas, 25.5 x 32in, Pierre Matisse Gallery, New York
145 See Gilles Plazy: *Dorothea Tanning*, Paris 1969; Dorothea Tanning: *Abyss*; *Dorothea Tanning*: Exposition Retrospective, Knokke-le-Zoute, Casino Communale 1977
146 Dorothea Tanning: *Eine Kleine Nachtmusik*, 1946, oil on canvas, 16.2 x 24in, private collection; *Guardian Angels*, 1946, oil on canvas, 48 x 55in, New Orleans Museum of Art, New Orleans
147 See Octavio Paz & Roger Callois: *Remedios Varo*, Mexico City 1973; Edouard Jaguer: *Remedios Varo*, Paris 1980; *Remedios Varo*, Museo de Arte Moderno, Mexico City 1983
148 Remedios Varo: *Creation of the Birds*, 1958, oil on masonite, 20.6 x 24.6in, private collection; *Harmony*, 1956, oil on masonite, 30 x 37in, private collection

writes Janet Kaplan.[149]

The most celebrated female Surrealist is Frida Kahlo, whose amazing self-portraits with their cutaway images of her body, are among the most ruthless explorations of sexuality in modern 'high art'.[150] Kahlo's *The Broken Column*, *The Two Fridas*, and the astonishing *My Birth*, investigate forms of (female) suffering, the relation of sexuality to violence, sexuality to self-image, sexuality to emotions (hatred, self-loathing, insecurity, rage).[151]

For Andrea Dworkin, Frida Kahlo is 'the great painter of primal female pain' whose 'paintings are the most vivid renderings by any woman of the female screwed, gashed, wounded', who, married to Diego Rivera, the Mexican artist, 'painted what it was like being fucked by him'.[152] Dworkin quotes Diego Rivera's testament of his relationship with Kahlo: '[i]f I loved a woman, the more I loved her, the more I wanted to hurt her. Frida was only the most obvious victim of this disgusting trait.'[153] For Dworkin, as for many feminists, Kahlo's paintings are the astonishing record of a woman's incredibly painful relationship with a man:

> She painted the suffering, enraged; she created an iconography of the
> *chingada* [literally the "screwed one"] that was resistance, not
> pornography; knowing herself to be the screwed one, she made an art
> of passionate rebellion that shows the pain of inferiority delivered
> into your body – the violence of the contempt... Kahlo paints the
> woman vividly wounded, dripping blood; in one, *A Few Small Nips*,
> painted in 1935, a naked woman (except for one sock and one shoe) is
> on a bed, gashed all over; she is alive, wide-eyed, her body animated
> in curves and subtle, living contortion; a man stands upright next to
> the bed, he is fully dressed, even wearing a hat, and he holds a knife in

149 J. Kaplan: "Remedios Varo: Voyages and Visions", *Woman's Art Journal*, 1, no.2, Autumn 1980/ Winter 1981, 13
150 See Hayden Herrera: *Frida: A Biography of Frida Kahlo*, Harper & Row, New York 1983; "Frida Kahlo: Her Life, Her Art", *Artforum*, 14, May 1976, 38-4; Gloria Orenstein: "Frida Kahlo: Painting For Miracles", *Feminist Art Journal*, Autumn 1973, 7-9; Terry Smith: "From the Margins: Modernity and the Case of Frida Kahlo", *Block*, 8, 1983, 14;
151 Frida Kahlo: *My Birth*, oil on sheet metal, 12.2 x 14in, collection: Edgar J. Kaufmann, New York; *The Broken Column*, 1944, oil on masonite, 15.8 x 12.2in, collection: Dolores Olmedo, Mexico City; *The Two Fridas*, 1939, oil on canvas, 67 x 67in, Museo de Arte Moderno, Mexico City
152 Andrea Dworkin: *Intercourse*, 211-2
153 Rivera, quoted in Hayden Herrera: *Frida*, op.cit., 183

his hand; he is aloof, indifferent, blank; and the blood in blotches and smears is all over her body and spreads out over the walls and over the floor in spots and smears even past the boundaries of the canvas to the frame. Kahlo shows the unspeakable pain of being *alive* and female, penetrated like this.[154]

Kahlo's art is that of an outsider, someone who inhabits the edges of society, a place that is perhaps the feminist 'wild zone'. As Whitney Chadwick wrote: '[w]hen it came to sharing in the collective mythology of Surrealism, women experienced themselves as outsiders.'[155] Léonor Fini saw herself as that archetypal female outsider, Lilith, the mythic witch of Western religion: 'I know that I belong with the idea of Lilith, the anti-Eve, and that my universe is that of the spirit.'[156] Looking at Surrealist concepts of eroticism from the alienated viewpoint of the female Surrealist artist, Ithel Colquhoun painted some ironic parodies of Surrealist sexuality, such as her *The Pine Family*, which depicts three male torsos made of pine logs, each with the penis lopped off.[157] Colquhoun's painting sends up Freudian psychoanalysis and the grotesque notion of castration.

But while Kahlo creates a powerful and idiosyncratic art, completely her own world, there were women Surrealists who produced disappointing art, art which did not veer from the patriarchal norms of masculine art. Nusch Eluard's collages, for instance, replay patriarchal views of women without much irony.[158]

154 Dworkin: *Intercourse*, 212, 223

155 Whitney Chadwick, *Women Artists and the Surrealist Movement*, 129

156 Léonor Fini, quoted in Xavière Gauthier: *Léonor Fini*, op.cit., 74

157 Ithell Colquhoun: *The Pine Family*, 1941, oil on canvas, 18 x 20in, private collection. See *Ithell Colquhoun*, Leva Gallery, London 1974; Dawn Ades: "Notes on Two Women Surrealist Painters: Eileen Agar and Ithell Colquhoun", *Oxford Art Journal*, 3, no.1, April 1980

158 Nusch Eluard: *Photo-Collages*, c. 1935, photo-collage postcard, 5.4 x 3.5in, collection: Timothy Baum, New York. See Nusch Eluard: *Collage Dreams*, Nadada Editions, New York 1978

Among non-figurative, abstract or partially-figurative artists, people such as Nancy Graves are absolutely astonishing, with her superb multi-media constructions.[159] Nancy Graves' skeletal, fossil-like works combine fantasy and natural forms in 'one exuberantly open-form, polychrome, freestanding construction after another' (Daniel Wheeler, 303).

The archetypal Minimal painter, Agnes Martin, might appear to be quite 'uninteresting'. Her paintings, though, are deeply poetic. They are, like Ryman's and Reinhardt's, flat squares in a human-scale (five foot square, for instance). They have poetic titles: *Mountain II, Drift of Summer* and *Night Sea*.[160] Martin's white paintings are not all they seem at first, as with Robert Ryman's work. They are in fact covered with a faint but strictly controlled grid, usually made with a pencil. *Night Sea* is, unusually in Martin's *oeuvre*, a light blue, hinting at nature, at skies and seas. Martin's painterly reductionism seems austere, but in fact poeticizes the world, as with Ryman or Marden. Martin writes: '[m]y paintings have neither objects, nor space, nor time, not anything – no forms. They are light, lightness, about merging, about formlessness, breaking down forms.'[161] Martin's paintings go beyond being simply graphs made in graphite on oil paint; they shimmer, phosphoresce, they are, as Martin says, about lightness and formlessness. They embrace a physicality of light and are not 'abstract' in the sense of being 'unreal'. Rather, they are grounded in reality, in nature, as with the oil and wax panels of Brice Marden.

Painters such as Thérèse Oulton are as sensuous and powerful

---

159 Nancy Graves: *Zaga*, 1983, cast bronze with polychrome chemical patination, 6' x 4'1" x 2'8", Nelson-Atkins Museum of Art, Kansas City; *Cantileve*, 1983, bronze with polychrome patina, 999 x 67 x 55in, M. Knoedler & Co, New York. See Avis Berman: "Nancy Graves", *Art News*, Feb 1986, 57-64; Debra Bricker Balken and Linda Nochlin: *Nancy Graves: Painting, Sculpture, Drawing 1980-5*, Vassar College Art Gallery, Poughkeepsie, 1986; E.A. Carmean *et al*: *The Sculpture of Nancy Graves*, Fort Worth 1987; Amy Fine Collins and Bradley Collins: "The Sum of the Parts [Nancy Graves]", *Art in America*, 1988, 113-8; L. Cathcart: *Nancy Graves: A Survey 1969-1980*, Albright-Knox Gallery, catalogue, 1981
160 Agnes Martin: *Night Sea*, 1963, oil and gold leaf on canvas, 72 x 72in, Saatchi Collection, London; *Drift of Summer*, 1965, acrylic and graphite on canvas, 72 x 72in, Saatchi Collection, London; *Mountain II*, 1966, oil and pencil on canvas, 72 x 72in, collection: R. Solomon, New York
161 Agnes Martin, quoted in Peter Schjedahl, 26

in their technique and subjects as any male painter. Oulton's canvases are as luscious and romantic as anything by, say, Titan, Rembrandt van Rijn, Diego Velásquez or Michelangelo Merisi da Caravaggio. Oulton's *Spinner*, painted in 1986, is a voluptuous, abstract creation, recalling the energetic gestures of the Expressionists and the Abstract Expressionists, while the colours, which melt from earth and ochre to white and pale, cerulean blue, recall landscape painters such as J.M.W. Turner, John Constable and Thomas Girtin.[162] The surface of Oulton's canvases – *Voice, The Heart of the Matter, In Fidelity, Countenance, The Passions, Mortal Coil* a n d *Space for Leda* – are extraordinarily sumptuous.[163] 'Oulton's work has a strong but non-specific erotic power,' writes Wendy Beckett (82), while John Griffiths describes Oulton's work thus:

> Highly textured 'wild' landscapes of the emotions, painted on a grand scale which suggest possible figurative images only to subvert the meanings suggested by the intrusion of quasi-abstract forms without obvious significance. Above all a sense of mystery and openness of spirit emerges underpinned by a strange, new, unlocated sense of landscape.[164]

And, as with Turner, her textures are always moving, never fixed. But, for all its surface sensuality, its iridescent but shadowy hues, Thérèse Oulton's work is religious, with spiritual goals. As with Turner, Oulton's canvases hint at a radiance busting out from behind shadows and darkness, as in her *Old Gold*,[165] which, like so many of Oulton's paintings, features a sense of over-arching structures, perhaps something of the sky or a mountainscape, as it might be in one of Turners' boiling, stormy

162 Thérèse Oulton: *Spinner*, 1986, oil on canvas, 234 x 213.5cm, private collection. See Gidal Lampert: *Thérèse Oulton Fools' Gold*, Gimpel Fils, catalogue, 1984; S. Morgan: *Thérèse Oulton: Skin Deep*, Galerie Thomas, Munich, 1986.
163 Thérèse Oulton: *Mortal Coil*, 1984, oil; *In Fidelity*, 1987, oil; *Countenance*, 1986, *oil*, all Marlborough Fine Art Gallery, London; *Voice*, 1984, oil on canvas, 92 x 84in, private collection; *Space for Leda*, 1983, oil on canvas, 269 x 228.5cm, collection: the artist
164 John Griffiths: "New Romantic Artists", in Papadakis: *The New Romantics*, 60
165 Oulton: *Old Gold*, 1984, oil on canvas, 205.7 x 259.1cm, Frankel Collection, Philadelphia

seas, or a storm in the Alps. In Oulton's work such direct connections are hinted at but not made dogmatic. Her abstraction hovers between hints of figuration and post-painterly abstraction. A sense of mystery is always retained, that spiritual 'openness' which renders her art so exciting. Critics call it 'romantic', and certainly it describes an area as far away as possible from the so-called 'real world' of socialist realistic, political, issue-based art. The colours Oulton uses repeatedly – whites, yellows, browns, ochres – are those of the Earth, of landscape. Oulton gives them an alchemical transmutation, where, as in alchemy, the 'base' metals or materials mined from the ground are transformed into something quite different, something spiritual. In Oulton's fervently mobile canvases we see the ferment of alchemy taking place. Her paintings are alchemical crucibles or vessels, you might say, in which the viewer is a witness to those supremely magical processes by which the life-stuff of the Earth (rocks, minerals, gold, soil, plants) becomes the life-stuff of the spirit (spiritual riches, spiritual gold). Oulton paints a 'landscape of the soul', where there is more emphasis, ultimately, on the soul than on the landscape, where the landscape (i.e. 'Nature') is the nourishment of the soul, after it has been 'processed', alchemically, by the artist, into a new kind of nourishment. The driving force behind this alchemical transmutation is Oulton's painterly sensuality, the eroticism of oil on canvas.

If you have doubts about there being any 'great' or powerful women painters about, painters who can more than look good when set against Julian Schnabel, Anselm Keifer, Robert Longo, Eric Fischl, Gerard Richter, David Salle, Jeff Koons and Francesco Clemente – then look at Thérèse Oulton's work, or Agnes Martin, or Helen Frankenthaler. If you want luscious sensuality in art, or a metaphysical, transcendent dimension, or rigorous formalism, or explorative abstraction, then you don't need to go to the revered 'modern masters' of contemporary art (Hockney, Kitaj, LeWitt, Scully, Stella, Johns, Rauschenberg, Warhol). You can find it aplenty in women artists such as Oulton, Nancy Graves, Jennifer Bartlett, Niki de Sant-Phalle, Mary Beth Edelson, Helen Frankenthaler, Elizabeth Catlett, Alison Wilding, Barbara Kruger, Lynn Malcolm, Agnes Martin, Elizabeth Murray, Judy Rifka, Katherine Porter, Susan Rothenberg, Eva Hesse, Lee Bontecou, Rebecca Horn, Magdalena Abakanowicz, Judy Pfaff and Pat Steir.

Lynda Benglis has produced three dimensional works which

develop the ironic objects of Claes Oldenburg, such as the wonderful, twisted *Aldebaran*.[166] Edward Lucie-Smith writes of Lynda Benglis thus:

> Oldenburg's drooping flaccid forms become emblems of impotence. Bengliss's rosettes are successors to an earlier group of sculptures in the shape of giant dildoes or penises. If we read what she is doing in the context supplied by Oldenburg's work, she still seems to be concerned with sexual issues – her comment is no longer one about men's fears of female aggression, but about women's need to adorn and at the same time 'cheapen' themselves, because they live in a man's world.' (*American Art Now*, 57)

The photographer Robert Mapplethorpe produced many pictures of penises: a penis on a pedestal, a black man's penis hanging out of a polyester suit, and so on.[167] These images were heavily contextualized as part of a homoerotic discourse. Women artists, such as Benglis have taken the phallus and put it into ironic, satirical contexts. Judith Bernstein produced thirty-foot high phallic drawings in the late 1960s, entitled *Phallic Screws. Of* these gigantic phalluses, Laurie Anderson wrote: '[t]he scale of Bernstein's seven new drawings, *Phallic Screws*, made Claes Oldenberg look like a miniaturist.'[168] Bernstein's aim was to appropriate some of the power of the phallus, an impossible goal to achieve for some feminists. Bernstein wrote: 'I feel the phallus has stood for power for so many centuries, and I feel that we women want to be part of that power.'[169] Bernstein's other pieces include *Supercock* (Superman with a penis twice as big as his body), and *Union Jack-Off Series* (flags with penises). Such feminist or 'women's ' art is forever marginalized by the art historical/ critical establishment. The arts establishment hasn't even really begun to address 'women's/ feminist art, perhaps because the issues it raises are simply too difficult/ complex/ troubling to deal with. Perhaps 'women's/ feminist art will always be marginalized and decentred because the establishment of arts

---

166 Lynda Benglis: *Aldebaran*, 1983, bronze, zinc, copper, aluminium, 167.5 x 134.5cm, Paula Cooper Gallery, New York
167 Mapplethorpe: *Man in Polyester Suit*, 1980, photograph, Estate of Robert Mapplethorpe
168 Anderson: "Judith Bernstein (AIR)", *Art News*, December 1973, 94
169 Bernstein in Jeanie Weiffenback: "Interview with Judith Bernstein", *Criss-Cross Art Communications*, January 1977, 228

criticism can only discuss a narrow range of issues. Anything outside of that confined discourse is threatening, too problematic, too confusing, too unnerving. It's not a question of not having an 'æsthetic framework' with which to analyze 'women's/ feminist art. There are plenty of theoretical/ æsthetic approaches available. It is, rather, that 'women's'/ feminist art speaks from and towards a creative cultural space on the boundaries of dominant culture, the 'wild zone'. And most critics and commentators, and nearly all critical discourse, simply does not want to have anything to do with a 'female'/ feminist 'wild zone'.

BIBLIOGRAPHY

All books are published in London, England, unless otherwise stated

Dorothy Aaron: *About Face: Towards a Positive Image of Women in Advertizing*, Ontario Status of Women Council, Toronto, 1975

Isobel Armstrong, ed. *New Feminist Discourses: Critical Essays on Theories and Texts*, Routledge, London, 1992

Karen Armstrong: *The Gospel According to Woman; Christianity's Creation of the Sex War in the West*, Pan, London, 1987

Geoffrey Ashe: *The Virgin: Mary's Cult and the Re-emergence of the Goddess*, Arkana, 1987

Alison Assister & Avedon Carol, eds. *Bad Girls and Dirty Pictures: The Challenge to Reclaim Feminism*, Pluto Press, London, 1993:

—. ed. *Althusser and Feminism*, Pluto Press, London, 1990

John Atkins: *Sex in Literature,* volume 2: *The Classical Experience of the Sexual Impulse*, Calder & Boyars, 1973

Patrick Bade: *Femme Fatale: Images of Evil and Fascinating Women*, Ash & Grant, 1979

Aliki Barnstone & Willis Barnstone, eds. *A Book of Women Poets: From Antiquity to Now*, Schocken Books, New York, NY, 1980

Kathleen Barry: *Female Sexual Slavery*, Prentice-Hall, NJ, 1979

Georges Bataille: *Literature and Evil*, tr. Alistair Hamilton, Calder, 1973

James Beck. *Italian Renaissance Painting*, Harper & Row, New York, NY, 1981

Ean Begg. *The Cult of the Black Virgin*, Routledge, London, 1985

Catherine Belsey: *Critical Practice*, Routledge, London, 1980

Nicola Bennett. *The British Art Show: Old Allegiances and New Directions, 1979-1984*, Orbis, 1984

Pamela Berger. *The Goddess Obscured*, Robert Hale, 1988

Leo Bersani: *A Future For Astynanax*, Marion Boyars, London, 1978

Frances Bonner, Lizbeth Goodman, Richard Allen, Linda Jones & Catherine King, eds. *Imagining Women Cultural Representations and Gender*, Polity Press, Cambridge, 1992

R. Braidotti: *Patterns of Dissonance: A Study of Contemporary Philosophy*, Polity Press, Cambridge, 1991

Serge Bramly. *Leonardo: The Artist and the Man*, Michael Joseph, 1992

Jan Bremmer, ed. *From Sappho to de Sade: Moments in the History of Sexuality*, Routledge, London, 1989

Robert Briffault: *The Mothers: A Study of the Origins of Sentiments and Institutions*, Allen & Unwin, 3 vols, 1927

Susan Brownmiller: *Against Our Will: Men, Women and Rape*, Bantam, New York, NY, 1976

J. Butler: *Gender Trouble: Feminism and the Subversion of Identity*, Routledge, London, 1990

—. & J.W. Scott, eds. *Feminists Theorise the Political*, Routledge, London, 1992

Deborah Cameron, ed. *The Feminist Critique of Language: A Reader*, Routledge, London, 1990

Joseph Campbell: *The Power of Myth*, with Bill Moyers, ed. Betty Sue Flowers, Doubleday, New York, NY, 1988

—. *The Hero With a Thousand Faces*, Paladin, London, 1988

Michael P. Carroll: *The Cult of the Virgin Mary*, Princeton University Press, NJ, 1986

Whitney Chadwick: *Women, Art, and Society*, Thames & Hudson, London, 1990

—. *Women Artists and the Surrealist Movement*, Thames & Hudson, London, 1991

Gail Chester & Julienne Dickey, ed. *Feminism and Censorship: The Current Debate*, Prism Press, Bridport, Dorset, 1988

Laura Chester, ed. *Deep Down: New Sensual Writing By Women, 1987*

Hélène Cixous: *A Hélène Cixous Reader*, ed. Susan Sellers, Routledge, London, 1994

—. & Catherine Clément: *The Newly Born Woman*, tr. Betsy Wing, Manchester University Press, Manchester, 1986

Frances Colpitt: *Minimal Art: The Critical Perspective*, University of Washington Press, Seattle, 1990

Gail Cunningham: *The New Woman and the Victorian Novel*, Macmillan, London, 1978

Magdalena Dabrowski. *Contrasts of Form: Geometric Abstract Art, 1910-80*, MOMA, New York, NY, 1985

Mary Daly: *Pure Lust: Elemental Feminist Philosophy*, Women's Press, London, 1984

—. *Gyn/ Ecology: The Metaethics of Radical Feminism*, Women's Press, London, 1979

—. *Beyond God the Father*, Women's Press, London, 1985

G. Day & C. Bloch, eds. *Perspectives on Pornography: Sexuality in Film and Literature*, Macmillan, London, 1988

—. *Readings in Popular Culture: Trivial Pursuits?*, Macmillan, London, 1990

M. de Certeau: *The Practice of Everyday Life*, University of California Press, Berkeley, CA, 1984

Christine Delphy: *The Main Enemy: A Materialist Analysis of Women's Oppression*, Women's Research and Resources Centre, 1977

—. "Andrea Dworkin", in Dworkin, 1993

Enno Develing & Lucy Lippard. *Minimal Art*, Städtische Kunsthalle, Düsseldorf, 1969

Jonathan Dollimore & Alan Sinfield, eds. *Political Shakespeare*, Manchester University Press, Manchester, 1985

John Drakakis, ed. *Alternative Shakespeares*, Routledge, London, 1988

Lene Dresen-Coenders, ed. *Saints and She-Devils: Images of Women in the 15th and 16th Centuries*, Rubicon Press, 1987

Steven C. Dubin: *Arresting Images: Impolitic Art and Uncivil Actions*, Routledge, London, 1992

Georges Duby & Michele Perrot: *Power and Beauty: Images of Women in Art*, Tauris Parke Books, 1989

Andrea Dworkin: *Mercy*, Arrow, 1990

—. *Ice and Fire*, Flamingo, 1987

—. *Intercourse*, Arrow, 1988

—. *Pornography: Men Possessing Women*, Women's Press, London, 1984

—. and Catherine MacKinnon: *Pornography and Civil Rights: A New Day for Women's Equality*, Organizing Against Pornography, Minneapolis, 1988

—. *Our Blood*, Harper & Row, New York, NY, 1976

—. *Right-Wing Women: The Politics of Domesticated Females*, Women's Press, London, 1983

—. *Letters From a War Zone*, Secker & Warburg, London, 1988

—. "Andrea Dworkin parle d'Israël", *Nouvelles Questions Féministes*, 14, 2, 1993

Richard Dyer: *Only Entertainment*, Routledge, London, 1992

Mary Eagleton, ed. *Feminist Literary Criticism*, Longman, London, 1991

—. ed. *Feminist Literary Theory: A Reader*, Blackwell, Oxford, 1986

Hester Eisenstein: *Contemporary Feminist Thought*, Unwin Paperbacks, 1984

Mircea Eliade: *Ordeal by Labyrinth*, University of Chicago Press, Chicago, IL, 1984

—. *Symbolism, the Sacred and the Arts*, Crossroad, New York, NY, 1985

M. Ellman, ed. *Thinking about Women*, Virago, London, 1979

Julius Evola: *The Metaphysics of Sex*, East-West Publications, 1985

R. Felski: *Beyond Feminist Aesthetics: Feminist Literature and Social Change*, Hutchinson, London, 1989

Feminist Review, eds. *Sexuality: A Reader*, Virago, London, 1987

Peter Fingesten: *The Eclipse of Symbolism*, University Press of California, 1970

John Fletcher & Andrew Benjamin, ed. *Abjection, Melancholia and Love: the Work of Julia Kristeva*, Routledge, London, 1990

Michel Foucault: *The History of Sexuality*, vol. 1, Penguin, London, 1981

—. *The Use of Pleasure: The History of Sexuality*, vol. 2, Penguin, London, 1987

Constance Franklin, ed. *Erotic Art by Living Artists*, Directors Guild Publishers, Renaissance, California, 1988

S. Franklin *et al*, eds. *Off Centre: Feminism and Cultural Studies*, HarperCollins, New York, NY, 1992

R.H. Fuchs. *Richard Long*, Thames & Hudson, London, 1986

Elinor Gadon: *The Once and Future Goddess*, Aquarian Press, London, 1990

Lorraine Gamman & Margaret Marshment, eds. *The Female Gaze: Women as Viewers of Popular Culture*, Women's Press, London, 1988

Pamela Church Gibson & Roma Gibson, ed. *Dirty Looks: Women, Pornography, Power*, British Film Institute, London, 1993

Marija Gimbutas: *The Language of the Goddess*, Thames & Hudson, London, 1989

Rona Goffen. *Giovanni Bellini*, Yale University Press, New Haven, CT, 1989

Erving Goffmann: *Gender Advertisements*, Macmillan, London, 1979

Robert Goldwater & Marco Treves, eds. *Artists on Art*, John Murray, 1975

Eugene Goodheart: *Desire and Its Discontents*, Columbia University Press, New York, NY, 1991

G. Greene & C. Kahn, eds. *Making a Difference: Feminist Literary Criticism*, Methuen, London, 1985

Clement Greenberg: *Art and Culture*, Beacon Press, Boston, MA, 1961

Germaine Greer: *The Obstacle Race: The Fortunes of Women Painters and Their Work*, Secker & Warburg, London, 1979; Picador, London, 1981

Gabriele Griffin *et al*, eds. *Stirring It: Challenges For Feminism*, Taylor & Francis, 1994

Susan Griffin: *Pornography and Silence: Culture's Revenge Against Nature*, Women's Press, London, 1981

Mary Beth Haralovitch: "Advertising Heterosexuality", *Screen*, 23, 2, 1982

M. Esther Harding: *Women's Mysteries*, Rider, 1989

Nancy G. Heller. *Women Artists. An Illustrated History*, Virago, London, 1987

Marianne Hester: *Lewd Women and Wicked Witches: A Study of the Dynamics of Male Domination*, Routledge, London, 1992

Janet Hobhouse: *The Bride Stripped Bare: The Artist and the Nude in the Twentieth Century*, Cape, London, 1988

David Holbrook, ed. *The Case Against Pornography,* Tom Stacey, 1972

Anne Hollander: *Seeing Through Clothes,* Viking Press, New York, NY, 1980

Maggie Humm: *Feminisms: A Reader,* Harvester Wheatsheaf, Hemel Hempstead, 1992

—. ed. *The Dictionary of Feminist Theory,* Harvester Wheatsheaf, Hemel Hempstead, 1989

— . *Feminist Criticism: Women as Contemporary Critics,* Harvester Wheatsheaf, Hemel Hempstead, 1986

Luce Irigaray: *The Irigaray Reader, ed.* Margaret Whitford, Blackwell, Oxford, 1991

—. *Je, tu, nous: Toward a Culture of Difference,* tr. Alison Martin, Routledge, London, 1993

— . *Thinking the Difference: For a Peaceful Revolution,* Athlone Press, London, 1994

Mary Jacobus, ed. *Women Writing and Writing About Women,* Croom Helm, 1979

Nancy G. Heller. *Women Artists. An Illustrated History,* Virago, London, 1987

Donald Judd. *Complete Writings, 1975-1986,* Van Abbemuseum, Eindhoven, Netherlands, 1987

J. Juffer. *At Home With Pornography,* New York University Press, New York, 1998

Philippe Julian. *Dreamers of Decadence: Symbolist Painters of the 1890s,* tr. Robert Baldick, Pall Mall Press, London, 1971

C.G. Jung: *Memories, Dreams, Reflections,* Collins, London, 1967

C. Kaplan: *Sea Changes: Essays on Culture and Feminism,* Verso, London, 1986

S. Kappeler: *The Pornography of Representation,* Polity Press, Cambridge, 1986

Bruce Kawin: *How Movies Work,* Macmillan, New York, NY, 1987

David Kinsley: *The Goddess's Mirror: Visions of the Divine From East and West,* State University of New York Press, Albany, NY, 1989

Cheris Kramarae & Paula A.Treichler, eds. *A Feminist Dictionary,* Pandora Press, London, 1987

Rosalind E. Krauss. *Passages in Modern Sculpture,* Thames & Hudson, London, 1977

Julia Kristeva: *The Kristeva Reader, ed.* Toril Moi, Blackwell, Oxford, 1986

—. *Desire in Language: A Semiotic Approach to Literature and Art,* ed. Leon Roudiez, tr. Thomas Gora, Alice Jardine & Leon Roudiez, Blackwell, Oxford, 1982

Annette Kuhn: *The Power of the Image: Essays on Representation and Sexuality,* Routledge, London, 1985

—. *Women's Pictures: Feminism and the cinema,* Routledge & Kegan Paul,

London, 1982

Weston La Barre: *The Ghost Dance,* Allen & Unwin, London, 1972

—. *Muelos,* Columbia University Press, New York, NY, 1985

Jacques Lacan and the *Ecole Freudienne: Feminine Sexuality,* ed. Juliet Mitchell and Jacqueline Rose, Macmillan, London, 1982

Marghanita Laski: *Ecstasy,* Cresset Press, London, 1961

D.H.Lawrence: *A Selection from Phoenix,* ed. A.A.H. Inglis, Penguin, London, 1971

—. *Selected Essays,* Penguin, London, 1950

—. *Lady Chatterley's Lover,* Penguin, London, 1960

—. *The Rainbow,* Penguin, London, 1981

—. *Phoenix,* Heinemann, London, 1956

—. *Phoenix II,* Heinemann, London, 1968

Antoinette Le Normand-Romain *et al,* eds. *Sculpture: The Adventure of Modern Sculpture in the Nineteenth and Twentieth Centuries,* Skira, Geneva, 1986

Carolyn Ruth Swift Lenz *et al,* eds. *The Woman's Part: Feminist Criticism of Shakespeare,* University of Illinois Press, Urbana, 1980

Lucy Lippard: *From the Center: feminist essays on women's art,* Dutton, New York, NY, 1976

—. *Six Years: The Dematerialization of the Art Object from, 1966 to, 1972,* Praeger, New York, NY, 1973

Edward Lucie-Smith: *Sexuality in Western Art,* Thames & Hudson, London, 1991

Fiona MacCarthy: *Eric Gill,* Faber, London, 1989

Catherine MacKinnon: *Towards a Feminist Theory of the State,* Harvard University Press, Cambridge, MA, 1989

—. *Feminism Unmodified: Discourses on Life and Law,* Harvard University Press, Cambridge, MA, 1987

Angela McRobbie, ed. *Zoot Suits and Second-Hand Dresses: An Anthology of Fashion and Music,* Macmillan, London, 1989

—. & M. Nava, eds. *Gender and Generation,* Macmillan, London, 1984

Elaine Marks & Isabelle de Courtivron, eds. *New French Feminisms: an Anthology,* Harvester Wheatsheaf, Hemel Hempstead, 1981

Gerardine Meaney: *(Un)Like Subjects: Women, Theory, Fiction,* Routledge, London, 1993

Nancy Miller, ed. *The Poetics of Gender,* New York, NY, 1986

Kate Millett: *Sexual Politics,* Doubleday, New York, NY, 1970

—. *The Prostitution Papers,* Avon Books, New York, NY, 1973

Toril Moi: *Sexual/ Textual Politics: Feminist Literary Theory,* Routledge, London, 1988

—. ed. *French Feminist Thought: A Reader,* Blackwell, Oxford, 1987

Moira Monteith, ed. *Women's Writing: A Challenge to Theory,* Harvester Press, Brighton, Sussex, 1986

Michael Moorcock: *Casablanca,* Gollancz, 1989

Robin Morgan: *The Word of a Woman: Selected Prose, 1968-1992*, Virago, London, 1993

Edward Mullins: *The Painted Witch: Female Body, Male Art*, Secker & Warburg, London, 1985

Laura Mulvey: *Visual and Other Pleasures*, Macmillan, London, 1989

Sally Munt, ed. *New Lesbian Criticism: Literary and Cultural Readings*, Harvester Wheatsheaf, Hemel Hempstead, 1992

Lynda Nead: *Female Nude: Art, Obscenity and Sexuality*, Routledge, London, 1992

Erich Neumann: *The Great Mother*, Princeton University Press, NJ, 1972

Shirley Nicholson, ed. *The Goddess Re-awakening: The Goddess Principle Today* Theosophical Publishing House, New York, NY, 1989

Onlywomen, ed. *Love Your Enemy? The Debate Between Heterosexual Feminism and Political Lesbianism*, Onlywomen Press, London, 1981

P. O'Toole. *Pornocopia*, Serpent's Tail, London, 1998

Ursula Owen, ed. *Index on Censorship*, Writers & Scholars International, 1/2, May June, 1994

Rozsika Parker & Griselda Pollock: *Old Mistresses: Women, Art and Ideology*, Routledge & Kegan Paul, London, 1981

Michael Payne: *Reading Theory: An Introduction to Lacan, Derrida, and Kristeva*, Blackwell, Oxford, 1993

Constance Penley, ed. *Feminism and Film Theory*, Routledge, New York, NY, 1988

Karen Petersen & J.J. Wilson: *Women Artists: Recognition and Reappraisal from the Early Middle Ages to the Twentieth Century* Women's Press, London, 1978

Griselda Pollock: *Vision and Difference: femininity, feminism and histories of art*, Routledge, London, 1988

H.L. Radtke & H.J. Stam, eds. *Gender and Power*, Sage, 1994

Janice Radway: *Reading the Romance: Feminism and the Representation of Women in Popular Culture*, University of North Carolina Press, Chapel Hill, 1984

Peter Redgrove. *The Black Goddess and the Sixth Sense*, Bloomsbury, London, 1987

J.L. Reich: "Genderfuck: The Law of the Dildo", *Discourse: Journal of Theoretical Studies in Media and Culture*, vol. 15, 1, 1992

Kathleen J. Reiger, ed. *The Spiritual Image in Modern Art*, Theosophical Publishing House, Wheaton, Illinois, 1987

Patrice Retro: "Mass Culture and the Feminine", *Cinema Journal*, 25, 1986

Philip Rice & Patricia Waugh, eds. *Modern Literary Theory: A Reader*, Arnold, London, 1992

Adrienne Rich: *Blood, Bread and Poetry*, Virago, London, 1980

Corrine Robbins, ed. *The Pluralist Era: American Art, 1968-1981*, Harper & Row, New York, NY, 1984

Franz Roh. *German Art in the Twentieth Century: Painting, Sculpture,*

` Architecture`, Thames & Hudson, London, 1968

Barbara Rose. *American Art Since, 1900*, Thames & Hudson, London, 1967

—. *American Painting*, Skira/Razzoli International, New York, NY, 1986

Robert Rosenblum. *Modern Painting and the Northern Romantic Tradition*,Thames & Hudson, London, 1978

Mark Roskill. *What is Art History?*, Thames & Hudson, London, 1976

John Ruskin. *Works*, ed. E.T. Cook & A. Wedderburn, 39 vols, Allen, 1903-12

Bertrand Russell: *A History of Western Philosophy*, Allen & Unwin, London, 1971

Gill Saunders: *The Nude: a new perspective*, Herbert Press, London, 1989

Janet Sayers: *Biological Politics*, London, 1982

C. Schwichtenberg, ed. *The Madonna Connection: Representational Politics, Subcultural Identities, and Cultural Theory*, Westview Press, Boulder, 1993

Eve Sedgwick: *Between Men: English Literature and Male Homosexual Desire*, Columbia University Press, New York, NY, 1985

L. Segal & M. McIntosh, eds. *Sex Exposed: Sexuality and the Pornographic Debate*, Virago, London, 1992

Eric Shanes: *Constantin Brancusi*, Abbeville, New York, NY, 1989

Ruth Sherry: *Studying Women's Writings: An Introduction*, Edward Arnold, London, 1988

Elaine Showalter, ed. *The New Feminist Criticism*, Virago, London, 1986

—. ed. *Speaking of Gender*, Routledge, London, 1989

—. *Sexual Anarchy: Gender and Culture at the* Fin de Siècle, Virago, London, 1992

Penelope Shuttle & Peter Redgrove: *The Wise Wound*, Paladin/ Grafton, 1978/86

Monica Sjöo & Barbara Mor: *The Great Cosmic Mother*, Harper & Row, San Francisco, CA, 1987

Dale Spender: *Man-Made Language*, Routledge & Kegan Paul, London, 1980

—. *The Writing or the Sex? why you don't have to read women's writing to know it's no good*, Pergamon Press, New York, NY, 1989

Nikos Stangos, ed. *Concepts of Modern Art*, Thames & Hudson, London, 1981

Frank Stella. *Working Space*, Harvard University Press, Cambridge, MA, 1986

Judith Still & Michael Worton, eds. *Textuality and Sexuality: Reading Theories and Practices*, Manchester University Press, Manchester, 1993

Susan Rubin Suleiman, ed. *The Female Body in Western Culture: Contemporary Perspectives*, Harvard University Press, Cambridge, MA, 1986

J. Stoltenberg: *Refusing To Be a Man*, Fontana, 1990

Andrew Tilly. *Erotic Drawings*, Phaidon, 1986

William Thompson: *The Time Falling Bodies Take to Light: Mythology, Sexuality and the Origins of Culture*, St Martin's Press, New York, NY, 19811

Maurice Tuchman. *The New York School*, Thames & Hudson, London, 1971

—. *The Spiritual in Art: Abstract Painting 1880-1985*, Los Angeles County Museum of Art/ Abbeville Press, New York, NY, 1986

William Tucker. *The Language of Sculpture*, Thames & Hudson, London, 1974

Maurice Valency: *In Praise of Love: An Introduction to the Love-Poetry of the Renaissance*, Macmillan, New York, NY, 1961

Kirk Varnedoe. *Vienna, 1900: Art, Architecture & Design*, Museum of Modern Art, New York, NY, 1986

Lionello Venturi. *Renaissance Painting, from Leonardo to Dürer*, Skira/ Macmillan, London, 1979

—. *Italian Paintings*, Zwemmer, 1950

—. *Botticelli*, Phaidon, 1964

Peter Vergo. *Art in Vienna: 1898-1918: Klimt, Kokoschka, Schiele and Their Contemporaries*, Phaidon, 1975

Paul Vogt. *Contemporary Painting*, Abrams, New York, NY, 1981

Benjamin Walker: *Body Magic*, Paladin, London, 1979

R. Warhol & D.P. Herndl: *Feminisms*, Rutgers University Press, New Brunswick, NJ

Marina Warner: *Alone Of All Her Sex: The Myth and Cult of the Virgin Mary*, Picador, London, 1985

—. *Monuments and Maidens*, Weidenfeld & Nicolson, London, 1985

Valerie Wayne, ed. *The Matter of Difference: Materialist Feminist Criticism of Shakespeare*, Harvester Wheatsheaf, Hemel Hempstead, 1991

Peter Webb: *The Erotic Arts*, Secker & Warburg, London, 1983

Daniel Wheeler: *Art Since Mid-Century:, 1945 to the Present*, Thames & Hudson, London, 1991

Margaret Whitford: *Luce Irigaray: Philosophy of the Feminine*, Routledge, London, 1991

S. Wilkinson & C. Kitzinger, eds. *Heterosexuality: A Feminism and Psychology Reader*, Sage, 1993

Judith Williamson: *Consuming Passion: The Dynamics of Popular Culture*, Marion Boyars, 1986

Colin Wilson: *The Sexual Misfits: A Study of Sexual Outsiders*, Collins, London, 1989

Heinrich Wolfflin. *Classic Art*, Phaidon, 1952/80

Gerard Woods *et al*, eds. *Art Without Boundaries*, Thames & Hudson, London, 1972

Manfred Wudram. *Art of the Renaissance*, Weidenfeld & Nicolson, 1985

Malcolm Yorke. *Eric Gill: Man of Flesh and Spirit*, Constable, 1981

THE ART OF
ANDY GOLDSWORTHY

COMPLETE WORKS: SPECIAL EDITION
(PAPERBACK and HARDBACK)

by William Malpas

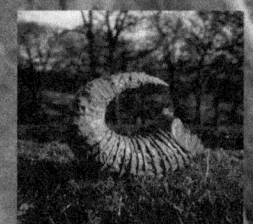

A new, special edition of the study of the contemporary British sculptor,
Andy Goldsworthy, including a new introduction, new bibliography and many
new illustrations.

This is the most comprehensive, up-to-date, well-researched and in-depth
account of Goldsworthy's art available anywhere.

Andy Goldsworthy makes land art. His sculpture is a sensitive, intuitive
response to nature, light, time, growth, the seasons and the earth. Goldsworthy's environmental art is becoming ever more popular: 1993's art book
Stone was a bestseller; the press raved about Goldsworthy taking over a
number of London West End art galleries in 1994; during 1995 Goldsworthy
designed a set of Royal Mail stamps and had a show at the British Museum.
Malpas surveys all of Goldsworthy's art, and analyzes his relation with other
land artists such as Robert Smithson, Walter de Maria, Richard Long and
David Nash, and his place in the contemporary British art scene.

The Art of Andy Goldsworthy discusses all of Goldsworthy's important and
recent exhibitions and books, including the *Sheepfolds* project; the TV documentaries; *Wood* (1996); the New York Holocaust memorial (2003); and
Goldsworthy's collaboration on a dance performance.

Illustrations: 70 b/w, 1 colour. 330 pages. New, special, 2nd edition.
Publisher: Crescent Moon Publishing. Distributor: Gardners Books.

ISBN 1-86171-059-3 (9781861710598) (Paperback) £25.00 / $44.00

ISBN 1-86171-080-1 (9781861710802) (Hardback) £60.00 / $105.00

ANDY GOLDSWORTHY
IN CLOSE-UP

SPECIAL EDITION (HARDBACK and PAPERBACK)

by William Malpas

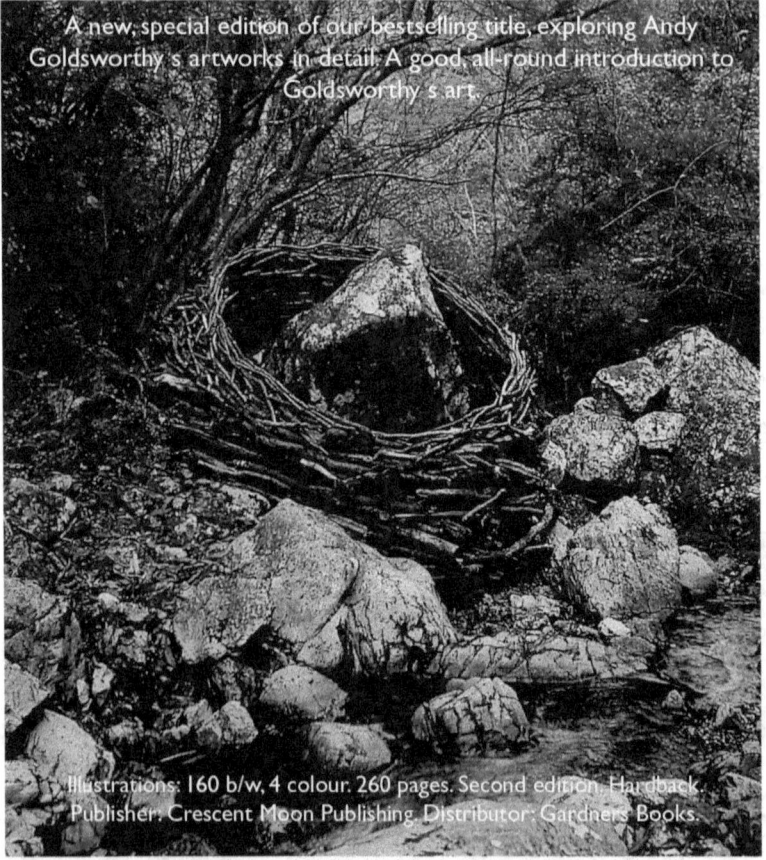

A new, special edition of our bestselling title, exploring Andy Goldsworthy's artworks in detail. A good, all-round introduction to Goldsworthy's art.

Illustrations: 160 b/w, 4 colour. 260 pages. Second edition. Hardback. Publisher: Crescent Moon Publishing. Distributor: Gardners Books.

ISBN 1-86171-094-1 (9781861710949) (Hbk) £60.00 / $105.00

ISBN 1-86171-091-7 (9781861710919) (Pbk) £25.00 / $44.00

Available from bookstores. amazon.com, play.com, tesco.com, and other websites.
In the United States from Baker & Taylor, (800) 7753760 or (800) 7751100
or (908) 5417062. electser@btol.com or btinfo@btol.com.

ANDY GOLDSWORTHY

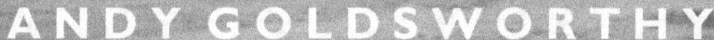

TOUCHING NATURE:
SPECIAL EDITION

(PAPERBACK and HARDBACK)

by William Malpas

A new, special and updated edition of our bestselling title, providing
an excellent general introduction to the art of Andy Goldsworthy.

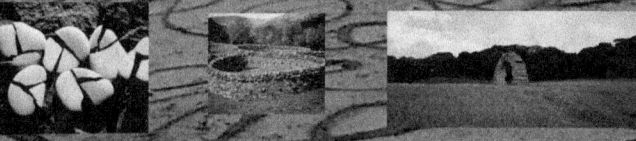

Illustrations: 75 b/w, 2 colour. 354 pages. Third edition. Paperback.

Publisher: Crescent Moon Publishing. Distributor: Gardners Books.

ISBN 1-86171-056-9 (9781861717) (Paperback) £25.00 / $44.00

ISBN 1-86171-087-9 (9781861710871) (Hardback) £60.00 / $105.00

THE ART OF
RICHARD LONG

COMPLETE WORKS : SPECIAL EDITION
(HARDBACK and PAPERBACK)

by William Malpas

A new study of the British artist Richard Long, an important contemporary international artist. The most detailed, in-depth
exploration of Richard Long's art currently available.

Illustrations: 48 b/w, 2 colour. 439 pages.
First edition. Hardback and paperback editions.

Publisher: Crescent Moon Publishing. Distributor: Gardners Books.

ISBN 1-86171-079-8 (9781861710796) (Hardback) £60.00 / $105.00

ISBN 1-86171-081-X (9781861710819) (Paperback) £25.00 / $44.00

LAND ART

A COMPLETE GUIDE TO LANDSCAPE, ENVIRONMENTAL, EARTHWORKS, NATURE, SCULPTURE AND INSTALLATION ART

by William Malpas

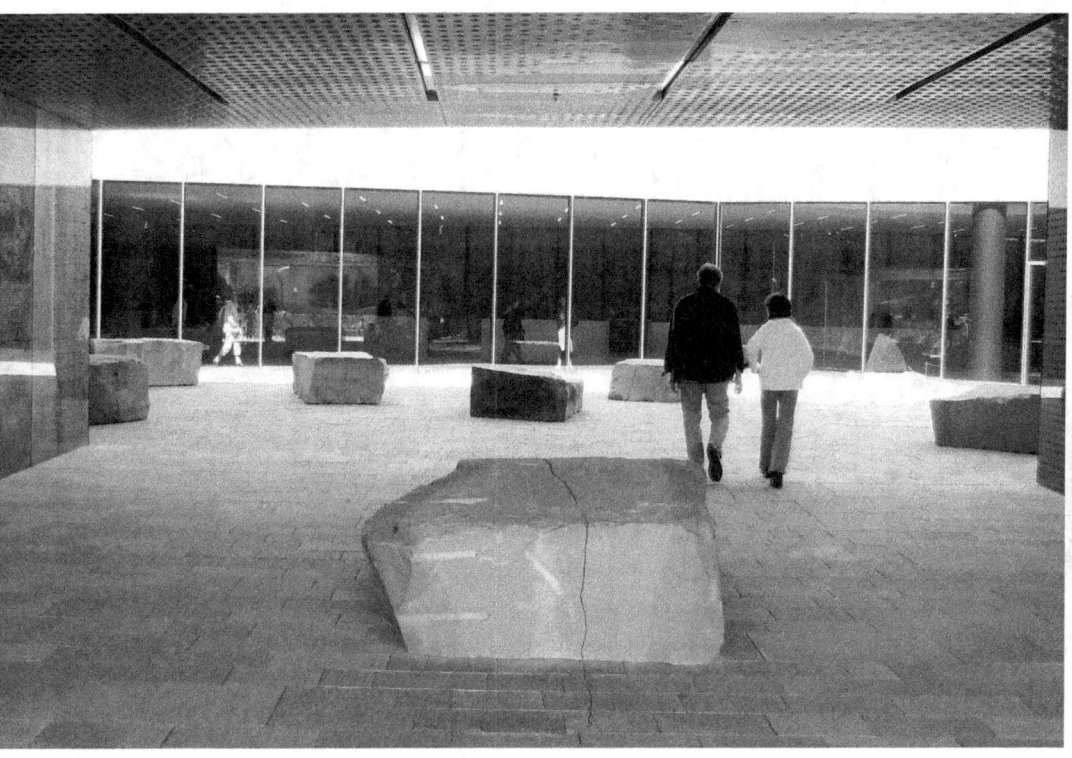

A new, special edition of our popular book on land art.
Chapters on land artists such as Robert Smithson, Walter de Maria, Christo,
Michael Heizer, Richard Long and Andy Goldsworthy.

Illustrations: 35 b/w, 2 colour. 314 pages. First edition. Paperback.

Publisher: Crescent Moon Publishing. Distributor: Gardners Books.

ISBN 1-86171-062-3 (9781861710628) £25.00 / $44.00

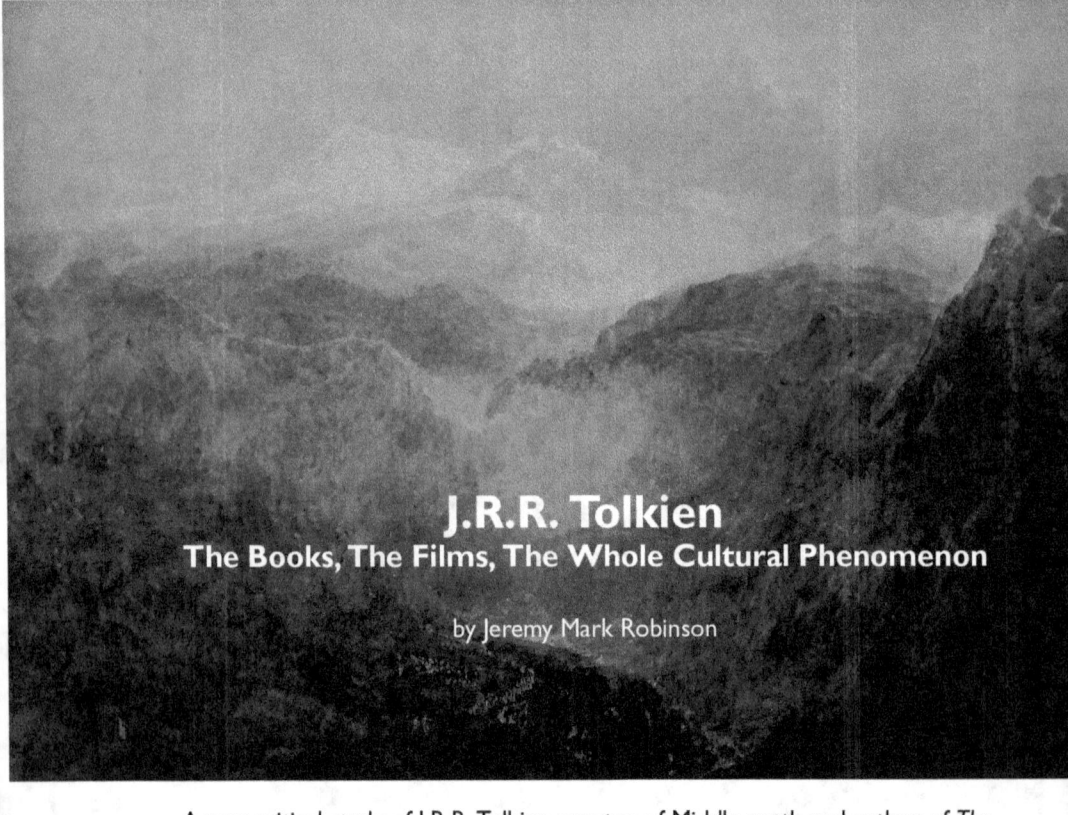

J.R.R. Tolkien
The Books, The Films, The Whole Cultural Phenomenon

by Jeremy Mark Robinson

A new critical study of J.R.R. Tolkien, creator of Middle-earth and author of *The Lord of the Rings*, *The Hobbit* and *The Silmarillion*, among other books.

This new critical study explores Tolkien's major writings (*The Lord of the Rings, The Hobbit, Beowulf: The Monster and the Critics, The Letters, The Silmarillion* and *The History of Middle-earth* volumes); Tolkien and fairy tales; the mythological, political and religious aspects of Tolkien's Middle-earth; the critics' response to Tolkien's fiction over the decades; the Tolkien industry (merchandizing, toys, role-playing games, posters, Tolkien societies, conferences and the like); Tolkien in visual and fantasy art; the cultural aspects of The Lord of the Rings (from the 1950s to the present); Tolkien's fiction's relationship with other fantasy fiction, such as C.S. Lewis and *Harry Potter*; and the TV, radio and film versions of Tolkien's books, including the 2001-03 Hollywood interpretations of *The Lord of the Rings*.

This new book draws on contemporary cultural theory and analysis and offers a sympathetic and illuminating (and sceptical) account of the Tolkien phenomenon. This book is designed to appeal to the general reader (and viewer) of Tolkien: it is written in a clear, jargon-free and easily-accessible style.

754pp ISBN 1-86171-057-7 £25.00 / $37.50

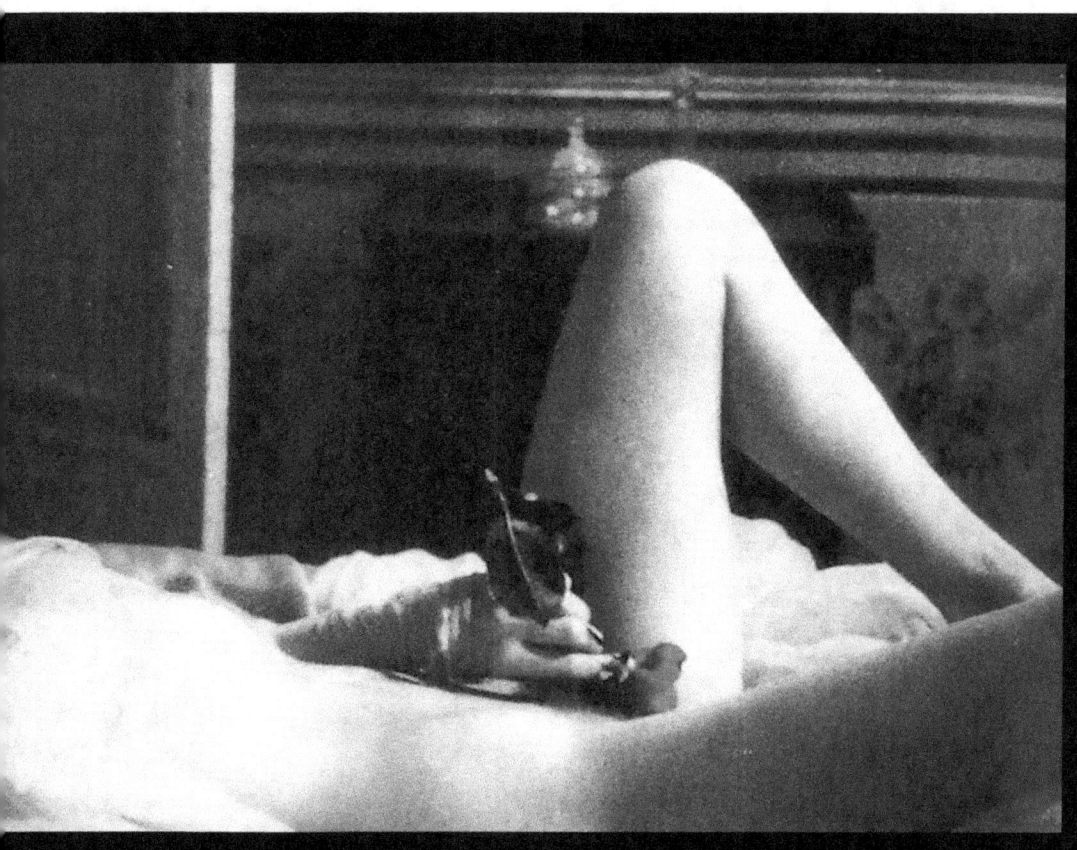

Walerian Borowczyk

Cinema of Erotic Dreams

by Jeremy Mark Robinson

Walerian Borowczyk (1923-2006) was a Polish artist, animator and filmmaker who lived in France for much of his life. He is the author of European art cinema masterpieces Goto: Island of Love, Blanche and Immoral Tales, some surreal animated shorts, and controversial films such as The Beast. This new book concentrates on Borowczyk's feature films, from Goto to Love Rites, which contain some of the most extraordinary images and scenes in recent cinema. Erotica for some, porn for others, Borowczyk's films are highly idiosyncratic and unforgettable.

Bibliography, notes, illustrations 240pp.
Paperback ISBN 9781861712301 £15.00 / $30.00

Jean-Luc Godard

The Passion of Cinema /
Le Passion de Cinéma

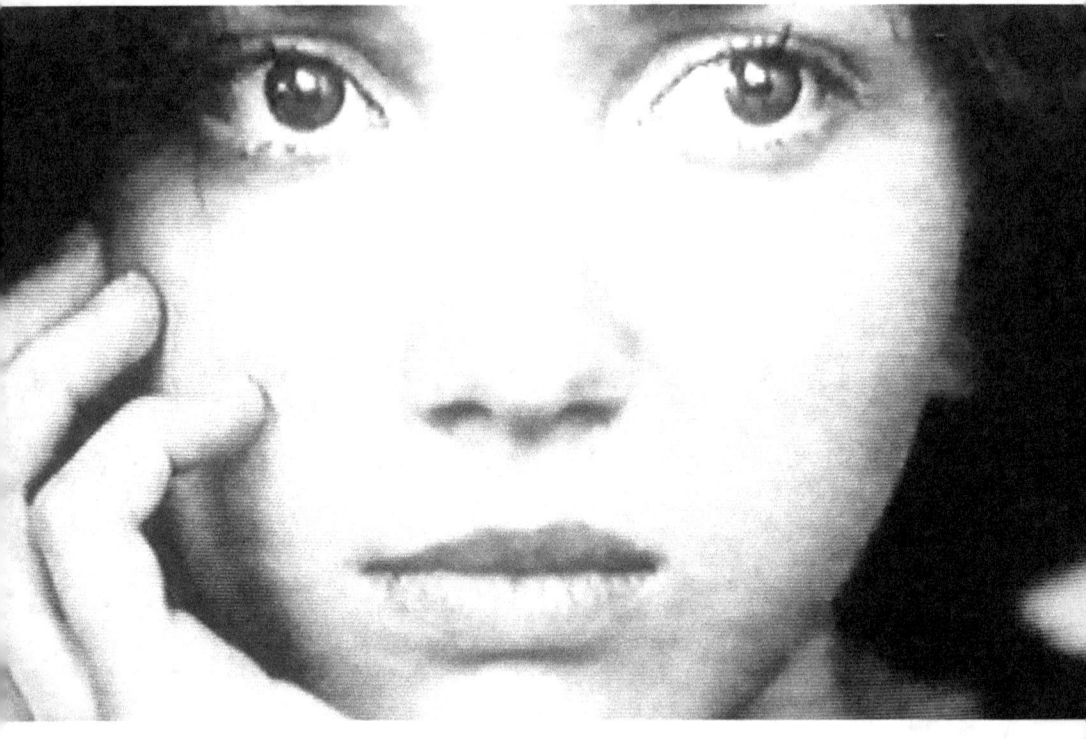

by Jeremy Mark Robinson

A new study of the French filmmaker Jean-Luc Godard (b. 1930),
director of iconic films such as *Breathless, Weekend, Pierrot le Fou,
Passion* and *Vivre Sa vie*. This book explores 27 of Godard's major films,
from *Breathless* to *Notre Musique*, and includes a scene by scene
analysis of Godard's controversial 1985 movie of the Virgin Mary,
Je Vous Salue, Marie.

Bibliography, notes, illustrations   420pp
Hardback   ISBN 9781761712271   £50.00 / $100.00

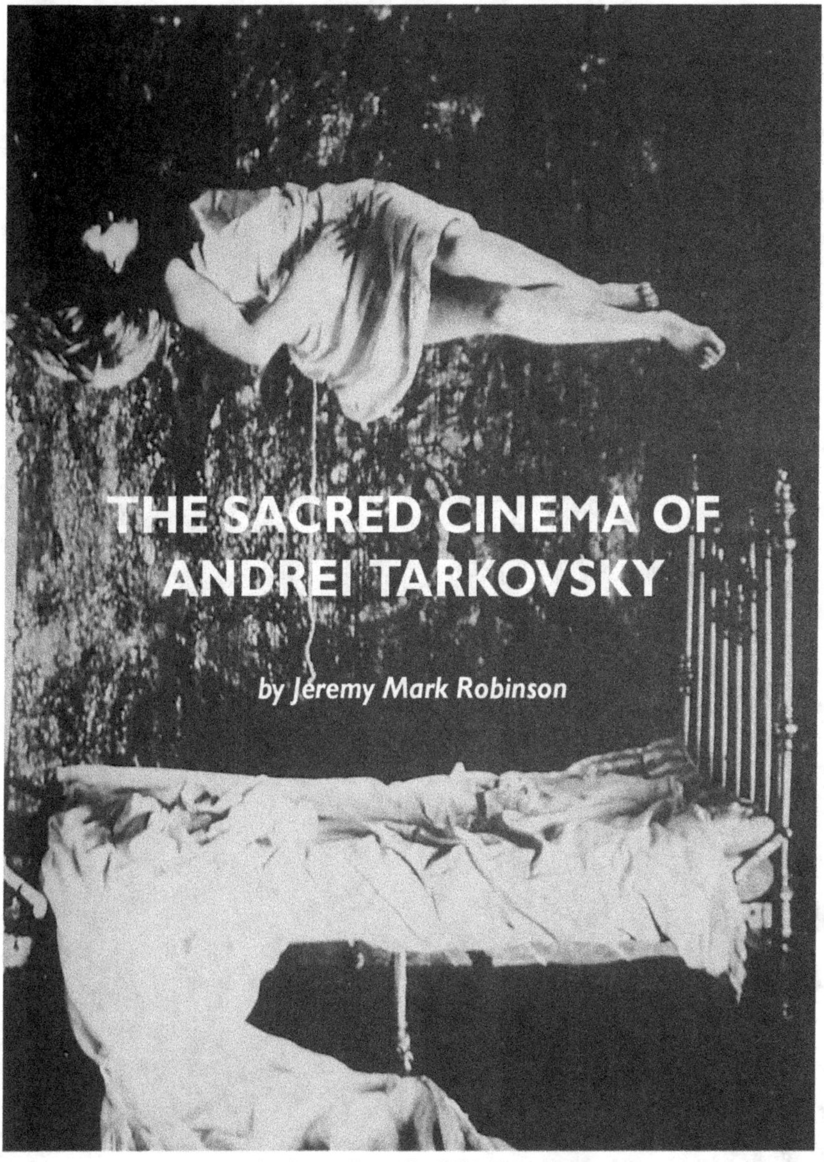

THE SACRED CINEMA OF ANDREI TARKOVSKY

by Jeremy Mark Robinson

A new study of the Russian filmmaker Andrei Tarkovsky (1932-1986), director of seven feature films, including *Andrei Roublyov, Mirror, Solaris, Stalker* and *The Sacrifice*.

This is one of the most comprehensive and detailed studies of Tarkovsky's cinema available. Every film is explored in depth, with scene-by-scene analyses. All aspects of Tarkovsky's output are critiqued, including editing, camera, staging, script, budget, collaborations, production, sound, music, performance and spirituality. Tarkovsky is placed with a European New Wave tradition of filmmaking, alongside directors like Ingmar Bergman, Carl Theodor Dreyer, Pier Paolo Pasolini and Robert Bresson.

An essential addition to film studies.

Illustrations: 150 b/w, 4 colour. 682 pages. First edition. Hardback.

Publisher: Crescent Moon Publishing. Distributor: Gardners Books.

ISBN 1-86171-096-8 (9781861710963) £60.00 / $105.00

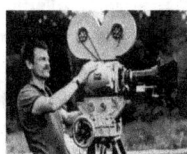

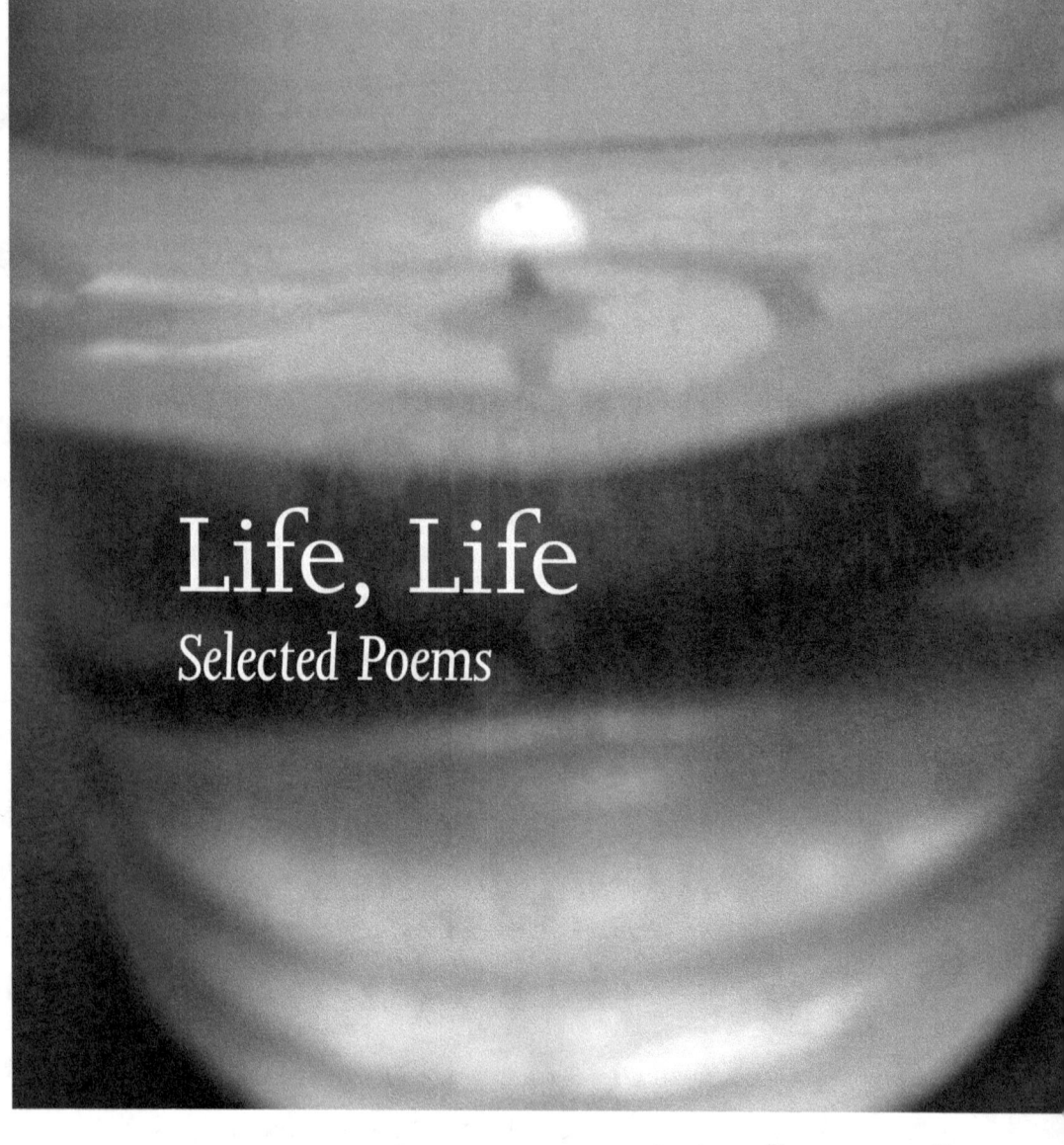

Life, Life
Selected Poems

Arseny Tarkovsky

translated and edited by Virginia Rounding

Arseny Tarkovsky is the neglected Russian poet, father of the acclaimed film director
Andrei Tarkovsky. This new book gathers together many of Tarkovsky's most lyrical
and heartfelt poems, in Rounding's clear, new translations. Many of Tarkovsky's poems
appeared in his son's films, such as *Mirror, Stalker, Nostalghia and The Sacrifice.*
There is an introduction by Rounding, and a bibliography of both Arseny and Andrei Tarkovsky.

Bibliography and notes   110pp   2nd ed   ISBN 1-86171-114-X   £10.00 / $20.00

In the Dim Void

Samuel Beckett's Late Trilogy:
Company, Ill Seen, Ill Said and *Worstward Ho*

by Gregory Johns

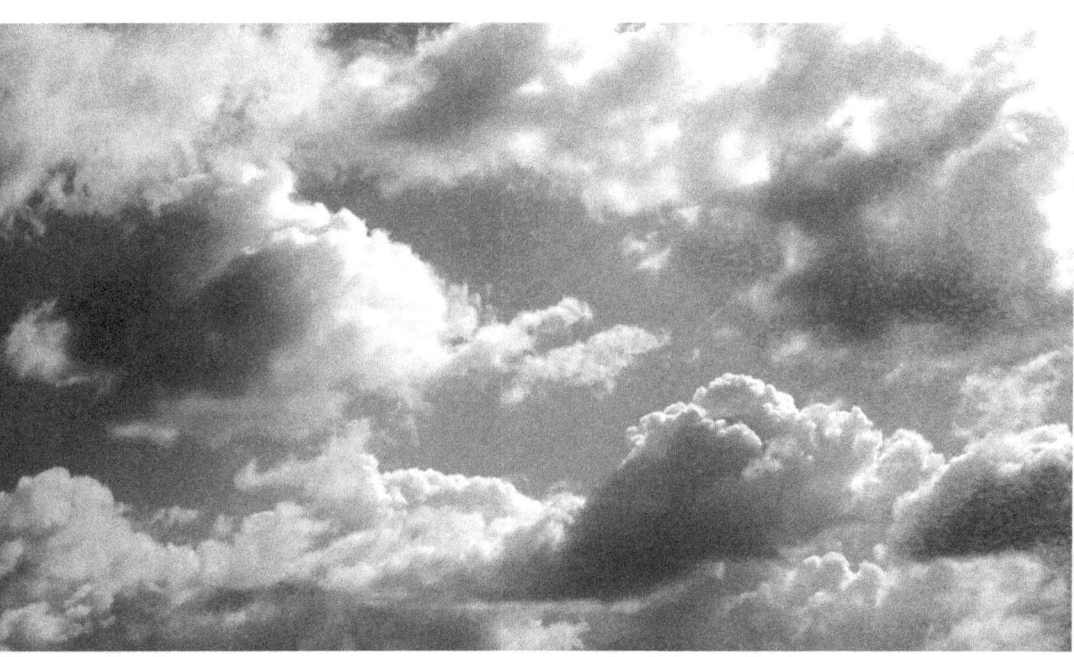

This book discusses the luminous beauty and dense, rigorous poetry of Beckett's late works, *Company, Ill Seen, Ill Said* and *Worstward Ho*. Johns looks back over Beckett's long writing career, charting the development from the *Molloy-Malone Dies-Unnamable* trilogy through the 'fizzles' of the 1960s to the elegiac lyricism of the *Company* series. Johns compares the trilogy with late plays such as *Ghosts, Footfalls* and *Rockaby*.

Bibliography, notes. 120pp
ISBN 1861710712 and ISBN 1861712356   £10.00 / $20.00

CRESCENT MOON PUBLISHING

ARTS, PAINTING, SCULPTURE

The Art of Andy Goldsworthy: Complete Works
Andy Goldsworthy: Touching Nature
Andy Goldsworthy in Close-Up
Andy Goldsworthy: Pocket Guide
Andy Goldsworthy In America

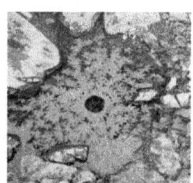

Land Art: A Complete Guide
Richard Long: The Art of Walking
The Art of Richard Long: Complete Works
Richard Long in Close-Up
Richard Long: Pocket Guide

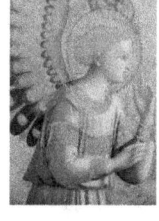

Land Art In the UK
Land Art in Close-Up
Land Art In the U.S.A.
Land Art: Pocket Guide
Installation Art in Close-Up

Minimal Art and Artists In the 1960s and After
Colourfield Painting
Land Art DVD, TV documentary
Andy Goldsworthy DVD, TV documentary
The Erotic Object: Sexuality in Sculpture From Prehistory to the Present Day
Sex in Art: Pornography and Pleasure in Painting and Sculpture
Postwar Art
Sacred Gardens: The Garden in Myth, Religion and Art
Glorification: Religious Abstraction in Renaissance and 20th Century Art
Early Netherlandish Painting
Leonardo da Vinci
Piero della Francesca
Giovanni Bellini

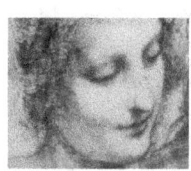

Fra Angelico: Art and Religion in the Renaissance
Mark Rothko: The Art of Transcendence
Frank Stella: American Abstract Artist
Jasper Johns: Painting By Numbers
Brice Marden

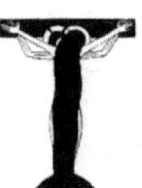

Alison Wilding: The Embrace of Sculpture
Vincent van Gogh: Visionary Landscapes
Eric Gill: Nuptials of God
Constantin Brancusi: Sculpting the Essence of Things
Max Beckmann

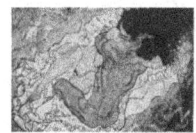

Egon Schiele: Sex and Death In Purple Stockings
Delizioso Fotografico Fervore: Works In Process 1
Sacro Cuore: Works In Process 2
The Light Eternal: J.M.W. Turner
The Madonna Glorified: Karen Arthurs

LITERATURE

J.R.R. Tolkien: The Books, The Films, The Whole Cultural Phenomenon
The *Earthsea* Books of Ursula Le Guin
Beauties, Beasts and Enchantment: Classic French Fairy Tales
Tolkien's Heroic Quest
Sexing Hardy: Thomas Hardy and Feminism
Thomas Hardy's *Tess of the d'Urbervilles*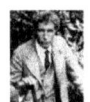
Thomas Hardy's *Jude the Obscure*
Thomas Hardy: The Tragic Novels
Love and Tragedy: Thomas Hardy
The Poetry of Landscape in Hardy
Wessex Revisited: Thomas Hardy and John Cowper Powys
Wolfgang Iser: Essays
Petrarch, Dante and the Troubadours
Maurice Sendak and the Art of Children's Book Illustration
Andrea Dworkin
Cixous, Irigaray, Kristeva: The *Jouissance* of French Feminism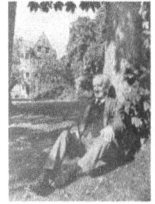
Julia Kristeva: Art, Love, Melancholy, Philosophy, Semiotics and Psychoanalysis
Hélène Cixous I Love You: The *Jouissance* of Writing
Luce Irigaray: Lips, Kissing, and the Politics of Sexual Difference
Peter Redgrove: Here Comes the Flood
Peter Redgrove: Sex-Magic-Poetry-Cornwall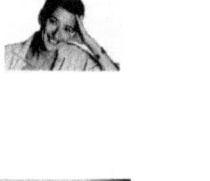
Lawrence Durrell: Between Love and Death, East and West
Love, Culture & Poetry: Lawrence Durrell
Cavafy: Anatomy of a Soul
German Romantic Poetry: Goethe, Novalis, Heine, Hölderlin
Feminism and Shakespeare
Shakespeare: Love, Poetry & Magic
The Passion of D.H. Lawrence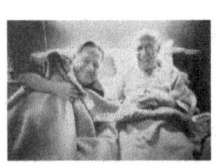
D.H. Lawrence: Symbolic Landscapes
D.H. Lawrence: Infinite Sensual Violence
Rimbaud: Arthur Rimbaud and the Magic of Poetry
The Ecstasies of John Cowper Powys
Sensualism and Mythology: The Wessex Novels of John Cowper Powys
Amorous Life: John Cowper Powys and the Manifestation of Affectivity (H.W. Fawkner)
Postmodern Powys: New Essays on John Cowper Powys (Joe Boulter)
Rethinking Powys: Critical Essays on John Cowper Powys
Paul Bowles & Bernardo Bertolucci
Rainer Maria Rilke
Joseph Conrad: *Heart of Darkness*
In the Dim Void: Samuel Beckett
Samuel Beckett Goes into the Silence
André Gide: Fiction and Fervour
Jackie Collins and the Blockbuster Novel
Blinded By Her Light: The Love-Poetry of Robert Graves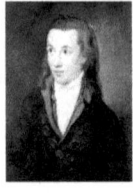
The Passion of Colours: Travels In Mediterranean Lands
Poetic Forms

POETRY

Ursula Le Guin: Walking In Cornwall
The Best of Peter Redgrove's Poetry
Peter Redgrove: Here Comes The Flood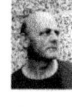
Peter Redgrove: Sex-Magic-Poetry-Cornwall
Dante: Selections From the Vita Nuova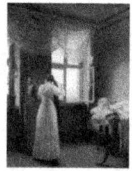
Petrarch, Dante and the Troubadours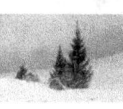
William Shakespeare: Sonnets
William Shakespeare: Complete Poems
Blinded By Her Light: The Love-Poetry of Robert Graves
Emily Dickinson: Selected Poems
Emily Brontë: Poems
Thomas Hardy: Selected Poems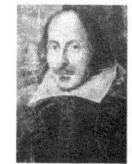
Percy Bysshe Shelley: Poems
John Keats: Selected Poems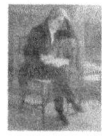
D.H. Lawrence: Selected Poems
Edmund Spenser: Poems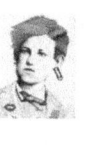
Edmund Spenser: Amoretti
John Donne: Poems
Henry Vaughan: Poems
Sir Thomas Wyatt: Poems
Robert Herrick: Selected Poems
Rilke: Space, Essence and Angels in the Poetry of Rainer Maria Rilke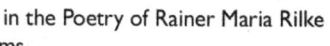
Rainer Maria Rilke: Selected Poems
Friedrich Hölderlin: Selected Poems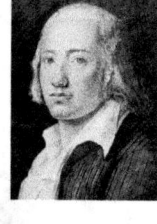
Arseny Tarkovsky: Selected Poems
Arthur Rimbaud: Selected Poems
Arthur Rimbaud: A Season in Hell
Arthur Rimbaud and the Magic of Poetry
Novalis: Hymns To the Night
Paul Verlaine: Selected Poems
D.J. Enright: By-Blows
Jeremy Reed: Brigitte's Blue Heart
Jeremy Reed: Claudia Schiffer's Red Shoes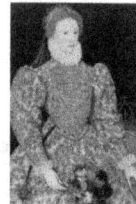
Gorgeous Little Orpheus
Radiance: New Poems
Crescent Moon Book of Nature Poetry
Crescent Moon Book of Love Poetry
Crescent Moon Book of Mystical Poetry
Crescent Moon Book of Elizabethan Love Poetry
Crescent Moon Book of Metaphysical Poetry
Crescent Moon Book of Romantic Poetry
Pagan America: New American Poetry

MEDIA, CINEMA, FEMINISM and CULTURAL STUDIES

J.R.R. Tolkien: The Books, The Films, The Whole Cultural Phenomenon
Cixous, Irigaray, Kristeva: The *Jouissance* of French Feminism
Julia Kristeva: Art, Love, Melancholy, Philosophy, Semiotics and Psychoanalysis
Luce Irigaray: Lips, Kissing, and the Politics of Sexual Difference
Hélène Cixous I Love You: The *Jouissance* of Writing
Andrea Dworkin
'Cosmo Woman': The World of Women's Magazines
Women in Pop Music
Discovering the Goddess (Geoffrey Ashe)
The Poetry of Cinema
The Sacred Cinema of Andrei Tarkovsky
Walerian Borowczyk: Cinema of Erotic Dreams
Jean-Luc Godard: The Passion of Cinema
John Hughes and Eighties Cinema
The Cinema of Richard Linklater
Liv Tyler: Star In Ascendance
The Cinema of Donald Cammell
The Cinema of Hayao Miyazaki
Blade Runner and the Films of Philip K. Dick
Paul Bowles and Bernardo Bertolucci
Media Hell: Radio, TV and the Press
An Open Letter to the BBC
Detonation Britain: Nuclear War in the UK
Feminism and Shakespeare
Wild Zones: Pornography, Art and Feminism
Sex in Art: Pornography and Pleasure in Painting and Sculpture
Sexing Hardy: Thomas Hardy and Feminism

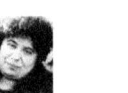
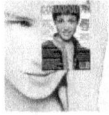
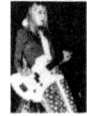
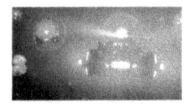
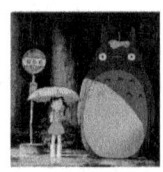
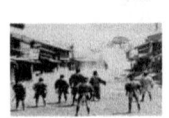
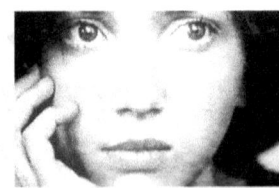
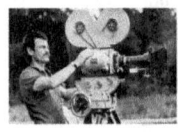

In my view *The Light Eternal* is among the very best of all the material I read on Turner. (Douglas Graham, director of the Turner Museum, Denver, Colorado)

The Light Eternal is a model monograph, an exemplary job. The subject matter of the book is beautifully organised and dead on beam. (Lawrence Durrell)

It is amazing for me to see my work treated with such passion and respect. (Andrea Dworkin)

Sex-Magic-Poetry-Cornwall is a very rich essay... It is like a brightly-lighted box. (Peter Redgrove)

CRESCENT MOON PUBLISHING
P.O. Box 393, Maidstone, Kent, ME14 5XU, United Kingdom.
01622-729593 (UK) 01144-1622-729593 (US) 0044-1622-729593 (other territories)
cresmopub@yahoo.co.uk   www.crescentmoon.org.uk